T0073906

Human-Centered AI

HUMAN-CENTERED AI

BEN SHNEIDERMAN

OXFORD
UNIVERSITY PRESS

OXFORD
UNIVERSITY PRESS

Great Clarendon Street, Oxford, OX2 6DP,
United Kingdom

Oxford University Press is a department of the University of Oxford.
It furthers the University's objective of excellence in research, scholarship,
and education by publishing worldwide. Oxford is a registered trade mark of
Oxford University Press in the UK and in certain other countries

Published in the United States of America by Oxford University Press
198 Madison Avenue, New York, NY 10016, United States of America

British Library Cataloguing in Publication Data
Data available

Library of Congress Control Number: 2021940444

ISBN 978–0–19–284529–0

DOI: 10.1093/oso/9780192845290.001.0001

Printed in Great Britain by
Bell & Bain Ltd., Glasgow

PREFACE

This book grew out of more than forty public lectures at leading research centers, universities, and government agencies, in which I refined my presentations to clarify three central ideas. These ideas were presented in three refereed papers, giving me still more feedback leading to the specific and constructive guidance in this book. As I worked, the primacy of human values such as rights, justice, and dignity grew steadily, even as I described more specific design guidelines.

Human-Centered AI offers fresh thinking for designers to imagine new strategies that support human self-efficacy, creativity, responsibility, and social connections. A greater emphasis on human-centered AI will reduce fears of AI's existential threats and increase benefits for users and society in business, education, healthcare, environmental preservation, and community safety.

The first idea is a framework for thinking about technology design, which shows how creative designers can imagine highly automated systems that preserve human control. The examples include familiar devices, such as elevators, self-cleaning ovens, and cellphone cameras, as well as life critical applications, such as highly automated cars, tele-operated surgical robots, and patient-controlled pain relief. The guidelines and examples clarify how designers can support *high levels of human control* and *high levels of automation*.

The second idea is to show how the two central goals of AI research—emulating human behavior and developing useful applications—are both valuable. They generate four pairs of metaphors that could be combined in developing products and services:

1) Intelligent agents and supertools,
2) Teammate and tele-bots,
3) Assured autonomy and control centers, and
4) Social robots and active appliances.

The third idea bridges the gap between widely discussed ethical principles of HCAI and the realistic steps needed to realize them. The book describes how to adapt proven technical practices, management strategies, and independent oversight methods. It guides software team leaders, business managers, and organization leaders in developing:

1) *Reliable* systems based on sound software engineering practices,

2) *Safety* culture through business management strategies, and

3) *Trustworthy* certification by independent oversight.

Technical practices for programmers, designers, software engineers, and team leaders include audit trails to enable analysis of failures, just like the flight data recorders (aviation black boxes, which are really orange boxes) that have made civil aviation such a success story. Then *Human-Centered AI* explains software engineering workflows, verification and validation testing, bias testing to enhance fairness, and explainable HCAI user interfaces.

Management strategies for creating a safety culture begin with leadership commitment to safety that leads to better hiring practices and training oriented to safety. Other management strategies are extensive reporting of failures and near misses, internal review boards for problems and future plans, and alignment with industry standard practices.

Trustworthy certification comes from accounting firms that conduct independent audits, insurance companies that compensate for failures, nongovernmental and civil society organizations that advance design principles, and professional organizations that develop voluntary standards and prudent policies. Then government interventions and regulation will play important roles, especially when they are designed to accelerate innovation, as they have done with automobile safety and fuel efficiency.

Many research and development challenges remain, but I hope my efforts provide a guidebook to hope and a roadmap to realistic policies.

ACKNOWLEDGEMENTS

Writing a book is a consuming experience that takes over my life in mostly energizing and satisfying ways. Each book I have done draws me in with excitement and the challenge of doing my best, because I believe in the importance and value of the project.

This book was especially meaningful as I have been thinking about the distinctive qualities that make us human for most of my adult life. Yes, I have been deeply involved in developing new technologies and have the satisfaction of seeing some of my contributions become widely used, but I always thought of the technology as serving human needs. I advocated for human–computer interaction, information visualization, and design thinking, with occasional excursions to challenge those who thought the goal of technology was to mimic or replace humans. I believed in the responsibility of those who design and use technology. For those interested, I tell some of my story in the Personal Epilogue.

In writing this book, I became aware that I could get beyond the past controversies by offering a positive vision of how to design potent future technologies. I embraced the contributions of artificial intelligence (AI) researchers, while suggesting how their breakthroughs could be put to work in successful products and services that were reliable, safe, and trustworthy. The book begins with some familiar controversies, then offers the fresh idea of the human-centered AI (HCAI) framework that shows how it is possible to have high levels of human control and high levels of computer automation, as is done in digital cameras.

The second vital idea is to offer new metaphors for describing technology design, which include supertools, tele-bots, active appliances, and control centers. The third idea is a set of recommendations for governance structures to bridge the gap between ethics and practice, such as audit trails, explainable designs, and independent oversight.

Throughout the book guidelines, examples, and references are meant to guide readers in how they could think differently, enabling them to create better products and services that actually serve human needs. I read avidly, taking in about a hundred books, a thousand papers, and a thousand websites to ensure I was in touch with the current state of research, development, innovation, and commercial practice. When appropriate, I contacted about a hundred authors and practitioners for email comments and phone or zoom discussions. I worked hard to credit and cite those whose work I admired, but I am aware that there is much more thoughtful work that I have yet to read. My work favors research, reports, websites, and videos that are in English, so I hope others can fill in what is missing from other languages, countries, and cultures.

I have been fortunate to have a large circle of colleagues and friends who sent me relevant work and commented on my drafts. They taught me a great deal about these topics, so I am grateful for their generous help.

I begin my thank yous with my dear wife, friend, and partner Jennifer Preece, who did more than accept and support my devotion to this book. She was my most trusted and reliable reader who clearly told me what needed to be improved and shifted my writing to ever more positive themes of how AI and HCAI could work together. I smile in appreciation of her love every day.

Other dedicated readers who went through the entire book include my former doctoral student, now valued colleague, Harry Hochheiser. His sharp and skeptical views were a healthy corrective to my sometimes overly optimistic self. Alan Mackworth, a leader in AI research, has become a trusted colleague who helped me appreciate the value and nature of AI science and engineering research. He was warmly open to reading every chapter and energetically engaged with long discussions.

Two new colleagues emerged to become cheerleaders and guides to further research and different perspectives. Sean Koon and Sean McGregor gave generous comments in the drafts and lengthy emails, which did much to improve the book. My new relationships with them during the COVID crisis were entirely electronic—we have never met, but I hope we will have some celebratory meals together in the future.

Some colleagues read and commented on large sections, such as Mary Czerwinski, Gregory Falco, Gerhard Fischer, Daniel Jackson, Jonathan Lazar, Benjamin Mueller, and Daniel Schiff. They gave me fresh ideas, new references, helpful corrections, and supportive feedback. I appreciated the prompt sanity checks about ideas from trusted friends, Robert Hoffman, Catherine Plaisant, and Gary Klein, whose frank comments made me smile and see my work from different perspectives.

Others gave terrific analyses of chapters or specific topics, including Connor Brooks, Margaret Burnett, Linda Candy, Lucas Cardiell, Hal Daume, Nick Diakopoulos, Susan Dumais, Ernest Edmonds, Robert Fraser, Guy Hoffman, Bonnie John, Jeff Johnson, Karrie Karahalios, Joseph Konstan, Amanda Lazar, Dinesh Manocha, Joanna McGrenere, Robin Murphy, Mor Naaman, Yvonne Rogers, Kacper Sokol, Jonathan Stray, Daniel Szafir, and Wei Xu.

Many physical meetings, fruitful emails, Zoom calls, and phone conversations enriched my knowledge, broadened my understanding, and cheered me on. Notable exchanges were with Maneesh Agrawala, Michael Bernstein, Alan Blackwell, Rafael Calvo, Ryan Carrier, Sumeet Chabria, Jessica Cicchino, William Clancey, Cristina Conati, Nancy Cooke, Ernest Davis, John Dickerson, Tom Dietterich, Aaron Dworkin, Mica Endsley, Will Griffin, Peter Hancock, Fox Harrell, Christopher Hart, Shanee Honig, Matt Jones, Malte Jung, Hernisa Kacorri, James Landay, Carl Landwehr, Jaron Lanier, Vera Liao, Guru Madhavan, Gary Marcus, John Markoff, Meredith Ringel Morris, Michael Nelson, Peter Norvig, Michael O'Connell, Brian O'Neill, Tal Oron-Gilad, Frank Pasquale, Gill Pratt, Adela Quinones, Lionel Robert, Steve Rosen, Marc Rotenberg, Cynthia Rudin, Ariel Sarid, Daniel Sarid, Helen Sarid, Jeffrey Schnapp, Ted Selker, Tom Sheridan, Brian Cantwell Smith, Marc A. Smith, Mark Smith, Harold Thimbleby, Ufuk Topcu, Katrien Verbert, Fernanda Viegas, Hanna Wallach, Martin Wattenberg, Lorne Whitehead, Alan Winfield, and David Woods.

The early work on this book began with three foundational journal articles, which were published during 2020, giving me a chance to get formative feedback to refine my thinking. Gavriel Salvendy and Constantine Stephanidis sympathetically conducted a careful refereeing process for the *International Journal of Human–Computer Interaction*. Then Katina Michael gave me the chance to publish a second article in the new *IEEE Transactions on Technology and Society*. The third paper was shepherded through the publication process for the *ACM Transactions on Interactive and Intelligent Systems* by editor-in-chief Michelle Zhou.

A review paper that summarized the three papers for business school researchers was helped through their refereeing process by the timely and scholarly work of Fiona Nah, editor-in-chief of the Association for Information Systems's *Transactions on Human-Computer Interaction*. Another summary paper for policy leaders was thoroughly revised by editor-in-chief Daniel Sarewitz for the National Academy of Sciences/Arizona State University journal *Issues in Sciences and Technology*.

The Oxford University Press team provided the help that every author needs. Dan Taber arranged for early reviews, responded promptly to my many questions, and personally commented on much of the book. Katherine Ward, Darcy Ahl, and Charles Lauder did their best to ensure high quality during the production process.

Family members and friends encouraged my work and stressed that I should use non-technical language where possible. My daughters and their spouses, grandchildren, sister, nephews, and my wide family circle make life meaningful every day and remind me about why I work so hard to find a path to a brighter future.

Ben Shneiderman
October 2021

CONTENTS

PART I WHAT IS HUMAN-CENTERED
ARTIFICIAL INTELLIGENCE?

1 Introduction: High Expectations   7

2 How Do Rationalism and Empiricism Provide Sound
   Foundations?   17

3 Are People and Computers in the Same Category?   25

4 Will Automation, AI, and Robots Lead to Widespread
   Unemployment?   33

5 Summary and Skeptic's Corner   39

PART 2 HUMAN-CENTERED AI FRAMEWORK

6 Introduction: Rising Above the Levels of Automation   45

7 Defining Reliable, Safe, and Trustworthy Systems   53

8 Two-Dimensional HCAI Framework   57

9 Design Guidelines and Examples   69

10 Summary and Skeptic's Corner   79

PART 3 DESIGN METAPHORS

11 Introduction: What Are the Goals of AI Research?   87

12 Science and Innovation Goals   93

13 Intelligent Agents and Supertools   99

14 Teammates and Tele-bots   105

15 Assured Autonomy and Control Centers   111

16 Social Robots and Active Appliances   117

17 Summary and Skeptic's Corner   137

PART 4 GOVERNANCE STRUCTURES

18 Introduction: How to Bridge the Gap from Ethics
    to Practice   145

19 Reliable Systems Based on Sound Software Engineering
    Practices   151

20 Safety Culture through Business Management Strategies   179

21 Trustworthy Certification by Independent Oversight   195

22 Government Interventions and Regulations   213

23 Summary and Skeptic's Corner   223

PART 5 WHERE DO WE GO FROM HERE?

24 Introduction: Driving HCAI Forward   229

25 Assessing Trustworthiness   245

26 Caring for and Learning from Older Adults   259

27 Summary and Skeptic's Corner   273

    Personal Epilogue: How I Became Passionate about
    Human-Centered Approaches   275

    Notes   281
    Bibliography   327
    Name Index   359
    Subject Index   367

PART I

What Is Human-Centered Artificial Intelligence?

1 Introduction: High Expectations

2 How Does Rationalism or Empiricism Provide Sound Foundations?

3 Are People and Computers in the Same Category?

4 Will Automation, AI, and Robots Lead to Widespread Unemployment?

5 Summary and Skeptic's Corner

Researchers, developers, business leaders, policy-makers, and others are expanding the technology-centered scope of artificial intelligence (AI) to include human-centered AI (HCAI) ways of thinking. This expansion from an algorithm-focused view to embrace a human-centered perspective can shape the future of technology so as to better serve human needs. Educators, designers, software engineers, product managers, evaluators, and government agency staffers can build on AI-driven technologies to design products and services that make life better for the users, enabling people to care for each other. Humans have always been tool builders, and now they are super-tool builders, whose inventions can improve our health, family life, education, business, the environment, and much more. The remarkable progress in algorithms for machine and deep learning during the past decade has opened the doors to new opportunities, and some dark possibilities. However, a bright future awaits AI researchers, developers, business leaders, policy-makers, and others who build on AI algorithms by including HCAI strategies of design and testing. This enlarged vision can shape the future of technology so as to better serve human values and needs. As many technology companies and thought leaders have said, the goal is not to replace people but to empower them by making design choices that give humans control over technology.

James Watts' steam engine, Samuel Morse's telegraph, and Thomas Edison's electric light were technology breakthroughs that were put to work to open up new possibilities for transportation, communications, business, and families. They all moved beyond the existing and familiar technologies to demonstrate new products and services that enhanced life while suggesting ever more potent possibilities. Each positive step is also embraced by malicious actors such as criminals, hate groups, terrorists, and oppressive rulers, so careful attention to how technologies are used can reduce these threats. The human capacity for frontier thinking, to push beyond current examples, is amply visible in the Wright brothers' airplane, Tim Berners-Lee's World Wide Web, and Jennifer Doudna and Emmanuelle Charpentier's genome editing. Now, as new technologies blossom into ever more potent breakthroughs we have a choice to make about how these technologies will be applied.

The high expectations and impressive results from AI, such as the AlphaGo program winning at the game of Go, have triggered intense worldwide activity by researchers, developers, business leaders, and policy-makers. The promise of startling advances from machine learning and other algorithms energizes discussions while eliciting huge investments in medical, manufacturing, and military innovations.

The AI community's impact is likely to grow even larger by embracing a human-centered future, filled with supertools that amplify human abilities, empowering people in remarkable ways. This compelling prospect of HCAI builds on AI methods, enabling people to see, think, create, and act with extraordinary clarity. HCAI technologies bring superhuman capabilities, augmenting human creativity, while raising human performance and self-efficacy. These capabilities are apparent in familiar HCAI applications such as digital cameras that have high levels of human control but many AI supports in setting aperture, adjusting focus, and reducing jitter from hand movements. Similarly, HCAI navigation systems give walkers, bikers, drivers, and public transport users control over the many choices that are derived from AI programs which use real-time data to predict travel times.

Extending the power of AI-driven algorithms, *Human-Centered AI* shows how to make successful technologies that amplify, augment, empower, and enhance human performance. This expanded mindset should please readers as it describes a safer, more understandable, and more manageable future. A human-centered approach will reduce the out-of-control technologies, calm fears of robot-led unemployment, and give users the rewarding sense of mastery and accomplishment. Beyond individual experiences, HCAI will enable better control of privacy/security to limit misinformation and counter malicious actors. The dangers from AI and HCAI systems are legitimate concerns—any technology that empowers people to do good also empowers those who would do evil. Carefully designed controls, audit trails, and supervised autonomy are some of the strategies that stakeholders can adopt to achieve, reliable, safe, and trustworthy systems.

This book makes a coherent presentation of the fresh HCAI methods with numerous examples to guide researchers, developers, business leaders, and policy-makers. It offers an HCAI framework to guide innovation, design metaphors to combine disparate views, and governance structures to advance a human-centered approach. Benefitting people becomes the driving force for making ever more potent supertools, tele-bots, active appliances, and control centers that empower users with extraordinary capabilities.

Reframing established beliefs with a fresh vision is among the most powerful tools for change. It can liberate researchers and designers, building on the past while allowing them to adopt new beliefs. The vast number of people embracing AI technologies are beginning to align with HCAI themes with an openness to human-centered thinking. I hope that the traditional AI technology-centered community, who have made so many important breakthroughs, will take in the human-centered perspectives, which offer a different vision of human destiny. A human-centered strategy will bring AI wider acceptance and higher impact by providing products and services that serve human needs. By encouraging a passionate devotion to empower people, enrich communities, and inspire hope, *Human-Centered AI* offers a vision of future technologies that values human rights, justice, and dignity.

CHAPTER 1

Introduction: High Expectations

The Analytical Engine has no pretensions whatever to originate anything. It can do whatever we know how to order it to perform.

Ada Lovelace *(1843)*

T his book proposes a new synthesis in which AI-based intelligent algorithms are combined with human-centered thinking to make HCAI. This approach will increase the chance that technology will empower rather than replace people. In the past, researchers and developers focused on building AI algorithms and systems, stressing machine autonomy and measuring algorithm performance. The new synthesis gives equal attention to human users and other stakeholders by raising the value of user experience design and by measuring human performance. Researchers and developers for HCAI systems value meaningful human control, putting people first by serving human values such as rights, justice, and dignity, and supporting goals such as self-efficacy, creativity, responsibility, and social connections.[1]

This new synthesis reflects the growing movement to expand from technology-centered thinking to include human-centered aspirations that highlight societal benefit. The interest in HCAI has grown stronger since the 2017 Montreal Declaration for Responsible Development of AI. That declaration called for devotion to human well-being, autonomy, privacy, and creation of a just and equitable society. Enthusiasm for these human-centered goals is also part of the AI4GOOD movement,[2] DataKind,[3] and the IBM Watson AI XPRIZE Foundation,[4] which seek to apply AI methods, such as machine learning, "to solve some of society's biggest challenges." This admirable devotion to societal needs is aligned with the HCAI approach that applies rigorous design and evaluation methods to produce high-impact research. AI4GOOD sets appropriate goals which can be pursued with HCAI methods that guide researchers and developers to determine how to effectively address genuine human needs, including meaningful problems in government, and vital challenges for businesses, schools, and healthcare systems. However, every opportunity for doing good is balanced by the dangers from the increased power of AI and HCAI systems, which can equally be used by malicious actors such as criminals, hate groups, terrorists, and oppressive politicians.

This movement towards setting societal goals for AI is aligned with the United Nations AI for Good Global Summit, an annual gathering of ardent research leaders, serious business executives, and conscientious policy-makers since 2017. The conference organizers state that their "goal is to identify practical applications of AI and scale those solutions for global impact."[5] The efforts of United Nations agencies and member countries are guided by the seventeen United Nations' Sustainable Development Goals (SDGs), which were established in 2015 to set aspirations for 2030 (Figure 1.1).[6] These goals include elimination of poverty, zero hunger, quality education, and reduced inequalities. Other ambitions address environmental issues such as climate action, life on land, life below water, and sustainable cities and communities. While many social, political, and psychological changes are needed, technology will play a role in finding solutions, including AI and HCAI.

Fig 1.1 The seventeen United Nation's Sustainable Development Goals (SDGs)

Source: https://sdgs.un.org/goals

Policy-makers assess progress toward these goals by 169 target indicators for each country, such as proportion of population living in households with access to basic services, maternal mortality ratio, and proportion of population using safely managed drinking water services.[7]

A related set of goals is captured in the notion of human *well-being,* which is the basis for a recent IEEE P7010 standard whose authors hope will encourage HCAI researchers and developers to "assess, manage, mitigate, and improve the well-being impacts on human and societal well-being, extending from individual users to the public."[8] Successful HCAI methods and applications could do much to advance these efforts. Human-centered methods and design thinking for all technologies will be helpful, but HCAI could be a potent combination that proves to be especially valuable for these grand challenges.

A key question is what do we mean by HCAI and what makes it different from AI? There are many definitions, but there are two key aspects:

1) Process: HCAI builds on user experience design methods of user observation, stakeholder engagement, usability testing, iterative refinement, and continuing evaluation of human performance in use of systems that employ AI and machine learning.

2) Product: HCAI systems are designed to be supertools which amplify, augment, empower, and enhance human performance. They emphasize human control, while embedding high levels of automation by way of AI and machine learning. Examples include digital cameras and navigation systems, which give humans control yet have many automated features.

The goal is to increase human self-efficacy, creativity, responsibility, and social connections while reducing the impact of malicious actors, biased data, and flawed software.

This book has three fresh ideas for changing technology design so as to bring about a new synthesis with its human-centered orientation.

HCAI framework that guides creative designers to ensure human-centric thinking about highly automated systems. The examples include familiar devices, such as thermostats, elevators, self-cleaning ovens, and cellphone cameras, as well as life critical applications, such as highly automated cars and patient-controlled pain relief devices. The new aspiration is to have *high levels of human control AND high levels of automation.*

Design metaphors suggest how the two central goals of AI research, science and innovation, are both valuable, but researchers, developers, business leaders, and policy-makers will need to be creative in finding effective ways of combining them to benefit the users. There are four design metaphors that can be used to combine the two goals of AI research:

1) intelligent agents and supertools;
2) teammates and tele-bots;
3) assured autonomy and control centers; and
4) social robots and active appliances.

Journalists, headline writers, graphic designers, and Hollywood producers are entranced by the possibilities of robots and AI, so it will take a generation to change attitudes and expectations towards a human-centered view. With fresh thinking, researchers, developers, business leaders, and policy-makers can find combined designs that will accelerate HCAI thinking. A greater emphasis on HCAI will reduce unfounded fears of AI's existential threats and raise people's belief that they will be able to use technology for their daily needs and creative explorations. It will increase benefits for users and society in business, education, healthcare, environmental preservation, and community safety.

Governance structures bridge the gap between widely discussed ethical principles and the practical steps needed to realize them. Software team leaders, business managers, and organization leaders will have to adapt proven technical practices, management strategies, and independent oversight methods, so they can achieve the desired goals of:

1) **Reliable** systems based on proven software engineering practices;
2) **Safety** culture through business management strategies; and
3) **Trustworthy** certification by independent oversight and government regulation.

Technical practices for designers, software engineers, programmers, team leaders, and product managers include audit trails to enable analysis of failures, just like the flight data recorders (aircraft black boxes, which are really orange boxes) that have made civil aviation such a success story. Part 4 suggests how sound existing practices can be applied to software engineering workflows, verification and validation testing, bias testing to enhance fairness, and explainable user interfaces.

Management strategies for creating a safety culture begin with leadership commitment to safety that leads to better hiring practices and training oriented to safety. Other management strategies are extensive reporting of failures and near misses, which are collected internally from employee reports and gathered externally from users who make incident reports, internal review boards, and alignment with industry standard practices.

Trustworthy certification and clarity about liability comes from accounting firms that conduct independent audits and insurance companies that compensate for failures. Then there are non-governmental and civil society organizations that advance design principles, and professional organizations that develop voluntary standards and prudent policies. Further support for trustworthiness will come from government legislation and regulation, but advocates of certification and independent oversight will have to cope with resistance to regulation and "revolving door" movements in which corporate leaders make jobs in oversight organizations.

The three fresh ideas are covered in Parts 2, 3, and 4 of this book. They are the foundation for achieving the aspirations, goals, and human values shown in Figure 1.2, which is a compact overview of this book The stakeholders participate in every aspect, while the threats from malicious actors, bias, and flawed

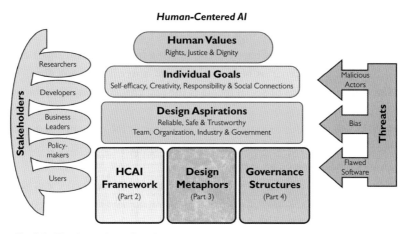

Fig 1.2 The three ideas of this book support the aspirations, goals, and human values, while recognizing the needs of stakeholders and the dangers of threats.

software remain prominent in stakeholder minds. The three fresh ideas are the HCAI framework, design metaphors, and governance structures.

Successful automation is all around us. Navigation applications give drivers control by showing times for alternative routes. E-commerce websites offer shoppers relevant options, customer reviews, and clear pricing so they can find and order the goods they need. Elevators, clothes-washing machines, and airline check-in kiosks, too, have meaningful controls that enable users to get what they need done quickly and reliably. When modern cameras assist photographers in taking properly focused and exposed photos, users have a sense of mastery and accomplishment for composing the image, even as they get assistance with optimizing technical details. These and millions of other mobile device applications and cloud-based web services enable users to accomplish their tasks with self-confidence and sometimes even pride.

In a flourishing automation-enhanced world, clear, convenient interfaces could let humans control automation to make the most of people's initiative, creativity and responsibility. The most successful machines could be powerful supertools that let users carry out ever-richer tasks with confidence, such as helping architects find innovative ways to design energy-efficient buildings and giving journalists tools to dig deeper into data to uncover fraud and corruption. Other HCAI supertools could enable clinicians to detect emerging medical conditions, industry watchdogs to spot unfair hiring decisions, and auditors to identify bias in mortgage loan approvals.

Designers of AI algorithms and HCAI user interfaces must work diligently to ensure that their work brings more benefits than harms. Charting a path between utopian visions of happy users, thriving businesses, and smart cities and the dystopian scenarios of frustrated users, surveillance capitalism, and political manipulations of social media is the real challenge we face. Training researchers, developers, business leaders, and policy-makers to consider downside risks will do much to limit harm. A good start is the growing database of more than a thousand AI incident and accident reports[9] that provide disturbing examples of what can go wrong.[10]

Humans are accomplished at building tools that expand their creativity— and then at using those tools in even more innovative ways than their designers intended. It's time to let more people be more creative more of the time. Technology designers who appreciate and amplify the key aspects of humanity are most likely to invent the next generation of what I call supertools, tele-bots, and active appliances. These designers will shift from trying to replace human

Human-Centered AI (HCAI) Stakeholders

Police,
Prosecutors,
Judges

Ages &
Genders

Abilities &
Expertise

Cultures &
Ethnicities

Users

Languages &
Personalities

Industrial
Researchers

Government
Staffers

**Policy-
makers**

Researchers

Professors

Regulators

Educators

Research
Funders

**Business
Leaders**

Developers

Post-Docs

Graduate
Research
Assistants

Journalists

Lawyers

Software
Engineers

Managers

Marketers

Chief Technology
Officers

Product
Managers

Designers

Evaluators

Programmers

Fig 1.3 HCAI stakeholders with core professionals who are researchers, developers, business leaders, and policy-makers.

behavior in machines to building the wildly successful applications that people love to use.

This book is intended for diverse readers who play a role in shaping technology and its uses. I refer to researchers, developers, business leaders, and policy-makers who shape HCAI systems and the users who benefit from them. Figure 1.3 names some of the larger set of diverse users and professionals who are all stakeholders with a role to play.

If AI technology developers increase their use of information visualization, their own algorithmic work will improve and they will help many stakeholders to better understand how to use these new technologies. The traditional AI research community favors statistical machine learning and neural net-inspired deep learning algorithms that do tasks automatically or autonomously. However, that attitude is changing as information visualization has proven its value in understanding deep learning methods, improving algorithms, and reducing errors. Visual user interfaces have become appreciated for providing developers, users, and other stakeholders with a better understanding of and more control over how algorithmic decisions are made for parole requests, hiring, mortgages, and other consequential applications.

My education about how AI systems could be evaluated came when serving on a National Academy of Sciences panel during 2006–2008, whose task was to prepare a report on *Protecting Individual Privacy in the Struggle Against Terrorists: A Framework for Program Assessment*.[11] This twenty-one person panel was filled with a diverse collection of impressive people and co-chaired by two remarkable individuals: William J. Perry, former US Secretary of Defense, and Charles M. Vest, President of the National Academy of Engineering and former President of MIT. Our job was to recommend evaluation methods for troubling technologies such as data mining, machine learning, and behavioral surveillance, so they could be used safely. The challenges were to protect individual privacy and limit inappropriate use by rigorously assessing the enthusiastic claims for these emerging technologies. One of my roles was to study independent oversight methods to clarify how they have been used and how they could be applied for these emerging technologies. Our statistical testing process, described as "a framework for evaluating information-based programs to fight terrorism or serve other important national goals," became a model for government agencies and others. The panel's recommendations included: "Any information-based counterterrorism program of the U.S. government should be subjected to robust, independent oversight ... All such programs should provide meaningful redress to any individuals inappropriately harmed by their operation." Our takeaway message was that careful evaluations coupled with independent oversight were strong partners in advancing safe use of technology.

In the time since that report, AI's success with machine and deep learning has catapulted it to the top of agendas for business leaders and government policy-makers. Bestselling books, such as Nick Bostrom's *Superintelligence: Paths, Dangers, Strategies* and Stuart Russell and Peter Norvig's textbook on *Artificial Intelligence: A Modern Approach*, celebrated the accomplishments, suggested continuing opportunities, and raised fears of what could go wrong.[12] Their work and many others led to intense interest from technology corporations, which quickly shifted to being AI corporations, and government commitments internationally of billions of dollars for AI applications in business, medical, transportation, military, and other applications.

On the other hand, cautionary voices sounded alarms. Cathy O'Neil's groundbreaking 2016 book *Weapons of Math Destruction: How Big Data Increases Inequality and Threatens Democracy* laid out the case of how numerous widely used algorithms were opaque and harmful.[13] As a Harvard-trained Wall Street analyst she is greatly respected, and her writing is powerful and clear. Her book and the European Union's General Data Protection and Regulation (GDPR) accelerated efforts to develop explainable AI (XAI) so that mortgage applicants, parole requestors, or job seekers who were rejected could get a meaningful explanation. Such explanations would help them adjust their requests or challenge an unfair decision. Information visualization methods became an increasing part of the designs in the growing XAI community.

The interest in HCAI blossomed with 500+ reports from public interest groups, professional societies, and governments encouraging responsible, ethical, and humane approaches. These efforts accelerated as the need to have better human control over computers was highlighted by stock market flash crashes, deadly failures of excessively autonomous Patriot missile systems in the 2003 Iraq War, and fatal accidents involving self-driving cars. While the two Boeing 737 MAX crashes in 2018 and a few months later in 2019 were not directly related to AI systems, the belief in autonomous systems misled designers and regulators. They believed that embedded algorithms could perform perfectly so that pilots were not even informed about their presence. When the angle of attack sensor failed, the embedded algorithms forced the plane to turn nose down, resisting the repeated attempts of the confused pilots to turn the nose up. The often mentioned ironies, dilemmas, conundrums, paradoxes, and myths of autonomy turned into a deadly tragedy of autonomy.

This book is meant as a guidebook to hope and a roadmap to realistic policies. To succeed, the HCAI community will have to change the language, metaphors, and images of technology that suggest human-like robots to collaboration among people who are using computers. The clichéd images of a human hand touching a robot hand or a humanoid robot walking with children already seem archaic and misguided. While control panels for washing machines or clothes dryers are a modest starting point, their successors are likely to become the next commercial successes. Tele-operated drones, remotely activated home controls, and precise surgical devices will spread. The ambitious control rooms for NASA's Mars Rovers, transportation management centers, patient-monitoring displays, and financial trading rooms are compelling prototypes for many applications. Medical monitors and implanted devices will be operated by smartphone apps, giving control to users and supervisory control to clinicians and product managers who can monitor thousands of these devices so as to improve their designs.

The future is human-centered—filled with supertools, tele-bots, and active appliances that amplify human abilities, empowering people in remarkable ways while ensuring human control. This compelling HCAI prospect enables people to see, think, create, and act in extraordinary ways by combining engaging user experiences with embedded AI algorithms to support services that users want.

However, I am well aware that my vision for the future is still a minority position, so there is much work to be done to steer researchers, developers, managers, and policy-makers to a human-centered agenda.

Underlying belief systems have long been at the heart of technology discussions. Three of those foundational issues are covered in the next three chapters:

- Chapter 2: How does rationalism or empiricism provide sound foundations?
- Chapter 3: Are people and computers in the same category?
- Chapter 4: Will automation, AI, and robots lead to widespread unemployment?

Then Chapter 5 summarizes this part and reminds readers of why they might be skeptical about my approach.

How Do Rationalism and Empiricism Provide Sound Foundations?

The contrast between AI and HCAI is a continuation of the 2000-year-old clash between Aristotle's rationalism, based on logical analyses, and Leonardo da Vinci's empiricism, based on sensory exploration of the world. Both are valuable and worthy of understanding.

The differences came through when using a Roomba robot vacuum cleaner from iRobot. I was eager to buy this device, which has been refined for thirty years and has sold 30 million of these active appliances. The online customer reviews were 70% positive ("I love it," "impressive") with only a few percent having a bad experience ("absolutely despise this product," "sending it back"). Roombas are a good model to follow, but there is room for improvement. The design goal was for it to vacuum your home or apartment on its own, so there are only three buttons with a few colored lights. The sparse "Owner's Guide" (instead of a "User's Guide") has only a few paragraphs on how to use the three buttons and what the lights mean.

In short, Roomba was designed to do the job on its own, which is what many users want, so maybe the stripped-down user interface was a good decision. An alternate design could give users meaningful controls so they know what it will do next and control the order it cleans rooms. The smartphone app shows a floor map that Roomba detects, but design improvements could give users more insight into what is happening, such as where it will go next and how long it will take. Roomba was designed by rationalist thinking to do the job on its own, rather than by empiricist thinking that would give users greater sense of control. By contrast, hugely successful, much loved, digital camera apps emerged from empiricist thinking, which puts the users first by giving them a simple point and shoot device, and also has easy-to-use controls so they can chose from many modes of operation, including selfies and portrait lighting, and then preview the image that they will get. Users can explore alternatives like videos or panoramic views, take dozens of photos, edit them or add annotations, and then immediately share them with friends and family. A few decades ago, only professional photographers could reliably take high-quality images and they might take days or weeks to print so they could mail copies out.

There are many nuanced discussions of rationalism and empiricism, but here's how I understand that debate. Rationalists believe in logical thinking, which can be accomplished in the comfort and familiarity of their office desk or research lab. They have confidence in the perfectability of rules and the strength of formal methods of logic and mathematical proofs. They assume the constancy of well-defined boundaries—like hot and cold, wet and dry. Aristotle recognized important distinctions, such as the differences between vertebrates and invertebrates, or the four categories of matter: earth, water, air, and fire. These categories are useful, but can become limiting in seeing other options, middle grounds, and newer patterns.

Aristotle's devotion to rational reflection rather than empirical observation, sometimes led him astray, as in his belief that women had only twenty-eight teeth, when a simple examination would have corrected his error. Followers of rationalism have included René Descartes, Baruch Spinoza, Immanuel Kant, and in the twentieth century, the famed statistician Ronald Fisher. His overly strong commitment to statistics led him to reject early data on smoking, so he continued his smoking habit, eventually dying of lung cancer. Rationalism, especially as embodied in logical mathematical thinking, is the basis for much of AI science research, in which logical thinking leads to algorithms that are treasured for their elegance and measured by their efficiency.

Rational thinking leads to medical information systems that require clinicians to enter reports about human health with a limited set of categories or codes. This formalization has benefits in forcing agreement about the categories, but has limitations because human health deserves more than a set of checkboxes or numeric ratings, which is why free text reports by clinicians are valued. Similarly, rules-based or decision tree models have their benefits and limitations. AI innovation researchers, who seek to make commercial products and services, realize that a rational approach may be a good start, but they know there are benefits from adding a human-centered empirical approach.

Empiricists believe that researchers must get out of their offices and labs to sense the real world in all its contextual complexity, diversity, and uncertainty. They understand that beliefs have to be continuously refined to respond to changing realities and new contexts. Leonardo da Vinci developed fluid dynamics principles by using his keen eyesight to study bird flight and generalized by watching water flowing around obstacles. Galileo Galilei followed da Vinci by noticing the rhythmic swaying of a chandelier in church, leading him to the formula for pendulum swing times. In the 1830s, Charles Darwin traveled to distant destinations, including the Galapagos, to observe the rich diversity of nature, which enabled him to develop the theory of evolution through natural selection.

Other empiricists were John Locke, David Hume, and, in the twentieth century, the statistician John Tukey, who believed in looking at data graphically. Empiricism and empathic observation of people are the basis for much of the user-experience design community, which assesses human performance so as to improve it. Empiricists question simple dichotomies and complex ontologies, because these may limit thinking, undermining analysts' capacity to see importance nuances and non-hierarchical relationships.

The rationalist viewpoint is a strong pillar of the AI community, leading researchers and developers to emphasize data-driven programmed solutions based on logic. Fortunately, an increasing component of AI research bends to the empirical approach, such as in affective computing, healthcare, and the conference on Empirical Methods in Natural Language Processing. The interest in empirical thinking grows when the goal is to build widely used consumer devices.

Rationalism also favors the belief that statistical methods and machine learning algorithms are sufficient to achieve AI's promise of matching or exceeding human intelligence on well-defined tasks. The strong belief in data-driven statistical methods is in contrast to deeply engaging with domain experts who understand causal relationships among variables. AI advocates have gone so far as to say that theories about causal relationships are no longer needed and that machine learning replaces expertise.[1] Others, such as Turing Award winner Judea Pearl, believe that the next step for AI will be to deal with causality.[2]

The troubling belief is that predictions no longer require causal explanations, suggesting that statistical correlations are sufficient to guide decisions.

Yes, machine learning can reveal patterns in the data used to "train" algorithms, but it needs to be extended to deal with surprising extreme cases, such as when the Tesla self-driving car that failed to distinguish a white truck from the sky and smashed into it, killing the driver. Furthermore, machine learning needs supplements that recognize hidden biases and the absence of expected patterns. Improvements to machine learning techniques could make them less brittle in novel situations, which humans cope with by human common sense and higher cognition.[3] Human curiosity and desire to understand the world means that humans are devoted to causal explanations, even when there is a complex set of distant and proximate causes for events.

Both philosophies, rationalism and empiricism, offer valuable insights, so I apply rational thinking for its strengths, but I know that balancing it with an empirical outlook helps me see other possibilities and use observational strategies. Watching users of technology has always led me to fresh insights, so I am drawn to usability studies, interviews, naturalistic observations, and repeated weeks-long case studies with users doing their work to complement the rationalist approach of controlled experiments in laboratory settings.

I think a design philosophy that begins with empathy for users and pushes forward with humility about the limits of machines and people will help build more reliable, safe, and trustworthy systems. Empathy enables designers to be sensitive to the confusion and frustration that users might have and the dangers to people when AI systems fail, especially in consequential and life-critical applications. Humility leads designers to recognize the need for audit trails that can be retrospectively analyzed when the inevitable failures occur. Rationalists tend to expect the best and design for optimal performance; empiricists are always on the lookout for what could go wrong and what could be made better. They thrive on feedback from users.

Implications for Design

Future technology designs are closely tied to beliefs in rationalism or empiricism. The sympathy for rationalism leads some researchers to favor autonomous designs in which computers operate reliably without human oversight. While critics have pointed out the ironies, paradoxes, conundrums, deadly myths, and dangers of imperfect autonomous devices, this approach is still favored by many people. The discussion about autonomy becomes especially fierce when lethal autonomous weapons systems (LAWS)[4] are debated by military thinkers who see them as an important option and those who fear the dangers of misuse.

Autonomous vehicles or self-driving cars are vigorous technology directions which could have adequate levels of safety if designers took an empiricist's outlook to enable meaningful human control, even as the levels of automation increase.[5] Shifting from *self-driving* to *safety-first* cars might lead to more rapid improvements of proven methods such as collision avoidance, lane following, and parking assist. The shift to using terms like advanced driver assistance systems (ADAS) is an indication of awareness that improving driver performance is a more constructive goal than pushing for self-driving cars. Then further improvements will come from vehicle-to-vehicle communication, improved highway construction, and advanced highway management control centers that build on the strategies of air traffic control centers.

Many AI thinkers continue to imagine a future where social robots will become our teammates, partners, and collaborators. But making machines that pretend to have emotions seems counterproductive and focuses AI designers on a questionable goal. Computers don't have emotions; people do. Today, human-like social robots remain novelties, mostly confined to entertainment.

The AI community's sympathy for rationalism continues to lead developers to favor autonomous designs in which computers operate reliably without human oversight. While there is a growing choir who chant the chorus of a "human-in-the-loop," this phrase often implies a grudging acceptance of human control panels. Those who seek a complete and perfect system are resistant to the idea that there needs to be human intervention, oversight, and control.

A more compelling chorus for me would recognize that humans are happily woven into social networks and that computers should play a supportive role. Humans thrive in social structures of supervisors, peers, and staff whom they want to please, inspire, and respect. They also want feedback, appreciation for their accomplishments, and supportive guidance about how to do better. They use computers to amplify their ability to work in competent, safe, or extraordinary ways. This attitude fits nicely into a bumper sticker "Humans in the group; computers in the loop" (Figure 2.1).

Progress in technology design is likely to accelerate as recognition spreads that humans must have meaningful control of technology and are clearly responsible for the outcomes of their actions. This human-centered, empiricist-driven strategy would seem to be appropriate in military applications where responsibility within a chain of command is a core value.

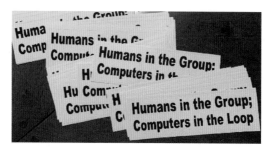

Fig 2.1 The bumper sticker "Humans in the Group; Computers in the Loop" reminds us that people are social and that they can use computers to support their performance.

Automation is invoked by humans, but they must be able to anticipate what happens, because they are responsible. One effective way to enable users to anticipate what happens is with direct manipulation designs—the objects and actions are represented on the screen; humans choose which actions to carry out; the actions and objects are all visible. Users drop a file into the trash can, accompanied by a clanging sound to signal that it has arrived. Touch screen pinches, taps, and swipes left and right become natural quickly. Visual interfaces provide an overview first, then allow users to zoom in on what they want and filter out what they don't want, and then get details on demand. Where possible, humans are in control and computers are predictable.

Humans want feedback to know that their intent is being carried out by the computer. They want to know what the computer will do next, in enough time to stop or change the action. That's why dialog boxes have a "Cancel" button, so there is a way to stop performance of undesirable actions and go back to a previous state.

Devotees of autonomous design often assume machines will do the right thing, with little interest in giving adequate feedback and even less interest in logging activity to support retrospective review of failures. A better strategy would be to follow civil aviation by installing a "flight data recorder in every robot." Adding audit trails, also called activity or product logs, would signal appropriate humility in addressing consequential and life-critical applications, thereby enabling retrospective analyses of failures and near misses and review of aggregate patterns of usage.

As flaws in AI-driven systems emerged to shatter the belief in their perfectibility, AI researchers have been forced to address issues such as biased evaluations for mortgage applications or parole requests. They began to take on fairness, accountability, transparency, explainability, and other design features that gave human developers, managers, users, and lawyers a better understanding of what was happening than in the previously closed black boxes. The good news is that a growing community of AI and HCAI researchers are shifting to empirical thinking as they study how to detect bias, what kinds of explanations are successful, and what redress methods for grievances work well.

The HCAI community's belief in empiricism leads participants to design systems with users at the center of attention. HCAI designers start by observing users in their homes and workplaces, interviewing users to get their feedback, and testing hypotheses with empirical studies. Designers conduct user-experience tests to guide repeated design revisions, and follow through with continuous monitoring to gain user feedback during use. HCAI thinking suggests incident reporting and suggestion box schemes, such as the FDA's Adverse Event Reporting System (AERS)[6] and the FAA's Aviation Safety Reporting System.[7]

While AI projects are often focused on replacing humans, HCAI designers favor developing information-rich visualizations and explanations built in, rather than added on. Today, the vast majority of apps are giving users more control—by showing highway navigation routes on maps, exercise histories in bar charts, and financial portfolios in line graphs. These information-abundant displays give users a clear understanding of what is happening and what they can do. Visual displays are now frequently complemented by audio interfaces based on speech recognition and generation, opening up new possibilities for diverse users to accomplish their tasks.

Those who share the rationalists' belief that computers are on the way to replacing people assume that future computers will be as intelligent as people, and also share human emotions. In short, they see no separation between people and what computers can become, so let me explain why I think people are in a different category from computers.

Are People and Computers in the Same Category?

A second contrast between AI and HCAI advocates is the issue of whether people are in the same category as computers or if they are distinct. The Stanford University AI-100 report states that "the difference between an arithmetic calculator and a human brain is not one of kind, but of scale, speed, degree of autonomy, and generality,"[1] which suggests that humans and computers are in the same category. In contrast, many HCAI sympathizers believe that there is a vast difference: "People are not computers. Computers are not people."

It's not that humans have a soul, a spirit, or are a mythical spark of life; it's just that the extraordinary human capabilities, formed by lengthy physical and cultural evolution, deserve appreciation. Human life can only be seen in the context of the remarkable tools people have refined over the generations, such as language, music, art, and mathematics, and technologies, such as clothing, housing, planes, and computers. Human creativity is also apparent in astonishing successes, such as agriculture, healthcare, cities, and legal systems. I believe that our historical role is to add to these technologies, tools for thinking, and cultural systems. Making a robot that simulates what a human does has value, but I'm more attracted to making supertools that dramatically amplify human abilities by a hundred- or thousand-fold. Past accomplishments have produced these kinds of astonishing technological advances, as do computers, the World Wide Web, email/texts, and mobile devices.

Maybe I should be more open to speculative discussions of what is possible in the long run. Maybe I should allow imaginative science fiction stories to open my mind to new possibilities of sentient computers, conscious machines, and superintelligent AI beings. I am driven by the assumption that people are uniquely creative and that my efforts are best directed towards making well-designed supertools that boost human performance.

Blurring the boundaries between people and computers diminishes appreciation of the richness, diversity, and creativity of people. I prefer to celebrate human accomplishments and treasure the remarkable cultural achievements in language, art, music, architecture, and much more, including machine learning and related algorithms, which are among the great human accomplishments. Clarifying the distinctions between people and computers increases respect for human responsibility and guides people in the appropriate ways to use computer power.[2]

Humans have bodies. Having a body makes you human. It puts us in touch with pain and pleasure, with sadness and joy. Crying and laughing, dancing and eating, love-making and thinking are all parts of being human. Emotions and passions are worth celebrating and fearing. Human emotions go far beyond the seven basic emotions that Paul Ekman described as universal: anger, contempt, disgust, enjoyment, fear, sadness, and surprise.[3] His work, which has been used in the AI community, oversimplifies the complexity of human emotions and their facial expressions. One direction for richer views of emotion is to do what many sentiment-analysis programs do, which is to assume that there are many more emotions (Figure 3.1).

Fig 3.1 Emotions, including the seven from Paul Ekman (blue), the negative emotions (red), the positive emotions (green), and some others (gray).

Source: Adapted from Susannah Paletz, Emotions Annotation Guide for Social Media, Version 3.32, January 21, 2020

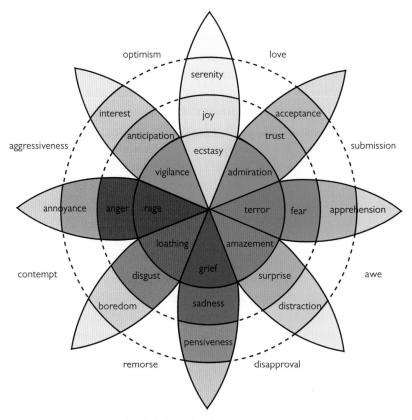

Fig 3.2 Wheel of human emotions.
Source: Robert Plutchik, 1980. Wiki Commons.
https://commons.wikimedia.org/wiki/Category:Plutchik%27s_Wheel_of_Emotions

For those who prefer a visual representation that also suggests stronger and weaker variations and the potential for emotions that fall between two categories, Robert Plutchik's wheel-like diagram with thirty-two emotions may be more appealing (Figure 3.2).

Another line of research sharply criticizes Paul Ekman's model, which might be called the classical view of emotions. In this mechanistic model of human behavior, internal emotional states of mind trigger accurate automatic expressions of emotion, which are the same for all humans. However, recent research, such as the work of Northeastern University psychologist Lisa Feldman-Barrett, favors a theory of *constructed emotions*, which are generated from sensory perceptions, cultural norms, and personal experiences, so expressions of emotions will be very different across individuals.[4] She describes emotional reactions as being constructed based on many factors, rather than automatically triggered and beyond human control. Therefore, facial expressions and body language are weak indicators of criminal intent, happiness, or fear. Human behavior is more complex than developers of simple algorithms for facial recognition programs assume. Measurable human actions, such as interrupting a speaker, moving closer to or farther away from someone, or making eye contact, can provide valuable feedback to help people change their behaviors.

Human emotions are extraordinarily complex and defy simple processes for recognizing them. Wikipedia's summary on emotions says: "There is currently no scientific consensus on a definition. Emotions are often intertwined with mood, temperament, personality, disposition, creativity, and motivation." Efforts to use facial recognition to determine personality, criminal intent, or political orientation can be as dangerous as the discredited ideas of phrenology, which suggested head and skull structures indicated mental abilities, personality, or criminal tendencies.[5]

While there is a large body of work on how computers can detect human emotional states and then respond to them, many researchers now question how accurate these can be. Even if it were possible, the idea of enabling social robots to express emotions in facial features, body language, and spoken language is troubling. Deceptive practices, whether banal or intended, can undermine the very trust that designers seek to build.[6] Emotional reactions by computers may be useful in entertainment or game applications, which may be enough to justify the research, but for most applications users want to get their tasks done with minimal distraction. Some users may be annoyed by or distrust computers that pretend to express emotion.

A more promising and reliable strategy is sentiment analysis, which analyzes text in social media posts, product reviews, or newspaper headlines. These aggregate data analyses, not attempt to identify the current emotions of an individual, can show differences in language usage by men and women, Democrats and Republicans, ethnic groups, or socioeconomic clusters. Sentiment analysis can also show changes over time, for example, to show that newspaper headlines have become increasingly negative.

Mimicking or imitating a human by computer is an enjoyable pursuit for some people, but a technology designer's imagination could be liberated by using other inspirations. More ambitious goals lead to valued innovations such as the World Wide Web, information visualization, assistive technology, Wikipedia, and augmented reality. These innovations extend human abilities to enable more people to be more creative more often.

Another central goal for me is to support human-to-human communication and cooperation, which have spawned success stories around email/texting, video conferencing, document sharing, and social media. Web-accessed videos, music, and game-playing are huge successes as well, often energized by going social to share favorites with friends, reach out to communicate with large audiences, and promote businesses to broad markets. All these successes have downsides of reducing face-to-face contacts, allowing mischievous scams, and permitting malicious actors to carry out crimes, spread hatred, or recruit terrorists. Just as residents can limit who comes into their homes, users should have rich controls to limit what kinds of messages they receive from autonomous anonymous bots. Social media platforms have yet to do their job to restrict misuses by giving users better controls over what they see.

Another question: what value is there in building computers that look and act like people? As we'll see in Part 3, there is a large community of people who believe that human-like, also called anthropomorphic, humanoid, or android, computers are the way of the future. This community wants to make social robots with human faces, arms, legs, and speech capabilities that could move around in a human world, maybe as older adult caretakers or disaster-response robots. This notion has lead to a long history of failures. Advocates say that this time is different because computers are so much more powerful and designers are so much more knowledgeable.

Human–human communication and relationships are just one model, and sometimes a misleading one, for the design of user interfaces. Humans relate to humans; humans operate computers. Improved interfaces will enable more people to carry out more tasks more rapidly and effectively. Voice is effective for human–human interaction, but visual designs of interfaces will be the dominant strategy because they enable users to operate computers rapidly. Voice user interfaces, such as Alexa and Siri, have an important role, especially when hands are busy and mobility is required (Chapter 16), even though the ephemeral and slow nature of voice communication limits its utility. Furthermore, human generation of speech commands requires substantial cognitive effort and working memory resources, limiting the parallel effort possible when using hand gestures and controls.

Interface designs that are consistent, predictable, and controllable are comprehensible, thus enabling mastery, satisfaction, and responsibility. They will be more widely used than ones that are adaptive, autonomous, and anthropomorphic.

Amplifying human abilities is a worthy goal. Telescopes and microscopes are extensions of the human eye that amplify human abilities. Calculators, digital libraries, and email enable users to do things that no human could do unaided. We need more powerful augmentation and amplification tools that empower people. One approach is the development of creativity support tools that give artists, musicians, poets, playwrights, photographers, and videographers more flexibility to explore alternatives and creatively produce something novel, interesting, and meaningful. Cameras and musical instruments have extended the possibilities of what people can do, but the human is still the driving creative source. Newer devices are likely to carry forward that tradition.

However, some researchers claim that AI technologies do more than empower people; these new technologies are the creators themselves. This claim goes back to the early days of computer art, at least to the time when Jasia Reichardt curated the Cybernetic Serendipity exhibition in London in 1968. Soon after that, Harold Cohen began working on a program he called AARON, which generated images of plants, people, and more abstract forms that were widely appreciated because they resembled watercolor paintings that appeared to have been made by a human. However, Harold Cohen was clearly the creator and therefore the recipient of the 2014 Lifetime Achievement Award in Digital Art from the largest computer graphics professional society, ACM's SIGGRAPH.

Other forms of computer-generated art has more geometric patterns in them, often with algorithmically generated features, adding to the suggestion that the art pieces go beyond the artist's imagination. Leading contributors such as Paul Brown[7] and Ernest Edmonds[8] have exhibited around the world and their work has been collected by major art galleries and museums. Brown uses evolving generative patterns and seeks art "that makes itself," but his books and exhibits list him as the artist. Edmonds, who is also a respected computer scientist, pursues interactive art that changes depending on who is viewing the art. He uses computation "to extend and amplify my creative process not to replace it." Like Harold Cohen, Ernest Edmonds received the ACM SIGGRAPH Lifetime Achievement Award in Digital Art in 2017.

Current AI art producers see their work as a step forward in that they create ever-more ambitious images that are surprising even to the programmers. These artists like, Alexander Mordvintsev,[9] produce something magical in that their Generative Adversarial Networks (GANs) use machine learning algorithms, trained on a set of images, so that the program can act autonomously to make novel images. Mordvintsev's DeepDream program[10] produces engaging and sometimes troubling images of distorted animals with multiple heads, eyes looking through furry limbs, and pets merging into their backgrounds in ways that challenge our view of reality.

While Harold Cohen considered AARON to be acting autonomously to generate images that were surprising to him, he told me that ultimately he was the creator of the artworks. While potent algorithms and technologies give artists new ways of producing art, the artists are still the source of the creative passion. AARON's work and recent AI art have gotten attention by being sold at auction, yet the proceeds and copyright still come to the artist-creator.

Computer-generated music also stimulates lively discussions of whether the music is produced by the human programmer or by the AI-driven computer program. Computer music algorithms have long been able to generate new music in the style of Bach or the Beatles, Mozart or Madonna, but critics disagree about whether the credit should go to the author or the algorithm. Some algorithms trained on databases of popular songs generate lyrics and music, giving a still richer sense of innovation. However, musicians, like jazz performer and musical therapist Daniel Sarid, suggest that these explorations are "an interesting exercise in understanding human cognition and esthetic organization as well as what constitutes musical language, but, has nothing to do with art." Sarid suggests that composers have a higher goal—they are on "a quest into the collective unconscious of the society/community within which he/she creates."[11]

Some enthusiasts would like to grant computer algorithms intellectual property rights for the images and music produced, but the US copyright office will only grant ownership to humans or organizations. Similar efforts have been made to have computer algorithms hold patents, which have yet to win legal approval. The debate continues, even though it is still unclear how algorithms would rise up to defend their intellectual property, pay damages, or serve jail time for violations.

As time passes, we will see more clearly that people are not computers and computers are not people. As people develop more ambitious embedded computerized applications, the computer as an object of attention will vanish, just as steel, plastics, and glass have become largely invisible parts of our surroundings. Even as computers become more powerful, the notion of computers being intelligent will be seen as naïve and quaint, just as alchemy and astrology are seen now.

That's the future, but let's examine the more immediate question that is on many people's minds: will automation, AI, and robots lead to widespread unemployment?

CHAPTER 4

Will Automation, AI, and Robots Lead to Widespread Unemployment?

The third discussion is over the issue of whether automation, AI, and robots will lead to widespread unemployment. Many books, including Martin Ford's 2015 book *The Robots Are Coming,*[1] spread the fears raised by an Oxford University report that 47% of US jobs were automatable by 2030.[2] These preposterous claims, suggesting widespread unemployment, were clearly wrong, as unemployment in the United States dropped to below 4% in 2020, even as automation, AI, and robots spread. Then the COVID-19 crisis arrived and unemployment rose because of the tragic and widespread epidemic. By 2021 the vaccine began to control COVID-19 cases and unemployment began to decline again.

Amazon bought Kiva Robotics in 2012, leading many to believe that it would trim its 125,000-person workforce, but by 2021, even with increased use of robots, Amazon employed more than a million people. The dramatic increase in demand, made even more extreme during the COVID crisis, led to much expanded labor needs in its supply chains, fulfillment centers, and delivery networks. Amazon's well-designed e-commerce websites and low prices brought benefits to many, thereby increasing demand. While Amazon has been criticized for its labor practices and its opposition to labor unions, it has led many companies by offering a $15 minimum wage, although often with reduced benefits.[3] Reports about demanding working conditions and higher rates of injuries than other companies have led many consumers to avoid shopping with Amazon. The controversies remain with protesters appearing at Amazon fulfillment centers, even as long lines of potential employees respond to job opportunities. The unknown factor is how many small store employees have lost their jobs and how many local suppliers and manufacturers have added jobs because of their capacity to sell by way of Amazon's extensive network. Yes, these changes have been disruptive, but the impact on employment is less clear and the benefits to consumers have increased sales.

Another dilemma is that unemployment is an imperfect measure since it does not count those who have dropped out of the job market and fails to tabulate the increasing fraction of minimum wage workers who have fewer benefits. Corporate owners may care more about market valuations than profits, so their goals are sales growth by way of low prices rather than better treatment of their workers.

Automation appears to increase concentration of wealth that produces ever-growing inequalities, with poorly educated workers suffering the most. The focus on growth at the cost of poor employee treatment is a serious danger of increased automation. Amazon has fought the introduction of labor unions, which have in the past enabled workers to get better wages, working conditions, health insurance, and benefits such as child care, sick pay, vacations, and pensions. The central question is how to distribute the benefits of automation more equitably.

Automation eliminates certain jobs, as it has for hundreds of years, from at least the time when Gutenberg's printing presses put scribes out of work. However, automation usually lowers costs and increases quality, leading to vastly expanded demand, which triggers expanded production to serve growing markets, bringing benefits to many people. The expanded production, broader distribution channels, and novel products lead to increased employment. Low-cost book production led to larger markets, growth of book distribution and sales networks, and greatly increased literacy. Another benefit of increased book production is the demand for authors to write books, leading to creative expressions, religious controversies, and political upheaval. Printed books were a powerful disruption but they are generally seen as an accelerator of education, business, better health, and much more.

Disruptions from AI-based automation follow a familiar historical pattern, leading to fear-provoking descriptions of never-before-seen widespread unemployment. The claim that this time the impact will be worse than ever before seems weak to me and to many economists. Agriculture accounted for 40% of employment in 1900, but now is only 4%, yet we don't see 36%

unemployment. Instead of working on farm food production, employment has grown in suppliers for agribusinesses, vast food distribution networks, and processed food manufacturers. New jobs have been generated in supermarkets that are now stocked with diverse produce and packaged goods at affordable prices. In addition, restaurants selling to rich and poor all create new employment possibilities. Here again, a troubling concern is how much the vast growth in automation increases inequality, which has surged to troubling levels.

As excitement about social robots matures, the latest surge of interest and fear is around robotic process automation (RPA), which continues the long history of accounting and back-office automation that did away with stock market trading and check-clearing clerks who filled vast halls on Wall Street and Main Street. RPA automates still more accounting and clerical jobs, which are painful disruptions for those affected, but well in line with the scale of previous waves of automation. The pressures of competition are a reality, but the reduced costs of transactions are a benefit to many. Respected socially responsive corporations can help these displaced workers share in the benefits of automation by providing training for better jobs in their corporations or helping them find job elsewhere.

The exaggerations about dramatic technology revolutions go back at least to the early days of telegraphy, automobiles, and aviation. Strong language was used in 1970 when Alvin Toffler's international bestseller, *Future Shock*, declared that "What is occurring now is, in all likelihood, bigger, deeper, and more important than the industrial revolution. . . . nothing less than the second great divide in human history, comparable in magnitude only with . . . the shift from barbarism to civilization."[4] Yes, it was true that tumultuous changes were happening in the 1970s, but similar periods of turmoil have and will continue to occur. The lessons of history are familiar and clear:

- Weaving machines led to the Luddite revolt early in the eighteenth century, which produced a dramatic drop in textile prices, triggering much greater demand. The expanded production of cloth, the growing fashion industry, and new clothing distribution channels increased employment, while enabling more people to own more clothes.

- When Louis Daguerre announced photography in 1839, famed French artist Louis Delaroche declared that "from today painting is dead," but the flourishing impressionist and other movements showed that there was much creative work to be done beyond photo-realistic landscapes and portraits. Photography, video, and visual communications expanded creative possibilities to become big businesses, enriching the lives of many people.

- In the 1960s, automated teller machines were supposed to put bank employees out of work, but the number of branches has increased as more people have taken advantage of expanded services such as mortgage loans and credit cards, thereby raising employment in banks. Now as online banking spreads, local branches may be disappearing, but bank and financial services employment keeps rising.

The main effect of automation is typically to lower costs and increase quality, which increases demand and expands production, bringing benefits to customers while increasing employment. Automation is also disruptive by making certain skills obsolete, so there are substantial challenges to technology innovators and policy-makers, especially in helping those whose jobs are destroyed and in ensuring greater fairness in distributing the benefits of automation so that workers can make a living wage and receive better treatment.

The need to ensure more equitable sharing of the benefits of automation was stressed in the thoughtful 2020 report from the MIT Work of the Future project, which called on policy-makers to build "a future for work that harvests the dividends of rapidly advancing automation and ever-more powerful computers to deliver opportunity and economic security for workers."[5] The report author team, led by David Autor, David Mindell, and Elisabeth Reynolds, recognized that changes would not come naturally, so pressures had to be put on business leaders: "to channel the rising productivity stemming from technological innovations into broadly shared gains, we must foster institutional innovations that complement technological change."[6]

The report reaffirmed that the future of work was bright:

we anticipate that in the next two decades, industrialized countries will have more job openings than workers to fill them, and that robotics and automation will play an increasingly crucial role in closing these gaps . . . innovations bring new occupations to life, generate demands for new forms of expertise, and create opportunities for rewarding work.[7]

While disruptions for those who lose their jobs is severe, the report goes on to say that "new goods and services, new industries and occupations demand new skills and offer new earnings opportunities."[8]

The US Bureau of Labor Statistics lists occupations that are expected to grow, especially in medical care, which has increased from 12% to 22% of employment with jobs such as home healthcare aides, registered nurses, medical therapists, medical managers, mental health counselors, and nursing assistants. Other growth areas are in starter jobs for younger, poorly educated, or immigrant populations such as food distribution, fast food workers, and warehouse staff. Better jobs are in technical fields such as software engineering, financial management, and renewable energy systems installation.

What forms of public pressure, corporate social responsibility, and government regulation will push business leaders and policy-makers to share the benefits of automation through higher minimum wages, better medical insurance, and expanded child care? How can these leaders be convinced that they will benefit if employees have better lives and become active participants in a growing economy, thereby reducing the harmful effects of growing income inequality? Ambitious efforts to create new opportunities for displaced workers, increase access to education, and develop job training with local businesses should be part of the response. Some workers may need skills training and encouragement to explore new possibilities. New jobs can help those ready to learn something new: healthcare, equipment maintenance, delivery services, and renewable energy installation. Growth will also come in the leisure, restaurant, personal services, and entertainment industries. These changes will take resources and imagination to realize, so technology companies and regulatory agencies have a responsibility to be more active in making serious commitments to worker welfare, while mitigating the effects of growth on environmental concerns.

CHAPTER 5

Summary and Skeptic's Corner

Theory without practice cannot survive and dies as quickly as it lives. He[/she] who loves practice without theory is like the sailor who boards a ship without a rudder and compass and never knows where he[/she] may cast.

Leonardo da Vinci

Forecasting the future is a risky business, so Alan Kay suggested that the best way to predict the future was to invent it. I take his encouragement seriously, so this book provides a vision of a technology future that is centered on increasing human control over ever more powerful supertools, telebots, active appliances, and control centers.

This vision suggests a new synthesis that values AI algorithms equally with human values that support rights, justice, and dignity. These AI and HCAI views emerge from an ongoing debate between the rationalists, who favor logical thinking based on laboratory research, and empiricists, who pursue real-world observations with an empathy for human needs. Both approaches have value, so I have come to blend rationalist thinking with an empiricist approach.

HCAI is based on processes that extend user-experience design methods of user observation, stakeholder engagement, usability testing, iterative refinement, and continuing evaluation of human performance in the use of systems that employ AI algorithms such as machine learning. The goal is to create products and services that amplify, augment, empower, and enhance human performance. HCAI systems emphasize human control, while embedding high levels of automation.

Many people still believe that computers can simulate, compete, and maybe replace people. I see people as being in a separate category, and that well-designed computers can help them do better, just as telescopes, electrocardio-grams, and airplanes have done in the past. Even as computers become more powerful and algorithms more sophisticated, the dominant design strategy will be to build supertools, tele-bots, active appliances, and control centers that empower people with more control over ever more advanced automation.

The disruptions to people's work lives from automation are real, so substantial efforts are needed to improve worker welfare and reduce inequality. While there are admirable corporate leaders, even they may have difficulty doing the right thing to pursue reliable, safe, and trustworthy systems in the face of stockholder pressure and their own ambitions. The challenges will come in difficult economic times and when competitors threaten their positions. Past history suggests that protections are needed for those with lower levels of education, wealth, power, and representation. While journalists, lawyers, and public interest groups can provide a counterforce, government intervention and regulation may also be needed.

There is growing support for human-centered thinking, but this new synthesis challenges existing practices. Skeptics doubt that the shift from an AI-centered thinking to a new HCAI synthesis that gives equal value to human-centered thinking will be more than a fringe trend. They believe that future technologies will come from further work on advanced algorithms that broaden the capabilities of machine learning and its many deep learning variations. Their solution to the problems of AI is more and better AI.

The large AI research community is focused on algorithmic advances, so they have little need for a human-centered approach. Journalists celebrate AI breakthroughs that feature machines doing tasks better than humans and intelligent autonomous systems that operate on their own. Celebrated neural network developer and Turing Award winner Geoff Hinton said in 2016 that "people should stop training radiologists now. It's just completely obvious that within five years deep learning is going to do better than radiologists."[1] I hope Hinton has come to appreciate that radiologists, who do much more than search for tumors, will be greatly empowered by having powerful deep learning tools, just as other doctors have gained much by having X-ray machines, electrocardiograms, and thousands of other supertools.

Another example of how fresh thinking could lead to new possibilities is with the large group of researchers who see an auspicious future for social robots which mimic human forms and behaviors. They believe that social robots will become our teammates, partners, and collaborators, but alternatively, tele-bots and active appliances could dramatically enhance human performance on common tasks. Many strong AI believers hold that common-sense reasoning, artificial general intelligence, and machine consciousness are possible, and even inevitable, but maybe the future is with ever more potent devices that expand human possibilities like airplanes, the World Wide Web, and DNA sequencers. These devices enable users to do things that no human has done before.

My challenge is to offer a convincing case that future technologies will be based on human-centered designs that increase human control, so as to amplify, augment, empower, and enhance people. At the same time, I fear that these advanced technologies will be used by cybercriminals, hate groups, terrorists, and oppressive governments, so these and other dangers need to be taken seriously. There is an old saying that "eternal vigilance is the price of liberty," which seems like good advice in thinking about how technology could enhance human autonomy.

However, my optimistic side recognizes that with all its potential dangers, technology has brought health, economic prosperity, safer communities, and continuing high levels of employment, as well as unimagined jobs in new industries. If those who are in positions to shape technology work to help those in need, support democratic institutions, and sustain the environment, then better lives for many are possible. In the longer run, further breakthroughs will increase human self-efficacy, creativity, responsibility, and social connections.

PART 2

Human-Centered AI Framework

6 Introduction: Rising above the Levels of Automation

7 Defining Reliable, Safe, and Trustworthy Systems

8 Two-Dimensional HCAI Framework

9 Design Guidelines and Examples

10 Summary and Skeptic's Corner

The success of AI algorithms has brought many new possibilities for improving design of widely used technologies. Researchers, developers, managers, and policy-makers who embrace human-centered approaches will accelerate the design and adoption of advanced technologies. The new synthesis that combines AI algorithms with human-centered design will take time.

Part 2 shows how human-centered AI ideas open up new possibilities for design of systems that offer high levels of human control and high levels of computer automation. It will take time to refine and disseminate this idea and respond to resistance. I believe that these designs can increase human performance by providing just the right automated features, which can be accomplished reliably, while giving users control of the features that are important to them.

The human-centered artificial intelligence (HCAI) framework clarifies how to (1) design for high levels of human control and high levels of computer automation so as to increase human performance, (2) understand the situations in which full human control or full computer control are necessary, and (3) avoid the dangers of excessive human control or excessive computer control. Achieving these goals will also support human self-efficacy, creativity, responsibility, and social connections.

The guidelines and examples show how to put the HCAI framework into practice.

CHAPTER 6

Introduction: Rising above the Levels of Automation

Unlike machines, human minds can create ideas. We need ideas to guide us to progress, as well as tools to implement them . . . Computers don't contain "brains" any more than stereos contain musical instruments . . . Machines only manipulate numbers; people connect them to meaning.

Arno Penzias, *Nobel Prize in Physics (1989)*

This chapter opens up new possibilities by way of a two-dimensional framework of human-centered artificial intelligence (HCAI) that separates levels of automation/autonomy from levels of human control. The new guideline is to seek both *high levels of human control* and *high levels of automation*, which is more likely to produce computer applications that are reliable, safe, and trustworthy. Achieving these goals, especially for complex, poorly understood problems, will dramatically increase human performance, while supporting human self-efficacy, creativity, responsibility, and social connections. This chapter focuses on the reliable, safe, and trustworthy goals, which may help to achieve other important goals such as privacy, cybersecurity, economic development, and environmental preservation.

I share the belief that computer autonomy is compelling for many applications. Who wouldn't want an autonomous device that would do a repetitive or difficult task reliably and safely? But what if it does that task correctly only 98% of the time? Or if it catches fire once in a hundred times?

Autonomy may be fine for some tasks, but dangerous for others. In consumer applications, like making recommendations, unusual films, or offbeat restaurants might lead to a welcome discovery, so the dangers of errors are low. For other tasks, like sensor-based pattern recognition for flushing a toilet in a bathroom, incorrect activations or failure to activate are minor annoyances. However, if the task is driving you to work, would you accept a car that once a month took an hour to start or a car that occasionally parked itself a mile from your workplace? For lightweight tasks like toilet flushing, failures are just an annoyance, but for transportation, health, financial, and military applications higher levels of reliability, safety, and trustworthiness are needed to gain the high levels of user acceptance that lead to commercial success.

But maybe there are designs of recommender systems, toilet flushing, or car driving in which users can take more control of what the machine does, prevent failures, and take over when user intent is not fulfilled. In a study of a news recommender system, users were given three sliders to allow them to indicate their interest in reading politics, sports, or entertainment articles. As users move the sliders, the list of recommended articles changes immediately so users can explore alternatives, leading to users clicking on recommendations more often and expressing "a strong desire for having more control."[1] A second study of two different control panels for a news recommender showed similar strong results favoring user control.[2]

Some recommender systems allow users to register their dissatisfaction with a recommendation, so that over time the recommender systems become more accurate. Automated toilets typically have a button to push to force flushing when the system has not activated automatically.

Despite many good designs, there is room for improvement in existing systems. I had an annoying experience at a swimming pool I go to regularly. While I was getting dressed, the changing room toilet flushed unnecessarily eight times, but I could see no way of stopping the automated device that used pattern recognition technologies from AI's early days. By contrast, I often had trouble activating the sink and the hand dryer, which became a nuisance. These pattern recognition devices were neither reliable or trustworthy. A remedy would be a standard icon, approved by all manufacturers, placed just at the spot where the pattern recognition sensor would be sure to spot it or a button to turn the sink or dryer on.

The black mats in front of automatic doors are usually not the sensor, but they are a clear indicator that stepping on to the mat will put you in the place where the camera sensor will pick up your image. Override buttons for users with handicaps enable them to activate the door on demand and keep the door open for longer, so they can get through safely. Greater user control, even in these relatively low-tech applications, make for a more reliable, safe, and trustworthy system.

In summary, automated systems can be wonderful, but strategies to ensure activation when needed and prevent inadvertent activations contribute to reliable, safe, and trustworthy operation that increases user acceptance. Good design also includes ways for maintenance staff to gather performance data to know whether the operation is correct and adjust controls to make sure the device functions correctly.

These issues become vital in life-critical applications such as airbag deployment. Airbags explosively deploy in two-tenths of a second to save about 2500 lives a year in the United States. However, in the early years more than 100 infants and elders were killed by inadvertent deployments, until design changes reduced the frequency of these tragedies. The important lesson is that collecting data on unsuccessful and inadvertent deployments provides the information necessary for refinements that make systems reliable, safe, and trustworthy. When autonomous systems' failures and near misses are tracked to support improved designs and when public websites enable reporting of incidents, quality and acceptance increase.

For consequential applications such as car driving, safety comes first. I might be willing to buy a car that would not let me drive if my breath alcohol was above legal levels. I would be even more eager to require that all cars had such a system so as to prevent others from endangering me. On the other hand, if that system made an incorrect measurement when I was excitedly getting in my car to drive my injured child to the hospital, I would be very angry, because the car was not trustworthy.

The first lesson about autonomous systems, which we will return to later, is that user controls to activate, operate, and override can make for more reliable, safe, and trustworthy systems. The second lesson is that performance histories, called audit trails or product logs, provide valuable data that lead to continuous design refinements. Maybe the most important lesson is that humility is an important quality for designers, who will be more successful if they think carefully about the possibilities of failures.

Enthusiasm has long been high about automated/autonomous systems using technologies such as machine learning, neural nets, statistical methods, recommenders, adaptive systems, and speech, facial, image, and pattern recognition. The goal of computer autonomy was central in the minds of MIT professor Tom Sheridan and his graduate student William Verplank in 1978 when they wrote

Table 6.1 *Summary of the widely cited, but one-dimensional levels of automation/autonomy*

Level	Description
	The Computer:
10 (High)	decides everything and acts autonomously, ignoring the human
9	informs the human only if the computer decides to
8	informs the human only if asked
7	executes automatically, then necessarily informs the human
6	allows the human a restricted time to veto before automatic execution
5	executes the suggestion, if the human approves
4	suggests one alternative
3	narrows the selection down to a few
2	offers a complete set of decision-and-action alternatives
1 (Low)	offers no assistance; the human must take all decisions and actions

Adapted from Parasuraman et al.[4]

about ten levels from human control to computer autonomy (Table 6.1).[3] Their widely cited one-dimensional list continues to guide much of the research and development, suggesting that increases in automation must come at the cost of lowering human control. But this zero-sum assumption limits thinking about ways to increase human control and the level of automation. There is a better way.

Sheridan and Verplank's ten levels of autonomy have been widely influential, but critics noticed that it was incomplete, missing important aspects of what users do. Over the years, there have been many refinements such as recognizing that there were at least four *stages* of automation: (1) information acquisition, (2) analysis of information, (3) decision or choice of action, and (4) execution of action.[5] These stages open the door to thinking about whether users might have greater control during some of the stages, especially during the decision-making stage. Computers could present choices to the human operators, who might select the option for the computer to carry out. This nuanced approach was on the right track towards identifying the combined strategy that gives human control for decisions and supports automation when it is reliable. The human operators may also make a note to suggest additional options or clarifications that could be added to the next software update.

The four stages were an important refinement that helped keep the levels of autonomy alive, even as critics continued to be troubled by the simple one-dimensional framework, which assumed that more automation meant less human control. Shifting to the two-dimensional framework for HCAI, presented in Chapter 8, could liberate design thinking so as to produce

Table 6.2 *Persistent, but still misleading, one-dimensional thinking about levels of autonomy for self-driving cars*[6]

Level	Description
5 (High)	**Full autonomy**: equal to that of a human driver, in every driving scenario.
4	**High automation**: fully autonomous vehicles perform all safety-critical driving functions in certain areas and under defined weather conditions.
3	**Conditional automation**: driver shifts "safety critical functions" to the vehicle under certain traffic or environmental conditions.
2	**Partial automation**: at least one driver assistance system is automated. Driver is disengaged from physically operating the vehicle (hands off the steering wheel AND foot off the pedal at the same time).
I	**Driver assistance**: most functions are still controlled by the driver, but a specific function (like steering or accelerating) can be done automatically by the car.
0 (Low)	**No automation**: human driver controls all: steering, brakes, throttle, power.

computer applications that increase automation, while amplifying, augmenting, empowering, and enhancing people to apply systems innovatively and creatively refine them.

Even Tom Sheridan commented with concern that "surprisingly, the level descriptions as published have been taken more seriously than were expected."[7] Robert R. Hoffman and Matt Johnson provide a fascinating history of how researchers struggled to preserve the levels of autonomy idea.[8] However, despite the many critiques, the one-dimensional level of autonomy, which only represents situations where increased automation must come with less human control, is still widely influential. For example, the US Society of Automotive Engineers adopted the unnecessary trade-off in its six levels of autonomy for self-driving cars (Table 6.2).[9] A better approach would be to clarify what features could be automated, like collision avoidance or parking assist, and what activities required human control, like dealing with snow-covered roads, sensor failures, or verbal instructions from police officers.

Critics of autonomy have repeatedly discussed the ironies,[10] deadly myths,[11] conundrums,[12] or paradoxes[13] of autonomy. The strong team of Jeff Bradshaw, Robert R. Hoffman, David D. Woods, and Matt Johnson from the Institute for Human and Machine Cognition wrote a sharply worded article: "The Seven Deadly Myths of Autonomous Systems."[14] They point to myths such as "once achieved, full autonomy obviates the need for human machine collaboration," which they mock as an obvious misunderstanding of how teams collaborate in interdependent ways. The "Deadly Myths" article cautions designers who "have succumbed to myths of autonomy that are not only damaging in their own right but are also damaging by their continued propagation . . . because they engender a host of other serious misconceptions and consequences."[15] Their article and many others make the strong point that humans must monitor what autonomous systems are doing, so design effort is needed to let humans know what an autonomous system is doing and what it will do next.

The US Defense Science Board report describes the ten levels of autonomy this way: "though attractive, the conceptualization of levels of autonomy as a scientific grounding for a developmental roadmap has been unproductive."[16] A later US Defense Science Board report described many opportunities and dangers with autonomy.[17] Cognitive science researchers like Robert R. Hoffman and his colleagues point to the failures and costs of autonomous weapons, which have had unintended deadly consequences.[18] A clear example of excessive autonomy with deadly outcomes was with the Patriot missile system, which inadvertently shot down British and American aircraft during the 2003 Iraq War.[19]

Another tragic case of excessive automation was the two Boeing 737 MAX crashes in October 2018 and March 2019 causing 346 deaths.[20] While there are many problems that led to these crashes, I choose to focus on the autonomous control system which failed because of a malfunctioning sensor, causing the control system to point the plane's nose down. The frantic pilots tried to pull the plane up more than twenty times in the minutes before the crash. The developers of the autonomous control system believed it was so reliable that pilots were not even informed about its presence in their training or user manuals, so they could not figure out what to do to restore their control of the aircraft.

Autonomous systems and humans can both fail, so recovery from failures, such as loss of power, communication, mobility, or sensors, needs to be a primary concern.[21] Until highways become controlled spaces like elevator shafts, there will likely be a need for a human operator to deal with fallen trees on roadways, construction crews that halt traffic, or vandals who spray paint over sensors.

The problems brought by autonomy are captured in Texas A&M professor Robin Murphy's law of autonomous robots: "any deployment of robotic systems will fall short of the target level of autonomy, creating or exacerbating a shortfall in mechanisms for coordination with human problem holders."[22]

Critics of human control make two strong claims. The first claim is that humans make mistakes, so automation can prevent such mistakes, working tirelessly and consistently. There is value in this concern, so designers include interlocks and other safety-ensuring features where possible from safety razors to nuclear reactor control rods. Understanding mistakes and how to prevent them takes research, which leads to design of appropriate features. There can always be unanticipated human mistakes, changing contexts of use, and adversarial attacks, so design vigilance is needed continuously over the lifetime of a product or service. The second claim is that even if controls are included, only a small number of users will learn how to use them and bother to use them. While some controls are of little interest to users, many controls are poorly designed, making them difficult to use. When controls are desired and well-designed, they are widely used, as in the case of adjustments for car seats, driving wheel positions, and rear- and side-view mirrors. Environmental controls in cars are necessary to set preferences for lighting, radio volume, window-opening position, and heating, ventilation, or air-conditioning level. The large number of controls in word processors, spreadsheets, and photo, video, and music editing programs add evidence that when features are desired and well-designed they are used.

Fortunately, there is growing awareness by leading artificial intelligence researchers and developers that human-centered designs are needed. Fei-Fei Li, a Stanford University computer science professor and the chief scientist for AI research at Google Cloud, wrote in a March 2018 *New York Times* opinion piece about the need to "make AI that's good for people." She sees a "trend toward automating those elements of jobs that are repetitive, error-prone and even dangerous. What's left are the creative, intellectual and emotional roles for which humans are still best suited." Professor Li concludes: "However autonomous our technology becomes, its impact on the world—for better or worse—will always be our responsibility."[23]

Fei-Fei Li also aligned behind the term "human-centered AI," which became the name of the Stanford University Institute that she co-founded with John Etchemendy, a Stanford philosophy professor who served as provost. They wrote: "As creators of this new technology, it is our collective responsibility to guide AI so that it has a positive impact on our planet, our nations, our communities, our families and our lives."[24]

Michael Jordan, a top machine learning researcher at the University of California-Berkeley, wrote a powerful statement in April 2018, saying that "the principles needed to build planetary-scale inference-and-decision-making systems of this kind, blending computer science with statistics, and taking into account human utilities, were nowhere to be found in my education."[25] He claimed: "What we're missing is an engineering discipline with its principles of analysis and design," which surprised me because he surely knows about human–computer interaction. He goes on to rightly question whether "working on classical human-imitative AI is the best or only way to focus on these larger challenges?" Jordan recommends that, what seems like a wise path forward: "We will need well-thought-out interactions of humans and computers to solve our most pressing problems. And we will want computers to trigger new levels of human creativity, not replace human creativity."[26]

Chapter 7 discusses the strategies for achieving reliable, safe, and trustworthy systems. Chapter 8 lays out the novel two-dimensional HCAI framework, describing different design objectives and the path to high levels of human control and high levels of automation. The HCAI framework rises above the belief in the one-dimensional levels of autonomy, which has been widely used for the past forty years. Chapter 9 provides design principles that guide thinking about novel systems plus examples to clarify what has been done and what is needed. Chapter 10 summarizes the HCAI framework and its limitations.

CHAPTER 7

Defining Reliable, Safe, and Trustworthy Systems

While machine autonomy remains a popular goal, the goal of human autonomy should remain equally strong in designers' minds. Machine and human autonomy are both valuable in certain contexts, but a combined strategy uses automation when it is reliable and human control when it is necessary. To guide design improvements it will be helpful to focus on the attributes that make HCAI systems *reliable, safe, and trustworthy*. These terms are complex, but I choose to define them with four levels of recommendations (see Part 4): (1) reliable systems based on sound software engineering practices, (2) safety culture through business management strategies, (3) trustworthy certification by independent oversight, and (4) regulation by government bodies.

These four communities are eager to accelerate development of reliable, safe, and trustworthy systems. Software engineers, business managers, independent oversight committees, and government regulators all care about the three goals, but I suggest practices that each community might be most effective in supporting.

Reliable[1] systems produce expected responses when needed. Reliability comes from appropriate technical practices for software engineering teams (Chapter 19). When failures occur, investigators can review detailed audit trails, much like the logs of flight data recorders, which have been so effective in civil aviation. The technical practices that support human responsibility, fairness, and explainability include:

- Audit trails and analysis tools
- Software engineering workflows
- Verification and validation testing
- Bias testing to enhance fairness
- Explainable user interfaces

Ample testing of software and analyses of training data used in machine learning promotes fairness. Explainability comes from many design features, but I focus on visual user interfaces that prevent or reduce the need for explainability.

Cultures of *safety*[2] are created by managers who focus on these strategies (Chapter 20):

- Leadership commitment to safety
- Hiring and training oriented to safety
- Extensive reporting of failures and near misses
- Internal review boards for problems and future plans
- Alignment with industry standard practices

These strategies guide continuous refinement of training, operational practices, and root-cause failure analyses. In software engineering communities, the thirty-five-year-old Capability Maturity Models, developed by the Software Engineering Institute at Carnegie Mellon University, help team managers in applying the practices that support safety.[3] Managers can work to move their organization up through five levels of maturity, which are marked by increasingly consistent policies and measurement strategies that lead to increased software quality. The Capability Maturity Models are not perfect, but they remain in use, especially for military projects and cybersecurity.

Trustworthy systems are discussed more frequently than ever, but there is a long history of discussions to define *trust*. An influential contribution was political scientist Francis Fukuyama's book *Trust: The Social Virtues and the Creation of Prosperity*, which focused on social trust "within a community of regular, honest, and cooperative behavior, based on commonly shared norms, on the part of the members of that community."[4] He focused on human communities, but there are lessons for design of trust in technology.

However, public expectations go beyond trust or trusted systems; users want *trustworthy* systems. A system could be mistakenly trusted, but a trustworthy system is one that deserves trust, even though stakeholders struggle to measure that attribute. I take the position that trustworthiness is assessed by respected independent oversight. Since most consumers do not have the skill and cannot invest the effort to assess the trustworthiness of a system, they rely on established organizations, such as Consumer's Report or Underwriters Laboratory. If a respected accounting firm, insurance company, or consumer advocacy group gives its seal of approval to a product or service, then consumers are likely to see it as trustworthy. The list of independent oversight organizations (Chapter 21) includes:

- Accounting firms conducting external audits
- Insurance companies compensating for failures
- Non-governmental and civil society organizations
- Professional organizations and research institutes

Government intervention and regulation also play an important role as protectors of the public interest, especially when large corporations elevate their agendas above the needs of residents and citizens (Chapter 22). Governments can encourage innovation as much as they can limit it, so learning from successes and failures will help policy-makers to make better decisions.

I chose to focus on reliable, safe, and trustworthy to simplify the discussion, but the rich literature on these topics advocates other attributes of systems, their performance, and user perceptions (Figure 7.1). These twenty-five attributes are all difficult to measure and resistant even to basic assessments, such as whether design changes would increase or decrease these attributes. Still, these are the attributes that are frequently used in discussions and ethical, responsible, or humane AI. Chapter 25 deals with the difficult issue of assessment.

Users of mature technologies such as elevators, cameras, home appliances, or medical devices know when these devices are reliable, safe, and trustworthy. They appreciate the high levels of automation but think of themselves as operating these devices in ways that give them control so as to accomplish their goals. Designers who adopt the HCAI mindset will emphasize strategies for enabling diverse users to steer, operate, and control their highly automated devices, while inviting users to exercise their creativity to refine designs. Well-designed automation can ensure finer human control, such as in surgical robots that enable surgeons to make precise incisions in difficult to reach organs.

Successful technologies enable humans to work in interdisciplinary teams so as to coordinate and collaborate with managers, peers, and subordinates. Since humans are responsible for the actions of the technologies they use, they

Fig 7.1 Some of the many attributes proposed as goals for HCAI systems.

are more likely to adopt technologies that show current status on a control panel, provide users with a mental model to predict future actions, and allow users to stop actions that they can't understand. Well-designed user interfaces provide vital support for human activities in ways that reduce workload, raise performance, and increase safety. The special cases requiring fully automatic action or fully human control demand additional design review, as discussed in Chapter 8.

Designers of reliable, safe, and trustworthy systems will also promote resilience, clarify responsibility, increase quality, and encourage creativity.[5] Human creativity is needed to extend existing designs, come up with wholly new approaches, and coordinate collaboration when needed to deal with unanticipated problems. Still broader goals are to ensure privacy, increase cybersecurity, support social justice, and protect the environment.

The HCAI framework (Chapter 8) guides designers and researchers to consider new possibilities that advance reliable, safe, and trustworthy systems. After all, most consumers, industrial supervisors, physicians, and airplane pilots are not interested in computer autonomy; what they want are systems to increase their performance dramatically, while simplifying their effort, so they can devote themselves to their higher aspirations. The HCAI framework shows how careful design leads to computer applications that enable high levels of human control while also providing high levels of automation.

CHAPTER 8

Two-Dimensional HCAI Framework

The HCAI framework steers designers and researchers to ask fresh questions and rethink the nature of autonomy. As designers get beyond thinking of computers as our teammates, partners, or collaborators, they are more likely to develop technologies that dramatically increase human performance.[1] Novel designs will take stronger advantage of unique computer features such as sophisticated algorithms, voluminous databases, advanced sensors, information abundant displays, and powerful effectors, such as claws, drills, or welding machines.

Clarifying human responsibility also guides designers to support the human capacity to invent creative solutions in novel contexts with incomplete knowledge. The HCAI framework clarifies how design excellence promotes human self-efficacy, creativity, and responsibility, which is what managers and users seek. The goals of reliable, safe, and trustworthy are useful for lighter weight recommender systems for consumers and consequential applications for professionals, but they are most relevant for life-critical systems:

Recommender systems: These are widely used in consumer services, social media platforms, and search engines, and have brought strong benefits to consumers.[2] Consequences of the frequent mistakes by recommender systems are usually less serious, possibly even giving consumers interesting suggestions of movies, books, or restaurants. However, malicious actors can manipulate these systems to influence buying habits, change election outcomes, spread hateful messages, and reshape attitudes about climate, vaccinations, gun control, etc. Thoughtful designs that improve user control through simple control panels could increase consumer satisfaction and limit malicious use.

Other applications of automation include common user tasks, such as search query completion or spellchecking. These tasks are carefully designed to preserve user control and avoid annoying disruptions, while offering useful assistance. Jeffrey Heer has broken new ground by offering ways of using automation in support of human control by seeking "a promising design space: one in which computational assistance augments and enriches, rather than replaces, people's intellectual work."[3] He writes that his "goal is to productively employ AI methods while ensuring people remain in control: unconstrained in pursuing complex goals and exercising domain expertise."[4] Jeff Heer's paper shows user-interface examples from data cleaning to remove errors and organize data, exploratory data visualization in which users can choose from a set of recommendations, and natural language translation with expanded user control.

Consequential applications: Getting correct outcomes is more important in medical, legal, environmental, or financial systems that can bring substantial benefits but also have risks of serious damage. A well-documented case is the flawed Google Flu Trends, which was designed to predict flu outbreaks based on user searches on terms such as "flu," "tissues," or "cold remedies." It was intended to enable public health officials to assign resources more effectively.[5] The initial success did not persist and after two years, Google withdrew the website, because the programmers did not anticipate the many changes in search algorithms, user behavior, and societal context. David Lazer and his team describe the harmful attitude of programmers as "algorithmic hubris," suggesting that some programmers have unreasonable expectations of their capacity to create foolproof autonomous systems, akin to what happened in the two crashes of the Boeing 737 MAX.

The financial flash crashes in public stock markets and currency exchanges caused by high-frequency trading algorithms triggered losses of billions of dollars in just a few minutes. However, with adequate logs of trades, market managers can often repair the damage. Another saving grace for the middle range of consequential applications in medical care, portfolio management, or legal advice is that there may be time for alert decision-makers to reflect on the algorithm's recommendation, consult with colleagues, or probe more deeply to understand the recommendation.

Life-critical systems: Moving up to the challenges of life-critical applications, we find the physical devices like self-driving cars, pacemakers, and implantable defibrillators, as well as complex systems such as military, medical, industrial, and transportation applications. These applications sometimes require rapid actions and may have irreversible consequences. Designing life-critical systems is a serious challenge, but a necessary one as these systems can avoid dangers and save lives.

Designers of recommender systems, consequential applications, and life-critical systems were guided by the one-dimensional levels of autonomy, which grew from Tom Sheridan and William Verplank's early paper, discussed in Chapter 6. Their model was repeated in many articles and textbooks, including my own textbook in 1987.[6] I shared the belief that more automation was better and that to increase automation, designers had to reduce human control. In short, designers had to choose a point on the one-dimensional line from human control to computer automation (Figure 8.1).

The mistaken message was that more automation necessarily meant less user control. Over the years, this idea began to trouble me so I eventually shifted to the belief that it was possible to ensure human control while increasing computer automation. Even I wrestled with this puzzling notion, till I began to see examples of designs that had high levels of human control for some features and high levels of automation for other features.

The decoupling of these concepts leads to a two-dimensional HCAI framework, which suggests that achieving high levels of human control and high levels of computer automation is possible (yellow triangle in Figure 8.2). The two axes go from low to high human control and from low to high computer automation. This simple expansion to two dimensions is already helping designers imagine fresh possibilities.

The desired goal is often, but not always, to create designs that are in the upper right quadrant. Most reliable, safe, and trustworthy systems are on the right side. The lower right quadrant is home to relatively mature, well-understood systems for predictable tasks, for example, automobile automatic transmission or skid control on normal highways. For poorly understood and complex tasks with varying contexts of use, the upper right quadrant is needed.

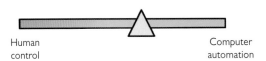

Human control   Computer automation

Fig 8.1 Misleading one-dimensional thinking suggests that designers must choose between human control and computer automation.

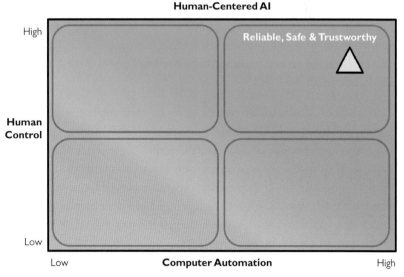

Fig 8.2 Two-dimensional framework with the goal of reliable, safe, and trustworthy designs, which are achieved by a high level of human control and a high level of computer automation (yellow triangle).

These tasks involve creative decisions, making them currently at the research frontier. As contexts of use are standardized (e.g. elevator shafts) these tasks can come under greater computer control with high levels of automation.

The lower right quadrant (Figure 8.3), with high computer automation and low human control, is the home of computer autonomy requiring rapid action, for example, airbag deployment, anti-lock brakes, pacemakers, implantable defibrillators, or defensive weapons systems. In these applications, there is no time for human intervention or control. Because the price of failure is so high, these applications require extremely careful design, extensive testing, and monitoring during usage to refine designs for different use contexts. As systems mature, users appreciate the effective and proven designs, paving the way for higher levels of automation and less human supervision.

The upper left quadrant, with high human control and low automation, is the home of human autonomy where human mastery is desired to enable competence building, free exploration, and creativity. Examples include bicycle riding, piano playing, baking, or playing with children where errors are part of the experience. During these activities, humans generally want to derive pleasure from seeking mastery, improving their skills, and feeling fully engaged. A safe bike ride or a flawless violin performance are events to celebrate. They may elect to use computer-based systems for training, review, or guidance, but many

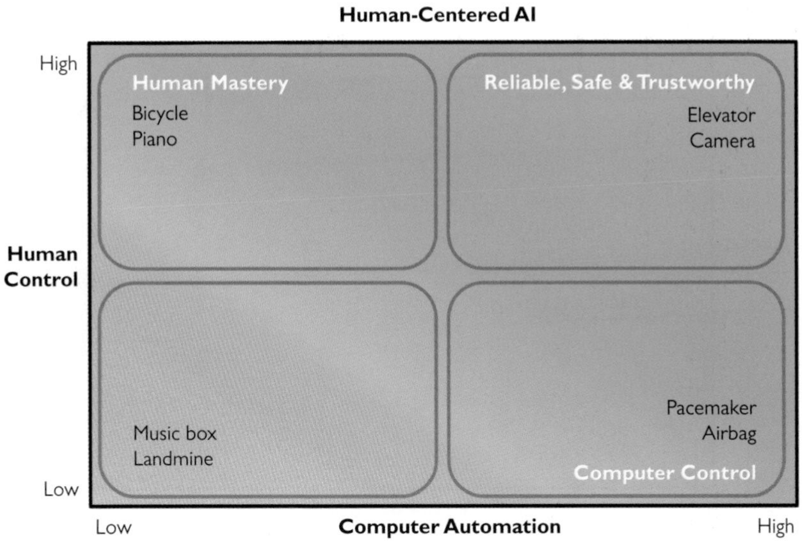

Human-Centered AI

Fig 8.3 Regions requiring rapid action (high automation, low human control) and human mastery (high human control, low automation).

humans desire independent action to achieve mastery that builds self-efficacy. In these actions, the goal is in the doing and the personal satisfaction that it provides, plus the potential for creative exploration.[7] The lower left quadrant is the home of simple devices such as clocks, music boxes, or mousetraps, as well as deadly devices such as land mines.

Two other implementation aspects greatly influence reliability, safety, and trustworthiness: the accuracy of the sensors and the fairness of the data. When sensors are unstable or data sources incomplete, error-laden, or biased, then human controls become more important. On the other hand, stable sensors and complete, accurate, and unbiased data favor higher levels of automation.

The take-away message for designers is that, for certain tasks, there is value in full computer control or full human mastery. However, the challenge is to develop effective and proven designs, supported by reliable practices, safety cultures, and trustworthy oversight.

In addition to the extreme cases of full computer and human autonomy, there are two other extreme cases that signal danger—excessive automation and excessive human control. On the far right of Figure 8.4 is the region of excessive automation, where there are dangers from designs such as the Boeing 737 MAX's MCAS system, which led to two crashes with 346 deaths in October 2018 and March 2019. There are many aspects to this failure, but some basic design principles were violated. The automated control system took the readings

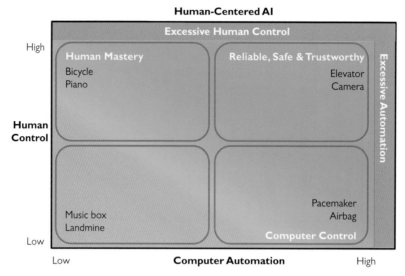

Fig 8.4 Designers need to prevent the failures from excessive automation and excessive human control (gray areas).

from only one of the two angle of attack sensors which indicate whether the plane is ascending or descending. When this sensor failed, the control system forced the plane's nose downwards, but the pilots did not know why, so they tried to pull the nose up more than twenty times in the minutes before the crash, which killed everyone on board. The aircraft designers made the terrible mistake in believing that their autonomous system for controlling the plane could not fail. Therefore, its existence was not described in the user manual and the pilots were not trained in how to switch to manual override. The unnecessary tragedies were entirely avoidable. The IBM AI Guidelines wisely warns that "imperceptible AI is not ethical AI."[8]

While the four quadrants suggest neat separations, the relationship between human control and computer automation is more complex. Human control may require vigilance over many hours as in cars, aircraft, or power station control centers, but human attention can lapse, requiring alerts or alarms to get operators to focus on emerging problems. The human vigilance problem grows as computer controls become more reliable, so that operators only rarely need to intervene, which eventually leads to the deskilling of operators, so they can no longer intervene quickly and correctly.

Excessive human control allows people to make deadly mistakes. Sometimes control panels are so complex that users are confused and uncertain how to operate a device. Swansea University's Harold Thimbleby tells troubling stories of how medical devices used by nurses and doctors can lead to "human errors," which should be seen as design failures.[9] In one example, nurses used a default setting on an intravenous medication system which led to patients receiving deadly overdoses of pain-killing medication. Default settings should select the safe options, but this device misled the nurses to make a deadly choice.

Home appliances also have guards, such as the interlock on self-cleaning ovens to prevent homeowners from the dangers of opening oven doors when temperatures are above 600° F. Poorly designed interlocks can be annoying, such as the overly ambitious automobile systems that lock doors too often. Formal methods and software-based constraints, such as range checking, generalize the interlocks and guards, ensuring that algorithms have permissible inputs and produce only acceptable outcomes.

Interlocks or guards are helpful in preventing mistakes, but additional design and monitoring features are needed to ensure reliable, safe, and trustworthy designs. One example is positive train control systems to limit trains from traveling at high speeds on curves or in terminal areas. The challenging question is how to integrate HCAI designs into life-critical systems like aviation, flexible manufacturing systems, and implantable pacemakers. Numerous interlocks in aviation prevent pilots from making mistakes; for example, reverse thrusters on jet engines can only be engaged once the strain gauge in the landing gear indicates that the plane has touched down on the ground.

Similar perils come from excessive computer automation, such as detailed in the US National Transportation Safety Board's report on the deadly 2016 crash of a Tesla car.[10] That report cautioned that "automation 'because we can' does not necessarily make the human-automation system work better. . . . This crash is an example of what can happen when automation is introduced 'because we can' without adequate consideration of the human element." The Tesla "Autopilot" system name suggests greater capability than is available. Tesla claims that it is "designed to be able to conduct short and long distance trips with no action required by the person in the driver's seat... in almost all situations."[11] This seems to overstate Autopilot's current capabilities, which is dangerous since it can encourage drivers to become less vigilant.

While power steering, automatic transmission, and anti-lock brake systems are mature automations that are widely accepted, cruise control and adaptive cruise control are more complex, but they give drivers better control over their vehicle's speed. Newer automations that augment human abilities to increase safety include parking assistance, lane following, and collision avoidance. Researcher Jessica Cicchino of the independent nonprofit Insurance Institute for

Highway Safety[12] reports that effective lane following would do the most to reduce fatalities, while rear-end collision avoidance would do the most to reduce
the number of accidents. Her research team provides detailed design recommendations, including visual reminders, audible cues, and physical alerts. Their
work also covers ways of detecting whether drivers are paying sufficient attention and how to keep them engaged.[13] Cars that display intended actions to
drivers in a step-by-step process, such as the Mercedes-Benz Active Parking Assist, give drivers a clear understanding of what will happen so they can accept or
reject the plan. An even better design would be to show the expected path of the
car. University of Colorado's Connor Brooks and Daniel Szafir demonstrated
that predictive planning displays lead to greater task accuracy and higher user
satisfaction.[14]

Some driving situations allow for predictions and warnings for drivers to
pay attention to dangers that are 30–60 seconds away, for example when approaching a busy fast-moving merge, while other situations have much shorter
warning times, making it very difficult for drivers involved in other tasks to take
over safely. Those dangerous situations should be avoided as much as possible
by using data from how other cars avoided the problem or simply by slowing the
car down. Car systems can't predict whether a boulder will roll down a hillside,
but they can alert drivers to sharp turns ahead, emergency vehicles on the road
a mile ahead, or the presence of a fast-driving, lane-weaving nearby vehicle. Reduced lane changing may become common, enabling convoys of electronically
linked cars to move as a group in a speedy and safe way, while staying in the
same lane.

A better design goal than self-driving may be a safety-first car. Some contexts of use can be made safer, such as convoys on limited access highways
or slowing cars as they approach intersections that have a high frequency of
previous accidents or when bright sunlight late in the day reduces the efficacy
of computer vision systems. These changes can then be refined and adapted
in ways that increase safety, eventually leading to less need for driver control,
with greater supervisory control from regional centers, akin to air-traffic control centers. These control centers signal human involvement, as opposed to
assured autonomy, suggesting that the computer works entirely on its own.
Car traffic controllers might manage traffic flow of thousands of vehicles by
changing speed limits to respond to weather and traffic conditions, dispatching
police, fire, and ambulance services, and tracking frequent near misses to guide
road redesign or car-driving algorithm improvements. Car manufacturers are
exploring the possibility of tele-bot cars, which would allow a remote driver to

take over control of a car if the driver is injured, has a medical problem, or falls asleep.

The notion of full car autonomy is productively giving way to a human-centered approach, which provides appropriate controls to improve safety, while addressing the numerous special cases of snow-covered roads, unusual vehicles, vandalism, malicious interference, and construction zones. Another set of concerns is how to design cars to deal with emergency guidance from police officers giving verbal instructions, or the special needs of firefighters or ambulance teams. A possible solution is to equip authorized police, fire, and ambulance crews to control nearby cars, in the same way that they have special keys to take over control of elevators and activate apartment fire control displays in emergency situations. As car sensors, highway infrastructure, and car-to-car communication improve, strategies to make cars as safe as elevators will become easier to implement.

Waymo, spun off from Google, has shifted from using the term self-driving to "fully autonomous driving" technology, now being tested as "robotaxis" in Phoenix, AZ. Their goal is not to build cars ("Waymo is building a driver—not a car"), but to provide the highly automated technology to be built by other companies into cars, taxis, and trucks.[15] Their tests show good progress, although even with limited car speeds, they have reported some accidents, but their open reporting is an admirable trust-building approach. Waymo's designers follow human-centered thinking to develop and test "user interfaces so that passengers can clearly indicate their destination, direct the vehicle to pull over, and contact Waymo rider support."[16] Waymo's strategies sometimes include trained drivers in the cars to serve as backup drivers if needed. Waymo also has a simple user interface for passengers with a "PULL OVER" button to stop the vehicle quickly and easily contact a Rider Support Agent to get help if needed.[17] Finally, Waymo uses a supervisory control strategy in regional centers to monitor every car remotely whenever it is on the road, provide support when needed, and collect performance data. Waymo's balanced approach—highly automated with human supervisory control—is likely to lead to steady improvements, but the timetable is uncertain.

Figure 8.5 shows the relative positions of 1940 and 1980 cars, 2020 self-driving cars, and the proposed goal of reliable, safe, and trustworthy cars in 2040 by way of mature automation and supervisory control.

The four quadrants may be helpful in suggesting differing designs for a product or service, as in this example. Patient-controlled analgesia (PCA) devices allow post-surgical, severe cancer, or hospice patients to select the amount and frequency of pain control medication. There are dangers and problems with

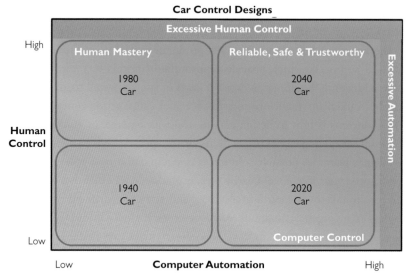

Fig 8.5 1980 cars had modest computer automation with high levels of human control, while 2020 self-driving cars have high computer automation, but inadequate human control. Achieving reliable, safe, and trustworthy self-driving cars by 2040 is possible.

young and old patients, but with good design and management, PCA devices deliver safe and effective pain control.[18] A simple morphine drip bag design for the lower left quadrant (low computer automation and low human control) delivers a fixed amount of pain control medication (Figure 8.6). A more automated design for the lower right quadrant (increased computer automation, but little human control) provides machine-selected doses that vary by time of day, patient activity, and data from body sign sensors, although these do not assess perceived pain.

A human-centered design for the upper left quadrant (higher human control, with low computer automation) allows patients to squeeze a trigger to control the dosing, frequency, and total amount of pain control medication. However, the dangers of overdosing are controlled by an interlock that prevents frequent doses, typically with lockout periods of 6–10 minutes, and total dose limits over one- to four-hour periods. Finally, a reliable, safe, and trustworthy design for the upper right quadrant allows users to squeeze a trigger to get more pain medicine but uses machine learning to choose appropriate doses based on patient and disease variables, while preventing overdosing. Patients are able to get information on why limiting pain medication is important with explanations of how they operate the PCA device (Figure 8.7). The design includes a hospital control center (Figure 8.8) to monitor usage of hundreds of PCA devices so as to ensure safe practices, deal with power or other failures, review audit trails, and collect data to improve the next generation of PCA devices.[19]

The rich possibilities of design variations for a single product are nicely demonstrated in the work of Pieter Desmet and Steven Fokkinga of Delft

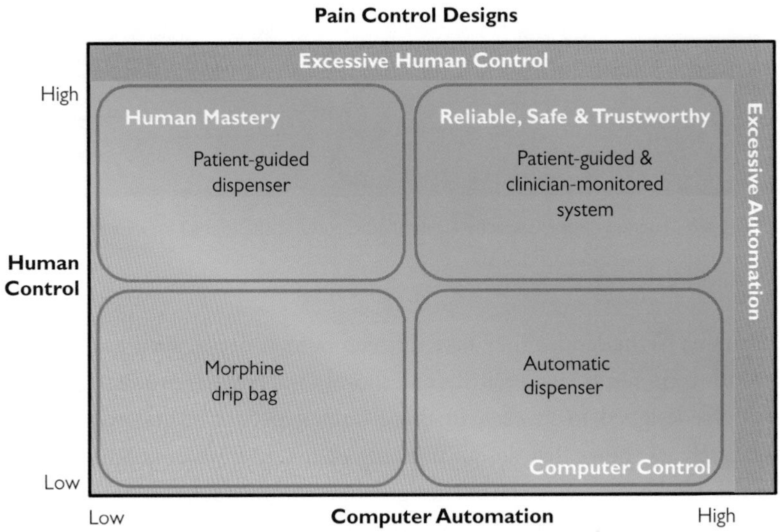

Pain Control Designs

Fig 8.6 Four approaches to pain control designs.

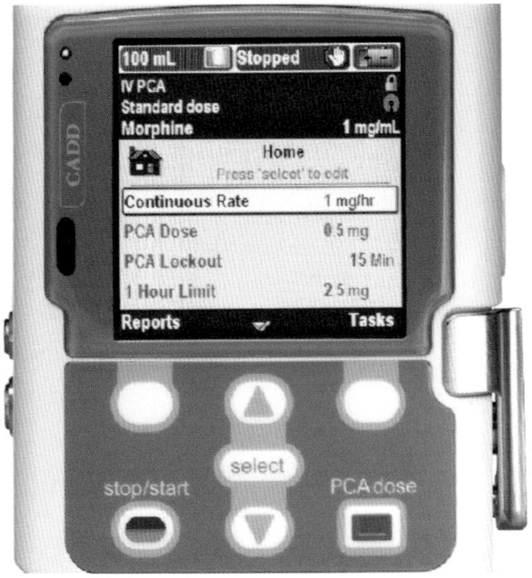

Fig 8.7 Administrator control panel for patient-controlled analgesia.

Source: Courtesy of Smith's-Medical CADD-Solis

Fig 8.8 The Judy Reitz Capacity Command Center at the Johns Hopkins Hospital.

Source: Photo courtesy of the Johns Hopkins Hospital

University, Netherlands. They take thirteen human needs, such as autonomy, comfort, community, and security, and show how a familiar product like chairs can be redesigned to fit each of those human needs.[20] Their work on appealing chairs shows that design thinking opens up fresh possibilities, which could be applied in diverse HCAI designs for recommender, consequential, and life-critical systems. With fresh thinking in mind, Chapter 9 describes design guidelines and shows HCAI examples in familiar applications.

CHAPTER 9

Design Guidelines and Examples

This new goal of HCAI resolves the fifty-year debate, lucidly described by *New York Times* technology writer John Markoff, between those who sought artificial intelligence and those who sought intelligence augmentation (IA).[1] This debate over AI versus IA now seems like arguing about iron horses versus horses or how many angels can fit on a pinhead. Designers can produce HCAI by integrating artificial intelligence algorithms with user interface designs in ways that amplify, augment, empower, and enhance people.

The current version of Google's design guidebook buys into the need to choose: "Assess automation vs. augmentation ... One large consideration is if you should use AI to automate a task or to augment a person's ability to do that task themselves ... For AI-driven products, there's an essential balance between automation and user control."[2] However, the authors of the Google design guidebook are open to the possibility that "[w]hen done right, automation and augmentation work together to both simplify and improve the outcome of a long, complicated process." That's the right message—do both!

Google's complementary website gives guidelines for responsible AI that are well-aligned with my principles.[3]

- Use a human-centered design approach
- Identify multiple metrics to assess training and monitoring
- When possible, directly examine your raw data
- Understand the limitations of your data set and model
- Test, Test, Test
- Continue to monitor and update the system after deployment

Other early guidelines, such as those from Microsoft Research leader Eric Horvitz,[4] paved the way for Microsoft's *Guidelines for AI-Human Interaction*.[5] These eighteen guidelines, which were presented with appealing graphics and even distributed as a deck of playing cards, cover initial use, normal use, coping with problems, and changes over time.[6] They are on the right track with their emphasis on user understanding and control, while addressing ways for the system to "make clear why the system did what it did" and "learn from user behavior."

IBM's Design for AI website discusses issues more broadly, offering a high-level tutorial that covers design foundations, technology basics, ethical concerns, accountability, explainability, and fairness.[7] However, I publicly questioned its suggestion that a system should "endear itself to the user" and "form a full emotional bond." Those phrases were changed, but the description of trust still includes the questionable encouragement to get users "to invest in an emotional bond with the system."

Mica Endsley's "Guidelines for the Design of Human-Autonomy Systems" has twenty thoughtful items that cover human understanding of autonomous systems, minimizing complexity, and supporting situation awareness.[8] Her guidelines include: "Use automated assistance for carrying out routine tasks rather than higher-level cognitive functions" and "Provide automation transparency," each of which she explains in detail.

Successful designs are comprehensible, predictable, and controllable, thereby increasing the users' self-efficacy, leading to reliable, safe, and trustworthy systems. These successes require careful design of the fine structure of interaction, which emerges from validated theories, clear principles, and actionable guidelines.[9] In turn, this knowledge becomes easy to apply when it is embedded in programming tools that favor human control. I playfully developed a compact set of Eight Golden Rules (Table 9.1) of user interface design, which I have updated in successive editions of *Designing the User Interface*.[10] These Eight Golden Rules remain valid for HCAI systems.[11]

User experience designer Euphemia Wong encouraged designers to follow these rules so as "to design great, productive and frustration-free user interfaces."[12] YouTube videos present these rules in many languages and parodies poke fun at them, which is just fine with me.

The design decisions to craft user interfaces based on the Eight Golden Rules typically involve trade-offs,[13] so careful study, creative design, and rigorous testing will help designers to produce high-quality user interfaces.

Table 9.1 *Eight Golden Rules for design*[14]

1. Strive for consistency
2. Seek universal usability
3. Offer informative feedback
4. Design dialogs to yield closure
5. Prevent errors
6. Permit easy reversal of actions
7. Keep users in control
8. Reduce short-term memory load

Then the implemented designs must be continuously monitored by domain experts to understand problems and refine the designs. There is always room for improvement and new demands require redesigned user interfaces.

The examples that follow clarify the key ideas of supporting users to express their intent through visual interfaces. In addition, auditory and haptic interfaces are also valuable in many situations and for users with disabilities (the second Golden Rule). These designs give users informative feedback about the machine state, with progress indicators and completion reports. Many real-world designs are flawed, but these positive examples describe how it is possible to support both high levels of human control and high levels of automation. Part 3 will expand on these examples by describing supertools, tele-bots, active appliances, and control centers. For now, here are some examples:

Example 9.1 Simple thermostats allow residents to take better control of the temperature in their homes. They can see the room temperature and the current thermostat setting, clarifying what they can do to raise or lower the setting. Then they can hear the heating system turn on/off or see a light to indicate that their action has produced a response. The basic idea is to give residents an awareness of the current state, allow them to reset the control, and then give informative feedback (the third Golden Rule) that the computer is acting on their intent. There may be further feedback as the residents see the thermometer rise in response to their action, and maybe an indication when their desired goal has been achieved. Thermostats offer still further benefits—they continue to keep the room temperature at the new setting automatically. In summary, while some thermostats may lack the features necessary that give clear feedback, well-designed thermostats give users an understanding of how they have controlled the automation to get the temperature they desire in their homes (Figure 9.1). Newer programmable thermostats, such as Google's Nest, apply

Fig 9.1 Honeywell thermostat shows status clearly and offers simple up and down markers to increase or decrease the temperature. Tele-operation is supported by way of a user's smartphone.

machine learning to allow residents to accommodate their schedules better and save energy. However, human behavior can be variable, undermining the utility of machine learning, as when residents change their schedules, adopt new hobbies such as baking, or have visitors with different needs. Getting the balance between human and machine control remains a challenge.

Example 9.2 Home appliances, such as dishwashers, clothes washers/dryers, and ovens allow users to choose settings that specify what they want, and then turn control over to sensors and timers to govern the process. When well-designed, these appliances offer users comprehensible and predictable user interfaces. They allow users to express their intent, with controls that let them monitor the current status and they can stop dishwashers to put in another plate or change from baking to broiling to brown their chicken (the seventh Golden Rule). These automations give users better control of these active appliances to ensure that they get what they want (Figure 9.2).

Example 9.3 Well-designed user interfaces in elevators enable substantial automation while providing appropriate human control. Elevator users approach a simple two-button control panel and press up or down. The button lights to

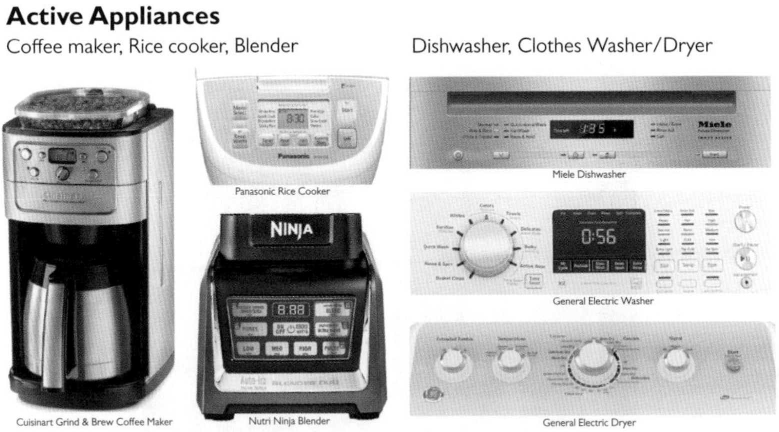

Active Appliances

Coffee maker, Rice cooker, Blender   Dishwasher, Clothes Washer/Dryer

Fig 9.2 Active appliances operate automatically, but show their status and allow user control.

indicate that the users' intent has been recognized. A display panel indicates the elevator's current floor so users can see progress, which lets them know how long they will have to wait. The elevator doors open, a tone sounds, and the users can step in to press a button to indicate their choice of floors. The button lights up to indicate their intent is recognized and the door closes. The floor display shows progress towards the goal. On arrival, a tone sounds and the door opens. The automated design which replaced the human operator ensures that doors will only open while on a floor, while triply redundant safety systems prevent elevators from falling, even under loss of power or broken cables. Machine learning algorithms coordinate multiple elevators, automatically adjusting their placement based on time of day, usage patterns, and changing passenger loads. Override controls allow firefighters or moving crews to achieve their goals. The carefully designed experience provides users with a high level of control over relevant features supported by a high level of automation. There are many refinements, such as detectors to prevent doors from closing on passengers (the fifth Golden Rule), so that the overall design is reliable, safe, and trustworthy.

Example 9.4 Digital cameras in most cell phones display an image of what the users would get if they clicked on the large button (Figure 9.3). The image is updated smoothly as users adjust their composition or zoom in. At the same time, the camera makes automatic adjustments to the aperture and focus, while compensating for shaking hands, a wide range of lighting conditions (high dynamic

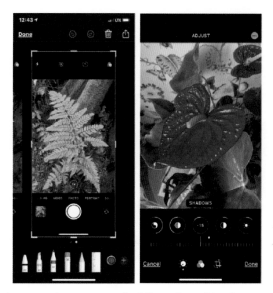

Fig 9.3 Digital cameras give users great flexibility such as taking photos and editing tools to mark up photos, adjust color, change brightness, crop photos, and much more.

range), and many other factors. Flash can be set to be on or off, or automatically set by the camera. Users can choose portrait modes, panorama, or video, including slow motion and time lapse. Users also can set various filters and once the image is taken they can make further adjustments such as brightness, contrast, saturation, vibrance, shadows, cropping, and red-eye elimination. These designs give users a high degree of control while also providing a high level of automation. Of course, there are mistakes, such as when the automatic focus feature puts the focus on a nearby bush, rather than the person standing just behind it. However, knowledgeable users can touch the desired focus point to override this mistake.

Example 9.5 Auto-completion is a form of recommender system that suggests commonly used ways to complete phrases or search terms, as in the Google search system. In Figure 9.4, the user begins a term and gets popular suggestions based on searches by other users. This auto-completion method does more than speed performance; it reminds users of possible search topics that they might find useful. Users can ignore the recommendation or choose one of the suggestions.

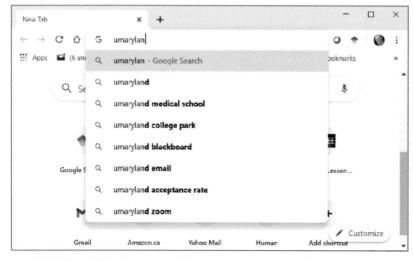

Fig 9.4 Google Search auto-completion suggests search terms, but users can ignore and continue their typing.

Fig 9.5 Spellchecker shows a possible mistake with a red wiggly line. When clicked on, it offers a suggested fix, but leaves users in control to decide whether they want to repair the mistake and when.

Example 9.6 Spelling and grammar checkers as well as natural language translation systems offer useful suggestions in subtle ways, such as a red wiggly line under the error, as in Figure 9.5, or the list of possible translations in Figure 9.6. These are examples of good interaction design that offers help to users while letting them maintain control. At the same time, autocorrecting text messaging systems regularly produce mistakes, alternately amusing and annoying senders and recipients alike. Still, these applications are widely appreciated when implemented in a non-intrusive and optional way so they can be easily ignored.

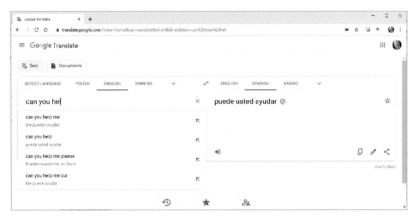

Fig 9.6 A natural language translation user interface that allows users to select the source and target languages, offers a choice of complete sentences, and invites feedback on the translation, by way of the pencil icon.

The Eight Golden Rules for design help designers develop the comprehensible, predictable, and controllable interfaces. Many of the principles are embedded in human interface guidelines documents, such as Apple's, which stipulates that "User Control: . . . people—not apps—are in control" and "Flexibility: . . . (give) users complete, fine-grained control over their work."[15] These guidelines and others that emphasize human control offer very different advice than the pursuit of computer autonomy.[16] The Eight Golden Rules are a starting point in leading to what I believe is desired by most users: reliable, safe, and trustworthy systems.

There is room to build on these Eight Golden Rules with an *HCAI pattern language* (Table 9.2). Pattern languages have been developed for many design challenges from architecture to social media systems. They are brief expressions of important ideas that suggest solutions to common design problems. Patterns remind designers of vital ideas in compact phrases meant to provoke more careful thinking.

1) **Overview first, zoom and filter, then details-on-demand**: The first one will be a familiar information visualization mantra that suggests users should be able to get an overview of all the data, possibly as a scattergram, geographic map, or a network diagram. This overview shows the scope and context for individual items, and allows users to zoom in on what they want, filter out what they don't want, and then click for details-on-demand.

Table 9.2 *An HCAI pattern language*

---

1. Overview first, zoom and filter, then details-on-demand
2. Preview first, select and initiate, then manage execution
3. Steer by way of interactive control panels
4. Capture history and audit trails from powerful sensors
5. People thrive on human-to-human communication
6. Be cautious when outcomes are consequential
7. Prevent adversarial attacks
8. Incident reporting websites accelerate refinement

---

2) **Preview first, select and initiate, then manage execution**: For temporal sequences or robot operations the second pattern is to show a preview of the entire process; it allows users to select their plan, initiate the activity, and then manage the execution. This is what navigation tools and digital cameras do so successfully.

3) **Steer by way of interactive control panels**: Enable users to steer the process or device by way of interactive control panels. This is what users do when driving cars, flying drones, or playing video games. The control panel can include joysticks, buttons, or onscreen buttons, sliders, and other controls, often placed on maps, rooms, or imaginary spaces. Augmented and virtual reality extend the possibilities.

4) **Capture history and audit trails from powerful sensors**: Aircraft sensors record engine temperature, fuel flow, and dozens of other values, which are saved on the flight data recorder, but are also useful for pilots who want to review what happened 10 minutes ago. Cars and trucks record many items for maintenance reviews; so should applications, websites, data exploration tools, and machine learning models, so users can review their history easily.

5) **People thrive on human-to-human communication**: Applications are improved when users can easily share content, ask for help, and jointly edit documents. Remember the bumper sticker: Humans in the Group; Computers in the Loop (Figure 2.1).

6) **Be cautious when outcomes are consequential**: When applications can affect people's lives, violate privacy, create physical damage, or cause injury, thorough evaluations and continuous monitoring become vital. Independent oversight helps limit damage. Humility is a good attribute for designers to have.

7) **Prevent adversarial attacks**: Failures can come not only from biased data and flawed software but also from attacks by malicious actors or vandals who would put technology to harmful purposes or simply disrupt normal use.

8) **Incident reporting websites accelerate refinement**: Openness to feedback from users and stakeholders will bring designers information about failures and near misses, which will enable them to continuously improve their technology products and services.

These patterns are discussed in Parts 3 and 4. The examples in this chapter show successful designs for user interfaces that give users the benefits of AI methods with the control they want.

In summary, design thinking is a powerful way of putting AI algorithms to work as vital components of HCAI systems that will amplify, augment, empower, and enhance human performance. These examples of supertools and active appliances are familiar and easy to understand, and they convey how the popular Eight Golden Rules from the past are applied, while showing how a newer pattern language for HCAI systems could become just as valuable in guiding designers.

Future users, including those with disabilities, will have supertools and active appliances to enable them to take care of more of the activities of daily life, explore creative possibilities, and help others. They will benefit from augmented and virtual realities to see more clearly, make better decisions, and have enriching entertainment experiences. Novel three-dimensional printing devices will give users options to make new devices that they want, repair existing devices, and fabricate custom jewelry or decorations. HCAI services will guide them to what they want to do, share products more easily with others, or start new businesses.

CHAPTER 10

Summary and Skeptic's Corner

We should stand in awe of the capacity of the human mind, and of the achievements of human culture.

Brian Cantwell Smith, *The Promise of Artificial Intelligence: Reckoning and Judgment (2019)*

M y aim is to help designers to make better AI systems by taking a human-centered approach. The HCAI framework separates the issue of human control from computer automation, making it clear that high levels of human control and high levels of automation can be achieved by good design. The design decisions give human operators a clear understanding of the machine state and their choices. Designers are guided by concerns such as the consequences and reversibility of mistakes. Well-designed automation preserves human control where appropriate, thereby increasing performance and enabling creative improvements.

The HCAI framework clarifies when computer control for rapid automated action is necessary, when human desire for mastery is paramount, and when there are dangers of excessive automation or excessive human control. It clarifies design choices for (1) consumer and professional applications, such as widely used recommender systems, e-commerce services, social media platforms, and search engines, which have brought strong benefits to consumers; (2) consequential applications in medical, legal, environmental, or financial systems that can bring substantial benefits and harms; and (3) life-critical applications such as cars, airplanes, trains, military systems, pacemakers, or intensive care units.

The HCAI framework is based on the belief that people are different from computers. Therefore, designs which take advantage of unique computer features, including sophisticated algorithms, voluminous databases, advanced sensors, information-abundant displays, and powerful effectors are more likely to increase human performance. Similarly designs and organizational structures which recognize the unique capabilities of humans will have advantages such as encouraging innovative use, supporting continuous improvement, and promoting breakthroughs to vastly improved designs.

An important research direction is to develop objective measures of the levels of control and autonomy. Such measures would stimulate more meaningful design discussions, which would lead to improved guidelines, evaluations, and theories.

Human responsibility for mistakes is another powerful driver of design advancements such as the inclusion of detailed audit trails, consistent informative feedback about machine state, and strategies to collect incidents and accidents. Then retraining of users and redesign of systems can proceed to reduce failures and near misses. Difficult questions remain, such as how to deal with the deskilling effects that undermine the very human skills which may be needed when automation fails. Another difficult question is how to enable operators to remain vigilant as their actions become less frequent—how can a human in a self-driving car stay engaged enough to take over when needed?

Ethical questions, such as considerations of responsibility, fairness, and explainability, are helpful in developing general principles. When these general principles are combined with deep knowledge of and experience with the complexities of product and service design, they can yield actionable guidelines.[1] The HCAI framework lays a foundation for responsibility, fairness, and explainability. Recommendations for bridging the gap between ethics and practice are collected in Part 4.

A human-centered system will be made better because of (1) improved reliability from sound software engineering practices, (2) safety culture through business management strategies, (3) trustworthy certification by independent oversight, and (4) regulation by government agencies. HCAI systems will evolve rapidly because mechanisms for monitoring failures and near misses support rapid improvements.

The HCAI framework and the examples seem modest to some readers who have bolder aspirations of synthesizing human intelligence, perception, decision-making, and autonomous action. They prefer to design systems that perform without human attention or intervention, focusing on machine autonomy rather than human autonomy. They believe that fully reliable systems can be built, so they ignore or reject efforts to add audit trails, control panels, failure reporting, and other features in existing systems, especially in consequential and life-critical applications.

Other skeptics see the two-dimensional HCAI framework as too modest. They envision three-dimensional models and more elaborate models. This is fine, so they should build the case for these extensions. Others complain that the example user interfaces are too simple and that they represent only modest cases of what AI systems can accomplish. Maybe so. I welcome examples of what novel designs of more autonomous systems would look like and how they would perform. Dealing with fundamental failures, such as loss of power, loss of wireless connections, and breakage of components, is a key part of design excellence. Other failures come from adversarial attacks by malicious actors, so substantial effort is needed to prevent or deal with them.

AI researchers and developers who shift from one-dimensional thinking about levels of automation/autonomy to the two-dimensional HCAI framework may find fresh solutions to current problems. The HCAI framework guides designers to give users appropriate control while providing high levels of automation. When successful, these technologies amplify, augment, enhance, and empower users, dramatically increasing their performance.

Then designers can imagine future supertools, tele-bots, active appliances, and control centers that improve life for many and advance efforts to achieve the UN's Sustainable Development Goals. Their designs may be guided by the original Eight Golden Rules or the new HCAI pattern language.

PART 3

Design Metaphors

11 Introduction: What Are the Goals of AI Research?

12 Science and Innovation Goals

13 Intelligent Agents and Supertools

14 Teammates and Tele-bots

15 Assured Autonomy and Control Centers

16 Social Robots and Active Appliances

17 Summary and Skeptic's Corner

Steve Jobs famously described a computer as "a bicycle for our minds," clearly conveying that computers were best designed to amplify human abilities, while preserving human control. Current computers may be more like a Harley-Davidson for our minds, but some suggest that in the future, computers will be chauffeur-driven limousines for our minds, taking us to our destinations automatically. The contrast between riding a bicycle and being driven can be understood by using the HCAI framework. The human-controlled bicycle ride may be pleasurable and healthy exercise, but the automated limousine with a chauffeur metaphor suggests comfort and maybe safety. However, how does a passenger convey intent about destination and influence performance, especially if the driver is unresponsive to requests to slow down or to stop? Human needs are complex and changing; sometimes people prefer to enjoy the pleasure of driving, exercising their driving skills; other times, they may appreciate being able to rest, read, or have a discussion with others.

Building on the transportation metaphor, we might think about computers as being large commercial jets that take many passengers to their destination in comfort, quickly, and safely, without having passengers learn how to fly. The plane is responsive to air-traffic controllers who monitor performance and to agencies that certify the aircraft, inspired by the upper right quadrant of the HCAI framework (Figure 8.4).

Readers may reflect on how civil aviation is safe because of the combination of automated features and the supervision from pilots and air traffic controllers. The answer is that both are needed. Automated features can take a plane from Washington, DC to Paris, France on a routine flight, allowing pilots to monitor aircraft systems more closely, but occasionally on-board fires, passengers with heart attacks, bird strikes that shut down engines, or hundreds of other problems require a skilled pilot to make difficult decisions rapidly.

While all metaphors, including this one, have their limits, they do have their value in conveying ideas that may open minds to fresh possibilities. Part 3 builds on the HCAI framework in Part 2 by directly dealing with the two design goals of AI and HCAI research:

1) Science goal: University of British Columbia professors David Poole and Alan Mackworth write that the science goal is to study "computational agents that act intelligently." They want to "understand the principles that make intelligent behavior possible in natural or artificial systems . . . by designing, building, and experimenting with computational systems that perform tasks commonly viewed as requiring intelligence."[1] Often, the science goal is based on research to understand human perceptual, cognitive, and motor skills so as to build systems that perform tasks as well as or better than humans, such as playing chess or identifying a cancer tumor.

2) Innovation goal: develop computers that amplify human abilities so people can do the job themselves. The innovation goal comes from research to build widely used products and services. Poole and Mackworth write that innovations "are built to be useful for an application domain."[2] Success stories include map-based navigation systems, natural language translation, and search query completion.

Both goals have value in thinking about design metaphors for future technologies. The challenge is to understand when each goal is most appropriate, and how to combine these goals. Some features may be best handled automatically, such as setting the focus and aperture in a digital camera, while other features may be best given to human control such as composing the image and choosing when to click—what photographers call "the decisive moment."

These two goals lead us to four pairs of design metaphors that describe AI and HCAI research. All are valuable, but for different reasons: high levels of computer autonomy allow unattended activity and high levels of human control enable human intervention. One of the pairs of metaphors is intelligent agents, which suggests competent independent action, and supertools, which suggests human control in use of a machine. The second pair is teammates, hinting at human-like action, and a tele-bots (tele-operated devices), indicating human operation. The third pair is assured autonomy, which promises to be safe because of its design, and control centers, which promise safety because human controllers can monitor and intervene. The fourth pair of metaphors is social robots, designed to behave like a person, and active appliances, designed to be like a dishwasher or clothes dryer.

These pairs of design metaphors refine the HCAI framework by suggesting solutions that are tuned to the needs of diverse contexts, some favoring more automation while others favor greater human control. A key idea is combined designs that take an automated approach for tasks that can be carried out reliably, and a user-controlled approach for tasks that users want to manage. Combined designs enable more nuanced decisions about which features can be carried out reliably by a computer and which features humans want or need to be in control.

Users of recommender, question-answering, and game-playing systems may ignore imperfect responses and maybe even enjoy the occasional surprise. However, with consequential or life-critical applications in medical care, transportation, or financial systems, correct responses become essential and predictable behavior is vital in building trust.

This book favors a new synthesis, which combines a human-centered approach with AI algorithms as essential components of successful designs for advanced systems.

CHAPTER 11

Introduction: What Are the Goals of AI Research?

When a person delegates some task to an agent, be it artificial or human, the result of that task is still the responsibility of the delegating person, who is the one who will be liable if things do not go as expected. . . . an interactive system that is autonomous and adaptable is hard to verify and predict, which in turn can lead to unexpected activity.

Virginia Dignum, *"Responsibility and Artificial Intelligence,"* in The Oxford Handbook of Ethics of AI *(2020), edited by Markus D. Dubber, Frank Pasquale, and Sunit Das*

G oals for AI science and engineering research were proposed at least sixty years ago, when early conferences brought together those who believed in pursuing Alan Turing's question "Can Machines Think?"[1] A simple description is that AI science research is devoted to getting computers to do what humans do, matching or exceeding human perceptual, cognitive, and motor abilities.

A starting point is satisfying the Turing Test, which gives observers a keyboard and display to have a typed conversation. If the observers cannot tell if they are connected to a human or a machine, then the machine has satisfied the Turing Test. Many variants have been developed over the years, such as creating computer-generated images which are indistinguishable from photos of people. Another variant is to make a robot that speaks, moves, and looks like a human. Stuart Russell, a University of California-Berkeley computer scientist, energetically embraced the dual goals of human emulation science and societally beneficial innovations.[2] He wrote that AI is "one of the principal avenues for understanding how human intelligence works but also a golden opportunity to improve the human condition—to make a far better civilization." Russell sees "problems arising from imbuing machines with intelligence."[3]

Science research on perceptual, cognitive, and motor abilities includes pattern recognition (images, speech, facial, signal, etc.), natural language processing, and translation from one natural language to another. Other research challenges have been to make accurate predictions, get robots to perform as well as a person, and have applications recognize human emotions so the application can respond appropriately. Yet another goal is to play popular games, such as checkers, chess, Go, or poker, as well as or better than human players.

As the early science research evolved, useful innovations became possible, but the science research that emphasized symbolic manipulation gave way to statistical approaches, based on machine learning and deep learning, which trained neural networks from existing databases. Neural network strategies were refined in later implementations of generative adversarial networks (GANs), convolutional neural networks (CNN), recurrent neural networks (RNN), inverse reinforcement learning (IRL), and newer foundation models and their variants.

The visionary aspirations of AI researchers have led to a range of inspiring projects. Proponents claim that the emergence of AI has been an historical turning point for humanity showing great promise. Critics pointed out that many projects have failed, as is common with ambitious new research directions, but other projects have led to widely used applications, such as optical character recognition, speech recognition, and natural language translation. While critics say that AI innovations remain imperfect, nevertheless many applications are impressive and commercially successful.

Bold aspirations can be helpful, but another line of criticism is that the AI science methods have failed, giving way to more traditional engineering solutions, which have succeeded. For example, IBM's famed Deep Blue chess-playing program, which defeated world champion Garry Kasparov in 1997, is claimed as an AI success. However, the IBM researcher who led the Deep Blue team, Feng-hsiung Hsu, has made an explicit statement that they did not use AI methods.[4] Their brute force hardware solution used specialized chips to rapidly explore moves that each player could make, up to twenty moves ahead.

As another example, in many business applications AI-guided knowledge-based expert systems have failed, but carefully engineered rule-based systems with human-curated rule sets have succeeded.[5] For example, many companies maintain complex pricing and discount policies that vary by region, product, and purchase volume, with favored customers getting lower prices. Keeping track of these so that all sales personnel quote the same price is important in maintaining trust.

Recent criticisms have focused on the brittleness of deep learning methods, which may work well in laboratory experiments but fail in real world applications.[6] New York University professors Gary Marcus and Ernest Davis have reported on the high expectations of early AI researchers, like Marvin Minsky, John McCarthy, and Herb Simon, which have not been realized.[7] Herb Simon's memorable 1965 prediction was that "machines will be capable, within twenty years, or doing any work a man [or woman] can do." Marcus and Davis describe the many failures of AI systems, which make mistakes in interpreting photos, become racist chatbots, fail at healthcare recommendations, or crash self-driving cars into fire trucks. However, they remain optimistic about the future of AI, which they believe will be brightened by the development of common-sense reasoning. They call for a reboot, based on more and better AI.

Science writer Mitchell Waldrop says, "there is no denying that deep learning is an incredibly powerful tool," but he also describes failures that highlight "just how far AI still has to go before it remotely approaches human capabilities."[8] Waldrop closes with possible solutions by improving deep learning strategies, expanding the training data sets, and taking a positive view of the challenges that lie ahead.

Even after sixty years, AI is in its early days. I want AI to succeed, and see the way forward is to adopt HCAI design processes that involve stakeholders in design discussions and iterative testing for user interfaces and control panels. The second component is to make products with more transparency and human control over the algorithms. I envision explainable user interfaces, audit trails to analyze failures and near misses, and independent oversight to guide decisions (Part 4). In short, a new synthesis of human-centered design thinking with the best of AI methods will do much to deliver meaningful technologies that benefit people.

These debates about AI research dramatically influence government research funding, major commercial projects, academic research and teaching, and public impressions. This chapter simplifies the many goals of AI researchers into these two, science and innovation, and then describes four pairs of design possibilities which could be fruitfully combined (Figure 11.1). Combined designs may result in more automation in some contexts, more human control in others. Combined designs will also have more nuanced choices over the features that can be reliably done by a computer and those that should remain under human control.

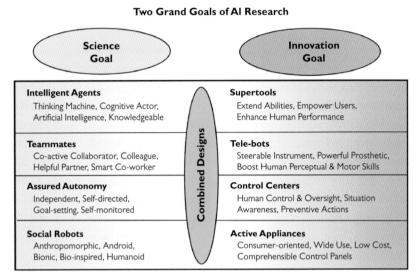

Fig 11.1 Terminology and design metaphors for the science goal and innovation goal, with the possibility of combined designs that take the useful features from each goal.

The four pairs of design possibilities are a guide to what might work in different contexts or they can suggest combined designs that lead to reliable, safe, and trustworthy systems, especially for consequential and life-critical applications. Design excellence can bring widespread benefits for users and society, such as in business, education, healthcare, environmental preservation, and community safety.

Chapter 12 describes the science goal of studying computational agents that think, which often means understanding human perceptual, cognitive, and motor abilities so as to build computers that autonomously perform tasks as well as or better than humans. It summarizes the innovation goal of developing widely used products and services by using AI methods, which keep humans in control. Both goals require science, engineering, and design research.

Chapter 13 focuses on ways to combine the best features of each goal. Those who pursue the science goal build cognitive computers that they describe as smart, intelligent, knowledgeable, and capable of thinking. The resulting human-like products may succeed on narrow tasks, but these designs can exacerbate the distrust, fears, and anxiety that many users have about their computers. The innovation goal community believes that computers are best designed to be supertools that amplify, augment, empower, and enhance humans. The combined strategy could be to design familiar HCAI user interfaces with AI technologies for services such as text messaging suggestions and search query completion. AI technologies would also enable internal operations to manage storage and transmit optimally across complex networks.

Chapter 14 raises these questions: do designers benefit from thinking of computers as being teammates, partners, and collaborators? When is it helpful and when is there a danger in assuming human–human interaction is a good model for human–robot interaction? Innovation goal researchers and developers want to build tele-bots that extend human capabilities while providing superhuman perceptual and motor support, thereby boosting human performance, while allowing human–human teamwork to succeed. The combined strategy could be to use science goal algorithms to implement automatic internal services that support the innovation goal of human control. This approach is implemented in the many car-driving technologies such as lane following, parking assist, and collision avoidance. The idea is to give users the control they desire by putting "AI inside," which provides valuable services to users based on machine and deep learning algorithms. In this way users have the benefit of AI optimizations, an understanding of what is happening, a clear model of what will happen next, and the chance to take control if needed.

Chapter 15 discusses the science goal for products and services that are autonomous with no human intervention. Rather than assured autonomy systems acting alone, innovation goal researchers want to support control centers and control panels (sometimes called human-in-the-loop or humans-on-the-loop), in which humans operate highly automated devices and systems. The combined strategy could be to have science goal algorithms provide highly automated features, with user interface designs that support human control and oversight. This combined strategy is in use in many NASA, industrial, utility, military, and air-traffic control centers, where rich forms of AI are used to optimize performance but the operators have a clear mental model of what will happen next. Predictable behavior from machines is highly valued by human operators.

Chapter 16 covers the many attempts by science goal advocates to build social robots over hundreds of years, which have attracted widespread interest. At the same time, active appliances, mobile devices, and kiosks are widespread consumer successes. Innovation goal champions prefer designs that are seen as steerable instruments, which increase flexibility or mobility, while being expendable in rescue, disaster, and military situations. The combined design could be to start with human-like services, which have proven acceptance, such as voice-operated virtual assistants. These services could be embedded in active appliances which give users control of features that are important to them.

Innovation goal thinking also leads to better than human performance in active appliances, such as using four-wheeled or treaded robots to provide the mobility over rough terrain or floods, maneuverability in tight spaces, and heavy-lifting capacity. Active appliances can also have superhuman sensors, such as infrared cameras or sensitive microphones, and specialized effectors, such as drills on Mars Rovers and cauterizing tools on surgical robots.

Awareness of the different goals can stimulate fresh thinking about how to deal with different contexts by creating combined designs that leads to reliable, safe, and trustworthy systems.[9] Chapter 17 summarizes the design trade-offs so as to find happy collaborations between the science goal and innovation goal communities.

CHAPTER 12

Science and Innovation Goals

A I researchers and developers have offered many goals such as this one in the popular textbook by Stuart Russell and Peter Norvig: "1. Think like a human. 2. Act like a human. 3. Think rationally. 4. Act rationally."[1] A second pair of textbook authors, David Poole and Alan Mackworth, write that the science goal is to study "computational agents that act intelligently." They want to "understand the principles that make intelligent behavior possible in natural or artificial systems . . . by designing, building, and experimenting with computational systems that perform tasks commonly viewed as requiring intelligence."[2]

Others see AI as a set of tools to augment human abilities or extend their creativity. For simplicity, I focus on two goals: science and innovation. Of course, some researchers and developers will be sympathetic to goals that fall in both communities or even other goals that fall in between. The sharply defined science and innovation goals are meant to clarify important distinctions, but individuals are likely to have more complex beliefs.

Science Goal

A shortened version of the science goal is to understand human perceptual, cognitive, and motor abilities so as to build computers that perform tasks as well as or better than humans. This goal includes the aspirations for social robots, common-sense reasoning, affective computers, machine consciousness, and artificial general intelligence (AGI).

Those who pursue the science goal have grand scientific ambitions and understand that it may take 100 or 1000 years, but they tend to believe that researchers will eventually be able to understand and model humans faithfully.[3] Many researchers in this AI community believe that humans are machines, maybe very sophisticated ones, but they see building exact emulations of humans as a realistic and worthwhile grand challenge. They are cynical about claims of human exceptionalism or that humans are a separate category from computers. The influential *AI 100 Report* states that "the difference between an arithmetic calculator and a human brain *is not one of kind* [emphasis added], but of scale, speed, degree of autonomy, and generality," which assumes that human and computer thinking are in the same category.[4]

The desire to build computers that match human abilities is an ancient and deep commitment. Elizabeth Broadbent, a medical researcher at the University of Auckland, NZ, wrote thoughtfully about "Interactions with robots: The truths we reveal about ourselves."[5] She pointed out: "Humans have a fundamental tendency to create, and the ultimate creation is another human." This phrase could be playfully interpreted as a desire to be a typical human parent, but it is also a barbed reminder that the motivation of some AI researchers is to create an artificial human.

The desire to create human-like machines influences the terminology and metaphors that the science goal community feels strongly about. They often describe computers as smart machines, intelligent agents, knowledgeable actors, and are attracted to the idea that computers are learning and require training, much as a human child learns and is trained. Science goal researchers often include performance comparisons between humans and computers, such as the capability of oncologists versus AI programs to identify breast cancer tumors. Journalists, especially headline writers, are strongly attracted to this competition idea, which make for great stories such as "How Robot Hands are Evolving to Do What Ours Can" (*New York Times*, July 30, 2018) or "Robots Can Now Read Better than Humans, Putting Millions of Jobs at Risk" (*Newsweek*, January 15, 2018). In their book *Rebooting AI*, Gary Marcus and Ernest Davis worry that "[t]he net effect of a tendency of many in the media to over report technology results is that the public has come to believe that AI is much closer to being solved than it really is."[6]

Many science goal researchers and developers believe that robots can be teammates, partners, and collaborators and that computers can be autonomous systems that are independent, capable of setting goals, self-directed, and self-monitoring. They see *automation* as merely carrying out requirements anticipated by the programmers/designs, while *autonomy* is a step beyond automation to develop novel goals based on new sensor data. Science goal protagonists promote embodied intelligence through social (human-like or anthropomorphic) robots, which are bio-inspired (or bionic) to resemble human forms.

Some researchers, legal scholars, and ethicists envision a future in which computers will have responsibility and legal protection of their rights, much as individual humans and corporations.[7] They believe that computers and social robots can be moral and ethical actors and that these qualities can be built into algorithms. This controversial topic is beyond the scope of this book, which focuses on design issues to guide near-future research and develop the next generation of technology.

Innovation Goal

The innovation goal, some would call it the engineering goal, drives researchers to develop widely used products and services by applying HCAI methods. This goal typically favors tool-based metaphors, tele-bots, active appliances, and control centers. These applications are described as instruments, apps, appliances, orthotics, prosthetics, utensils, or implements, but I'll use the general term *supertool*. These AI-guided products and services are built into clouds, websites, laptops, mobile devices, home automation, kiosks, flexible manufacturing, and virtual assistants. A science goal airport assistant might be a mobile human-like robot that greets travelers at the entrance to guide them to their check-in and departure gate. Some airport scenarios show robots who engage in natural language conversation, offering help and responding to questions. By contrast, an innovation goal airport supertool would be a smartphone app with a map tailored to guide travelers, a list of security line wait times, and current information on flights.

Researchers and developers who pursue innovations study human behavior and social dynamics to understand user acceptance of products and services. These researchers are typically enthusiastic about serving human needs, so they often partner with professionals to work on authentic problems and take pride in widely adopted innovations. They regularly begin by clarifying what the tasks are, who the users are, and the societal/environmental impacts.[8]

The innovation goal community frequently supports high levels of human control and high levels of computer automation, as conveyed by the two-dimensional HCAI framework from Part 2. They understand that there are innovations that require rapid fully automatic operation (airbag deployment, pacemakers, etc.) and there are applications in which users prefer full human control (bicycle riding, piano playing, etc.). Between these extremes lies a rich design space that combines high levels of human control and high levels of automation. Innovation researchers normally recognize the dangers of excessive automation and excessive human control, which were described in the HCAI framework of Part 2. These HCAI researchers and developers introduce interlocks that prevent human mistakes and controls that prevent computer failures, while striving to find a balance that produces reliable, safe, and trustworthy systems.

The desire to make commercially successful products and services means that human–computer interaction methods such as design thinking, observation of users, user experience testing, market research, and continuous monitoring of usage are frequent processes employed by the innovation goal community. They recognize that users often prefer designs that are comprehensible, predictable, and controllable because they are eager to increase their own mastery, self-efficacy, and creative control. They accept that humans need to be "in-the-loop" and even "on-the-loop," respect that users deserve explainable systems, and recognize that only humans and organizations are responsible, liable, and accountable.[9] They are sympathetic to audit trails, product logs, or flight data recorders to support retrospective forensic analysis of failures and near misses so as to improve reliability and safety, especially for life-critical applications such as pacemakers, self-driving cars, and commercial planes.[10]

Sometimes those pursuing innovations start with science-based ideas and then do what is necessary to create successful products and services. For example, science-based speech recognition research was an important foundation of successful virtual assistants such as Apple's Siri, Amazon's Alexa, Google's Home, and Microsoft's Cortana. However, a great deal of design was necessary to make successful products and services that deftly guided users and gracefully dealt with failures. These services deal with common requests for weather, news, and information by steering users to existing web resources, like Wikipedia, news agencies, and dictionaries.[11]

Similarly, natural language translation research was integrated into well-designed user interfaces for successful websites and services. A third example is that image understanding research enabled automatic creation of alt-tags, which are short descriptions of images that enable users with disabilities and others to know what is in a website image.

Autonomous social robots with bipedal locomotion and emotionally responsive faces, inspired by the science goal, make appealing demonstrations and videos. However, these designs often give way to four-wheeled rovers, tread-based vehicles, or tele-operated drones without faces, which are needed for success in the innovation goal.[12] The language of robots may remain popular, as in "surgical robots," but these are tele-bots that allow surgeons to do precise work in tight spaces inside the human body.

Many science goal researchers believe that a general purpose social robot can be made, which can serve tea to elders, deliver packages, and perform rescue work. By contrast innovation goal researchers recognize that they have to tune their solutions for each context of use. Nimble hand movements, heavy lifting, or movement in confined spaces require specialized designs which are not at all like a generic multipurpose human hand.

Lewis Mumford's book *Technics and Civilization* has a chapter titled "The Obstacle of Animism" in which he describes how first attempts at new technologies are misled by human and animal models.[13] He uses the awkward term "dissociation" to describe the shift from human forms to more useful designs, such as recognizing that four wheels have large advantages over two feet in transporting heavy loads over long distances. Similarly, airplanes have wings, but they do not flap like bird wings. Mumford stressed that "the most ineffective kind of machine is the *realistic* mechanical imitation of a man or other animal." He continues with this observation "circular motion, one of the most useful and frequent attributes of a fully developed machine, is, curiously, one of the least observable motions in nature" and concludes "for thousands of years animism has stood in the way of . . . development."[14]

As Mumford suggests, there are better ways to serve people's needs than making a human-like device. Many innovation goal researchers seek to support human connections by collaborative software, such as Google Docs to enable collaborative editing, shared databases to foster scientific partnerships, and improved media for better communications. For example, tele-conferencing services, like Zoom, Webex, and Microsoft Teams, expanded dramatically during the COVID crisis as universities shifted to online instruction with live instructors trying innovative ways to create engaging learning experiences, complemented by automated massive online open courses (MOOCs). MOOC designs, such as those from Khan Academy, edX, or Coursera, led learners through their courses by providing regular tests that gave learners feedback about their progress, enabling them to repeat material that they still had to master. Learners could choose to pace their progress and challenge themselves with more difficult material when they were ready.

The COVID crisis also led businesses to quickly expand working from home (WFH) options for their employees so they could continue to operate. Similarly, family, friends, and communities adopted services, such as Zoom, to have dinners together, weddings, funerals, town meetings, and much more. Some talk about Zoom fatigue from hours of online meetings, while others find it liberating to have frequent conversations with distant colleagues or family. New forms of online interaction are quickly emerging that have new game-like user interfaces, like Kumospace and Gather.town, which allow more flexibility, and meeting organizers are finding creative ways to make engaging large group events, while supporting small group side discussions.

Many forms of collaboration are supported by social media platforms, such as Facebook, Twitter, and Weibo, which employ AI-guided services. These platforms have attracted billions of users, who enjoy the social connections, benefit from the business opportunities, connect communities in productive ways, and support teamwork as in citizen science projects. However, many users have strong concerns about privacy and security as well as the misuse of social media by political operatives, criminals, terrorists, and hate groups to spread fake news, scams, and dangerous messages. Privacy invasion, massive data collection about individuals, and surveillance capitalism excesses are substantial threats. AI algorithms and user interface designs have contributed to these abuses, but they also can contribute to the solutions, which must include human reviewers and independent oversight boards.

Mumford's thinking about serving human needs leads naturally to new possibilities: *orthotics*, such as eyeglasses, to improve performance; *prosthetics*, such as replacements for missing limbs; and *exoskeletons* that increase a human's capacity to lift heavy objects. Users of orthotics, prosthetics, or exoskeletons see these devices as amplifying their abilities.

The next four chapters address the four pairs of metaphors that are guiding AI and HCAI researchers, developers, business leaders, and policy-makers. They offer diverse perspectives, which can be useful in different contexts, and can guide designers in combining features that put these metaphors to work.

CHAPTER 13

Intelligent Agents and Supertools

By the 1940s, as modern electronic digital computers emerged, the descriptions included "awesome thinking machines" and "electronic brains." George Washington University Professor Dianne Martin's extensive review of survey data includes her concern:

> The attitude research conducted over the past 25 years suggests that the "awesome thinking machine" myth may have in fact retarded public acceptance of computers in the work environment, at the same time that it raised unrealistic expectations for easy solutions to difficult social problems.[1]

In 1950, Alan Turing provoked huge interest with his essay "Computing Machinery and Intelligence" in which he raises the question: "Can Machines Think?"[2] He proposed what has come to be known as the Turing Test or the imitation game. His thoughtful analysis catalogs objections, but he ends with "[w]e may hope that machines will eventually compete with men [and women] in all purely intellectual fields." Many artificial intelligence researchers who pursue the science goal have taken up Turing's challenge by developing machines that are capable of carrying out human tasks such as playing chess, understanding images, and delivering customer support. Critics of the Turing Test think it is a useless distraction or publicity stunt with poorly described rules, but the Loebner Prize has attracted participants and media attention since 1990 with prizes for the makers of the winning program.[3] The January 2016 issue of *AI Magazine* was devoted to articles with many new forms of Turing Tests.[4] Media theorist Simone Natale of the University of Turin sees the Turing Test as a banal deception which builds on the readiness of people to accept devices that simulate intention, sociality, and emotions.[5]

An early, more nuanced vision came in J. C. R. Licklider's 1960 description of "man–computer symbiosis," which acknowledged differences between humans and computers, but stated that they would be cooperative interaction partners with computers doing the routine work and humans having insights and making decisions.[6]

The widespread use of terms such as smart, intelligent, knowledgeable, and thinking helped propagate terminology such as machine learning, deep learning, and the idea that computers were being trained. Neuroscience descriptions of human brains as neural networks was taken up enthusiastically as a metaphor for describing AI methods, further spreading the idea that computers were like people.

IBM latched onto the term cognitive computing to describe their work on the Watson system. However, IBM's Design Director for AI transformation reported in 2020 that it "was just too confusing for people to understand" and added that "we say AI, but even that, we clarify as augmented intelligence."[7] Google has long branded itself as strong on AI, but their current effort emphasizes "People and AI Research" (PAIR).[8] It appears that those pursuing the innovation goal increasingly recognize that the suggestion of computer intelligence should be tempered with a human-centered approach for commercial products and services.

Journalists have often been eager proponents of the idea that computers were thinking and that robots would be taking our jobs. Cover stories with computer-based characters have been featured in popular magazines, such as *Newsweek* in 1980, which reported on "Machines That Think," and *Time Magazine* in 1996, which asked "Can Machines Think?"

Graphic artists have been all too eager to show thinking machines, especially featuring human-like heads and hands, which reinforce the idea that humans and computers are similar. Common themes were a robot hand reaching out to grasp a human hand and a robotic human sitting in the pose of Auguste Rodin's The Thinker sculpture. Popular culture in the form of Hollywood movies has offered sentient computer characters, such as HAL in the 1968 film *2001: A Space Odyssey* and C3PO in the 1977 *Star Wars*. Human-like robotic characters have also played central roles in terrifying films such as *The Terminator* and the *The Matrix*, in charming films such as *Wall-E* and *Robot & Frank*, and in thought provoking films such as *Her* and *Ex Machina*.[9]

Computers have been increasingly portrayed as independent actors or agents that ("who") could think, learn, create, discover, and communicate. University of Toronto professor Brian Cantwell Smith highlights words that should be avoided when discussing what computers can do, such as know, read, explain, or understand.[10] However, journalists and headline writers are attracted to the idea of computer agency and human-like capabilities, producing headlines such as:

Machines Learn Chemistry (ScienceDaily.com)

Hubble Accidentally Discovers a New Galaxy in Cosmic Neighborhood (NASA)

The Fantastic Machine That Found the Higgs Boson (*The Atlantic*)

Artificial Intelligence Finds Disease-Related Genes (ScienceDaily.com)

These headlines are in harmony with the more popular notion that computers are gaining capabilities to match or exceed humans.[11] Other writers have voiced the human-centered view that computers are supertools that can amplify, augment, empower, and enhance people (see Figure 11.1). Support for the idea of computers as supertools comes from many sources, including Professor Daniela Rus, head of the MIT Computer Science and Artificial Intelligence Laboratory, who has said: "It is important for people to understand that AI is nothing more than a tool . . . [with] huge power to empower us."[12]

The supertool community included early HCAI researchers, such as Douglas Engelbart,[13] whose vision of what it meant to augment human intellect was shown in his famed demonstration at the 1968 Fall Joint Computer Conference.[14] *New York Times* technology journalist John Markoff traces the history of artificial intelligence versus intelligence augmentation (AI versus IA), in his popular book *Machines of Loving Grace: The Quest for Common Ground between Humans and Robots*.[15] He describes controversies, personalities, and motivations, suggesting that there is a growing belief that there are productive ways to pursue both the science and innovation goals.

These issues were the heart of my 1997 debates with MIT Media Lab's Pattie Maes. Our positions represented two views of what future computers would be like, well before there were ubiquitous smartphones and 3 million touchscreen-driven apps.[16] My examples, based on the ideas of direct manipulation, showed users operating control panels with buttons, checkboxes, and sliders, so as to change visual displays with maps, textual lists, arrays of photos, bar charts, line graphs, and scatterplots.[17] By contrast, Maes described how "a software agent knows the individual user's habits, preferences, and interests." She argued that "a software agent is proactive. It can take initiative because it knows what your interests are." Simply put, I argued for designs which gave users a high level of control of potent automation, while Maes believed that software agents could reliably take over and do the work for the users.[18] Even after twenty-five years of progress that debate continues in ever-evolving forms.

Innovation goal developers are more likely to pursue designs of tool-like products and services. They are influenced by many guidelines documents, such as The Apple Human Interface Design Guidelines, which included two clear principles: "User Control: . . . people—not apps—are in control . . . it's usually a mistake for the app to take over the decision-making" and "Flexibility: . . . (give) users complete, fine-grained control over their work."[19] These guidelines and others from IBM, Microsoft, and the US government[20] have led to greater consistency within and across applications, which makes it easier for users, especially those with disabilities, to learn new applications on laptops, mobile devices, and web-based services.

On airplane flights it is common to see people using laptops for work, but I was impressed when a blind woman with a white cane came to sit next to me. Just after takeoff, she took out her laptop and began working on a business report. She listened to the text through her earphones as she deftly revised and formatted the document. When I spoke to her, she said she was head of accessibility for the state of Utah. She confirmed that the accessibility guidelines and features as implemented on common laptops enabled her to participate fully as a professional.

The guidelines stressing user control, even for users with disabilities, have led to widespread adoption of computing, but the attraction of robotic and intelligent terminology and metaphors from the science goal remains prominent, especially at the numerous AI conferences. The conference papers may describe innovations but their approach is often to have a computer carry out the task automatically, as in reading mammograms or self-driving cars. However, there are strong innovation goal viewpoints which describe designs in which humans operate supertools and active appliances. These viewpoints are more likely to emerge at conferences such as Augmented Humans[21] and the dozens of human–computer interaction conferences run by groups such as the ACM's SIGCHI,[22] User Experience Professionals Association,[23] and similar groups around the world. Events such as World Usability Day[24] have promoted academic, industry, and government activities. Combined ideas come at conferences such as the ACM's Intelligent User Interfaces.[25]

Application developers, who produce the 3 million applications in the Apple and Google Play stores, have largely built tool-like user interfaces, even when there is ample AI technology at work internally. These developers appreciate that users often expect a device that is comprehensible, predictable, and under their control.

The combined design could be to build science goal technologies for internal operations, while the users see empowering interfaces that give them clear choices, as in GPS navigation systems, web search, e-commerce, and recommender systems. AI-guided systems offer users suggestions in spelling and grammar checkers, web search, and email writing. University of Washington professor Jeffrey Heer shows three ways of using AI-guided methods in support of human control in more advanced applications such as data cleaning, exploratory data visualization, and natural language translation.[26] Many others have proposed similar strategies for giving users control panels to operate their AI-guided recommender systems, such as sliders to choose music or check boxes to narrow e-commerce searches. These are covered in Chapter 19's section "Explainable User Interface."

A second way to combine the goals is seen in the familiar example of the well-designed integration of automated features and human control of the cell phone digital camera. These widely used devices employ AI features such as high dynamic range lighting control, jitter removal, and automatic focus, but give users control over composition, portrait modes, filters, and social media postings.

A third way to combine goals is to provide supertools with added features that come from intelligent agent designs. Recommender systems fit this approach by using AI algorithms to recommend movies, books, spelling corrections, and search query possibilities. Users benefit from the improved supertools but remain in control, since they can choose whether or not to follow a recommendation.[27] Novel recommendations could be in the form of suggested meals based on the contents of your refrigerator or dietary shifts based on what you have eaten. Another class of recommenders have been called coaches, such as reviews of your piano playing to indicate where you strayed from the music score or feedback to show you when your knee should have been bent further during yoga practice. These coaching suggestions are best presented when you complete your effort and on request in a gentle way that makes it your choice to accept or ignore.

In summary, there are ways to combine the enthusiasm for intelligent agents with the idea of human-controlled supertools that are consistent, comprehensible, predictable, and controllable. Skillful combinations of AI with HCAI thinking can improve the value and acceptance of products and services. Chapter 14 takes on the second pair of metaphors that guides design possibilities: teammates and tele-bots.

CHAPTER 14

Teammates and Tele-bots

A common theme in designs for robots and advanced technologies is that human–human interaction is a good model for human–robot interaction,[1] and that emotional attachment to embodied robots is an asset.[2] Many designers never consider alternatives, believing that the way people communicate with each other, coordinate activities, and form teams is the only model for design. The repeated missteps stemming from this assumption do not deter others who believe that this time will be different, that the technology is now more advanced, and that their approach is novel.

Numerous psychological studies by Clifford Nass and his team at Stanford University showed that when computers are designed to be like humans, users respond and engage in socially appropriate ways.[3] Nass's fallacy might be described as this: since many people are willing to respond socially to robots, it is appropriate and desirable to design robots to be social or human-like.

However, what Nass and colleagues did not consider was whether other designs, which were not social or human-like, might lead to superior performance. Getting beyond the human teammate idea may increase the likelihood that designers will take advantage of unique computer features, including sophisticated algorithms, huge databases, superhuman sensors, information-abundant displays, and powerful effectors. I was pleased to find that in later work with grad student Victoria Groom, Nass wrote: "Simply put, robots fail as teammates."[4] They elaborated: "Characterizing robots as teammates indicates that robots are capable of fulfilling a human role and encourages humans to treat robots as human teammates. When expectations go unmet, a negative response is unavoidable."

Lionel Robert of the University of Michigan cautions that human-like robots can lead to three problems: mistaken usage based on emotional attachment to the systems, false expectations of robot responsibility, and incorrect beliefs about appropriate use of robots.[5] Still, a majority of researchers believe that robot teammates and social robots are inevitable.[6] That belief pervades the human–robot interaction research community which "rarely conceptualized robots as tools or infrastructure and has instead theorized robots predominantly as peers, communication partners or teammates."[7]

Psychologist Gary Klein and his colleagues clarify ten realistic challenges to making machines behave as effectively as human teammates.[8] The challenges include making machines that are predictable, controllable, and able to negotiate with people about goals. The authors suggest that their challenges are meant to stimulate research and also "as cautionary tales about the ways that technology can disrupt rather than support coordination." A perfect teammate, buddy, assistant, or sidekick sounds appealing, but can designers deliver on this image or will users be misled, deceived, and disappointed?[9] Can users have the control inherent in a tele-bot while benefiting from the helpfulness suggested by the teammate metaphor?

My objection is that human teammates, partners, and collaborators are very different from computers. Instead of these terms, I prefer to use tele-bots to suggest human controlled devices (see Figure 11.1). I believe that it is helpful to remember that "computers are not people and people are not computers." Margaret Boden, a long-term researcher on creativity and AI at the University of Sussex, makes an alternate but equally strong statement: "Robots are simply not people."[10] I think the differences between people and computers include the following:

Responsibility Computers are not responsible participants, neither legally nor morally. They are never liable or accountable. They are a different category from humans. This continues to be true in all legal systems and I think it will remain so. Margaret Boden continues with a straightforward principle: "Humans, not robots, are responsible agents."[11] This principle is especially true in the military, where chain of command and responsibility are taken seriously.[12]

Pilots of advanced fighter jets with ample automation still think of themselves as in control of the plane and responsible for their successful missions, even though they must adhere to their commander's orders and the rules of engagement. Astronauts rejected designs of early Mercury capsules which had no window to eyeball the re-entry if they had to do it manually—they wanted to be in control when necessary, yet responsive to Mission Control's rules. Neil Armstrong landed the Lunar Module on the Moon—he was in charge, even though there was ample automation. The Lunar Module was not his partner. The Mars Rovers are not teammates; they are advanced automation with an excellent integration of human tele-operation with high levels of automatic operation.

It is instructive that the US Air Force shifted from using the term unmanned autonomous/aerial vehicles (UAVs) to remotely piloted vehicles (RPVs) so as to clarify responsibility. Many of these pilots work from a US Air Force base in Nevada to operate drones flying in distant locations on military missions that often have deadly outcomes. They are responsible for what they do and suffer psychological trauma akin to what happens to pilots flying aircraft in war zones. The Canadian Government has a rich set of knowledge requirements that candidates must have to be granted a license to operate a remotely piloted aircraft system (RPAS).[13] Designers and marketers of commercial products and services recognize that they and their organizations are the responsible parties; they are morally accountable and legally liable.[14] Commercial activity is further shaped by independent oversight mechanisms, such as government regulation, industry voluntary standards, and insurance requirements.

Distinctive capabilities Computers have distinctive capabilities of sophisticated algorithms, huge databases, superhuman sensors, information-abundant displays, and powerful effectors. To buy into the metaphor of "teammate" seems to encourage designers to emulate human abilities rather than take advantage of the distinctive capabilities of computers. One robot rescue design team described their project to interpret the robot's video images through natural language text messages to the operators. The messages described what the robot was "seeing" when a video or photo could deliver much more detailed information more rapidly. Why settle for a human-like designs when designs that make full use of distinctive computer capabilities would be more effective.

Designers who pursue advanced technologies can find creative ways to empower people so that they are astonishingly more effective—that's what familiar supertools have done: microscopes, telescopes, bulldozers, ships, and planes. Empowering people is what digital technologies have also done, through cameras, Google Maps, web search, and other widely used applicataions. Cameras, copy machines, cars, dishwashers, pacemakers, and heating, ventilation, and air conditioning systems (HVAC) are not usually described as teammates—they are supertools or active appliances that amplify, augment empower, and enhance people.

Human creativity The human operators are the creative force—for discovery, innovation, art, music, etc. Scientific papers are always authored by people, even when powerful computers, telescopes, and the Large Hadron Collider are used. Artworks and music compositions are credited to humans, even if rich composition technologies are heavily used. The human qualities such as passion, empathy, humility, and intuition that are often described in studies of creativity are not readily matched by computers.

Another aspect of creativity is to give human users of computer systems the ability to fix, personalize, and extend the design for themselves or to provide feedback to developers for them to make improvements for all users. The continuous improvement of supertools, tele-bots, and other technologies depends on human input about problems and suggestions for new features.

Those who promote the teammate metaphor are often led down the path of making human-like designs, which have a long history of appealing robots, but succeed only as entertainment, crash test dummies, and medical mannequins (Chapter 16). I don't think this will change. There are better designs than human-like rescue robots, bomb disposal devices, or pipe inspectors. In many cases four-wheeled or treaded vehicles are typical, usually tele-operated by a human controller.

The DaVinci surgical robot is not a teammate. It is a well-designed tele-bot that enables surgeons to perform precise actions in difficult to reach small body cavities (Figure 14.1). As Lewis Mumford reminds designers, successful technologies diverge from human forms.[15] Intuitive Surgical, the developer of the DaVinci systems for cardiac, colorectal, urological, and other surgeries, makes clear that "Robots don't perform surgery. Your surgeon performs surgery with Da Vinci by using instruments that he or she guides via a console."[16]

Many robotic devices have a high degree of tele-operation, in which an operator controls activities, even though there is a high degree of automation. For example, drones are tele-bots, even though they have the capacity to automatically hover or orbit at a fixed altitude, return to their take-off point, or follow a series of operator-chosen GPS waypoints. The NASA Mars Rover vehicles also have a rich mixture of tele-operated features and independent movement capabilities, guided by sensors to detect obstacles or precipices, with

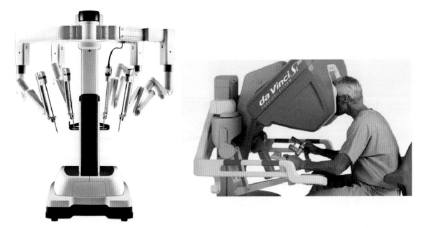

Fig 14.1 DaVinci Surgical System from Intuitive Surgical
Source: http://www.intusurg.com

plans to avoid them. The control centers at NASA's Jet Propulsion Labs have dozens of operators who control various systems on the Rovers, even when they are hundreds of millions of miles away. It is another excellent example of combining high levels of human control and high levels of automation.

Terms like tele-bots and telepresence suggest alternative design possibilities. These instruments enable remote operation and more careful control of devices, such as when tele-pathologists control a remote microscope to study tissue samples. Combined designs take limited, yet mature and proven features of teammate models and embed them in devices that augment humans by direct or tele-operated controls.

Another way that computers can be seen as teammates is by providing information from huge databases and superhuman sensors. When the results of sophisticated algorithms are displayed on information-abundant displays, such as in three-dimensional medical echocardiograms with false color to indicate blood flow volume, clinicians can be more confident in making cardiac treatment decisions. Similarly, users of Bloomberg Terminals for financial data see their computers as enabling them to make bolder choices in buying stocks or rebalancing mutual fund retirement portfolios (Figure 14.2). The Bloomberg Terminal uses a specialized keyboard and one or more large displays, with multiple windows typically arranged by users to be spatially stable so they know where to find what they need. With tiled, rather than overlapped, windows users can quickly find what they want without rearranging windows or scrolling. The voluminous data needed for a decision is easily visible and

Fig 14.2 A Bloomberg Terminal for financial analysts shows abundant data, arranged to be spatially stable with non-overlapping windows.

clicking in one window produces relevant information in other windows. More than 300,000 users pay $20,000 per year to have this supertool on their desks.

In summary, the persistence of the teammate metaphor means it has appeal for many designers and users. While users should feel fine about describing their computers as teammates, designers who harness the distinctive features of computers, such as sophisticated algorithms, huge databases, superhuman sensors, information-abundant displays, and powerful effectors may produce more effective tele-bots that are appreciated by users as supertools.

CHAPTER 15

Assured Autonomy and Control Centers

C omputer autonomy is an attractive science goal for many AI researchers, developers, journalists, and promoters. Past descriptions of computer autonomy are giving way to discussions that feature stronger statements about assured autonomy, which contrast with the increasing use of control centers (see Figure 11.1).

Computer autonomy has become a widely used term to describe an independently functioning machine, not directly under human control. The US Defense Science Board makes this definition:

Autonomy results from delegation of a decision to an authorized entity to take action within specific boundaries. An important distinction is that systems governed by prescriptive rules that permit no deviations are automated, but they are not autonomous. To be fully autonomous, a system must have the capability to independently compose and select among different courses of action to accomplish goals based on its knowledge and understanding of the world, itself, and the situation.[1]

However, the US Defense Science Board cautioned that:

Unfortunately, the word "autonomy" often conjures images in the press and the minds of some military leaders of computers making independent decisions and taking uncontrolled action ... It should be made clear that all autonomous systems are supervised by human operators at some level, and autonomous systems' software embodies the designed limits on the actions and decisions delegated to the computer ... Autonomy is, by itself, not a solution to any problem.[2]

This warning highlights the reality that humans and machines are embedded in complex organizational and social systems, making interdependence an important goal as well. Since humans remain as the responsible actors (legally, morally, ethically), shouldn't computers be designed in ways that assure user control? The combined design position is that some features can be made autonomous if they are comprehensible, predictable, and controllable, while giving users control over the features that are not reliable and those that are important to them.

While enthusiasm for fully autonomous systems remains high and may be valuable as a research goal, the realities of usage have been troubling. Autonomous, high-speed financial trading systems have produced several billion-dollar financial crashes, but more troubling are deadly outcomes such as the Patriot missile system shooting down two friendly aircraft during the Iraq War[3] or the 2016 crash of a Tesla while on autopilot.[4] Maybe the most dramatic examples are the late 2018 and early 2019 crashes of the Boeing 737 MAX, caused by the autonomous maneuvering characteristics augmentation system (MCAS) system, which took over some aircraft controls without even informing the pilots.[5]

Some of the problems caused by autonomy are captured in Texas A&M University professor Robin Murphy's law of autonomous robots: "any deployment of robotic systems will fall short of the target level of autonomy, creating or exacerbating a shortfall in mechanisms for coordination with human problem holders."[6]

Those who faced the realities of dealing with innovation goals have repeatedly described the dangers of full computer autonomy. An early commentary in 1983 gently described the ironies of autonomy, which instead of lightening the operator's workload increased their workload because continuous monitoring of the autonomous computer was necessary.[7] These operators are in the unhappy situation of being unsure of what the computer will do, yet they are responsible for the outcome.[8]

Other concerns were the difficulty of humans remaining vigilant when there was little for them to do, the challenge of rapidly taking over when problems arose, and the struggle to maintain skills for the times when they need to take over operations. These ironies of vigilance, rapid transition, and deskilling of operators remain relevant because the operators are responsible for the outcomes.[9]

The team of Jeff Bradshaw, Robert R. Hoffman, David D. Woods, and Matt Johnson make forceful comments in a strongly worded paper: "The Seven Deadly Myths of Autonomous Systems."[10] They make the bold statement that "there's nothing worse than a so-called smart machine that can't tell you what it's doing, why it's doing something, or when it will finish. Even more frustrating—or dangerous—is a machine that's incapable of responding to human direction when something (inevitably) goes wrong." These authors also make the devastating remark that believers in full computer autonomy "have succumbed to myths of autonomy that are not only damaging in their own right but are also damaging by their continued propagation . . . because they engender a host of other serious misconceptions and consequences."

Even human factors leaders, like Mica Endsley, who support the autonomy goal describe conundrums: "as more autonomy is added to a system, and its reliability and robustness increase, the lower the situation awareness of human operators and the less likely that they will be able to take over manual control when needed."[11] Endsley's work on situational awareness in autonomous systems allows for some kinds of supervisory control, a blend that seems like a realistic combined design. Peter Hancock, another leader in human factors, raised further danger signs in his strongly worded 2022 opinion piece: "Avoiding Adverse Autonomous Agent Actions."[12] He fears that autonomous devices are "virtually inevitable," leading him to call for their elimination or severe restrictions on their capabilities.

A consequential debate continues around the dangers of lethal autonomous weapons (LAWS) which could select targets and launch deadly missiles without human intervention. A vigorous effort to ban these weapons, much as land mines have been banned, has attracted almost 5000 signatures.[13] A regular United Nations Convention on Certain Conventional Weapons in Geneva attracts representatives of 125 countries who are drafting a treaty restricting use of LAWS. Their case is bolstered by reports from cognitive science researchers,[14] who document the failures, dangers, and costs of autonomous weapons. However, some military leaders do not wish to be limited when they fear that adversaries will adopt autonomous weapons. Progress has been slow in making any agreement to limit application of autonomous defensive or offensive weapons.

I share the belief that computer autonomy is compelling for many applications. I would be eager to have an autonomous device that would do repetitive, dangerous, or difficult tasks reliably and safely. I wish I had a self-driving car that would have avoided my scraping our car on a pillar in a narrow garage. This and other human slips could be avoided by designs that prevent human errors. A safety-first approach seems to be the wise choice in consequential and life-critical applications.

The notion of assured autonomy is increasingly discussed, such as at the Computing Research Association workshop on the topic that I participated in during February 2020 in Phoenix, AZ. The spirited discussion led to a balanced report that retained the term "assured autonomy" and advocated human-centered approaches, formal methods for proving correctness, extensive testing, and independent certification.[15] The report accepts that "since legal and moral responsibility for failures of autonomous systems resides only in humans and organizations, designers and developers should be trained to understand the legal doctrines of liability and accountability."

I supported these balanced statements, but I prefer to use the term "supervised autonomy," implemented as control panels and control centers. Supervised autonomy signals that humans are monitoring performance by way of visual control panels on devices or at remote control centers, so that they can intervene in a timely manner to ensure vital outcomes. Another component of supervised autonomy is that audit trails and product logs are collected to support retrospective failure analysis (see the section "Audit Trails and Analysis Tools" in Chapter 19). In some situations, a remote control center monitors operation of many cars or trains, hospital intensive care units (ICUs), or communications networks.

The term assured autonomy continues to gather support, as indicated by the formation of the Johns Hopkins Institute for Assured Autonomy.[16] Its website states that "the trustworthiness of future autonomous systems will depend on reliable technology, rigorous systems and human engineering, and principled public policy." The UK's Research and Innovation Council has given major funding to several universities to pursue "Trustworthy Autonomous Systems."[17] My worry is that the terms assured or trustworthy autonomy promise more than is possible, misleading developers to believe that they can construct a reliable, safe, and trustworthy system with minimal human supervision.

By contrast, terms like supervised, flexible, shared, parallel, and distributed autonomy suggest that human autonomy is an equally important goal. An alternate vision is that control centers can provide human oversight, support continuous situation awareness, and offer a clear model of what is happening and what will happen next. Control centers provide information-abundant control panels, extensive feedback for each action, and an audit trail to enable retrospective reviews. Supervisory control, tele-robotics, and automation were extensively described by Sheridan,[18] who sought to define the space between detailed manual and fully automatic control, thereby clarifying human responsibility for operation of industrial control centers, robots, elevators, and washing machines.

The control center metaphor suggests human decision-making for setting goals, supported by computers carrying out predictable tasks with low-level physical actions guided by sensors and carried out by effectors. Automobile automatic transmissions are a familiar example of a successful mature autonomous system that largely operates on its own. In electronic systems, such as the social media or e-commerce, users carry out their tasks of posting messages or ordering products, getting feedback about what has happened, with alerts about posts from friends or if a product shipment is delayed. In mature systems, users have a clear mental model of what the device or system is doing, with interlocks to prevent unintended actions, alerts when problems arise, and the capacity to intervene when undesired actions occur or goals change.

Contemporary versions of control centers imply even more ambitious ideas. For example, in commercial aviation there may be several forms of human control, which begins with aircraft pilots and co-pilots, includes air-traffic controllers working in local centers (terminal radar approach control, TRACON) and extends to twenty regional control rooms (air route traffic control center, ARTCC) that coordinate the US national airspace. Further supervision of autonomous systems includes FAA certification of each aircraft, reviews of pilot training and performance, and retrospective analysis of flight data recorder information to study failures and successful recoveries from near misses. Similarly, hospital, transportation, power, stock market, military, and other complex systems have multiple control centers, within which there may be many AI-guided components.

Support grows for combined solutions such as the vision of Daniela Rus, who leads an MIT research group devoted to cars that have parallel autonomy, which means that humans are in control of the vehicle, with computers intervening only minimally during normal driving. However, the computer will act to prevent accidents by braking or avoiding collisions with cars, obstacles, or pedestrians.[19] This notion, the safety-first car, makes sense in other computer applications, especially with mobile and social robots, discussed in Chapter 16.

In summary, there is enthusiasm for the notion of assured autonomy, but for many applications control centers may provide more opportunities for human oversight. When rapid response necessitates autonomous activity, great care and constant review of performance will help make for safer operation. It may be that the terminology does not matter, as long as the designers find a reliable, safe, and trustworthy design strategy with adequate testing, feedback from users, audit trails, and open reporting of problems.

CHAPTER 16

Social Robots and Active Appliances

The fourth pair of metaphors brings us to the popular and durable ideas of social robots, sometimes called humanoid, anthropomorphic, or android, that are based on human-like forms. The contrast is with widely used appliances, such as kitchen stoves, dishwashers, and coffee makers. That's just the beginning; there are also clothes washers and dryers, security systems, baby monitors, and home heating, ventilation, and air-conditioning (HVAC) systems. Homeowners may also use popular outdoor active appliances or telebots that water gardens, mow lawns, and clean swimming pools. I call the more ambitious designs active appliances because they have sensors, programmable actions, mobility, and diverse effectors (see Figure 11.1). Active appliances do more than wait for users to activate them; they can initiate actions at specified times or when needed, such as when temperatures change, babies cry, or intruders enter a building.

History of Social Robots

Visions of animated human-like social robots go back at least to ancient Greek sources, but maybe one of the most startling successes was in the 1770s. Swiss watchmaker Pierre Jaquet-Droz created elaborate programmable mechanical devices with human faces, limbs, and clothes. The Writer used a quill pen on paper, The Musician played a piano, and The Draughtsman drew pictures, but these became only museum pieces for the Art and History Museum in

Neufchâtel, Switzerland. Meanwhile other devices such as printing presses, music boxes, clocks, and flour mills became success stories.

The idea of human-created characters gained acceptance with classic stories such as the Golem created by the sixteenth-century rabbi of Prague and Mary Shelley's *Frankenstein* in 1818. Children's stories tell of the puppet maker Geppetto whose wooden Pinocchio comes to life and the anthropomorphic Tootle the Train character who refuses to follow the rules of staying on the track. In German polymath Johann Wolfgang von Goethe's "Sorcerer's Apprentice," the protagonist conjures up a broomstick character to fetch pails of water, but when the water begins to flood the workshop, the sorcerer cannot shut it down. Worse still, splitting it in half only generates twice as many broomsticks. In the twentieth century, the metaphors and language used to discuss animated human-like robots are usually traced back to Karel Capek's 1920 play *Rossum's Universal Robots*.

These examples illustrate the idea of social robots; some are mechanical, biological, or made from materials like clay or wood, but they usually have human characteristics such as two legs, a torso, arms, and a face with eyes, nose, mouth, and ears. They may make facial expressions and head gestures, while speaking in human-like voices, expressing emotion and showing personality.[1]

These captivating social robots have strong entertainment value that goes beyond mere puppetry because they seem to operate autonomously. Children and many adults are enthusiastic about robots as film characters, engaged with robot toys, and eager to build their own robots.[2] But moving from entertainment to devices that serve innovation goals has proven to be difficult, except for crash test dummies and medical mannequins.

One example of how human-like robot concepts can be misleading is the design of early robot arms. The arms were typically like human arms: 16 inches long, with five fingers and a wrist that rotated only $180°$. These robot arms could lift at most 20 pounds, limiting their scope of use. Eventually the demands of industrial automation led to flexible manufacturing systems and powerful dexterous robot arms, without human-like forms. Rather than just an elbow and wrist, these robots might have five to six joints to twist in many directions and lift hundreds of pounds with precision. Instead of five fingers, robot hands might have two grippers or suction devices to lift delicate parts. This shift from human-like to more sophisticated forms that are tailored to specific tasks is just as Lewis Mumford predicted.

Still, serious researchers, companies, and even government agencies created social robots. The US Postal Service built a life-sized human-like Postal

Buddy in 1993 with plans to install 10,000 machines. However, they shut down the project after consumers rejected the 183 Postal Buddy kiosks that were installed.[3] Many designs for anthropomorphic bank tellers, like Tillie the Teller, disappeared because of consumer disapproval. Contemporary banking systems usually shun the name automatic teller machines in favor of automatic transaction machines or cash machines, which support patrons getting their tasks done quickly without distracting conversations with a deceptive social robot bank teller avatar. Voice commands would also bring privacy problems since other people are waiting in line.

Nass's fallacy, delivered by his consulting, contributed to the failure of Microsoft's 1995 BOB, in which friendly onscreen characters would help users do their tasks. This cute idea got media attention but in a year Microsoft shut it down instead of bringing out version 2.0. Similarly, Microsoft's Office 1997 Clippy (Clippit) was a too chatty, smiling paperclip character that popped up to offer help, thereby interrupting the user's effort and train of thought.

Other highly promoted ideas included Ananova, a web-based news-reading avatar launched in 2000 but terminated after a few months. However, the idea of a human-like news reader was revived by Chinese developers for the state news agency Xinhua in 2018,[4] and an improved version was released in June 2020. Even cheerful onscreen characters, such as Ken the Butler in Apple's famed 1987 Knowledge Navigator video and avatars in intelligent tutoring systems, have vanished. They distracted users from the tasks they were trying to accomplish.

Manufacturer Honda created an almost-life-sized social robot named Asimo, which was featured at trade events and widely reported in the media, but that project was halted in 2018 and no commercial products are planned.[5] A recent dramatic news event was when David Hanson's Social Robotics company, whose motto is "We bring robots to life," produced a human-sized talking robot named Sophia, which gained Saudi Arabian citizenship.[6] These publicity stunts draw wide attention from the media, but they have not led to commercial successes. The company is shifting its emphasis to a 14-inch-high, low-priced programmable version, named "Little Sophia," which could be used for education and entertainment. It is described as a "robot friend that makes learning STEM [science, technology, engineering, math], coding and AI a fun and rewarding adventure for kids."

At the MIT Media Lab, Cynthia Breazeal's two decades of heavily promoted demonstrations of emotive robots, such as Kismet,[7] culminated in a business startup, Jibo, which closed in 2019. Other social robot startups, including Anki (maker of Cozmo and Vector) and Mayfield Robotics (maker of Kuri), also closed in 2019.[8] These companies found happy users, but not enough of a market with users who valued the social robot designs. Cornell University's Guy Hoffman wrote that "it now seems that three of the most viable contenders to lead the budding market of social home robots have failed to find a sustainable business model."[9] Hoffman remains optimistic that artists and designers could make improved models that might still succeed: "A physical thing in your space, moving with and around you, provides an emotional grip that no disembodied conversant can."

Guy Hoffman's Cornell colleague Malte Jung, who heads the Robots in Groups Lab, wrote me in an email, "I have trouble seeing a convincing design argument for anthropomorphic robots (except maybe for a very small set of use-cases). I think designing robots with anthropomorphic features of form or behavior has several disadvantages including unnecessary complexity and risk of raising expectations that can't be met." Jung sees opportunities in related directions: "cars are becoming more and more like robots . . . we can use HRI [human–robot interaction] design approaches to improve these systems."[10]

Another direction that has drawn publicity is the idea of sex robots, fashioned to be a human-sized, conversational companion that are a big step from the popular sex toys used by many couples. Female and male sex robots can have custom-tailored physical features with prices in the range of $3,000 to $50,000. Customers can choose color, shape, size, and texture of erogenous zones and facial features, with heated skin as an option. The Campaign Against Sex Robots has raised concerns about how these robots will harm women and girls, with strong warnings about the dangers of child sex robots.

Some companies are managing to turn impressive demonstrations of human-like robots into promising products that go beyond anthropomorphic inspirations. Boston Dynamics,[11] which began with two-legged two-armed social robots, has shifted to wheel-driven robots with vacuum suction for picking up hefty packages in warehouses (Figure 16.1). The Korean automobile giant Hyundai signaled support for Boston Dynamics' technology by taking it over in 2020, giving it a valuation of over $1 billion.

The Japanese information technology and investor giant Softbank, which was also a part owner of Boston Dynamics, is devoted to products that are "smart and fun!" Softbank acquired the French company, Aldebaran Robotics, in 2012 and in 2014 they introduced the Pepper robot that featured a four-foot-high human-like shape, with expressive head, arm, and hand movements, and a three-wheeled base for mobility. Softbank claims that Pepper "is optimized for human interaction and is able to engage with people through

Fig 16.1 Mobile robot for moving boxes in a warehouse from Boston Dynamics.
Source: Handle™ robot image provided courtesy of Boston Dynamics, Inc.

conversation and his touch screen."[12] Its appealing design and conversational capacity generated strong interest, leading to sales of more than 20,000 units. Pepper is promoted for tasks such as welcoming customers, product information delivery, exhibit or store guide, and satisfaction survey administration.[13] A ten-week study of Pepper in a German elder care home found that the "older adults enjoyed the interaction with the robot" in physical training and gaming, but they "made it clear that they do not want robots to replace caregivers."[14] During the COVID-19 crisis, Pepper robots, wearing masks, were used in shopping malls to remind customers to wear their masks. SoftBank Robotics acquired the 2-foot-high human-like NAO robot from Aldebaran Robotics in 2015. NAO is more sophisticated than Pepper and more expensive, yet it has sold more than 5000 units for healthcare, retail, tourism, and education applications. As an indication of the turbulence in social robotics, Softbank shut down production of Pepper in June 2021.

In Japan, a country that is often portrayed as eager for gadgets and robots, a robot-staffed hotel lasted only a few months, closing in 2019. It had robot cleaning staff and robot front-desk workers, including crocodile-like receptionists. The company president remarked, "When you actually use robots you realize that there are places where they aren't needed—or just annoy people."[15] At the same time, traditional automated soft drink, candy, and other dispensers are widely successful in Japan and elsewhere. These have become more elaborate with heated and cooled versions dispensing food and drinks.

Controversy continues around uses of social robots for autism therapy. Some studies report benefits from using robots with children who have difficulty with human relationships. These studies suggest that some children on the autism spectrum may feel more comfortable engaging with robots, possibly paving the way for improved relationships with people.[16] Critics suggest that the focus on technology, rather than the child, leads to early successes but less durable outcomes. Neil McBride of De Monfort University worries that "if we view the human as something more than a machine, we cannot possibly devolve the responsibility for a therapeutic relationship to a mechanical toy."[17] However, play therapy with dolls and puppets could evolve to include robotic characters.

The tension between believers and skeptics has grown stronger. David Watson at the Oxford Internet Institute raises strong concerns: "the temptation to fall back on anthropomorphic tropes . . . is at best misleading and at worst downright dangerous."[18] He addresses the ethical issues of responsibility as well: "The temptation to grant algorithms decision-making authority in socially sensitive applications threatens to undermine our ability to hold powerful individuals and groups accountable for their technologically-mediated actions."[19] The believers in human-like social robots remain strong and hopeful that they will find successful designs and large markets.[20]

Animal Robots

Although human-like social robots are appreciated by some users but are not yet successful, many developers suggest that animal-like pet robots may be appealing enough to find enthusiasm from consumers.

The PARO therapeutic robot is a synthetic fur-covered white seal-like robot (Figure 16.2) that has touch, light, sound, temperature, and posture sensors, so that it "responds as if it is alive, moving its head and legs, making sounds, and . . . imitates the voice of a real baby harp seal."[21]

PARO has been approved by the US Food and Drug Administration as a Class 2 medical device. Some studies conducted during the past fifteen years report successes in producing positive responses from patients ("it's like a buddy," "it's a conversation piece," and "it makes me happy") and indications of potential therapeutic improvements.[22] However, these are typically short-term studies at the introduction of PARO, when patients are intrigued by the novelty, but the long-term use is still to be studied. Some reports suggest that the

Fig 16.2 Dr. Takanori Shibata holding his creation, PARO, a robot therapy device, in June 2018.

novelty is an attraction, which stimulates discussion among residents, giving them satisfying exchanges with their friends.

Other robot pets include SONY's dog robot, AIBO, first released in 1999 and then shut down in 2006. Since the early models cannot be repaired, failed AIBO robots had to be disposed of; however in Japan, owner devotion to their robot pets led to hundreds of Buddhist funeral services to give a compassionate farewell ceremony for a much appreciated companion. One temple's head priest commented sympathetically that Buddhism honors inanimate objects so "even though AIBO is a machine and doesn't have feelings, it acts as a mirror for human emotions."[23]

In 2018, SONY produced an updated version with a $2900 price tag that has impressive performance, even supporting robo-friendship between pairs of AIBOs. These robots could be entertaining, as the website says: "AIBO's eyes—sparkling with a clever twinkle—speak volumes, constantly giving you a window into its feelings" (Figure 16.3).[24] The new version remains a popular demonstration, but has had modest commercial success.

In the same high price category as AIBO is the doglike MiRO-E from Consequential Robots, which has a programming language to teach children coding skills. A much cheaper alternative is the $129 Joy for All companion dog robot developed by toymaker Hasbro in 2015 as a soft, cuddly, responsive companion

Fig 16.3 SONY AIBO robot dog.
Source: photo by Ben Shneiderman

for older adults with mild to moderate dementia or loneliness. Ageless Innovation was spun out as a separate company in 2018, devoted to making enjoyable toys for older adults (Figure 16.4).[25] More than ten studies by independent researchers report satisfaction and benefits for many users of the dog or cat pet robots. Their founder and chief executive officer, Ted Fischer, told me that their sales have exceeded half a million pet companion robots. The low price means older adults in nursing homes can have their own pet robot, rather than only access to an expensive device for a few hours a week. The Joy for All companion pet barks or meows, moves its head and body, has a heartbeat, and responds to voice, touch, and light.

An emerging option is the Tombot dog robot designed for older adults suffering from mild to moderate dementia and other problems.[26] The dog robot, covered with a synthetic fur, rests in place, but has rich behaviors of head, mouth, tail, and ear movements (Figure 16.5). It makes gentle barking and growling sounds when left alone but is responsive to voice, touch, stroking, and caresses. The dog robot was designed by Jim Henson's Creature Shop for Tombot and prototype-tested by university researchers. Deliveries to pre-paid

Fig 16.4 Joy for All Companion pet dog barks, responds to voice, and has a heartbeat.

buyers will begin in 2022 and then sales will open to a long waiting list of people who have expressed interest in buying it at the $400 price.

I found dozens of robot animals in online toy stores, so I thought I would try one. I bought a programmable robot dog from Fisca that was more like the famed AIBO, but priced at just $60. It had hundreds of five-star ratings, so it seemed like a worthwhile purchase (Figure 16.6). Its handheld remote controller enabled me to make it go forward or back, turn left or right, shake its head, blink its eyes, play music, and make dog-like sounds. Its plastic body is durable and mobility on wheels was amusing, but it lacked the soft cuddly qualities of other pet robots. I was able to program it to move around and dance, but after an hour, I had enough of it. I felt it was good value and performed as advertised, but I didn't have further use for it.

A vastly different programmable dog robot comes from Boston Dynamics. Their $70,000 dog-like four-legged robot called Spot, has impressive capabilities to walk, run, turn, and hop in outdoor environments to avoid objects and climb stairs (Figure 16.7). It comes with a well-designed game-like controller that resembles a drone controller, making it easy to learn to operate.

Fig 16.5 Tombot with CEO Tom Stevens.
Source: http://www.tombot.com

Spot's multiple cameras and sensors enable it to perform complex actions autonomously on rough terrain, recover from falls, and navigate narrow passages. It offers yet another example of a combined design in which rapid actions, such as movement and stability preservation, are done autonomously, while longer term functions and planning are carried out by human operators. It can conduct security patrols with sound or fire sensors, be fitted with cameras for pipeline inspection, or carry equipment to support military missions.[27]

However, the Spot User Manual cautions, "Spot is not suitable for tasks that require operation in close proximity to people. People must stay a safe distance (at least two meters) from Spot during operation to avoid injury. . . . Spot may sometimes move unpredictably or fall. Only use Spot in areas where a fall or collision will not result in an unacceptable risk."

A review of eighty-six papers with seventy user studies during the period 2008–2018 showed the persistent research interest in social robots, but revealed the sparseness of long-term studies of acceptance which would indicate interest past the novelty stage.[28] However, this review suggests potential for social robots in motivating children to be more physically active.

(a)   (b)

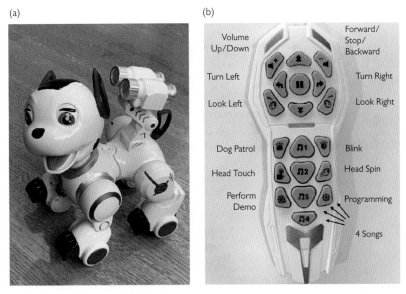

Volume Up/Down

Turn Left

Look Left

Dog Patrol

Head Touch

Perform Demo

Forward/ Stop/ Backward

Turn Right

Look Right

Blink

Head Spin

Programming

4 Songs

Fig 16.6 Programmable dog robot from Fisca with controller to make it move, play music, make head movements, and record sequences of actions to be replayed.

Fig 16.7 Boston Dynamics' Spot robot and remote controller.

Source: https://www.bostondynamics.com/spot.

In summary, human-like social robots have yet to be successful, but pet dog or cat robots appear to be gaining acceptance for older adults, and possibly for some children. The key to success seems to be to find a genuine human need that can be served by an animal-like robotic device.

Active Appliances

Another category that is different from social and animal robots might be called appliance robots, although I will call them active appliances. This large

Fig 16.8 Google Nest Learning Thermostat.

Source: https://store.google.com/product/nest_learning_thermostat_3rd_gen

class of successful consumer products do necessary tasks such as kitchen work, laundry chores, house cleaning, security monitoring, and garden maintenance. There are also many entertainment centers and a wide range of increasingly sophisticated exercise equipment. The control panels for these active appliances (examples in Chapter 9) have received increased attention as designers accommodate richer touchscreen controls, refined user needs, and more ambitious products. Increasingly home control devices depend on machine learning to recognize patterns of usage, such as for temperature control in the Google Nest Learning Thermostat (Figure 16.8).

An informal survey of AI colleagues showed me that about half of them accepted the idea of calling appliances robots, but the other half felt that the lack of mobility and human-like form disqualify them from being called robots.

I feel privileged that our kitchen has seven active appliances with sensors to detect and adjust activity. Most of them wait for me to activate them, but they can be programmed to start at preset times or when sensors indicate the need for activity. Increasingly they use AI methods to save energy, recognize users, increase home security, or communicate through voice user interfaces.[29]

Still there is much room for improvement in the frustrating designs which are often internally inconsistent, difficult to learn, and vary greatly across devices. They all have a clock on them, some also have a date display, but each has a different user interface for setting the time and date, even though several come from the same manufacturer. Dealing with changes due to daylight savings time is an unnecessary challenge because of the different designs and especially because that task could be automated. Setting timers on my oven, microwave, coffee maker, rice cooker, and other devices could be standardized, as could status displays of remaining time to completion or current device temperatures. Better still might be to have all these devices operable from my mobile phone or laptop, which would allow me to control them even while I was away from home.

Another category of home-based active appliances that could be made better with consistent user interfaces are medical devices. Commonly used devices include a thermometer, bathroom scale, step counter, blood pressure monitor, and pulse oximeter. Specialized devices include glucose monitors for insulin patients, menstrual cycle monitors for women, and continuous positive airway pressure devices for people dealing with sleep apnea. A large growth area is exercise machines, such as treadmills, elliptical exercise machines, standing bicycles, and rowing machines. Several manufacturers advertise "AI-powered" to indicate that the exercise sessions are personalized by machine learning techniques. Some of these devices have time and date settings with differing control panels and very different displays of data. Here again a consistent user interface and operation from a mobile device or laptop would be especially helpful. For these medical and well-being needs, users often have to record their history over months and years, so automatic recording would be especially valuable in helping users track their health and condition. These health histories could be analyzed to identify changes and shared with clinicians to improve treatment plans.

A prominent consumer success comes from iRobot, which makes the Roomba floor-cleaning machine (Figure 16.9).[30] They and other companies, such as Dyson, Samsung, and SONY, sell related products for mopping floors, mowing lawns, and cleaning swimming pools. These robots have mobility, sensors, and sophisticated algorithms to map spaces while avoiding obstacles. I'm a happy user of the Roomba irobot, which vacuums our floors and rugs, then returns to its base station to recharge and expel the dirt into a bag. It is controllable from my smartphone and can be tele-operated.

While the early Roomba designs were influenced by autonomous thinking with limited user control (only three simple buttons) and minimal feedback, the recent versions provide better user control by way of smartphone user interfaces. Users can schedule cleaning of the whole apartment or individual rooms,

Fig 16.9 Roomba 700 series robotic vacuum cleaner sold by iRobot.

but the Roomba sensors can detect that the house is vacant so it can clean. The smartphone app shows a history of activity, but the most impressive feature is the floor map that it generated after two to three cleaning sessions, including blank spaces where sofas and beds blocked Roomba's movement (Figure 16.10). With some effort I configured and labeled our apartment in meaningful ways so we could specify individual rooms for more frequent cleaning, like our hallway, which often collects dirt tracked in on our shoes.

The issues of control panels, user control, history keeping, and feedback on performance will grow as active appliances become more elaborate. A careful review of fifty-two studies of robot failures by Shanee Honig and Tal Oron-Gilad at Ben Gurion University in Israel provides guidance that could lead to greater success.[31] They discuss how robots might indicate that a failure has occurred, by way of a control panel on the robot, a voice message, or a display on a remote monitoring device. They also address the questions of how robots can report failures to users and how users can take steps to recover from a failure. Further work would be to develop systematic failure reporting methods, which could accelerate improvements. While they focused on academic research reports, incident reporting on robot failures in medical and industrial environments is growing. More recent work by Honig and Oron-Gilad analyzed online customer reviews on Amazon to understand failures of domestic robots, how often they occur, and how they influence customer opinions.[32]

Fig 16.10 Roomba home screen and generated apartment map with room labels supplied by the author.

Promising home services include cleaning, maintenance, and gardening technologies, which make life easier and expand the range of what people can do. Chapter 26 has a long list (Table 26.1) of older adult needs, such as entertainment, medical devices, and security systems, which are all candidates for active appliances in many homes.

Voice and Text User Interfaces

A notable success for the idea of active appliances are the speech-based virtual assistants such as Amazon's Alexa, Apple's Siri, Google's Home, and Microsoft's Cortana. The designers have produced impressive speech recognition and question answering systems, with high-quality speech generation that has gained consumer acceptance. When questions cannot be answered, links to web pages are offered to help users learn more about their questions. These devices avoid human forms, using pleasant-looking cylinders with textured surfaces to make them fit in many home settings. This means they don't fit strict definitions of social robots, but their success deserves attention and may suggest other opportunities for home-based devices that could be operated by voice.[33]

An ambitious study of users of eighty-two Amazon Alexa and eighty-eight Google Home devices revealed that more than a quarter of the usage was to find and play music. Searching for information and controlling home devices like lights and heating were other frequent tasks. Less frequent uses were for setting timers and alarms, requesting jokes, and getting weather conditions or predictions.[34]

Most users treat voice user interfaces as a way of getting tasks done; they are not friends, teammates, partners, or collaborators—they are supertools. Yes, users are likely to explore the range of possibilities by asking for a hug, making impossible requests, and posing probing questions like "Are you alive?" to which Siri replies: "I'm not a person, or a robot. I'm software, here to help."

Voice dictation is another success story, which allows text input and editing for users who have difficulty in typing due to injuries, loss of motor control, or visual disabilities. Another use case is users whose hands are busy such as doctors who can dictate their findings while they are examining patients or reviewing X-rays, lab reports, and other documents. The specialized terminology of medical care leads to higher rates of accurate speech recognition than with informal conversations.

Phone-based voice user interfaces have been another notable success, with generally good-quality speech recognition, even in noisy environments. The speaker independent design, which avoids the need to train the system, is usually effective, although speakers with accents and speech impediments have had problems.

Voice readers are a growing application with successes in electronic books and magazines, which can use synthesized voices, but human voices are popular because they convey appropriate emotion, accurate pronunciation, and appealing prosody. These voice readers help users with visual disabilities, but are also popular on long car trips or while taking a walk. Voice control over web browsers or other applications benefits users with visual disabilities and those who are temporarily disabled by injuries.

Cathy Pearl's book *Designing Voice User Interfaces* reminds readers that the goal "shouldn't be to fool people into thinking it's a human; it should be to solve the user's problem in an efficient easy-to-use way."[35] Voice can be quicker than typing, works when user's hands are busy, and can be operated at a distance. Of course, there are limitations to voice user interfaces: they can interfere with human conversations, are ephemeral, and deliver less information than visual user interfaces on mobile devices or larger screens. There is a vast difference between visual and voice user interfaces; both are valuable in different contexts.

Another caveat is that speaking is cognitively demanding, robbing users of some of their short-term and working memory, so that performing concurrent tasks becomes more difficult.[36] That is one reason voice user interfaces have not been used in high workload situations such as for fighter pilots who can plan their attack scenarios more effectively if they operate the plane with hand controls.

Despite the success of voice-based virtual assistants, talking dolls have failed to draw consumer success. Early efforts began with Thomas Edison in the 1880s and were regularly revived as toys, including the Mattell Talking Barbie in 1992 and a more ambitious Hello Barbie version in 2015.[37] Mattell has no further plans to pursue a talking Barbie.

Text user interfaces to chatbots are another path followed by researchers and entrepreneurs, especially in the form of customer service agents on mobile apps and websites. While text chatbots do not adhere to strict definitions of social robots because they are typically just text and may not have faces, they are designed with social conventions of politeness, humor, eagerness to help, and apologies for their failures. Microsoft's Tay chatbot was shutdown within a day because its algorithms began to make offensive statements, but its successor Zo lasted more than two years before it was shut down in 2019. A greater success is the Chinese Xiaoice, based on the same Microsoft technology, but now spun off as a Chinese company. Xiaoice has hundreds of millions of users, even though the Chinese government has forced its design to avoid politically sensitive topics. Xiaoice was given the personality of a cheerful female teenager, who reads news stories, sings songs, and makes art.

Replika, an "AI companion who cares . . . always here to listen and talk," has a human-like face, which users can configure.[38] Over time it absorbs your personality so as to become a sympathetic conversational friend (Figure 16.11), carrying forward Joseph Weizenbaum's ELIZA work from the 1960s. The design is meant to be helpful to those suffering losses, just as the founder Eugenia Kuyda did, so in addition to the chat window, it provides links to suicide hotlines.

Woebot is another chatbot project tied to human mental health: "we're building products that are designed to bring quality mental health care to all."[39] It uses cognitive behavioral therapy in textual chats designed to engage with people who are dealing with depression and anxiety. Its research trials, supported by the US National Institutes of Drug Abuse, have shown benefits with hundreds of users who felt improvements in two to four weeks, but more rigorous comparisons with other treatments is needed.

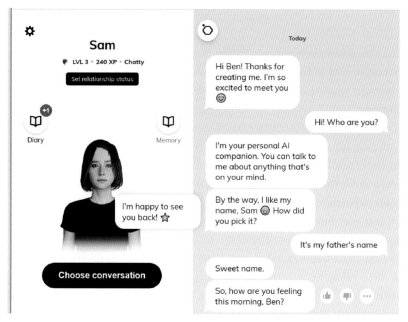

Fig 16.11 Replika chatbot with discussion session.
Source: https://replika.ai/

A common aspiration for chatbot developers is for customer support to answer questions about products and services, such as dinner reservations, banking rules, tourism, or e-commerce purchases. Early versions were flawed, but continued efforts suggest that some durable roles will emerge for text user interfaces to chatbots,[40] if only to identify user needs so as to steer them to the correct human customer service representative. The presence or absence of a chatbot avatar may also influence short-term acceptance, but long-term usage deserves more study. As with voice user interfaces, some degree of human-like personality features are appreciated, which appears to be different from embodied social robots where the reception is mixed.[41] However, even customer service chatbots defined by appealing metaphors will have to deliver genuine value, just as voice-controlled virtual assistant do. Engaging in a dialog is more challenging than answering a question, playing a song, or finding a website.

The Future of Social Robots

The modest commercial adoption of social robots has not deterred many researchers and entrepreneurs who still believe that they will eventually succeed. The academic research reports present a mixed view with studies from developers showing user satisfaction and sometimes delight, while others studies show preference for more tool-like designs, which adhere to the principles of giving users control of comprehensible, predictable, and controllable interfaces.[42] An academic survey of 1489 participants studied fear of autonomous robots and artificial intelligence (FARAI). This fear, dubbed robophobia,[43] was a minor issue for 20.1% and a serious issue for 18.5% of the participants.[44] Milder forms of concern about robots is over the uncanny valley, where near-human designs are distrusted.[45]

Human willingness to engage with social robots was the focus of dozens of studies conducted by Clifford Nass, a Stanford psychologist, and his students.[46] They found that people were quick to respond to social robots, accepting them as valid partners in interactions. However, the central question remains: Would people perform more effectively and prefer a supertool or active appliance design? Human control by way of comprehensible user interfaces is a key concept from developers of banking machines and most mobile devices, household appliances, kiosks, office technologies, and e-commerce websites. As mentioned earlier, the Apple Human Interface Design Guidelines advocate: "User Control: . . . people—not apps—are in control" and "Flexibility: . . . (give) users complete, fine-grained control over their work."[47] The fact that many users will treat active appliances as social robots is not surprising or disturbing to me—I do it myself. However, what is surprising and disturbing to me is that so many researchers and designers find it hard to open their imagination to go from social robots to active appliances.

The lessons of history are clear. Early anthropomorphic designs and social robots gave way to functional banking machines that support customer control, without the deception of having a human-like bank teller machine or screen representation of a human bank teller. This deception led bank customers to wonder how else their bank was deceiving them, thereby undermining the trust needed in commercial transactions. What customers wanted was to get their deposit or withdrawal done as quickly and reliably as possible. They wanted active appliances with control panels that they understood and enabled them to reliably and predictably get what they wanted. Even leading AI researchers, such as University of California-Berkeley's Stuart Russell, clearly state that "there is no good reason for robots to have humanoid form . . . they represent a form of dishonesty."[48]

These historical precedents can provide useful guidance for contemporary designers pursuing the innovation goal, since many still believe that improved designs of social robots based on the science goal will eventually succeed. A commonly mentioned application is elder care in which users wishing to live independently at home will need a human-like social robot to use kitchen implements designed for humans, to navigate hallways and stairs, and to perform tasks such as administering medications or offering a cup of tea. Another proposed application of social robots is disaster relief, but in that area the shift towards tele-bots has led to notable successes. Robin Murphy from Texas A&M University, who is a leader in developing, testing, and fielding rescue robots, advocates agile robots that can go under buildings or through ventilation ducts, and tele-operated drones that can fly into dangerous places to provide video for human decision-makers.[49]

Inspired by the science goal, social robot advocates continue to believe that they are needed, especially when the requirement is to work in environments built for human activity. However, I believe that if the imagination of these designers were more open they would see new possibilities, such as a small dishwasher built into, under, or near a dining table to help those who are physically challenged. If designers still want to try social robots, they would do well to understand what has been done in the past so they can build on the success stories.

A pointed scenario is that, if transported back to 1880, some designers might propose clothes-washing robots that pick up a bar of soap and a washboard to scrub clothes one at a time, rinse them in a sink, and hang them on a clothesline to dry. Designers of modern clothes washers and dryers have gone well beyond social robots to make active appliance successes that wash a week's worth of clothes and spin dry them in about an hour. Similarly, Amazon fulfillment centers have many robots for moving products and packing boxes, but none of them are human-like.[50]

The combined design strategy could be to use voice-based virtual assistants, which have proven successful, in active appliance and medical device designs. Text-based customer service chatbots could become successes, if dialogs can be carried out with low error rates. Exploration of pet-like devices for therapeutic applications and human-like guides for exercise sessions could be further refined with long-term studies to understand what solutions remain appealing and useful over time.

CHAPTER 17

Summary and Skeptic's Corner

The most damaging phrase in the language is: "It's always been done that way."

Grace Hopper, Commander, US Navy

The simplified review of AI research goals focused on just two. The first, based on AI science, is to study intelligent computational agents by designing, building, and testing systems that are based on human intelligence. Often, the science goal is to understand human perceptual, cognitive, and motor skills so as to build computers that match or exceed human performance. The second is the innovation goal, based on AI engineering, which does HCAI research for developing successful and widely used commercial products and services. Both make valuable contributions which researchers should pursue to bring increased societal benefits. These contributions could be bolstered with design thinking to raise the prominence of user experience methods and design of control panels and information-abundant visual displays.

Developers often discuss four pairs of design metaphors:

1) intelligent agents and supertools,

2) teammates and tele-bots,

3) assured autonomy and control centers, and

4) social robots and active appliances.

Successful designs seem to come from a combined strategy: employing automation for tasks for which machines produce reliable results, while leaving users the creative or safety choices that are important to them. Digital cameras offer a good example by using automated methods to choose the aperture, shutter speed, and reduce jitter, while allowing users to frame the photo, set the zoom, and click when they are pleased with the image preview.

Social robots remain a popular goal but they have had far less commercial success than active appliances or tele-bots. The science goal inspires many social robot researchers and creates widespread public interest.

Powerful AI methods include deep learning, recommender systems, speech recognition, image understanding, and natural language processing. Successful products often depend on combining these AI methods with user experience design methods, which include gathering user requirements, iterative design, user experience testing, and guidelines compliance. Many other principles lead to successful outcomes such as supporting human self-efficacy, encouraging human creativity, clarifying responsibility, and facilitating social connections.

While my critics tell me the separation into science and innovation goals is far from perfect, this simple dichotomy helps sort out different ways of thinking, allowing designers to consider both branches. Fervent devotees of either branch may be reluctant to think about combined designs. However, contrasting viewpoints often suggest new possibilities and illuminate design tradeoffs. For those who see other goals beyond these two, please follow them as diversity can bring fresh thinking.

Many researchers and entrepreneurs feel confident that social robots will be our future teammates, partners, and collaborators. I ask that they consider the alternatives in this chapter. Those who believe social robots are inevitable would benefit from studying the history and reasons for failures to help them find successes, such as voice user interfaces, medical mannequins, and crash test dummies. Maybe the large community working on social robots will find satisfaction in designing supertools, tele-bots, control centers, and active appliances, which give users a clear understanding, predictable behavior, and control over devices that serve identified human needs.

PART 4

Governance Structures

18 Introduction: How to Bridge the Gap from Ethics to Practice

19 Reliable Systems Based on Sound Software Engineering Practices

20 Safety Culture through Business Management Strategies

21 Trustworthy Certification by Independent Oversight

22 Government Interventions and Regulations

23 Summary and Skeptic's Corner

The viral spread of misinformation and outrageous conspiracy theories on popular news sites and social media exchanges have dramatically raised interest in the ethical issues of implementing widely used AI systems. To realize humane, responsible, and beneficial systems is more than a technical task; like writing a better computer program, it requires governance structures to bridge the gap between ethical principles of human-centered AI (HCAI) and practical steps. HCAI systems are developed and implemented by software engineering teams, managed within organizations, segmented by industry, and possibly regulated by government. These four levels of governance could provide the comprehensive attention that is already applied to technologies in vital sectors, such as transportation, medical care, and finance.

Moving from ethics to practice means that decision makers will need to take meaningful actions at the levels of team, organization, industry, and government. The recommendations in Part 4 are meant to increase the reliability, safety, and trustworthiness of HCAI systems by way of governance structures:

- *Software engineering practices* within teams, such as audit trails to enable retrospective analysis of failures, improved software engineering workflows that are tuned to HCAI systems, verification and validation testing to demonstrate correctness, bias testing to enhance fairness, and explainable user interfaces that offer all stakeholders an understanding of why decisions have been made.

- *Safety culture* within organizations through business management strategies that include leadership commitment to safety, hiring and training oriented to safety, extensive reporting of failures and near misses, internal review boards to assess problems and future plans, and alignment with industry standards and recommended practices.

- *Trustworthy certification* through industry-specific independent oversight efforts that include accounting firms conducting external audits, insurance companies compensating for failures, nongovernmental and civil society organizations advancing design principles, and professional organizations and research institutes developing standards, policies, and novel ideas.

- *Regulation by government agencies* to ensure fair business practices and public safety. While there is understandable concern from major technology companies that *government regulation* will limit innovation, well-designed regulation can accelerate innovation as it has done for automobile safety and fuel efficiency.

CHAPTER 18

Introduction: How to Bridge the Gap from Ethics to Practice

The vast majority of AI . . .will remain. . . subject to existing regulations and regulating strategies. . . . What we need to govern is the human application of technology, and what we need to oversee are the human processes of development, testing, operation, and monitoring.

> Joanna J. Bryson, *"The Artificial Intelligence of the Ethics of Artificial Intelligence,"* in **The Oxford Handbook of Ethics of AI** *(2020), edited by Markus D. Dubber, Frank Pasquale, and Sunit Das*

The widespread application of HCAI comes with high expectations of benefits for many domains, including healthcare, education, cyber security, and environmental protection. When it works as expected, HCAI could improve medical diagnoses, stop cybercriminals, and protect endangered species. However, there are equally dire predictions of out-of-control robots, unfair treatment of minority groups, privacy violations, adversarial attacks, and challenges to human rights. HCAI design and evaluation methods can address these dangers to realize the desired benefits.[1]

Part 3 made the case that traditional AI science research focused on studying and then emulating (some would use the term simulating) human behavior, while current AI innovation research emphasizes practical applications. Typical AI scientific foundations and technology-based innovations include pattern recognition and generation (images, speech, facial, signal, etc.), human-like robots, game playing (checkers, chess, Go, etc.), and natural language processing, generation, and translation.

HCAI research builds on these scientific foundations by using them to amplify, augment, and enhance human performance in ways that make systems reliable, safe, and trustworthy.[2] Typical HCAI scientific foundations and technology-based applications include graphical user interfaces, web-page design, e-commerce, mobile device apps, email/texting/video conferencing, photo/video editing, social media, and computer games. These systems also support human self-efficacy, encourage creativity, clarify responsibility, and facilitate social participation. HCAI designers, software engineers, and managers can adopt user-centered participatory design methods by engaging with diverse stakeholders. Then user experience testing helps ensure that these systems support human goals, activities, and values. The indicator of a shift to new thinking is the growing awareness that evaluating human performance and satisfaction is as important as measuring algorithm performance.

Multiple HCAI definitions come from prominent institutions such as Stanford University, which seeks "to serve the collective needs of humanity" by understanding "human language, feelings, intentions and behaviors."[3] While there is a shared belief that data-driven algorithms using machine and deep learning bring benefits, they also make it more difficult to know where the failure points may be. Explainable user interfaces and comprehensible control panels could help realize the HCAI's benefits in healthcare, business, and education.

The idea that HCAI represents a new synthesis conveys the significance of this change in attitudes and practices. In the past, researchers and developers focused on building AI algorithms and systems, stressing the autonomy of machines rather than human control through well-designed user interfaces. In contrast, HCAI puts human autonomy at the center of design thinking, emphasizing user experience design. Researchers and developers for HCAI systems focus on measuring human performance and satisfaction, valuing customer and consumer needs, and ensuring meaningful human control.[4] Leaders of existing businesses are adapting quickly to integrate HCAI systems.

This new synthesis may take decades until it is widely accepted, as it represents a fundamental shift to value both machine- and human-centered outlooks. The fifteen practical recommendations in Part 4 are meant to encourage discussion and actions that would accelerate this shift. However, at least two sources of HCAI system complexity make it difficult to implement all of these recommendations. First, individual components can be carefully tested, reviewed, and monitored by familiar software engineering practices, but complex HCAI systems, such as self-driving cars, social media platforms, and electronic healthcare systems are difficult to assess. That difficulty means that until engineering practices are refined, social mechanisms of independent oversight and reviews of failures and near misses are necessary. Second, HCAI systems are woven together from many products and services, including chips, software development tools, voluminous training data, extensive code libraries, and numerous test cases for validation and verification, each of which may change, sometimes on a daily basis. These difficulties present grand challenges for software engineers, managers, reviewers, and policy-makers, so the recommendations are meant to launch much-needed discussions, pilot tests, and scalable research that can lead to constructive changes.

There are more than 500 reports describing aspirational HCAI principles from companies, professional societies, governments, consumer groups, and non-government organizations.[5] A Berkman Klein Center report from 2020 discusses the upsurge of policy activity, followed by a thoughtful summary of thirty-six of the leading and most comprehensive reports. The authors identify eight HCAI themes for deeper commentary and detailed principles: privacy, accountability, safety and security, transparency and explainability, fairness and non-discrimination, human control of technology, professional responsibility, and promotion of human values.[6]

Other reports stress ethical principles, such as IEEE's far-reaching "Ethically Aligned Design," which emerged from a 3-year effort involving more than 200 people. The report offers clear statements about eight general principles: human rights, well-being, data agency, effectiveness, transparency, accountability, awareness of misuse, and competence. It went further with strong encouragement to ensure that advanced systems "shall be created and operated to respect, promote, and protect internationally recognized human rights".[7] Figure 18.1 shows the close match and the roughly similar principles in the two reports.

Human-Centered AI Principles

Berkman Klein Center	IEEE Ethically Aligned Design

Close Match

Accountability	Accountability
Transparency & explainability	Transparency
Promotion of human values	Human rights
Safety & security	Well-being

Similar

Human control of technology	Effectiveness
Fairness & non-discrimination	Awareness of misuse
Professional responsibility	Competence
Privacy	Data agency

Fig 18.1 Human-centered AI principles in the Berkman Klein Center Report and the IEEE Ethically Aligned Design Report.

These and other ethical principles are important foundations for clear thinking, but as Alan Winfield from the University of Bristol and Marina Jirotka from Oxford University note: "the gap between principles and practice is an important theme."[8] The four-layer governance structure for HCAI systems could help bridge this gap: (1) reliable systems based on sound software engineering practices, (2) safety culture through proven business management strategies, (3) trustworthy certification by independent oversight, and (4) regulation by government agencies (Figure 18.2). The inner oval covers the many software engineering teams which apply technical practices relevant to each project. These teams are part of a larger organization (second oval) where safety culture management strategies influence each project team. In the third oval, independent oversight boards review many organizations in the same industry, giving them a deeper understanding, while spreading successful practices.

The largest oval is government regulation, which provides another layer of thinking that addresses the public's interest in reliable, safe, and trustworthy HCAI systems. Government regulation is controversial, but success stories such as the US National Transportation Safety Board's investigation of plane, train, boat, and highway accidents has generally been seen as advancing

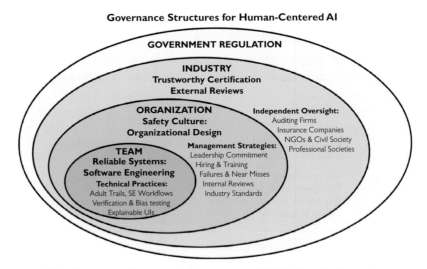

Fig 18.2 Governance Structures for human-centered AI: The four levels are shown as nested ovals: (1) Team: reliable systems based on software engineering (SE) practices, (2) Organization: a well-developed safety culture based on sound management strategies, (3) Industry: trustworthy certification by external review, and (4) Government regulation.

public interests. Government regulations in Europe, such as the General Data Protection Regulation, triggered remarkable research and innovation in explainable AI. The US regulations over automobile safety and fuel efficiency had a similar stimulus in improving design research.

Reliability, safety, and trustworthiness are vital concepts for everyone involved in technology development, whether driven by AI or other methods. These concepts and others, including privacy, security, environmental protection, social justice, and human rights are also strong concerns at every level: software engineering, business management, independent oversight, and government regulation.

While corporations often make positive public statements about their commitment to customer and employee benefits, when business leaders have to make difficult decisions about power and money, they may favor their corporate interests and stockholder expectations.[9] Current movements for human rights and corporate social responsibility are helpful in building public support, but these are optional items for most managers. Required processes for software engineers, managers, external reviewers, and government agencies, which are guided by clear principles and open reporting of corporate plans, will have more impact, especially when reviewed by internal and external review boards. This is especially true in emerging technologies, such as HCAI, where corporate managers may be forced by public pressure to acknowledge their societal responsibilities and report publicly on progress.

Similarly, most government policy-makers need to be more informed about how HCAI technologies work, and how business decisions affect the public interest. Congressional or parliamentary legislation governs industry practices, but government agency staffers must make difficult decisions about how they enforce the laws. Professional societies and non-governmental organizations (NGOs) are making efforts to inform government officials.

These proposed governance structures in Part 4 are practical steps based on existing practices, which have to be adapted to fit new HCAI technologies. They are meant to clarify who takes action and who is responsible. To increase chances for success, these recommendations will need to be put to work with a budget and a schedule. Each recommendation requires pilot testing and research to validate effectiveness.[10] These governance structures are a starting point. Newer approaches will be needed as technologies advance or when market forces and public opinion reshape the products and services that become successful. For example, public opinion dramatically shifted business practices over facial recognition technologies in 2020, when leading developers, including IBM, Amazon, and Microsoft, withdrew from selling these systems to police departments because of pressure over potential misuse and abuse.[11]

The next four chapters cover the four levels of governance. Chapter 19 describes five technical practices of software engineering teams that enable reliable HCAI systems: audit trails, workflows, verification and validation testing, bias testing, and explainable user interfaces.

Chapter 20 suggests how organizations that manage software engineering projects can develop a safety culture through leadership commitment, hiring and training, reporting failures and near misses, internal reviews, and industry standards.

Chapter 21 shows how independent oversight methods by external review organizations can lead to trustworthy certification and independent audits of products and services. These independent oversight methods create a trusted infrastructure to investigate failures, continuously improve systems, and gain public confidence. Independent oversight methods include auditing firms, insurance companies, NGOs and civil society, and professional organizations.[12]

Chapter 22 opens the larger and controversial discussion of possible government interventions and regulations. The summary in Chapter 23 raises concerns, but offers an optimistic view that well-designed HCAI systems will bring meaningful benefits to individuals, organizations, and society.

The inclusion of human-centered thinking will be difficult for those who have long seen algorithms as the dominant goal. They will question the validity of this new synthesis, but human-centered thinking and practices put AI algorithms and systems to work for commercially successful products and services. HCAI offers a hope-filled vision of future technologies that support human self-efficacy, creativity, responsibility, and social connections among people.

Reliable Systems Based on Sound Software Engineering Practices

Reliable HCAI systems are produced by software engineering teams that apply sound technical practices.[1] These technical practices clarify human responsibility, such as audit trails for accurate records of who did what and when, and histories of who contributed to design, coding, testing, and revisions.[2] Other technical practices are improved software engineering workflows that are tuned to the tasks and application domain. Then when prototype systems are ready, verification and validation testing of the programs, and bias testing of the training data can begin. Software engineering practices also include the user experience design processes that lead to explainable user interfaces for HCAI systems (see Figure 18.2).

Audit Trials and Analysis Tools

The success of flight data recorders (FDR) in making civil aviation remarkably safe provides a clear guide for the design of any product or service that has consequential or life-critical impacts. The history of FDRs and the cockpit voice recorders (CVR) demonstrates the value of using these tools to understand aviation crashes, which have contributed strongly to safe civil aviation.[3] Beyond accident investigations, FDRs have proven to be valuable in showing what was done right to avoid accidents, providing valuable lessons to improve training and equipment design. A further use of FDR data is to detect changes in equipment behavior over time to schedule preventive maintenance.

FDRs provide important lessons for HCAI designers of audit trails (also called product logs) to record the actions of robots.[4] These robot versions of aviation flight data recorders have been called smart, ethical, or black boxes, but the consistent intention of designers is to collect relevant evidence for retrospective analyses of failures.[5] Such retrospective analyses are often conducted to assign liability in legal decision-making and to provide guidance for continuous improvement of these systems. They also clarify responsibility, which exonerates those who have performed properly, as in the case of the unfairly accused nurses whose use of an intravenous morphine device was revealed to be proper.

Similar proposals have been made for highly automated (also called self-driving or driverless) cars.[6] These proposals extend current work on electronic logging devices, which are installed on many cars to support better maintenance. Secondary uses of vehicle logging devices are to improve driver training, monitor environmentally beneficial driving styles, and verify truck driver compliance with work and traffic rules. In some cases, these logs have provided valuable data in analyzing the causes of accidents, but controversy continues about who owns the data and what rights manufacturers, operators, insurance companies, journalists, and police have to gain access.

Industrial robots are another application area for audit trails, to promote safety and reduce deaths in manufacturing applications. Industry groups such as the Robotic Industries Association, now transformed into the Association for Advancing Automation, have promoted voluntary safety standards and some forms of auditing since 1986.[7]

Audit trails for stock market trading algorithms are now widely used to log trades so that managers, customers, and the US Securities and Exchange Commission can study errors, detect fraud, or recover from flash crash events.[8] Other audit trails from healthcare, cybersecurity, and environmental monitoring enrich the examples from which improved audit trails can be tuned to the needs of HCAI applications.

Challenging research questions remain, such as what data are needed for effective retrospective forensic analysis and how to efficiently capture and store high volumes of video, sound, and light detection and ranging (LIDAR) data, with proper encryption to prevent falsification. Logs should also include machine learning algorithms used, the code version, and the associated training data at the time of an incident. Then research questions remain about how to analyze the large volume of data in these logs. Issues of privacy and security complicate the design, as do legal issues such as who owns the data and what rights manufacturers, operators, insurance companies, journalists, and police have to access, benefit from, or publish these data sets. Effective user interfaces, visualizations, statistical methods, and secondary AI systems enable investigators to explore the audit trails to make sense of the voluminous data.

An important extension of audit trails are incident databases that capture records of publicly reported incidents in aviation, medicine, transportation, and cybersecurity. The Partnership on AI has started an AI Incident Database that has more than a thousand reports (see Chapter 20's section "Extensive Reporting of Failures and Near Misses").

Software Engineering Workflows

As AI technologies and machine learning algorithms are integrated into HCAI applications, software engineering workflows are being updated. The new challenges include novel forms of benchmark testing for verifying and validating algorithms and data (see this chapter's section "Verification and Validation Testing"), improved bias testing to enhance algorithm and data fairness (see this chapter's section "Bias Testing to Enhance Fairness"), and agile programming team methods.[9] All these practices have to be tuned to the different domains of usage, such as healthcare, education, environmental protection, and defense. To support users and legal requirements, software engineering workflows have to support explainable user interfaces (see this chapter's section "Explainable User Interface").

The international team of Jie M. Zhang, Mark Harman, Lei Ma, and Yang Liu describe five problem types for machine learning which may need software engineering workflows that are different from those for traditional programming projects:[10]

1) **Classification**: to assign a category to each data instance; e.g., image classification, handwriting recognition.

2) **Regression**: to predict a value for each data instance; e.g., temperature/age/income prediction.

3) **Clustering**: to partition instances into homogeneous regions; e.g., pattern recognition, market/image segmentation.

4) **Dimension reduction**: to reduce the training complexity; e.g., data-set representation, data pre-processing.

5) **Control**: to control actions to maximize rewards; e.g., game playing.

Workflows for all these tasks require expanded efforts with user requirements gathering, data collection, cleaning, and labeling, with use of visualization and data analytics to understand abnormal distributions, errors and missing data, clusters, gaps, and anomalies. Then model training and evaluation becomes a multistep process that starts with early in-house testing, proceeds to deployment, and maintenance. Continuous monitoring of deployed systems is needed to respond to changing contexts of use and new training data.

Software engineering workflows for HCAI systems will extend AI design methods to include user experience design so as to ensure that users understand how decisions are made and have recourse when they wish to challenge a decision. These traditional human–computer interaction methods of user experience testing and guidelines development are being updated by leading corporations and researchers to meet the needs of HCAI.[11]

A Virginia Commonwealth University team proposes a human-centered AI system lifecycle geared to deliver trustworthy AI by emphasizing fairness, interactive visual user interfaces, and privacy protection through careful data governance.[12] They raise the difficult issue of measuring trustworthiness by quantitative and qualitative assessment, which we will return to in Chapter 25.

Software engineering workflows have migrated from the *waterfall* model, which assumed that there was an orderly linear lifecycle, starting from requirements gathering and moving to design, implementation, testing, documentation, and deployment. The waterfall model, which may be appropriate when the requirements are well understood, is easy to manage, but can result in massive failures when delivered software systems are rejected by users. Rejections may be because requirements gathered a year ago at the start of a project are no longer adequate or because developers failed to test prototypes and early implementations with users.

The newer workflows are based on the *lean* and *agile* models, with variants such as *scrum*, in which teams work with the customers throughout the lifecycle, learning about user needs (even as they change), iteratively building and testing prototypes, then discarding early ideas as refinements are developed, and always being ready to try something new. Agile teams work in one- to two-week *sprints*, intense times when big changes are needed. The agile model builds in continuous feedback to ensure progress towards an effective system, so as to avoid big surprises.

Agile models demand strong collaboration among developers to share knowledge about each other's work, so they can discuss possible solutions and help when needed. Waterfall projects may deliver a complete system after a year of work, while agile projects could produce a prototype in a month. IBM encourages agile approaches to AI projects, because developers have to keep an open mind and explore alternatives more than in traditional projects.[13]

The *Manifesto for Agile Software Development*, first developed in 2001 by a group of seventeen people calling themselves the Agile Alliance, is based on twelve principles.[14] I've rephrased them for consistency:

1) Satisfy customers by early and continuous delivery of valuable software.

2) Welcome changing requirements, even in late development.

3) Deliver working software frequently, in weeks rather than months.

4) Cooperate closely with customers and their managers.

5) Shape projects around motivated, trusted individuals.

6) Ensure regular face-to-face conversation among developers and customers.

7) Make working software the primary measure of progress.

8) Work at a sustained pace for the project's duration.

9) Give continuous attention to technical and design excellence.

10) Keep projects simple—embrace minimalist design—write less code.

11) Enable self-organizing teams to pursue quality in architectures, requirements, and designs.

12) Reflect regularly on how to become more effective, and then do it.

The agile principles suggest a human-centered approach of regular contact with customers, but was less focused on issues such as user experience testing. The Agile Alliance website recognizes that "usability testing is not strictly speaking an Agile practice," but it goes on to stress its importance as part of user experience design.

Building on these agile principles, IBM recommends data set-related agility to explore data sets and run a proof-of-concept test early on to make sure the data sets can deliver the desired outcomes. Where necessary developers must clean the error-laden data, remove low relevance data, and expand the data to meet accuracy and fairness requirements.[15] Their recommendations could also be improved by inclusion of usability testing and user experience design methods.

Fig 19.1 Microsoft's nine-stage software engineering workflow
for machine learning projects.
Source: From Amershi et al. 2019a

Microsoft offers a nine-stage software engineering workflow for HCAI systems that looks like it is closer to a linear waterfall model than to agile methods (Figure 19.1), but their descriptions suggest more agile processes in its execution.[16] Microsoft is strong about maintaining connections with customers throughout their workflow. Their interviews with fourteen developers and managers found that they emphasize data collection, cleaning, and labeling, followed by model training, evaluation, and deployment. The report makes this important distinction: "software engineering is primarily about the code that forms shipping software, ML (machine learning) is all about the data that powers learning models."[17]

HCAI system developers can use the waterfall model, but agile methods are more common to promote early engagement with clients and users. With waterfall or agile methods, HCAI projects are different from traditional programming projects, since the machine learning training data sets play a much stronger role. Traditional software testing methods, such as static analysis of code, need to be supplemented by dynamic testing with multiple data sets to check for reliability in differing contexts of use and user experience testing to see if users can succeed in doing their tasks.

User experience testing in HCAI systems also has to address perceptions of how the machine learning system guides users to understand the process well enough so they know whether to challenge the outcomes. This is of modest importance with recommender systems, but consequential decisions such as mortgage or parole decisions have to be understandable to users. Understandability is vital for acceptance and effective use of life-critical systems used for medical, transportation, and military applications.

The next section covers verification and validation testing that ensures correct operation and the section after that covers bias testing to enhance fairness. A final point is that developers of HCAI systems will benefit from guidelines documents discussed in Chapter 20 that describe principles and show examples of diverse machine learning applications.

Verification and Validation Testing

For AI and machine learning algorithms embedded in HCAI systems, novel processes for algorithm verification and validation are needed, as well as user experience testing with typical users. The goal is to strengthen the possibility that HCAI systems do what users expect, while reducing the possibility that there will be unexpected harmful outcomes. Civil aviation provides good models for HCAI certification of new designs, careful verification and validation testing during use, and certification testing for pilots.

The US National Security Commission on AI stresses that "AI applications require iterative testing, evaluation, verification, and validation that incorporates user feedback."[18] This broad encouragement is refined by Jie M. Zhang and co-authors, who make important distinctions in testing for three forms of machine learning:

Supervised learning: a type of machine learning that learns from training data with labels as learning targets . . . Unsupervised learning: a learning methodology that learns from training data without labels and relies on understanding the data itself. Reinforcement learning: a type of machine learning where the data are in the form of sequences of actions, observations, and rewards.[19]

In each case, machine learning is highly dependent on the training data, so diverse data sets need to be collected for each context so as to increase accuracy and reduce biases. For example, each hospital will serve a distinct community that varies by age, income, common diseases, and racial makeup, so training data for detecting cancerous growths needs to come from that community.

During validation of an AI-based pneumonia detection system for chest X-rays, the results varied greatly across hospitals depending on what X-ray machine was used. Additional variations came from patient characteristics and the machine's position.[20] Documenting these multiple data sets, which may be updated regularly or even continuously, is vital, but it presents substantial challenges that go well beyond what programming code repositories currently accomplish. These repositories, such as the widely used GitHub,[21] track every change in programming statements. Data curation concepts such as provenance tracking with the unalterable blockchain method[22] and checking that the data are still representative in the face of change are promising possibilities. Finally, clarifying who is responsible for data-set curation puts a human in the loop to deal with unusual circumstances and new contexts of use.

At least five popular testing techniques can be applied to HCAI systems:

Traditional case-based The development team collects a set of input values and the expected output values, then verifies that the system produces the expected results. It takes time to construct input records, such as mortgage applications, with desired outcomes of acceptance or rejection, but the system should produce the expected results. Test cases of classifying animal images or translating sentences can be easily understood, since successes and failures are clear. Collecting a large enough set of test cases opens the minds of designers to consider extreme situations and possible failures, which by itself could lead to recognition of needed improvements. A common approach is to have several teams involving developers and those who are not developers to construct test cases with expected results.

In established fields, there are data sets of test cases that can be used to compare performance against other systems; e.g. ImageNet has 14 million images that have been annotated with the expected results. The NIST Text Retrieval Conference (TREC) has run annual workshops for almost thirty years with many test data sets that have annotated correct results.

A key part of verification is to develop test cases to detect adversarial attacks, which would prevent malicious use by criminals, hate groups, and terrorists. As new requirements are added or the context of use changes, new test cases must be added.[23]

Differential This strategy is commonly used to verify that an updated system produces the same results as earlier versions. The input test data sets are run on the earlier and updated system to produce results which can be automatically compared to make sure that the system is still working as it did before. The advantage of differential testing is that the test team does not have to create the expected results. There are at least two disadvantages: (1) incorrect performance in the earlier software will propagate to the updated software so both tests will have the same incorrect results, and (2) new features that accommodate different inputs cannot be compared with previous test results. Another version of differential testing is to compare two different systems, possibly developed by other teams or organizations. Differences in results lead to further study to see which system needs to be fixed. For machine learning, differential testing is widely used to compare performance with two different training data sets.

Metamorphic This clever approach is built on the idea of metamorphic relations among sets of results. In a simple example, an algorithm that finds paths in an undirected network, the shortest path from a to b should be the same as the one from b to a. Similarly, decreasing the amount of a mortgage application request should never reject someone who was approved for a larger amount. For e-commerce recommenders, changing the maximum price for a product from $100 to $60 should produce a subset of products. As with differential testing, the test team does not have to create expected results, since they are generated by the software. Applying metamorphic testing for training data sets is possible by adding or deleting records that should not change the results.

User experience   For HCAI applications which involve users, such as mortgage, parole, or job interview applications, user testing is needed to verify that they can deal with the system and get meaningful explanations. User testing is conducted by giving standard tasks to five to twenty-five users, who are asked to think aloud as they work through the tasks, typically in 30–120 minutes, explaining that they see, think, and do. The testing team records user comments and performance to generate a report about common problems, sometimes including suggested fixes. User testing is a practical approach used in system development to detect problems that users report. It is different from research-based controlled experiments that test alternate hypotheses to prove statistically significant differences between two or more designs.

Red teams   Beyond testing by development teams, an increasingly popular technique is to have a red team of outsiders stage attacks on HCAI systems. The idea of red teams came from military war-gaming exercises, grew dramatically in the cybersecurity community, and is used in aviation security testing, such as when government agents test airport screening systems by using different strategies to get deadly weapons past screening systems and onto airplanes.[24]

Red team testing for HCAI systems would probe weaknesses in the software and strategies for *poisoning* the training data by adding misleading records. Facial recognition systems are easily undermined by wearers of unusual T-shirts and self-driving car algorithms are misled by stickers on STOP signs or lines of salt crystals on a highway. Red team members would gain skill over time as they probe systems, developing an attacker mindset and sharing strategies with others.

The MITRE Corporation maintains a cybersecurity ATT&CK (note the unusual spelling) matrix that catalogs almost 300 tactics of attackers, organized into eleven categories, which reminds developers about the ways that adversaries might attack the systems they are building.[25] A similar matrix for the ways red teams could attack HCAI systems and data sets would be a helpful guide to developers about how to protect their systems. As a start, software engineers could individually catalog potential attacks and then combine their results with other team members. Comparisons with other teams could lead to further ideas of potential attacks. MITRE Corporation has begun a project to make such a catalog of AI failures.[26]

For all testing techniques, the history of testing should be recorded to enable reconstruction and document how repairs were made and by whom.[27] Microsoft's Datasheets for Datasets is a template to document data used in machine learning. It contains sections on the motivation and process for collecting and cleaning the data, who has used the data set, and contact information for the data curator.[28] This positive step quickly propagated to be used by many software engineering teams, and encouraged Google's Model Cards template for model reporting.[29] Lessons from database systems[30] and information visualization[31] about tracking provenance of data and histories of testing are also useful. These documentation strategies all contribute to transforming software engineering practices from early stage research to more mature professional practices.

For mobile robotic devices, which could inadvertently harm nearby human workers, deadly weapons, and medical devices, special care is needed during testing. Metrics for "safe operation, task completion, time to complete the task, quality, and quantity of tasks completed" will guide development.[32] Mature application areas such as aviation, medical devices, and automobiles, with a long history of benchmark tests for product certification, provide good models for newer products and services. Verifying and validating HCAI systems accuracy, correctness, usability, and vulnerability are important, but in addition since many applications deal with sensitive decisions that have consequences for people's lives, bias testing is needed to enhance fairness.

Bias Testing to Enhance Fairness

As AI and machine learning algorithms were applied to consequential applications such as parole granting, mortgage loan approval, and job interviewing, many critics arose to point to problems that needed fixing. A leader among these was the Wall Street statistician Cathy O'Neil, who was very familiar with the dangers. Her powerful book *Weapons of Math Destruction: How Big*

Data Increases Inequality and Threatens Democracy raises questions about how algorithms became dangerous when they had three properties:[33]

- *Opacity*: the algorithms are complex and hidden from view, making it hard to challenge decisions,
- *Scale*: the system is used by large companies and governments for major applications, and
- *Harm*: the algorithms could produce unfair treatment that impact people's lives.

A growing research community responded with influential conferences, such as the one on Fairness, Accountability, and Transparency in Machine Learning,[34] which studied gender, racial, age, and other potential biases. Commercial practices began to shift when serious problems emerged[35] from biased decisions that influenced parole granting, when hate-filled chatbots learned from malicious social media postings, and when job hiring biases were exposed.[36]

An early review by academics Batya Friedman and Helen Nissenbaum[37] described three kinds of bias: (1) *pre-existing bias* based on social practices and attitudes, such as mortgage loan rejections for lower income neighborhoods, making it more difficult for upwardly mobile residents to buy a better home; (2) *technical bias* based on design constraints in hardware and software, such as organ donor requests that are presented alphabetically on a scrolling list rather than ranked by severity of need; and (3) *emergent bias* that arises from changing the use context, such as when educational software developed in high literacy countries is put to work in low literacy countries that also may have different cultural values.

Professor Ricardo Baeza-Yates, whose roots are in Chile, Spain, and the United States, described additional forms of bias, such as geography, language, and culture, which were embedded in web-based algorithms, databases, and user interfaces.[38] He cautions that "bias begets bias" as when popular websites become even more popular, making it harder for marginal voices to be heard. Questions of bias are closely tied to the IEEE's Ethically Aligned Design report that seeks to build a strong ethical foundation for all AI projects. A comprehensive review of bias, from a University of Southern California team, extends the concept to cover statistical, user interaction, funding, and more than twenty other forms of bias.[39] Their review also moves forward to describe ways of mitigating bias, testing data sets, and advancing research.

HCAI researcher Meredith Ringel Morris raised concerns about how AI systems often make life more difficult for users with disabilities, but wrote "AI technologies offer great promise for people with disabilities by removing access barriers and enhancing users' capabilities."[40] She suggests that speech-based virtual agents and other HCAI applications could be improved by using training data sets that included users with physical and cognitive disabilities. However, since AI systems could also detect and prey on vulnerable populations such as those with cognitive disabilities or dementia, research is needed on how to limit such attacks.

Algorithmic bias in healthcare can lead to significant disparities in treatment, as shown in a study which found that "unequal access to care means that we spend less money caring for black patients than for white patients." The report claims that "remedying this disparity would increase the percentage of black patients receiving additional help from 17.7 to 46.5%."[41]

The long history of gender bias re-emerges in computing, which struggles to increase the numbers of women students, professors, and professionals. Lack of women participating in research and development can lead to inadequate consideration for bias, which has happened in hiring, education, consumer services, and mortgage applications. Limiting such biases is vital in efforts to increase equity.

Converting ethical principles and bias awareness into action is a challenge.[42] Development teams can begin with in-depth testing of training data sets to verify that the data are current and have a representative distribution of records for a given context. Then known biases in past performance can be tested, but beyond detecting biases, standard approaches to mitigating bias can be applied, so that future decisions are fairer. Academic researchers offer fairness-enhancing interventions, such as avoiding gender, race, or age that could bias a hiring decision.[43] Companies are developing commercial grade toolkits for detecting and mitigating algorithmic bias, such as IBM's Fairness 360.[44] These examples are a good start, but better outcomes are likely for development teams that appoint a bias testing leader who is responsible for assessing the training data sets and the programs themselves. The bias testing leader will study current research and industry practices and respond to inquiries and concerns. A library of test cases with expected results could be used to verify that the HCAI system did not show obvious biases. Continued monitoring of usage with reports returned to the bias testing leader will help to enhance fairness. However, since development teams may be reluctant to recognize biases in their HCAI systems, someone outside the team will also need to monitor performance and review reports (see Chapter 20 on safety culture management practices).

These constructive steps are a positive sign, but the persistence of bias remains a problem as applications such as facial recognition become more widely used for police work and commercial applications.[45] Simple bias tests for gender, race, age, etc. were helpful in building more accurate face databases, but problems remained when the databases were studied for intersections, such as black women.[46] Presenting these results in refereed publications and in widely seen media can pressure the HCAI systems builders to make changes that improve performance.

MIT's Joy Buolamwini, who founded the Algorithmic Justice League (see Chapter 21's Appendix A), was able to show gender and racial bias in facial recognition systems from Microsoft, IBM, and Amazon, which she presented in compelling ways through her high-energy public talks, sharply written op-eds, and theatrical videos.[47] Her efforts, with collaborator Timnit Gebru, led to improvements and then corporate withdrawal of facial recognition products from police departments, when evidence of excessive use of force became widespread in spring 2020.[48] Their efforts were featured in the full-length April 2021 documentary *Coded Bias*, which has drawn widespread interest.[49]

Ethics issues triggered a public scandal when Google fired Timnit Gebru, who co-led its Ethical AI team, triggering support for her from thousands of Google employees and others. The controversy included Gebru's outspoken stance about the low level of female and minority hiring at Google, which she suggests is related to deficiencies in understanding bias. Effective bias testing for machine learning training data is one contribution to changing the long history of systemic bias in treatment of minorities in many countries.[50]

The bias in algorithms is sometimes obvious as in this Google Images search for "professional hair" (Figure 19.2a) that shows mostly light-skinned women, which is notably different for the search for "unprofessional hair" (Figure 19.2b) that shows mostly dark-skinned women. These examples show how existing biases can propagate, unless designers intervene to reduce them.

The question of bias is vital to many communities that have suffered from colonial oppression, including Indigenous people around the world. They often have common shared values that emphasize relationships within their local context, foregrounding their environment, culture, kinship, and community. Some in Indigenous communities question the rational approaches of AI, while favoring empirical ways of knowing tied to the intrinsically cultural nature of all computational technology: "Indigenous kinship protocols can point us towards

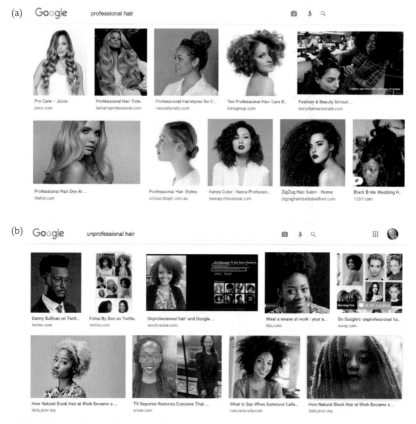

Fig 19.2 (a) Google Search for "Professional hair" shows mostly light-skinned women. (b) Google Search for "Unprofessional hair" shows mostly dark-skinned women.

potential approaches to developing rich, robust and expansive approaches to our relationships with AI systems and serve as guidelines for AI system developers."[51] MIT computer scientist and media scholar D. Fox Harrell reinforces the importance of cultural influences and assumptions that are usually left implicit.[52] His work is aligned with the claims of Indigenous authors that deeper understanding of cultural contexts will reduce bias, while enabling "new innovations based in cultures that are not currently privileged in computer science."

Explainable User Interfaces

Designers of HCAI systems have come to realize that consequential life decisions, such as rejections for mortgages, parole, or job interviews, often raise questions from those who are affected. To satisfy these legitimate needs, systems must provide comprehensible explanations that enable people to know what they need to change or whether they should challenge the decision. Furthermore, explanations have become a legal requirement in many countries based on the European Union's General Data Protection Regulation (GDPR) requirement of a "right to explanation."[53]

This controversial GDPR requirement is vague and difficult to satisfy in general, but international research efforts to develop explainable AI have blossomed.[54] A useful and practical resource are the three reports on "Explaining Decisions Made with AI" from the UK Information Commissioner's Office and the Alan Turing Institute.[55] The three reports cover: (1) The basics of explaining AI, (2) Explaining AI in practice, and (3) What explaining AI means for your organization. The first report argues that companies benefit from making AI explainable: "It can help you comply with the law, build trust with your customers and improve your internal governance."[56] The report spells out the need for explanations that describe the reason for the decision, who is responsible for the system that made the decision, and the steps taken to make fair decisions. Beyond that it stipulates that users should be given information about how to challenge a decision. The second and longest report has extensive discussions about different kinds of explanations, but it would inspire more confidence if it showed sample screen designs and user testing results.

Daniel S. Weld and Gagan Bansal from the University of Washington make a strong case for explainability (sometimes called interpretability or transparency) that goes beyond satisfying users' desire to understand and the legal requirements to provide explanations.[57] They argue that explainability helps designers enhance correctness, identify improvements in training data, account for changing realities, support users in taking control, and increase user acceptance. An interview study with twenty-two machine learning professionals documented the value of explainability for developers, testers, managers, and users.[58] A second interview study with twenty-nine professionals emphasized the need for social and organizational contexts in developing explanations.[59] However, explainability methods are only slowly finding their way into widely used applications and possibly in ways that are different from the research.

As the AI research community learns more about the centuries of relevant social science research, thoughtfully described by Tim Miller from the University of Melbourne, who complains that "most work in explainable artificial intelligence uses only the researchers' intuition of what constitutes a 'good' explanation."[60] Miller's broad and deep review of social science approaches and evaluation methods is eye-opening, but he acknowledges that applying it to explaining AI systems "is not a straightforward step."

The strong demand for explainable AI has led to commercial toolkits such as IBM's AI Explainability 360.[61] The toolkit offer ten different explanation algorithms, which can be fine-tuned by programmers for diverse applications and users. IBM's extensive testing and case studies suggest they have found useful strategies, which address the needs of developers, business decision-makers, government regulators, and consumers who are users.[62]

A review of current approaches to explainable AI by a team from Texas A&M University, Mengnan Du, Ninghao Liu, and Xia Hu, makes useful distinctions between intrinsically understandable machine learning models, such as decision trees or rule-based models, and the more common approach of post-hoc explanations.[63] But even the intrinsically understandable models are hard for most people to understand, and often challenging even to experts. They contrast these with the common approach of natural language descriptions of why a decision was made. These are called post-hoc (or retrospective) explanations because they come after the algorithmic decision has been made. The explanations are generated for users who are surprised by results and want to know why a certain decision was made. For example, a jewelry e-commerce site might report that "we made these recommendations because you ordered silver necklaces last year before Valentine's Day." These post-hoc explanations are the preferred approach among researchers, especially when deep learning neural nets and other black box methods are used. However, the work would be improved if follow-up questions were allowed and user tests were conducted.[64]

Margaret Burnett and her team at Oregon State University showed that adding well-designed post-hoc explanations for a sports-related natural language text classification application improved user satisfaction and understanding of the results.[65] The visual user interface design showed which terms were important in classifying a document as a hockey or baseball story (Figure 19.3). It also allowed users to provide feedback to the system by adding or removing words from the classification model, improving the machine learning algorithm.

Cynthia Rudin from Duke University makes a strongly worded case to "Stop explaining black box machine learning models."[66] She developed clever ways to make the machine learning models easier to interpret so that users can understand how they work. This is a worthy approach that pursues a fundamental goal of preventing the confusion that requires post-hoc explanations.

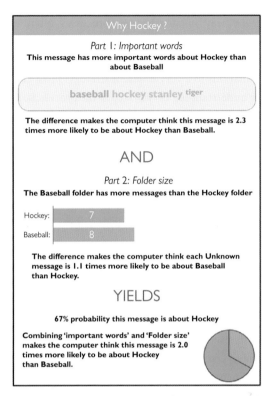

Fig 19.3 Part of the user interface of a text classification application that shows why a document was classified as being about hockey

Source: Revised version, based on Kulesza et al., 2015

Preventing the Need for Explanations

While post-hoc explanations can be helpful, this strategy was tried three decades ago in knowledge-based expert systems, intelligent tutoring systems, and user interface help systems. However, the difficulty in figuring out what kinds of explanations a confused user wants led to strategies that prevent or at least reduce the need for explanations. The favored strategies were to offer step-by-step processes which explain each step of a decision process before the final decision is made.

In knowledge-based expert systems, which were built by encoding rules from expert decision-makers, many projects struggled with providing post-hoc explanations. A famed series of projects began with the medically oriented diagnostic system, MYCIN, but expanded to domain independent systems.[67] William Clancey, then working at Stanford University,[68] describes his pursuit of explainability by way of step-by-step processes often using graphical overviews. Another example of changes to limit the need for explanations was in successful business rule-based systems. Designers moved from dependence on post-hoc explanations to a very different strategy: prospective designs that give users a better understanding of each step in the process, so they can prevent mistakes and the need for explanations.[69]

For intelligent tutoring systems, the idea of a human-like avatar explaining difficult topics and answering questions gave way to user-controlled strategies that emphasized the material they were learning. Rather than using screen space for an avatar image and distracting user attention from the text or diagram, the winning strategy turned out to be to let learners concentrate on the subject matter. Other lessons were to avoid artificial praise from the avatar and to give learners more control over their educational progress, so they felt a greater sense of accomplishment in mastering the subject matter. These lessons became key components of the success of massive open online courses (MOOCs), which gave users clear feedback about their mastery of test questions.

Similarly, in early user interface help systems, the designers found that *post-hoc* explanations and error messages were difficult to design, leading them to shift to alternative methods that focused on:[70]

1. Preventing errors so as to reduce the need for explanations: e.g. by replacing typing MMDDYYYY with selecting month, day, and year from a calendar. Replacing typing with selecting prevents errors, thereby eliminating the need for extensive error detection and numerous explanatory messages.

2. Using progressive step-by-step processes in which each question leads to a new set of questions. The progressive step-by-step processes guide users incrementally toward their goals, simplifying each step and explaining terminology, while giving them the chance to go back and change earlier decisions. Effective examples are in the Amazon four-step e-commerce checkout process and in the well-designed TurboTax system for income tax preparation.

Prospective Visual Designs for Exploratory User Interfaces

Since predictability is a fundamental principle for user interface design, it has been applied in many systems that involve different forms of AI algorithms.

These AI-based designs give users choices to select from before they initiate action, as in spelling correctors, text message autocompletion, and search query completion (see Figures 9.3 and 9.4). The same principle was productively applied by University of Colorado professor Daniel Szafir and his collaborators for robot operation. They showed that previews of the path and goals for intended actions of a dexterous robot arm resulted in improved task completion and increased satisfaction.[71] For robots the human control design principle for predictability might be the second pattern in Figure 9.2 preview first, select and initiate, then manage execution.

Navigation systems adhere to the predictability principle when they apply AI-based algorithms to find routes based on current traffic data. Users are given two to four choices of routes with estimated times for driving, biking, walking, and public transportation, from which they select the one they want. Then this supertool provides visual, textual, and speech-generated instructions (Figure 19.4).

In addition to AI-based textual, robot, and navigation user interfaces, similar *prospective* (or ante-hoc) methods can be used in recommender systems by offering exploratory user interfaces that enable users to probe the algorithm boundaries with different inputs. Figures 19.5a and 19.5b show a post-hoc explanation for a mortgage rejection, which is good, but could be improved. Figure 19.5c shows a prospective exploratory user interface that enables users to investigate how their choices affect the outcome, thereby reducing the need for explanations.

In general, prospective exploratory user interfaces are welcomed by users who spend more time developing an understanding of the sensitivity of variables and digging more deeply into aspects that interest them, leading to greater satisfaction and compliance with recommendations.[72] Further gains come from enabling adaptable user interfaces to fit different needs and personalities.[73]

For complex decisions, Fred Hohman, now an Apple researcher, showed that user interfaces and data analytics could clarify which features in a machine learning training data set are the most relevant.[74] His methods, developed as part of his doctoral work at Georgia Tech, also worked on explanations of deep learning algorithms for image understanding.[75] A Google team of eleven researchers built an interactive tool to support clinicians in understanding algorithmic decisions about cancers in medical images. Their study with twelve medical pathologists showed substantial benefits in using this slider-based

Fig 19.4 Navigation system for driving, public transportation, walking, and biking. The one-hour time estimate is for biking.

exploratory user interface, which "increased the diagnostic utility of the images found and increased user trust in the algorithm."[76]

Interactive HCAI approaches are endorsed by Weld and Bansal, who recommend that designers should "make the explanation system interactive so users can drill down until they are satisfied with their understanding."[77] Exploration

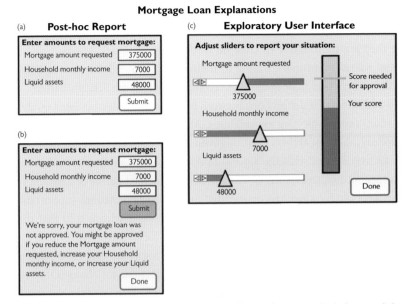

Fig 19.5 Mortgage loan explanations. (a) is a post-hoc explanation, which shows a dialog box with three fill-in fields and a submit button. (b) shows what happens after clicking the submit button. The feedback users get a brief text explanation, but insufficient guidance for next steps. (c) shows an exploratory user interface that enables users to try multiple alternatives rapidly. It has three sliders to see the impact of changes on the outcome score.

works best when the user inputs are actionable; that is, users have control and can change the inputs. Alternative designs are needed when users do not have control over the input values or when the input is from sensors such as in image and face recognition applications. For the greatest benefit, exploratory user interfaces should support accessibility by users with visual, hearing, motor, or cognitive disabilities.

The benefits of giving users more control over their work was demonstrated in a 1996 study of search user interfaces by Rutgers University professor Nick Belkin and graduate student Juergen Koenemann. They summarize the payoffs from exploratory interaction in their study of sixty-four participants who, they report, "used our system and interface quite effectively and very few usability problems . . . Users clearly benefited from the opportunity to revise queries in an iterative process."[78]

Supportive results about the benefits of interactive visual user interfaces come from a study of news recommenders in which users were able to move sliders to indicate their interest in politics, sports, or entertainment. As they moved the sliders the recommendation list changed to suggest new items.[79] Related studies added one more important insight: when users have more control, they are more likely to click on a recommendation.[80] Maybe being in control makes them more willing to follow a recommendation because they feel they discovered it, or maybe the recommendations are actually better.

In addition to the distinctions between intrinsically understandable models, post-hoc, and prospective explanations, Mengnan Du, Ninghao Liu, and Xia Hu follow other researchers in distinguishing between global explanations that give an overview of what the algorithm does and local explanations that deal with specific outcomes, such as why a prisoner is denied parole or a patient receives a certain treatment recommendation.[81] Local explanations support user comprehension and future actions, such as a prisoner who is told that they could be paroled after four months of good behavior or the patient who is told that if they lost ten pounds they would be eligible for a non-surgical treatment. These are actionable explanations, which are suggestions for changes that can be accomplished, rather than being told that if you were younger the results would be different.

An important statement about who would value explainable systems was in a US White House memorandum.[82] It reminded developers that "transparency and disclosure can increase public trust and confidence in AI applications" and then stressed that good explanations would allow "non-experts to understand how an AI application works and technical experts to understand the process by which AI made a given decision."

Increased user control through visual user interfaces is apparent in recommender systems that offer more transparent approaches, especially for consequential medical or career choices.[83] Our research team, led by University of Maryland doctoral student Fan Du, developed a visual user interface to allow cancer patients to make consequential decisions about treatment plans based on finding other "patients like me."

The goal was to enable users to see how similar patients fared in choosing chemotherapy, surgery, or radiation. But medical data were hard to obtain because of privacy protections, so our study used a related context. We tested eighteen participants making educational choices, such as courses, internships, or research projects, to achieve their goals, such as an industry job or graduate studies (Figure 19.6). The participants wanted to choose students who were similar to them by gender, degree program, and major, as well as having taken similar courses. The results showed that they took longer when they had control over the recommender system, but they were more likely to understand and

Fig 19.6 Visual user interface to enable users to find people who have similar past histories.
Source: Du et al., 2019

follow the recommendations. As one participant commented: "The advanced controls enable me to get more precise results."[84]

Professor Katrien Verbert and her team at the University of Leuven in Belgium have been studying exploratory user interfaces for AI-based recommender systems for almost a decade.[85] Their multiple papers in applications such as music recommendation and job seeking repeatedly show the benefits of simple slider controls to allow users to guide the selection.[86] In one study they used five of Spotify's fourteen dimensions for songs: acousticness, instrumentalness, danceability, valence, and energy. As users move the sliders to show increased or decreased preferences the song list reflects their choices (Figure 19.7). The results were strong: "the majority of the participants expressed positiveness towards having the ability to steer the recommendations . . . by looking at the relationship between the recommended songs and

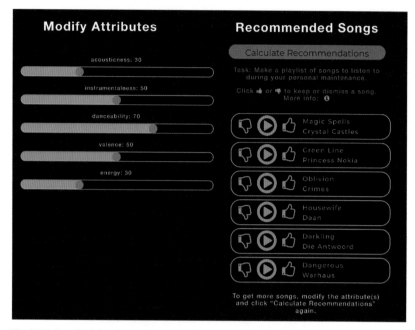

Fig 19.7 Simple sliders let users control the music recommender system by moving sliders for acousticness, instrumentalness, danceability, valence, and energy.

Source: Component from Millecamp et al., 2018

the attributes, they may better understand why particular songs are being recommended."[87]

Another example is in the OECD's Better Life Index website,[88] which rates nations according to eleven topics such as housing, income, jobs, community, and education (Figure 19.8). Users move sliders to indicate which topics are more or less important to them. As they make changes the list gracefully updates with a smoothly animated bar chart so they can see which countries most closely fulfill their preferences.

Yes, there are many users who don't want to be bothered with making choices, so they prefer the fully automatic recommendations, even if the recommendations are not as well tuned to their needs. This is especially true with discretionary applications such as movie, book, or restaurant recommendations, but the desire to take control grows with consequential and especially with life-critical decisions in which professionals are responsible for the outcomes.

There are many similar studies in e-commerce, movie, and other recommender systems but I was charmed by a simple yet innovative website to get

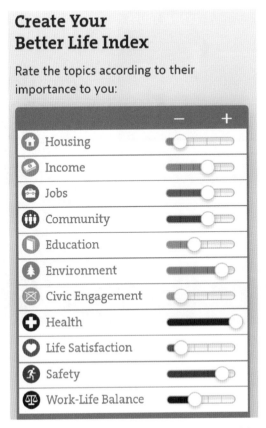

Fig 19.8 The OECD's Better Life Index with eleven sliders.

Source: http://www.oecdbetterlifeindex.org/

recommendations for novels to read. Users could select four of the twelve sliders to choose attributes such as funny/serious, beautiful/disgusting, or optimistic/bleak (Figure 19.9). As they move the sliders, the cover images of books would come and go on the right side. A click on the cover image produced a short description helping users to decide on what to read.[89] Other controls include a world map for location (which even shows imaginary locations) and check boxes for type of story (conflict, quest, revelation, etc.), race, age, gender, and sexual preference. I liked it—give it a try!

In summary, while post-hoc explanations to help confused users are a good idea and may be needed in some cases, a better approach may be to prevent or reduce the need for explanations. This idea of preventing rather than treating the disease is possible with prospective visual user interfaces that let users explore possibilities. Visual user interfaces help users understand the dimensions

Fig 19.9 Recommender system for novels based on attributes of the books. As users move the sliders the book covers appear or disappear.

Source: https://www.whichbook.net/

or attributes of a problem by easily exploring alternatives to understand the tradeoffs, find nearby items, and make some discoveries of their own. Since user needs are volatile over time and highly dependent on context, allowing users to guide the recommendations is helpful. The simple designs in this chapter won't always work, but there is growing evidence that, when done well, user controls are appreciated and produce more satisfied users and more successful usage than systems without user controls.

A University of Illinois team led by Karrie Karahalios surveyed seventy-five Facebook users and conducted a usability test and interview with thirty-six participants.[90] The issue was whether users understood their Facebook News Feed and how to control it. The disturbing results were that users were largely unaware of that these controls existed and were mostly unable to find the controls that were required to carry out the usability test tasks. Some became angry when they found that the settings were available but so difficult to find. The study makes recommendations such as to include a search feature and improve the menu design.

Skeptics of control panels point out that very few users learn to use the existing ones, but well-designed controls, such as in automobiles to adjust car seats, mirrors, lighting, sound, and temperature have gone from being a competitive advantage to required features. Instead of control panels, Jonathan Stray and colleagues at the Partnership on AI emphasize strategies to learn from users about what is needed to align automated recommendations more closely with their needs and well-being.[91] Newer designs which fit the many kinds of problems that HCAI serves are possible—they just require a little more imagination.

Safety Culture through Business Management Strategies

While every organization wants to perform flawlessly in all circumstances, the harsh reality is that pandemics overwhelm public health, nuclear power station failures trigger regional devastation, and terrorists threaten entire nations. Past accidents and incidents often had narrow impacts, but today's failures of massive technology-based interdependent organizations in globalized economies can have devastating effects for the health and economies of entire cities, regions, and continents. Preparing for failure by organizational design has become a major HCAI theme, with at least four approaches:

Normal accident theory Charles Perrow's influential book, *Normal Accidents*, makes a strong case for organizational responsibility for safety, rather than criticism of specific designs or operator error.[1] His analysis, which emerges from political science and sociology, emphasizes the dangers of *organizational complexity* and *overly tight coupling* of units with too much centralized control and insufficient redundancy to cope with disruptions. Tight coupling implies that there are standard operating procedures with well-crafted hierarchical chains of command, but when unexpected events occur, fluid collaboration across units can become vital. Supporting redundancy is difficult for organizations that seek minimum staff to handle daily operations, but when emergencies occur, additional experienced staff are needed immediately. How can an organization justify 20% or 30% more staff than is needed for daily operations, just to be ready for emergencies that happen once a year? How should organizations plan for the unavailability or death of key personnel, as highlighted by the case of three top executives of a firm who died in a small plane crash en route to a meeting—maybe organizations should ensure that key personnel fly on separate planes? Perrow's work is extended by psychologist Gary Klein and criticized by sociologist Andrew Hopkins who has pointed to the lack of metrics for the two dangers: tight coupling and insufficient redundancy.[2] Other critics found Perrow's belief in the inevitability of failure in complex organizations to be unreasonably pessimistic.

High reliability organizations This approach emerged from organizational design and business administration.[3] High reliability organizations have a "preoccupation with failure," studying possible ways that failures and near misses can occur, with a "commitment to resilience" by regularly running simulations of failures with relevant staff. Hilary Brown, who works on electricity transmission in Minnesota, writes that high-reliability organizations "develop reliability through redundancy, frequent training, emphasizing responsibility, and distributing decision-making throughout the group hierarchy, all of which reduce the impacts of complexity and tight coupling, as defined by Perrow."[4] In contrast to normal accident theory, high-reliability organization advocates are optimistic that a culture of mindfulness can prevent disasters.

Resilience engineering This approach grew out of cognitive science and human factors engineering.[5] Resilience engineering is about making organizations flexible enough to recover from unexpected events. David D. Woods of Ohio State University promotes resilience engineering by encouraging organizations to develop "architectures for sustained adaptability," drawing lessons from biological, social, and technological systems.[6] Resilience comes from planning about how to adapt to disasters that are natural (earthquakes, floods, storms), technology-based (power, telecommunications, water outage), adversarial (sabotage, terrorism, criminal), or design (system bugs, human error, management failure).

Safety cultures This approach came from responses to major disasters, such as the Chernobyl nuclear reactor and NASA's Space Shuttle *Challenger* disaster, which could not be attributed to an individual mistake or design failure. Leaders in this community seek to build organizations which cultivate staff attitudes,[7] by long-term commitment to open management strategies, a safety mindset among all staff, and validated organizational capabilities.[8] MIT's

Nancy Leveson has developed a systems engineering approach to safety engineering that includes design, hazard analysis, and failure investigations.[9] She thoughtfully distinguishes between safety and reliability, pointing out that they are separable issues, demanding different responses.

These four approaches share the goal of ensuring safe, uninterrupted performance by preparing organizations to cope with failures and near misses (see Figure 18.2).[10] Building on the safety culture approach, my distillation emphasizes the ways managers can support HCAI: (1) leadership commitment to safety, (2) hiring and training oriented to safety, (3) extensive reporting of failures and near misses, (4) internal review boards for problems and future plans, and (5) alignment with industry standards and accepted best practices.

Leadership Commitment to Safety

Top organizational leaders can make their commitment to safety clear with explicit statements about values, vision, and mission. Their preoccupation with failure is demonstrated by making positive statements about building a safety culture, which includes values, beliefs, policies, and norms. The durable safety culture can be shaken by the current safety climate, which includes the changing atmosphere, context, and attitudes because of internal conflicts and novel external threats.[11] Wise corporate leaders also know that a commitment to safety is more likely to succeed if the board of directors is also involved in decision-making, so that leaders recognize that their position depends on success with safety.

Leadership commitment is made visible to employees by frequent restatements of that commitment, positive efforts in hiring, repeated training, and dealing openly with failures and near misses. Reviews of incidents, such as monthly hospital review board meetings, can bring much increased patient safety. Janet Berry's team at an Ohio hospital report: "Improved safety and teamwork climate . . . are associated with decreased patient harm and severity-adjusted mortality."[12] Safety-focused leaders stress internal review boards for discussion of plans and problems, as well as adherence to industry standards and practices.

Safety cultures require effort and budget to ensure that there are sufficient and diverse staff involved with ample time and resources to do their work. This may imply redundancy to ensure knowledgeable people are available when problems emerge and a proactive mindset that anticipates dangers by conducting risk audits to prevent failures. Safety, reliability, and resilience raise ongoing costs, but the reduction of expensive failures is the payoff. In addition, safety efforts often result in increased productivity, reduced expenses for employee injuries, and savings on operations and maintenance costs. These benefits can be hard to prove to skeptics who want to cut costs by raising questions about spending to prepare for rare and unpredictable events.

While some literature on safety culture focuses on employee and facility safety, for HCAI systems, the focus must be on those whose lives are impacted by these systems. Therefore, a safety culture for HCAI systems will be built by strong connections with users, such as patients, physicians, and managers in hospitals or prisoners, lawyers, and judges in parole-granting organizations. Outreach to affected communities means two-way communications to inform stakeholders, continuous data collection on usage, and easy reporting of adverse events. Implementations of safety cultures in HCAI-based organizations are emerging with initial efforts to support AI governance in medical care.[13]

Safety for AI algorithms is a management problem, but it has technical implications for developers. Leaders will need to learn enough about the ways safety can be increased by careful design of algorithms, such as in choosing the right objective metrics, ensuring that supervisory controllers can stop dangerous actions, avoiding "distributional shift" (changes in context that invalidate the training data), and preventing adversarial attacks.[14] Leaders will need to verify that testing is done often enough during development and continues throughout deployment.

Skeptics fear that corporate safety culture pronouncements are merely public relations attempts to deal with unacceptable risks in many industries such as nuclear power, chemical production, healthcare, or social media platforms. They also point to cases in which failures were blamed on operator error rather than improper organizational preparation and inadequate operator training. One approach to ensuring safety is to appoint an internal ombudsperson to hear staff and stakeholder concerns privately, while enabling fair treatment of whistleblowers who report serious safety threats.

Hiring and Training Oriented to Safety

When safety is included in job-hiring position statements, that commitment becomes visible to current employees and potential new hires. Diversity in hiring also demonstrates commitment to safety by including senior staff who represent the diversity of employees and skills. Safety cultures may need experienced safety professionals from health, human resources, organizational design, ethnography, and forensics.

Safety-first organizations conduct training exercises regularly, such as industrial control room operators carrying out emergency plans, pilots flying simulators, and hospital workers running multiple day exercises for mass casualties or pandemics. When routine practices are similar to emergency plans, employees are more likely to succeed during the emergency. Thoughtful planning includes ranking of emergencies, based on past frequency of occurrence or severity, with an analysis of how many internal responders are needed in each situation, plus planning for how to engage external services when needed. Well-designed checklists can reduce errors in normal operations and remind operators what to do in emergencies.

The training needed for computer software and hardware designers has become easier due to the guidelines documents from leading technology companies such as Apple's Human Interface Guidelines[15] and Google's design guidebook,[16] which both contain useful example screen designs. In addition, Microsoft's eighteen guidelines for AI–human interaction,[17] and IBM's Design for AI website[18] rely on thoughtful general principles, which will need refinement.

These guidelines build on a long history of user interface design[19] and newer research on designing interfaces for HCAI systems.[20] However, guidelines have to be taught to user interface designers, programmers, AI engineers, product managers, and policy-makers, whose practices gain strength if there are organizational mechanisms for ensuring enforcement, granting exemptions, and making enhancements.

As HCAI systems are introduced, the training needs for consumers with self-driving cars, clinicians struggling with electronic healthcare systems, and operators of industrial control rooms become more complex. These users need to understand what aspects of the HCAI systems they control and how machine learning works, including its potential failures and associated outcomes.

Paul R. Daugherty and H. James Wilson's book *Human + Machine: Reimagining Work in the Age of AI* underlines the importance of training. They write that "companies must provide the employee training and retraining required so that people will be prepared and ready to assume any new roles . . . investing in people must be the core part of any company's AI strategy."[21]

Extensive Reporting of Failures and Near Misses

Safety-oriented organizations regularly report on their failures (sometimes referred to as adverse events) and near misses (sometimes referred to as "close calls").[22] Near misses can be small mistakes that are handled easily or dangerous practices that can be avoided, thereby limiting serious failures. These include near misses such as an occasional water leak, forced equipment restart, operator error, or electrical outage. If the errors of omission or commission in near misses are reported and logged, then patterns become clear to equipment and facility managers, so they can focus attention on preventing more serious failures. Since near misses typically occur much more often than failures, they provide richer data to guide maintenance, training, or redesign.

The US National Safety Council makes the surprising recommendation to avoid rewarding managers whose units have few failures, but rather to reward those managers whose units have high rates of near miss reports.[23] By making near miss reporting a common and virtuous practice, staff attention is more focused on safety and ready to make near miss reports, rather than cover them up.

Civil aviation has a much-deserved reputation for safety. This stems, in part, from a rich culture of near miss reporting such as through the US Federal Aviation Administration Hotline,[24] which invites passengers, air-traffic controllers, pilots, and the general public to report incidents, anonymously if they wish. The US National Transportation Safety Board, whose public reports are trusted and influential in promoting improvements, thoroughly investigates crashes with injuries or loss of life. In addition, the Aviation Safety Reporting System is a voluntary use website that "captures confidential reports, analyzes the resulting aviation safety data, and disseminates vital information to the aviation community."[25] These public reporting systems are good models for HCAI systems.

The US Food and Drug Administration's (FDA) Adverse Event Reporting System provides a model for the public reporting of problems with HCAI systems.[26] Their web-based public reporting system for healthcare professionals, consumers, and manufacturers invites reports on medications, medical devices, cosmetics, food, and other products (Figure 20.1).[27] The user interface walks users through seven stages to collect the data needed to make a credible

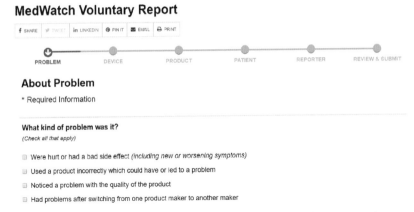

Fig 20.1 US Food and Drug Administration Voluntary Reporting Form invites adverse event reports from health professionals and consumers.

Source: https://www.accessdata.fda.gov/scripts/medwatch/index.cfm

and useful data set. The Public Dashboard presents information on the growing number of reports each year, exceeding 2 million in 2018, 2019, and 2020 (Figure 20.2).

Another US FDA reporting system, Manufacturer and User Facility Device Experience (MAUDE), captures adverse events in use of robotic surgery systems. Drawing on this data, a detailed review of 10,624 reports covering 2000–2013 reported on 144 deaths, 1,391 patient injuries, and 8,061 device malfunctions.[28] The report on these alarming outcomes recommends "improved human-machine interfaces and surgical simulators that train surgical teams for handling technical problems and assess their actions in real-time during the surgery." The conclusion stresses the value of "surgical team training, advanced human machine interfaces, improved accident investigation and reporting mechanisms, and safety-based design techniques."

For cybersecurity problems which threaten networks, hardware, and software, public reporting systems have also proven to be valuable. The MITRE Corporation, a company funded to work for the US government, has been keeping a list of common vulnerabilities and exposures since 1999, with more than 150,000 entries.[29] MITRE works with the US National Institutes of Standards and Technology to maintain a National Vulnerabilities Database,[30] which helps software developers understand the weaknesses in their programs. This allows more rapid repairs, coordination among those with common interests, and efforts to prevent vulnerabilities in future products and services. All of these open

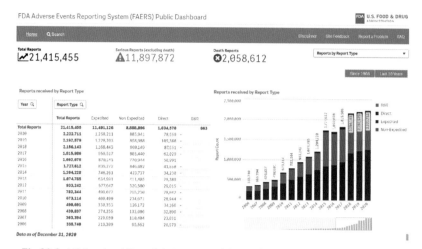

Fig 20.2 US Food and Drug Administration Adverse Event Reporting System (FAERS) Public Dashboard. Data as of December 31, 2020.

Source: https://fis.fda.gov/sense/app/d10be6bb-494e-4cd2-82e4-0135608ddc13/sheet/7a47a261-d58b-4203-a8aa-6d3021737452/state/analysis

reporting systems are good models to follow for HCAI failure and near miss reports.

In software engineering, code development environments, such as GitHub, record the author of every line of code and document who made changes.[31] GitHub claims to be used by more than 56 million developers in more than 3 million organizations. Then, when systems are in operation, bug reporting tools, such as freely available Bugzilla, guide project teams to frequent and serious bugs with a tracking system for recording resolution and testing.[32] Fixing users' problems promptly prevents other users from encountering the same problem. These tools are typically used by members of software engineering teams but inviting reports of problems from users is another opportunity.

The cybersecurity field has a long-standing practice of paying for vulnerability reports that could be adapted for HCAI systems. Bug bounties could be paid for individuals who report problems with HCAI systems, but the idea could be extended to bias bounties for those who report biased performance.[33] This crowdsourcing idea has been used by companies such as Google, which has paid from $100 to more than $30,000 per validated report for a total of more than $3 million. At least two companies make a business of managing such systems for clients: HackerOne[34] and BugCrowd.[35] Validating this idea in the HCAI context requires policies about how much is paid, how reports are evaluated, and how much information about the bug and bias reports are publicly disclosed.[36] These crowdsourced ideas build on software developer Eric Raymond's belief that "with enough eyes, all bugs are shallow," suggesting that it is valuable to engage more people in finding bugs.

Bug reporting is easier for interactive systems with comprehensible status displays than for highly automated systems without displays, such as elevators, manufacturing equipment, or self-driving cars. For example, I've regularly had problems with Internet connectivity at my home, but the lack of adequate user interfaces makes it very difficult for me to isolate and report the problems I've had. When my Internet connection drops, it is hard to tell if it was a problem on my laptop, my wireless connection to the router/modem, or the Internet service provider. I wish there was a status display and control panel so I could fix the problem or know whom to call. Server hosting company Cloudflare provides this information for its professional clients. Like many users, the best hope is to reboot everything and hope that in ten to fifteen minutes I can resume work.

Another model to follow is the US Army's method of after-action reviews, which have also been used in healthcare, transportation, industrial process control, environmental monitoring, and firefighting, so they might be useful for studying HCAI failures and near misses.[37] Investigators try to understand what was supposed to happen, what actually happened, and what could be done better in the future. A complete report that describes what went well and what could be improved will encourage acceptance of recommendations. As After-Action Review participants gain familiarity with the process, their analyses are likely to improve and so will the acceptance of their recommendations.

Early efforts in the HCAI community are beginning to collect data on HCAI incidents. Roman Yampolskiy's initial set of incidents has been included in a more ambitious project from the Partnership on AI.[38] Sean McGregor describes the admirable goals and methods used to build the database of more than 1000 incident reports sourced from popular, trade, and academic publications.[39] Searches can be done by keywords and phrases such as "mortgage" or "facial recognition," but a thoughtful report on these incidents remains to be done. Still, this is an important project, which could help in efforts to make more reliable, safe, and trustworthy systems.

Another important project, but more narrowly focused, is run by Karl Hansen, who collects public reports on deaths involving Tesla cars. He was a special agent with the US Army Criminal Investigation Command, Protective

Services Battalion, who was hired by Tesla as their internal investigator in 2018. He claims to have been wrongfully fired by Tesla for his public reporting of deaths involving Tesla cars.[40] The 209 deaths as of September 2021 is far more than most people expect, from what is often presented to the public. These reports are incomplete so it is difficult to determine what happened in each case or whether the Autopilot self-driving system was in operation. In August 2021, the US National Highway Transportation Safety Administration launched an investigation of eleven crashes of Tesla cars on autopilot that hit first responders on the road or at the roadside.

Other concerns come from 122 sudden unintended acceleration (SUA) events involving Teslas that were reported to the US National Highway Traffic Safety Administration by January 2020.[41] A typical report reads: "my wife was slowly approaching our garage door waiting for the garage door to open when the car suddenly lurched forward . . . destroying the garage doors . . . the car eventually stopped when it hit the concrete wall of the garage." Another report describes two sudden accelerations and ends by saying "fortunately no collision occurred, but we are scared now." Tesla claims that its investigations showed that the vehicle functioned properly, but that every incident was caused by drivers stepping on the accelerator.[42] However, shouldn't a safety-first car prevent such collisions with garage doors, walls, or other vehicles?

Internal Review Boards for Problems and Future Plans

Commitment to a safety culture is shown by regularly scheduled monthly meetings to discuss failures and near misses, as well as to celebrate resilient efforts in the face of serious challenges. Standardized statistical reporting of events allows managers and staff to understand what metrics are important and to suggest new ones. Internal and sometimes public summaries emphasize the importance of a safety culture.[43]

Review boards may include managers, staff, and others, who offer diverse perspectives on how to promote continuous improvement. In some industries, such as aviation, monthly reports of on-time performance or lost bag rates drive healthy competition, which serves the public interest. Similarly, hospitals may report patient care results for various conditions or surgeries, enabling the public to choose hospitals, in part, by their performance. The US Department of Health and Human Services has an Agency for Healthcare Research and

Quality, which conducts regular surveys on patient safety culture in hospitals, nursing homes, and community pharmacies.[44] The surveys raise staff awareness of patient safety and show trends over time and across regions.

A surprising approach to failures is emerging in many hospitals, which are adopting disclosure, apology, and offer programs.[45] Medical professionals usually provide excellent care for their patients, but when problems arise, there has been a tendency to do the best they can for the patient. However, fear of malpractice lawsuits limits physician willingness to report problems to patients, their families, or hospital managers. The emerging approach of disclosure, apology, and offer programs shifts to full disclosure to patients and their families with a clear apology and an offer of treatments to remedy the problem and/or financial compensation. While some physicians and managers feared that this would increase malpractice lawsuits, the results were dramatically different. Patients and their families appreciated the honest disclosure and especially the clear apology. As a result, lawsuits were often cut in half, while the number of medical errors decreased substantially because of physicians' awareness of these programs. Professional and organizational pride also increased.[46]

Internal review and auditing teams can also improve HCAI practices to limit failures and near misses. Google's five-stage internal algorithmic auditing framework, which is designed "to close the AI accountability gap," provides a good model for others to build on:[47]

1) **Scoping:** identify the scope of the project and the audit; raise questions of risk.

2) **Mapping:** create stakeholder map and collaborator contact list; conduct interviews and select metrics.

3) **Artifact collection:** document design process, data sets, and machine learning models.

4) **Testing:** conduct adversarial testing to probe edge cases and failure possibilities.

5) **Reflection:** consider risk analysis, failure remediation, and record design history.

The authors include a post-audit review for self-assessment summary report and mechanisms to track implementation. However, they are well aware that "internal audits are only one important aspect of a broader system of required quality checks and balances."

Initial corporate efforts include Facebook's oversight board, set up in mid-2020 for content monitoring and governance on their platform.[48] Microsoft's AI and Ethics in Engineering and Research (AETHER) Committee advises their leadership on responsible AI issues, technology, processes, and best practices that "warrant people's trust."[49] Microsoft's Office of Responsible AI implements company-wide rules for governance, team readiness, and dealing with sensitive use cases. They also help shape new HCAI-related "laws, norms, and standards . . . for the benefit of society at large."

Alignment with Industry Standard Practices

In many consequential and life-critical industries there are established industry standards, often promulgated by professional associations, such as the Association for Advancing Automation (AAA).[50] The AAA, founded in 1974 as the Robotics Industries Association (RIA), works with the American National Standards Institute[51] to drive "innovation, growth, and safety" by developing voluntary consensus standards for use by its members. Their work on advanced automation is a model for other forms of HCAI.

The International Standards Organization (ISO) has a Technical Committee on Robotics whose goal, since 1983, is "to develop high quality standards for the safety of industrial robots and service robots . . . by providing clear best practices on how to ensure proper safe installations, as well as providing standardized interfaces and performance criteria."[52] The emerging IEEE P7000 series of standards is directly tied to HCAI issues such as transparency, bias, safety, and trustworthiness.[53] These standards could do much to advance these goals by making more precise definitions and ways of assessing HCAI systems. The Open Community for Ethics in Autonomous and Intelligent Systems (OCEANIS) promotes discussions to coordinate multiple global standards efforts.[54]

A third source of standards is the World Wide Web Consortium (W3C), which supports website designers who pursue universal or inclusive design goals with the Web's Content Accessibility Guidelines.[55] Another source is the US Access Board, whose Section 508 standards guide agencies to "give disabled employees and members of the public access to information that is comparable to the access available to others."[56] These accessibility guidelines will be needed to ensure universal usability of HCAI systems, and they provide helpful models of how to deploy other guidelines for HCAI systems.

Characteristics of the Maturity levels

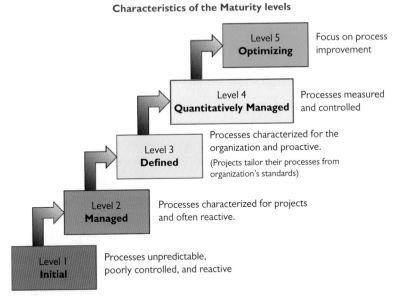

Fig 20.3 Characteristics of maturity levels: five levels in the Capability Maturity Model: (1) Initial, (2) Managed, (3) Defined, (4) Quantitatively Managed, and (5) Optimizing.

By working with organizations that develop these guidelines, companies can contribute to future guidelines and standards, learn about best practices, and provide education for staff members. Customers and the public may see participation and adherence to standards as indication of a safety-oriented company. However, skeptics are concerned that corporate participation in developing voluntary standards leads to weak standards whose main goal is to prevent more rigorous government regulation or other interventions. This process, *corporate capture*, indicates that corporate participants weaken standards to give them competitive advantages or avoid more costly designs. However, corporate participants also bring realistic experience to the process, raising the relevance of standards and increasing the chances for their widespread acceptance. The right blend is hard to achieve, but well-designed voluntary standards can improve products and services.

Another approach to improving software quality is the Capability Maturity Model (Figure 20.3), developed by the Software Engineering Institute (SEI) in the late 1980s[57] and regularly updated.[58] The SEI's goal is to improve software development processes, rather than setting standards for products and services. The 2018 Capability Maturity Model Integration version comes with the claim that it helps "integrate traditionally separate organizational functions, set process improvement goals and priorities, provide guidance for quality processes, and provide a point of reference for appraising current processes."[59]

The Capability Maturity Model Integration is a guide to software engineering organizational processes with five levels of maturity from Level 1 in which processes are unpredictable, poorly controlled across groups, and reactive to problems. Higher levels define orderly software development processes with detailed metrics for management control and organization-wide discussions of how to optimize performance and anticipate problems. Training for staff and management help ensure that the required practices are understood and followed. Many US government software development contracts, especially from defense agencies, stipulate which maturity level is required for bidders, using a formal appraisal process.

In summary, safety cultures take a strong commitment by industry leaders, supported by personnel, resources, and substantive actions, which are at odds with the "move fast, break things" ethic of early technology companies. To succeed, leaders will have to hire safety experts who use rigorous statistical methods, anticipate problems, appreciate openness, and measure performance. Other vital strategies are internal reviews and alignment with industry standards. Getting to a mature stage, where safety is valued as a competitive advantage will make HCAI technologies increasingly trusted for consequential and life-critical applications.

Skeptics question whether the Capability Maturity Models lead to top-heavy management structures, which may slow the popular agile and lean development methods. Still, proposals for HCAI Capability Maturity Models are emerging for medical devices, transportation, and cybersecurity.[60] The UK Institute for Ethical AI and Machine Learning proposes a Machine Learning Maturity Model based on hundreds of practical benchmarks, which cover topics such as data and model assessment processes and explainability requirements.[61]

HCAI Capability Maturity Models might be transformed into Trustworthiness Maturity Models (TMM). TMMs might describe Level 1 initial use of HCAI that is guided by individual team preferences and knowledge, making it unpredictable, poorly controlled, and reactive to problems. Level 2 use might call for uniform staff training in tools and processes, making it more consistent across teams, while Level 3 might require repeated use of tools and processes that are reviewed for their efficacy and refined to meet the application domain needs and organization style. Assessments would cover testing for biased data, validation and verification of HCAI systems, performance, user experience testing, and reviews of customer complaints. Level 4 might require measurement of HCAI systems and developer performance, with analysis of audit trails to understand how failures and near misses occurred. Level 5 might have repeated measures across many groups and over time to support continuous improvement and quality control.

Supporting the TMM idea, professional and academic attendees of a workshop produced a thorough report with fifty-nine co-authors who call for "AI developers to earn trust from system users, customers, civil society, governments, and other stakeholders that they are building AI responsibly, there is a need to move beyond principles to a focus on mechanisms for demonstrating responsible behavior."[62] The authors' recommendations of institutional structures and software workflows are in harmony with those in this book, and they also cover hardware recommendations, formal methods, and "verifiable claims" that are "sufficiently precise to be falsifiable."

Another growing industry practice is to develop templates for documenting HCAI systems for the benefit of developers, managers, maintainers, and other stakeholders. The 2018 idea of "datasheets for datasets" sparked great interest because it addresses the notion that machine learning data sets needed as much documentation as the programs that used them. The authors proposed a "standardized way to document how and why a data set was created, what information it contains, what tasks it should and should not be used for, and whether it might raise any ethical or legal concerns."[63] Their paper, which provided examples of datasheets for face recognition and sentiment classification projects, triggered strong efforts such as Google's Model Cards, Microsoft's Datasheets, and IBM's FactSheets.[64] The FactSheets team conducted evaluations by thirty-five participants of six systems, such as an audio classifier, breast cancer detector, and image caption generator, for qualities such as completeness, conciseness, and clarity. Combined with a second study, which required nineteen participants to create FactSheets, the team refined their design and evaluation methods. The FactSheets studies and much related material are available on an IBM website.[65] Following in this line of work, Kacper Sokol and Peter Flach of the University of Bristol, UK, developed "Explainability Fact Sheets" to describe numerous features of a system's explanations.[66] If these early documentation efforts mature and spread across companies, they could do much to improve development processes so as to improve reliability, safety, and trustworthiness.

Trustworthy Certification by Independent Oversight

The third governance layer is independent oversight by external review organizations (see Figure 18.2). Even as established large companies, government agencies, and other organizations that build consequential HCAI systems are venturing into new territory, so they will face new problems. Therefore, thoughtful independent oversight reviews will be valuable in achieving trustworthy systems that receive wide public acceptance. However, designing successful independent oversight structures is still a challenge, as shown by reports on more than forty variations that have been used in government, business, universities, non-governmental organizations, and civic society.[1]

The key to independent oversight is to support the legal, moral, and ethical principles of human or organizational responsibility and liability for their products and services. Responsibility is a complex topic, with nuanced variations such as legal liability, professional accountability, moral responsibility, and ethical bias.[2] A deeper philosophical discussion of responsibility is useful, but I assume that humans and organizations are legally liable (responsible) for the products and services that they create, operate, maintain, or use indirectly.[3] The report from the European Union's Expert Committee on Liability for New Technologies stresses the importance of clarifying liability for autonomous and robotic technologies.[4] They assert that operators of such technologies are liable and that products should include audit trails to enable retrospective analyses of failures to assign liability to manufacturer, operator, or maintenance organizations.

Professional engineers, physicians, lawyers, aviation specialists, business leaders, etc. are aware of their personal responsibility for their actions, but the software field has largely avoided certification and professional status for designers, programmers, and managers. In addition, contracts often contain "hold harmless" clauses that stipulate developers are not liable for damages, since software development is often described as a new and emerging activity, even after fifty years of experience. The HCAI movement has raised these issues again with frequent calls for algorithmic accountability and transparency,[5] ethically aligned design,[6] and professional responsibility.[7] Professional organizations, such as the AAAI, ACM, and IEEE, have ethical codes of conduct for their members, but penalties for unethical conduct are rare.

When damages occur, the allocation of liability is a complex legal issue. Many legal scholars, however, believe that existing laws are sufficient to deal with HCAI systems, although novel precedents will help clarify the issues.[8] For example, Facebook was sued for discrimination under existing laws since its AI algorithms allowed real estate brokers to target housing advertisements by gender, age, and zip code. Facebook settled the case and instituted changes to prevent advertising discrimination in housing, credit, and employment.[9]

Independent oversight is widely used by businesses, government agencies, universities, non-governmental organizations, and civic society to stimulate discussions, review plans, monitor ongoing processes, and analyze failures.[10] The goal of independent oversight is to review plans for major projects, investigate serious failures, and promote continuous improvement that ensures reliable, safe, and trustworthy products and services.

The individuals who serve on independent oversight boards need to be respected leaders whose specialized knowledge makes them informed enough about the organizations they review to be knowledgeable, but far enough away that they are independent. Conflicts of interest, such as previous relationships with the organization that is being reviewed, are likely to exist, so they must be disclosed and assessed. Diverse membership representing different disciplines, age, gender, ethnicity, and other factors helps build robust oversight boards.

Their capacity to investigate may include the right to examine private data, compel interviews, and even subpoena witnesses for testimony. The independent oversight reports are most effective if they are made public. Recommendations will have impact if there is a requirement to respond and make changes within a specified time period, usually measured in weeks or months.

Three independent oversight methods are common (Figure 21.1):[11]

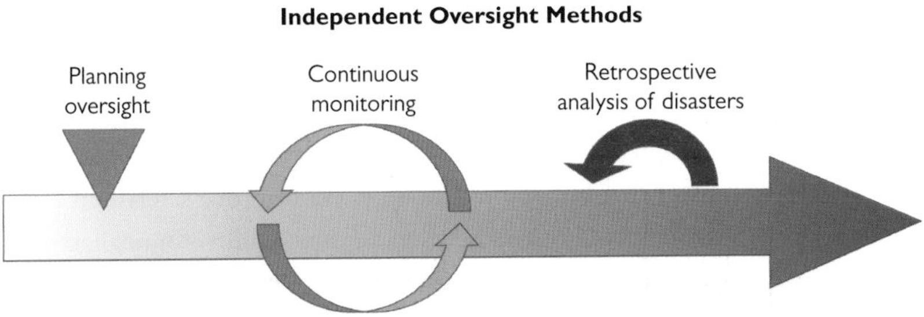

Independent Oversight Methods

Fig 21.1 Independent oversight methods. Three forms of independent oversight: planning oversight, continuous monitoring, and retrospective analysis of disasters.

Planning oversight proposals for new HCAI systems or major upgrades are presented for review in advance so that feedback and discussion can influence the plans. Planning oversight is similar to zoning boards, which review proposals for new buildings that are to adhere to building codes. A variation is the idea of algorithmic impact assessments, which are similar to environmental impact statements that enable stakeholders to discuss plans before implementation.[12] Rigorous planning oversight needs to have follow-up reviews to verify that the plan was followed.

Continuous monitoring this is an expensive approach, but the US Food and Drug Administration has inspectors who work continuously at pharmaceutical and meat-packing plants, while the US Federal Reserve Board continuously monitors practices at large banks. One form of continuous monitoring is periodic inspections, such as quarterly inspections for elevators or annual financial audits for publicly traded companies. Continuous monitoring of mortgage or parole granting HCAI systems would reveal problems as the profile of applicants' changes or the context shifts, such as has happened during the COVID-19 crisis.

Retrospective analysis of disasters the US National Transportation Safety Board conducts widely respected, thorough reviews with detailed reports about aircraft, train, or ship crashes. Similarly, the US Federal Communications Commission is moving to review HCAI systems in social media and web services, especially disability access and fake news attacks. Other agencies in the United States and around the world are developing principles and policies to enable study and limitation of HCAI failures. A central effort is to develop voluntary industry guidelines for audit trails and analysis for diverse applications.

Skeptics point to failures of independent oversight methods, sometimes tied to a lack of sufficient independence, but the value of these methods is widely appreciated.

In summary, clarifying responsibility for designers, engineers, managers, maintainers, and users of advanced technology will improve safety and effectiveness, since these stakeholders will be aware of their liability for negligent behavior. The five technical practices for software engineering teams (Chapter 19) are first steps to developing reliable systems. The five management strategies for organizations (Chapter 20) build on existing strategies to promote safety cultures across all the teams in their organization. This chapter offers four paths to trustworthy certification within an industry by independent oversight reviews, in which knowledgeable industry experts bring successful practices from one organization to another. Chapter 22 describes government interventions and regulations.

Accounting Firms Conduct External Audits for HCAI Systems

The US Securities and Exchange Commission (SEC) requires publicly traded businesses to have annual internal and external audits, with results posted on the SEC website and published in corporate annual reports. This SEC mandate, which required use of the generally accepted accounting principles (GAAP), is widely considered to have limited fraud and offered investors more accurate information. However, there were massive failures such as the Enron and MCI WorldCom problems, which led to the Sarbanes–Oxley Act of 2002, known as the Corporate and Auditing Accountability, Responsibility, and Transparency Act, but remember that no system will ever completely prevent malfeasance and fraud. New mandates about reporting on HCAI projects, such as descriptions of fairness and user experience test results, could standardize and strengthen reporting methods so as to increase investor trust by allowing comparisons across corporations.

Independent financial audit firms, which analyze corporate financial statements to certify that they are accurate, truthful, and complete, could develop reviewing strategies for corporate HCAI projects to provide guidance to investors. They would also make recommendations to their client companies about what improvements to make. These firms often develop close relationships with internal auditing committees, so that there is a good chance that recommendations will be implemented.

Leading independent auditing firms could be encouraged by public pressure or SEC mandate to increase their commitment to support HCAI projects. The big four firms are PricewaterhouseCoopers,[13] Deloitte,[14] Ernst & Young,[15] and KPMG;[16] all claim expertise in AI. The Deloitte website makes a promising statement that "AI tools typically yield little direct outcome until paired with human-centered design," which leans in the directions recommended by this chapter. Accounting firms have two potential roles, consulting and independent audit, but these roles must be kept strictly separated, as stipulated by the Sarbanes–Oxley Act.

A compelling example of independent oversight of corporate projects is contact tracing for COVID-19. Apple and Google partnered to produce mobile device apps that would alert users if someone they came in contact with developed COVID-19. However, the privacy threats immediately raised concerns, leading to calls for independent oversight boards and policies. One thoughtful proposal offers over 200 items for an independent oversight board of governance to assess and adjudicate during an audit.[17] For controversial projects that involve privacy, security, industry competition, or potential bias, independent oversight panels could play a role in increasing public trust.

If the big four auditing firms stepped forward, their credibility with corporations and general public trust could lead to independent HCAI audits that had substance and impact. A model to build on is the Committee of Sponsoring Organizations,[18] which brought together five leading accounting organizations to improve enterprise risk management, internal controls, and fraud deterrence. This form of auditing for HCAI could reduce pressures for government regulation and improve business practices. Early efforts could attract attention and enlist trusted public figures and organizations to join such review boards.

In addition to auditing or accounting firms, consulting companies could also play a role. Leaders like Accenture, McKinsey and Co., and Boston Consulting Group have all built their AI expertise and published white papers in order to advise companies on reliable, safe, and trustworthy systems.

Insurance Companies Compensate for Failures

The insurance industry is a potential guarantor of trustworthiness, as it is in the building, manufacturing, and medical domains. Insurance companies could specify requirements for insurability of HCAI systems in manufacturing, medical, transportation, industrial, and other domains. They have long played a key role in ensuring building safety by requiring adherence to building codes for structural strength, fire safety, flood protection, and many other features.

Building codes could be a model for software engineers, as described in computer scientist Carl Landwehr's proposal: "A building code for building code."[19] He extends historical analogies to plumbing, fire, or electrical standards by applying them to software engineering for avionics, medical devices, and cybersecurity, but the extension to HCAI systems seems natural.

Builders must satisfy the building codes to gain the inspector's approval, which allows them to obtain liability insurance. Software engineers could contribute to detailed software design, testing, and certification standards, which could be used to enable an insurance company to conduct risk assessment and develop insurance pricing. Requirements for audit trails of performance and monthly or quarterly reports about failures and near misses would give insurance companies data they need. Actuaries would become skillful in developing risk profiles for different applications and industries, with guidelines for compensation when damage occurs. Liability law from related technologies would have to be interpreted to HCAI systems.[20]

A natural next step would be for insurance companies to gather data from multiple companies in each industry they serve, which would accelerate their development of risk metrics and underwriting evaluation methods. This would also support the refinement of building codes for each industry to educate developers and publicly record expected practices. The development of building codes also guides companies about how to improve their HCAI products and services.

In some industries such as healthcare, travel, and car or home ownership, consumers purchase insurance which provides no-fault protection to cover damages for any reason. But in some cases, providers purchase insurance to cover the costs of medical malpractice suits, transportation accidents, and building damage from fire, floods, or storms. For many HCAI systems, it seems reasonable that the providers would be the ones to purchase insurance so as to provide protection for the large numbers of consumers who might be harmed. This would drive up the costs of products and services, but as in many industries, consumers are ready to pay these costs. Insurance companies will have to develop risk assessments for HCAI systems, but as the number of applications grow, sufficient data on failures and near misses will emerge to guide refinements.

Car insurance companies, including Travelers Insurance, produced a July 2018 paper on "Insuring Autonomy" for self-driving cars.[21] They sought a framework that "spurs innovation, increases public safety, provides peace of mind and protects ... drivers and consumers." The report endorsed the beliefs that self-driving cars would dramatically increase safety, but damage claims would increase because of the more costly equipment. Both beliefs influence risk assessment, the setting of premiums, and profits, as did their forecast that the number of cars would decrease because of more shared usage. This early report remains relevant because the public still needs data that demonstrate or refute the idea that self-driving cars are safer. Manufacturers are reluctant to report what they know and the states and federal government in the United States have yet to push for open reporting and regulations on self-driving cars.[22] The insurance companies will certainly act when self-driving cars move from demonstration projects to wider consumer use, but earlier interventions could be more influential.[23]

Skeptics fear that the insurance companies are more concerned with profits than with protecting public safety and they worry about the difficulty of pursuing a claim when injured by a self-driving car, mistaken medical recommendation, or biased treatment during job hiring, mortgage approval or parole assessment. However, as the history of insurance shows, having insurance will benefit many people in their difficult moments of loss. Developing realistic insurance from the damages caused by HCAI systems is a worthy goal.

Other approaches are to create no-fault insurance programs or victim compensation funds, in which industry or government provide funds to an independent review board that pays injured parties promptly without the complexity and cost of judicial processes. Examples include the September 11 Victim Compensation Fund for the 2001 terror attack in New York and the Gulf Coast Claim Facility for the Deepwater Horizon oil spill. Proposals for novel forms of compensation for HCAI system failures have been made, but none have yet gained widespread support.

Non-governmental and Civil Society Organizations

In addition to government efforts, auditing by accounting firms, and warranties from insurance companies, the United States and many other countries have a rich set of non-governmental and civil society organizations that have already been active in promoting reliable, safe, and trustworthy HCAI systems (Appendix A). These examples have various levels of support, but collectively they are likely to do much to promote improved systems and public acceptance.

These non-governmental organizations (NGOs) are often funded by wealthy donors or corporations who believe that an independent organization has greater freedom to explore novel ideas and lead public discussions in rapidly growing fields such as AI. Some of the NGOs were started by individuals who have the passion necessary to draw others in and find sponsors, but the more mature NGOs may have dozens or hundreds of paid staff members who share their enthusiasm. Some of these NGOs develop beneficial services or training courses on new technology policy issues that bring in funding and further expand their networks of contacts.

An inspiring example is how the Algorithmic Justice League was able to get large technology companies to improve their facial recognition products so as to reduce gender and racial bias within a two-year period. Their pressure also was likely to have been influential in the spring 2020 decisions of leading companies to halt their sales to police agencies in the wake of the intense movement to limit police racial bias.

NGOs have proven to be early leaders in developing new ideas about HCAI principles and ethics, but now they will need to increase their attention to developing new ideas about implementing software engineering practices and business management strategies. They will also have to expand their relationships with government policy-makers, liability lawyers, insurance companies, and auditing firms so they can influence the external oversight mechanisms that have long been part of other industries.

However, NGOs have limited authority to intervene. Their role is to point out problems, raise possible solutions, stimulate public discussion, support investigative journalism, and change public attitudes. Then, governmental agencies respond with policy guidance to staff and where possible new rules and regulations. Auditing companies change their processes to accommodate HCAI, and insurance companies update their risk assessment as they underwrite new technologies. NGOs could also be influential by conducting independent oversight studies to analyze widely used HCAI systems. Their reports could provide fresh insights and assessment processes tuned to the needs of diverse industries.

Professional Organizations and Research Institutes

Professional organizations have proven effective in developing voluntary guidelines and standards. Established and new organizations (Appendix B) are vigorously engaged in international discussions on ethical and practical design principles for responsible AI. They are already influential in producing positive outcomes. However, skeptics caution that industry leaders often dominate professional organizations, sometimes called *corporate capture*, so they may push for weaker guidelines and standards.

Professional societies, such as the IEEE, have long been effective in supporting international standards, with current efforts on the P7000 series addressing topics such as transparency of autonomous systems, algorithmic bias considerations, fail-safe design for autonomous and semi-autonomous systems, and rating the trustworthiness of news sources.[24] The ACM's US Technology Policy Committee has subgroups that address accessibility, AI/algorithmic accountability, digital governance, and privacy. The challenge for professional societies is to increase the low rates of participation of their members in these efforts. The IEEE has stepped forward with an Ethics Certification Program for Autonomous and Intelligent Systems, which seeks to develop metrics and certification methods for corporations to address transparency, accountability, and algorithmic bias.[25]

Academic institutions have long conducted research on AI, but they have now formed large centers to conduct research and promote interest in ethical, design, and research themes around HCAI. Early efforts have begun to add ethical concerns and policy-making strategies to education, but much more remains to be done so that graduates are more aware of the impact of their work. Examples of diverse lab names include these at prominent institutions:

- Brown University, US (Humanity Centered Robotics Initiative)
- Columbia University, US (Data Science Institute)
- Harvard University, US (Berkman Klein Center for Internet and Society)
- Johns Hopkins University, US (Institute for Assured Autonomy)
- Monash University, Australia (Human-Centered AI)
- New York University, US (Center for Responsible AI)
- Northwestern University, US (Center for Human–Computer Interaction + Design)
- Stanford University, US (Human-Centered AI (HAI) Institute)
- University of British Columbia, Canada (Human-AI Interaction)
- University of California-Berkeley, US (Center for Human-Compatible AI)

- University of Cambridge, UK (Leverhulme Centre for the Future of Intelligence)
- University of Canberra, Australia (Human Centred Technology Research Centre)
- University of Chicago, US (Chicago Human+AI Lab)
- University of Oxford, UK (Internet Institute, Future of Humanity Institute)
- University of Toronto, Canada (Ethics of AI Lab)
- Utrecht University, Netherlands (Human-Centered AI)

There are also numerous research labs and educational programs devoted to understanding the long-term impact of AI and exploring ways to ensure it is beneficial for humanity. The challenge for these organizations is to build on their strength in research by bridging to practice, so as to promote better software engineering processes, organizational management strategies, and independent oversight methods. University–industry–government partnerships could be a strong pathway for influential actions.

Responsible industry leaders have repeatedly expressed their desire to conduct research and use HCAI in safe and effective ways. Microsoft's CEO Satya Nadella proposed six principles for responsible use of advanced technologies.[26] He wrote that artificially intelligent systems must:

- Assist humanity and safeguard human workers.
- Be transparent . . . Ethics and design go hand in hand.
- Maximize efficiencies without destroying the dignity of people.
- Be designed for intelligent privacy.
- Have algorithmic accountability so that humans can undo unintended harm.
- Guard against bias . . . So that the wrong heuristics cannot be used to discriminate.

Similarly, Google's CEO Sundar Pichai offered seven objectives for artificial intelligence applications that became core beliefs for the entire company:[27]

- Be socially beneficial.
- Avoid creating or reinforcing unfair bias.

- Be built and tested for safety.
- Be accountable to people.
- Incorporate privacy design principles.
- Uphold high standards of scientific excellence.
- Be made available for uses that accord with these principles.

Skeptics will see these statements as self-serving corporate whitewashing designed to generate positive public responses. However, they can produce important efforts such as Google's internal review and algorithmic auditing framework[28] (see Chapter 20's section "Internal Review Boards for Problems and Future Plans"), but their 2019 effort to form a semi-independent ethics review committee collapsed in controversy within a week. Corporate statements can help raise public expectations, but the diligence of internal commitments should not be a reason to limit external independent oversight. Since support for corporate social responsibilities may be countered by pressures for a profitable bottom line, corporations and the public benefit from questions raised by knowledgeable journalists and external review boards.

Non-Governmental and Civil Society Organizations Working on HCAI

There are hundreds of organizations in this category, so this brief listing only samples some of the prominent ones.

Underwriters Laboratories, established in 1894, has been "working for a safer world" by "empowering trust." They began with testing and certifying electrical devices and then branched out worldwide to evaluate and develop voluntary industry standards. Their vast international network has been successful in producing better products and services, so it seems natural for them to address HCAI.[29]

Brookings Institution, founded in 1916, is a Washington, DC non-profit public policy organization, which is home to an Artificial Intelligence and Energy Technology (AIET) Initiative. It focuses on governance issues by publishing reports and books, bringing together policy-makers and researchers at conferences, and "seek to bridge the growing divide between industry, civil society, and policymagers."[30]

Electronic Privacy Information Center (EPIC), founded in 1994, is a Washington, DC-based public interest research that that focuses "public attention on emerging privacy and civil liberties issues and to protect privacy, freedom of expression, and democratic values in the information age." It runs conferences, offers public education, files amicus briefs, pursues litigation, and testifies before Congress and governmental organizations. Its recent work has emphasized AI issues such as surveillance and algorithmic transparency.[31]

Algorithmic Justice League, which stems from IT and Emory University, seeks to lead "a cultural movement towards equitable and accountable AI." The League combines "art and research to illuminate the social implications and harms of AI." With funding from large foundations and individuals it has done influential work on demonstrating bias, especially for face recognition systems. Its work productively has led to algorithmic and training data improvements in leading corporate systems.[32]

AI Now Institute at New York University "is an interdisciplinary research center dedicated to understanding the social implications of artificial intelligence." This institute emphasizes "four core domains: Rights & Liberties, Labor & Automation, Bias & Inclusion, Safety & Critical Infrastructure." It supports research, symposia, and workshops to educate and examine "the social implications of AI."[33]

Data and Society, an independent New York-based non-profit that "studies the social implications of data-centric technologies and automation . . . We produce original research on topics including AI and automation, the impact of technology on labor and health, and online disinformation."[34]

Foundation for Responsible Robotics is a Netherlands-based group whose tag line is "accountable innovation for the humans behind the robots." Its mission is "to shape a future of responsible (AI-based) robotics design, development, use, regulation, and implementation. We do this by organizing and hosting events, publishing consultation documents, and through creating public-private collaborations."[35]

AI4ALL, an Oakland, CA-based non-profit works "for a future where diverse backgrounds, perspectives, and voices unlock AI's potential to benefit humanity." It sponsors education projects such as summer institutes in the United States and Canada for diverse high school and university students, especially women and minorities to promote AI for social good.[36]

ForHumanity is a public charity which examines and analyzes the downside risks associated with AI and automation, such as "their impact on jobs, society, our rights and our freedoms." It believes that independent audit of AI systems, covering trust, ethics, bias, privacy, and cybersecurity at the corporate and public-policy levels, is a crucial path to building an infrastructure of trust. It believes that "if we make safe and responsible artificial intelligence and automation profitable whilst making dangerous and irresponsible AI and automation costly, then all of humanity wins."[37]

Future of Life Institute is a Boston-based charity working on AI, biotech, nuclear, and climate issues in the United States, United Kingdom, and European Union. It seeks to "catalyze and support research and initiatives for safeguarding life and developing optimistic visions of the future, including positive ways for humanity to steer its own course considering new technologies and challenges."[38]

Center for AI and Digital Policy is part of the Michael Dukakis Institute for Leadership and Innovation. Its website says that it aims "to ensure that artificial intelligence and digital policies promote a better society, more fair, more just, and more accountable—a world where technology promotes broad social inclusion based on fundamental rights, democratic institutions, and the rule of law."[39] The extensive report on AI and Democratic Values it produces assesses performance of twenty-five countries annually.

Professional Organizations and Research Institutes Working on HCAI

There are hundreds of organizations in this category, so this brief listing only samples some of the prominent ones. A partial listing can be found on Wikipedia.[40]

Institute for Electrical and Electronics Engineers (IEEE) launched a global initiative for ethical considerations in the design of AI and autonomous systems. It is an incubation space for new standards and solutions, certifications and codes of conduct, and consensus building for ethical implementation of intelligent technologies.[41]

IEEE Global Initiative on Ethics of Autonomous and Intelligent Systems (2019) originates with the large professional engineering society and collected more than 200 people over three years to prepare an influential report: "Ethically Aligned Design: A Vision for Prioritizing Human Well-being with Autonomous and Intelligent Systems."[42]

ACM, a professional society with 100,000 members working in the computing field, has been active in developing principles and ethical frameworks for responsible computing. ACM's Technical Policy Committee delivered a report with seven principles for algorithmic accountability and transparency.[43]

Association for the Advancement of Artificial Intelligence (AAAI) is a "non-profit scientific society devoted to advancing the scientific understanding of the mechanisms underlying thought and intelligent behavior and their embodiment in machines. AAAI aims to promote research in, and responsible use of, artificial intelligence." It runs very successful conferences, symposia, and workshops, often in association with ACM, that bring researchers together to present new work and train newcomers to the field.[44]

OECD AI Policy Observatory is a project of the Organisation for Economic Co-operation and Development. It works with policy professionals "to consider the opportunities and challenges" in AI and to provide "a centre for the collection and sharing of evidence on AI, leveraging the OECD's reputation for measurement methodologies and evidence-based analysis."[45]

Associaton for Advancing Automation, founded in 1974 as the Robotics Industries Association, is a North American trade group that "drives innovation, growth, and safety in manufacturing and service industries through education, promotion, and advancement of robotics, related automation technologies, and companies delivering integrated solutions."[46]

Machine Intelligence Research Institute (MIRI) is a research non-profit studying the mathematical underpinnings of intelligent behavior. Its mission is to develop formal tools for the clean design and analysis of general-purpose AI systems, with the intent of making such systems safer and more reliable when they are developed.[47]

Open AI is a San Francisco-based research organization that "will attempt to directly build safe and beneficial Artificial General Intelligence (AGI) . . . that benefits all of humanity." Their research team is supported by corporate investors, foundations, and private donations.[48]

The Partnership on AI, established in 2016 by six of the largest technology companies, has more than 100 industry, academic, and other partners who "shape best practices, research, and public dialogue about AI's benefits for people and society." It funded the Partnership on AI, which "conducts research, organizes discussions, shares insights, provides thought leadership, consults with relevant third parties, responds to questions from the public and media, and creates educational material."[49]

Montreal AI Ethics Institute is an international, non-profit research institute dedicated to defining humanity's place in a world increasingly characterized and driven by algorithms. Its website says: "We do this by creating tangible and applied technical and policy research in the ethical, safe, and inclusive development of AI. We're an international non-profit organization equipping citizens concerned about artificial intelligence to take action."[50]

Government Interventions and Regulations

Government leaders around the world have recognized that AI is a vital technology for economic growth, national security, and community safety. While there is principled resistance to government intervention and regulation, there is a growing recognition that it could be helpful and maybe necessary (see Figure 18.2). The United States is seen as a leader in AI research and development, but major efforts have also come from the United Kingdom, Europe, Canada, Russia, China, India, South Korea, and other countries. National policies from these and other countries have outlined their plans, but most impressively China's Next Generation Artificial Intelligence Development Plan has set ambitious goals to become the top center for AI basic research, product development, and commercial applications by 2030.

China's large and well-educated population gives the country advantages that make its plans for leadership in AI a realistic possibility. The Chinese government's centralized national economic policies and commitment of more than $100 billion means that their plans can have broad impacts. Their plan has little to say about HCAI or responsible AI, but a follow-on document from China's Ministry of Science and Technology does address some of the familiar principles of HCAI, such as fairness, justice, and respect for privacy, while adding open collaboration and agile governance.[1] China's large Internet companies such as Alibaba, WeChat, Tencent, and Baidu are huge successes in e-commerce, banking, social media, and communications, in part because of their strength in AI.

China's cultural differences lead to some advantages in broad application of AI. While privacy is stated as a Chinese value, so is community benefit. This means that government collection of personal information, such as medical data, is expected. The data from individual healthcare are used to support public health practices that will bring the greatest benefits to all. This contrasts with Western practices, especially in the European Union, which prioritize individuals and strongly protect their privacy. Similarly, widespread surveillance in China via a vast system of cameras enables local and national governments to track individuals. These data contribute to a Social Credit System, a national system for personal economic and social reputation for each individual. While some see this as an invasive surveillance system, it gives China huge databases that enable rapid progress on AI machine learning algorithms and scalable implementation techniques.[2]

However, the United States has strong assets in its academic centers, major companies that currently dominate several markets, and an innovative start-up culture. A high-level policy statement comes from a 2019 US White House report which emphasizes the need to "[e]nsure the safety and security of AI systems. Advance knowledge of how to design AI systems that are reliable, dependable, safe, and trustworthy."[3] The report stresses research to achieve these goals "but does not describe or recommend policy or regulatory actions related to the governance or deployment of AI." A related report retreats still further from government regulation: "The private sector and other stakeholders may develop voluntary consensus standards that concern AI applications, which provide nonregulatory approaches to manage risks associated with AI applications that are potentially more adaptable to the demands of a rapidly evolving technology." While such statements indicate past resistance to regulation, changes to policy are likely.

A broad review of US policy-making by Brookings Institution's Darrell M. West and John R. Allen pointed to AI's distinctive features of intentionality (capacity to form goals), intelligence (cognitive functioning approaching or exceeding human abilities), and adaptability (capacity to change behavior based on new data). The authors saw these as distinct enough from past technologies, so that new initiatives from government were needed.[4] They make familiar arguments about the need for responsible AI, transparency, and ethical principles, but their language becomes stronger when supporting oversight through AI impact assessments and advisory boards of relevant stakeholders for federal agencies. While their advice is more generic than specific, they speak up for HCAI by writing that "there needs to be avenues for humans to exercise oversight and control of AI systems."

Government research agency leaders are already making choices about what kind of AI research they should support. The US National Science Foundation's (NSF) $100M+ program for National AI Research Institutes seeks to accelerate "research, transforming society, and growing the American workforce." The request for proposals requires investigators to address foundational AI research while conducting "use-inspired research" that "drives innovations in related sectors of science and engineering, segments of the economy, or societal needs" while working with "external stakeholders such as industrial partners, public policy-makers, or international organizations."[5]

This vision breaks from much of the NSF's past that was guided by Vannevar Bush's 1945 manifesto, *Science, the Endless Frontier*, which argued for research funding to be curiosity driven, rather than focused on societal needs. Bush's widely influential manifesto has been challenged by many, but remains a firm lodestone for many researchers who seek to separate themselves from practitioners, societal needs, and policy topics.[6]

The encouragement for AI researchers to raise their emphasis on use-inspired research is aligned with the growing awareness of the benefits of partnering with non-academic organizations and researchers. When AI researchers partner with those who are close to realistic driving problems, the quality of foundational research is likely to increase, as are the benefits to society. Diverse organizations, such as the Center for Advancing Research Impact in Society,[7] HIBAR Research Alliance,[8] and the University–Industry Demonstration Partnerships,[9] support these principles, while growing evidence shows the increased impact of such partnerships.[10]

The NSF program for National AI Research Institutes includes as one of its eight themes "Human–AI Interaction and Collaboration." The commentary supports human-centered design by encouraging attention to "ethics, fairness, privacy, lack of deception, explainability, protection of vulnerable and protected populations, and participatory and inclusive design" so as to produce "trustworthy and safe" HCAI systems.[11]

Many nations, regional alliances, and international organizations are also funding research and addressing AI policy implications. The Canadian government promotes responsible use of AI by way of an algorithmic impact assessment to "mitigate the risks associated with deploying an automated decision system."[12]

European nations, especially the United Kingdom, France, Germany, and Italy, have put forward their statements, often aligned with European Union reports. The European Union's General Data Protection Regulation (GDPR) requirement of a "right to explanation,"[13] discussed in Chapter 19's section "Explainable User Interfaces," covers all industries, but there is a growing awareness that industry-specific oversight may be more appropriate. In the UK, the Royal Society recommended that existing industry-specific agencies should address AI systems, rather than having "an overarching framework for all uses of machine learning."[14] A useful strategy comes from the UK's Information Commissioners Office and the Alan Turing Institute, which released a carefully considered set of guidelines about how agencies should develop their industry-specific policies.[15]

The European Commission's White Paper on AI[16] proposes regulatory approaches and specific checklists for developers and managers.[17] The European effort, through its High-Level Expert Group, stresses seven principles for trustworthy AI:

1) human agency and oversight,

2) technical robustness and safety,

3) privacy and data governance,

4) transparency,

5) diversity, non-discrimination, and fairness,

6) environmental and societal well-being, and

7) accountability.

However, for now these principles are left for voluntary use by developers and deployers of AI systems.

An example of what regional alliances can accomplish, the Organisation of Economic Cooperation and Development's (OECD) developed a set of "Principles for responsible stewardship of trustworthy AI" that labeled their work as a human-centered approach.[18] These principles were supported by the Group of Twenty (G20), which includes nineteen countries and the European Union, to promote economic development and financial stability and then endorsed by more than fifty countries, making it the most widely shared principles. The OECD's HCAI principles, adopted in May 2019, begin with familiar values such as inclusive growth, sustainable development, well-being, transparency, explainability, and accountability.[19] Beyond these, the OECD principles encourage policy-makers to invest in research and development, build human capacity, deal with labor market transformation, and foster international cooperation.

The authors of the OECD principles recognized that follow-up efforts were needed to disseminate information, track implementation, and monitor outcomes. In 2020, they established a Policy Observatory with dashboards for sixty countries to track their policy initiatives, budgets, and academic research leaders. Then, by way of a Canadian and French partnership, the OECD convened a Global Partnership on AI (GPAI) to encourage policy-makers to pursue the principles. The GPAI makes a special mention of the COVID-19 crisis, with the hope of applying HCAI to respond and recover more effectively.

International initiatives, especially through the United Nations (UN), could also add weight to national HCAI policy efforts. The UN has generally been seen as a positive force in regulating atomic energy by way of monitoring of the 1970 Nuclear Non-proliferation Treaty. The UN's International Atomic Energy Agency (IAEA) sends inspectors to nuclear facilities in many of the 190 countries who signed the treaty to verify that they are not using their reactors to produce nuclear weapons. Critics point out that even after massive reductions, there are still more than 20,000 nuclear weapons in the world, although none have been used in warfare since 1945. Another concern is that a small number of nations with nuclear activities have not signed the treaty, so there are still serious threats that nuclear weapons might be used.

The UN's role as a potential regulator of HCAI stems from its international efforts on health, communications, food, agriculture, and other technologies. The UN's International Telecommunication Union (ITU) is active on AI topics with its annual AI for Good Global Summit.[20] That event focuses on supporting the UN's seventeen Sustainable Development Goals (see Figure 1.1),[21] but the ITU's effort so far is only to be helpful in bringing researchers, corporate leaders, and government policy-makers together to discuss their efforts. There is no enforcement or regulatory effort, even on issues such as lethal autonomous weapons systems (LAWS). Progress on outlawing LAWS has been slow, hampered by nations that oppose it, differences in attitudes about defensive and offensive weapons, and the difficulty of making enforceable policies. More vigorous efforts, akin to the IAEA, would have to be put in place to make the UN effective with HCAI.

Examples of enforcement or regulatory effort may emerge from individual countries. In the United States, government agencies already play key roles in improving automated systems, so they could begin to address HCAI systems.[22] The US National Transportation Safety Board (NTSB) has a long history as a trusted investigator of aviation, ship, train, and other disasters, in part because the US Congress funds it as an independent agency outside the usual executive branch departments. Their skilled teams arrive at accident scenes to collect data, which become the basis for thoughtful reports with recommendations for improvement.

For example, the NTSB report on the deadly May 2016 Tesla crash criticized the manufacturer's and operator's "overreliance on the automation and a lack of understanding of system limitations." The report recommended that future designs include audit trails in the form of "a standardized set of retrievable data . . . to enable independent assessment of automated vehicle safety and to foster automation system improvements."[23] Furthermore, the report cautioned "this crash is an example of what can happen when automation is introduced 'because we can' without adequate consideration of the human element."

It is reasonable that deadly automobile accidents gain government regulatory attention because there are so many of them and that airplane crashes are investigated because there are so many deaths. Government interventions and regulations are also likely in life-critical businesses such as medical device production, pharmaceutical manufacturing, and healthcare or eldercare facilities.

Resistance to government regulation is understandable, but for consequential and life-critical applications, some form of independent oversight seems likely to reduce harm and accelerate the continuous improvement of products and services. Oversight for consequential applications, such as in finance and credit granting, is important because so many people are affected. For lightweight recommender and many consumer applications, government regulation could be modest, except when these are used to limit competition or take advantage of vulnerable populations, such as users with disabilities, children, or older adults.[24]

Skeptics also point to regulatory capture of government agencies, the practice whereby corporate leaders having close connections with government agency staff gain appointments in regulatory agencies for their own industry. These corporate leaders who work in government may be informed professionals, but many people doubt that they will take strong positions which would anger their former colleagues.

A broad National Algorithms Safety Board proposal has provoked discussions,[25] but adding HCAI expertise to existing oversight and regulatory agencies is a more practical approach. This makes sense since existing regulatory agencies will push to extend their oversight role and because the policies need to be attuned to the needs of different industries. This is just what several

US government agencies have done in their current efforts to review HCAI projects.

A good example is the US Food and Drug Administration (FDA), which wrote a carefully considered plan for regulation of AI and machine learning software updates in medical devices, such as intensive care units (ICUs) and skin lesion image analysis apps. They invited discussion of how these approaches "have the potential to adapt and optimize device performance in real-time to continuously improve healthcare for patients" and recognized that the FDA had to act "to ensure that safe and effective technology reaches users."[26]

Similarly, the US Federal Aviation Administration (FAA) Software and Systems Branch has been dealing with AI-based adaptive software in cockpit systems that changes its behavior based on current data from aircraft sensors. Advocates see opportunities to improve safety and performance, but pilots, air-traffic controllers, and regulators worry about unpredictable behavior. The European Union Aviation Safety Agency pushed forward in 2020 with a fifteen-year roadmap for a "human-centric approach to AI in aviation," which emphasizes the need for trustworthiness based on accountability, oversight, and transparency.[27]

Starting in 2019, the US National Institute of Standards and Technology was given a major role in assessing AI trustworthiness and explainability. Their workshops, reports, and websites provide useful information.[28] Another major effort is the Final Report of the US National Security Commission on Artificial Intelligence,[29] which makes extensive recommendations about dramatically expanding research and implementation of AI systems to support national security. This report warns of the competition with China, seeking to preserve US leadership in AI, but it would have been stronger if it gave more credibility to partnerships, collaboration, and diplomatic approaches. The report suggests directions for implementing potential regulation, oversight, education, and substantially increased funding to pursue explainability, visualization, and enhanced human–AI interaction.

Another US government agency active in AI and algorithms is the Federal Trade Commission (FTC). It claims familiarity with automated decision-making, which goes back to their work on the Fair Credit Reporting Act of 1970, so it claims to be ready to deal with AI and machine learning. The FTC fights unfair and deceptive practices with strong and clear advice to financial and credit-granting companies that they must be transparent and be able to explain their AI-based decisions to consumers who are denied services. Their guideline for companies states: "This means that you must know what data is used in your model and how that data is used to arrive at a decision. And you must be able to explain that to the consumer."[30] Skeptics may question how strongly these guidelines are enforced, but their website provides data and visualizations that report on the return of more than $1 billion to more than 7 million consumers in the past two years.

Critics of the major technology companies have raised concerns about AI-based surveillance systems, which violate personal privacy using facial recognition and analysis of voluminous data sets of personal data. Harvard Business professor Shoshanna Zuboff and others use the term "surveillance capitalism" to describe the practices by which major companies, especially Facebook and Google, profit from their vast resources of personal data by selling targeted advertisements.[31] Their AI algorithms are especially effective in using personal data to predict which group of people will buy a product, respond to a political advertisement, or share a fake news story.

Zuboff claims that the business models of large technology companies are built on practices that invade privacy, surreptitiously persuade readers, and covertly reduce their choices. HCAI design strategies might give users better user interfaces with clearer choices about protecting their privacy so they can limit the data collected about them and can have easiser control over what information is presented to them. However, as Zuboff points out, the business models of these companies would be shaken by giving users more control, as shown by Facebook's fierce reaction when Apple gave their users ways to limit what data was sent to Facebook. While the European Union has taken steps to regulate some of these companies, the UK and United States are more reluctant to use regulatory powers.

Many AI industry leaders and government policy-makers fear that government regulation would limit innovation, but when done carefully, regulation can accelerate innovation as it did with automobile safety and fuel efficiency. A US government memorandum by Russell T. Vought, Director of the Office of Management and Budget, for Executive Branch Departments and Agencies offered ten principles for "stewardship of AI applications."[32] The memorandum suggests: "The private sector and other stakeholders may develop voluntary consensus standards that concern AI applications, which provide nonregulatory approaches to manage risks associated with AI applications that are potentially more adaptable to the demands of a rapidly evolving technology."

A 2020 White House report seeks to "ensure that regulations guiding the development and use of AI are supportive of innovation and not overly burdensome."[33] The principles were to "ensure public engagement, limit regulatory overreach, and promote trustworthy AI." Vought later updated his memorandum to reiterate this limited role of regulation: "Federal agencies must avoid regulatory or non-regulatory actions that needlessly hamper AI innovation and growth."[34] On the other hand, there is a need to protect the public from biased systems and regulatory capture, in which industry advocates set weak regulations.[35] Without regulation of social media platforms, hate speech, misinformation, and ethnical and racial attacks have spread widely because it serves the business interests of the platforms, rather than the public good. In some countries, regional, state, or local governments could become influential in trying fresh ideas that become valuable precedents. The future is likely to bring increased regulation of the companies and practices that are used in HCAI systems to ensure fair business practices, promote safe use by consumers, and limit misinformation and hate speech.

CHAPTER 23

Summary and Skeptic's Corner

As soon as algorithms—and especially robotics—have effects in the world, they must be regulated and their programmers subject to ethical and legal responsibility for the harms they cause…. Only human reviewers with adequate expertise and power can detect, defuse, and deflect most of these harms.

Frank Pasquale, *New Laws of Robotics (2020)*

Human-centered artificial intelligence (HCAI) systems represent a new synthesis that raises the importance of human performance and human experience. The fifteen recommendations for governance structures to create reliable, safe, and trustworthy systems will enable designers to translate widely discussed ethical principles into professional practices in large organizations with clear schedules. These recommendations are summarized in the four levels of governance structures: (1) reliable systems based on sound software engineering practices, (2) safety culture through business management strategies, (3) trustworthy certification by independent oversight, and (4) regulation by government agencies (Figure 18.2).

These diverse concerns mean that drawing researchers and practitioners from diverse disciplines is more likely to lead to success.[1] These HCAI systems will be well received if industry leaders go beyond positive statements about fairness, transparency, accountability, security, and privacy to support specific practices that demonstrate success in addressing the genuine concerns of many observers. Fairness is easy to say but hard to ensure, especially as contexts of use change. Transparency can be paraded by allowing access to code, but the complexity of real programs makes it difficult or impossible to know what it will accomplish. Beyond preventing failures, business leaders would do well to commit themselves to raise human self-efficacy, encourage creativity, clarify responsibility, and facilitate social connections. They should recognize that fairness, transparency, and other attributes are competitive advantages that will be increasingly valued.

The proposed governance structures face many challenges. No industry will implement all fifteen recommendations in the four levels. Each recommendation requires research and testing to validate effectiveness, and refinement based on the realities of each implementation. Another complexity is that real HCAI systems have many components from diverse providers, which means that some recommendations, such as software, data, and user experience testing can be accomplished for a component, but may be more difficult for a complete system. Formal methods and thorough testing may be possible for an airbag deployment algorithm, but independent oversight reviews may be more relevant for a self-driving car system.

Just as each home evolves over time, HCAI systems will be adapted to meet changing desires and demands. Adaptations will integrate new HCAI technologies, the needs of different application domains, and the changing expectations of all stakeholders.

Global interest in HCAI systems is demonstrated by the activities of the United Nations International Telecommunications Union and its thirty-five UN partner agencies. They seek to apply AI to the seventeen influential UN Sustainable Development Goals,[2] all of which combine technology developments with behavioral changes, to improve healthcare, wellness, environmental protection, and human rights. Global efforts on HCAI are tracked by the OECD Policy Observatory and the Michael Dukakis Center for AI and Digital Policy, which publishes an annual Social Contract Index documenting how well twenty-five countries pursue democratic policies for HCAI systems.[3]

The massive interest in ethical, social, economic, human rights, social justice, and responsible design is a positive sign for those who wish to see HCAI applied to social good and preserving the environment. Skeptics fear that poor design will lead to failures, bias, privacy violations, and uncontrolled systems, while malicious actors will misuse AI's powers to spread misinformation, threaten security, expand cybercrime, and disrupt utility services. More dire predictions come in discussions of lethal autonomous weapons systems, undermining of democratic institutions, racial bias, and surveillance capitalism. Critics, like Microsoft's Kate Crawford, see the extractive nature of AI, which threatens the environment, fosters unhealthy working conditions, and mistreats users.[4]

These are serious concerns that deserve ample attention, but the intense efforts by well-intentioned researchers, business leaders, government policy makers, and civil society organizations suggest more positive outcomes are possible. The new synthesis will take decades to be widely adopted, but human-centered design thinking can help to build successful future societies in which human values of rights, justice, and dignity are advanced. This book is devoted to fostering positive mindsets and constructive actions that support human self-efficacy, creativity, responsibility, and social connections.

PART 5

Where Do We Go from Here?

24 Introduction: Driving HCAI forward

25 Assessing Trustworthiness

26 Caring for and Learning from Our Older Adults

27 Summary and Skeptic's Corner

The main ideas of this book are the HCAI framework (Part 2), design metaphors (Part 3), and governance structures (Part 4). These ideas clarify how human-centered thinking will help bring the powerful AI algorithms into widespread use by way of reliable, safe, and trustworthy systems.

AI's expansion from a focus on algorithms to include user experience design methods is happening in practitioner and research communities, which now regularly discuss ethics, responsible AI, fairness, explainability, and other topics. Designers increasingly appreciate how the HCAI framework guides them to designs that enable high levels of human control and high levels of automation. The design metaphors that work well often combine features that bring reliable automation for some tasks and user-oriented control panels for others. Business leaders and policy-makers are coming to understand that HCAI governance structures bring competitive advantages because reliable, safe, and trustworthy systems are valued by users. Substantial global interest in governance structures is turning into actionable policies adopted by regional organizations, nations, industry leaders, and corporate managers.

There are many appealing directions for future HCAI research and development of products and services. Chapter 24 suggests a few HCAI projects and next steps to support adoption of HCAI thinking in academia, industry, government, and non-governmental organizations with courses, guidelines, and success stories.

Chapter 25 takes on the central challenge of assessing trustworthiness and other widely discussed attributes of HCAI systems. When objective measures are impossible, subjective measures of stakeholder perceptions become attractive. Chapter 26 puts the ideas from this book to work on the topic of caring for and learning from older adults. Chapter 27 closes with a summary and reaffirms the goals of this book.

CHAPTER 24

Introduction: Driving HCAI Forward

The real question before us lies here: do these instruments further life and enhance its values, or not? . . . The machine itself makes no demands and holds out no promises: it is the human spirit that makes demands and keeps promises.

Lewis Mumford, *Technics and Civilization (1934)*

The expansion of AI thinking to include HCAI methods is a central goal of this book. This means gathering user requirements, adherence to design guidelines, iterative testing with users, and continuous evaluation once the product or service is released. Including these methods in education and practice will take persistent efforts from many sources in academia, business, government, and civic society organizations. This chapter begins with a few examples of challenges for research and development projects. Then it suggests ways for universities, businesses, and governments to accelerate the adoption of HCAI.

Research Directions

HCAI topics offer vibrant research possibilities and lively application contexts which expand in many alluring directions. Technically oriented researchers will want to improve deep learning algorithms and their variations, while socially oriented researchers will reduce bias to ensure fair, accurate, and helpful systems. Ethicists will offer fresh interpretations, while practitioners build better tools for developers. Policy-makers will formulate national agendas, while agency staffers will sort out the realities of enforcing rules and regulations, and funding agencies will choose promising research proposals.

The seventeen UN's Sustainable Development Goals[1] are attractive to many researchers as are the fourteen Grand Challenges from the US National Academy of Engineering, but new goals are proposed with regularity.[2] A set of UK Grand Challenge missions, announced in 2021, address four topics: artificial intelligence and data, ageing society, clean growth, and the future of mobility.[3] Grand Challenges, which include HCAI themes, have also been issued in Canada, Japan, South Korea, Germany, and elsewhere. Separately, grand challenges have been issued by leaders in topics such as genomic research, cancer prevention, space exploration, and environmental protection. Another source of inspirational grand challenges are non-profit organizations like the Bill and Melinda Gates Foundation[4] and the XPRIZE Foundation.[5]

There are grand challenges that have been active for decades, such as controlled fusion reactions to generate electricity, weather control to bring or stop rain, and ways to reduce antibiotic resistance, all of which could benefit from AI algorithms and HCAI designs. Newer grand challenges are to use HCAI to optimize performance for wind turbines, solar panels, electric vehicle charging networks, and other technologies that respond to the climate crisis.

Three challenges that could benefit from HCAI are boosting citizen science, stopping misinformation, and finding new treatments and vaccines for major diseases. These applications will include AI algorithms and HCAI designs in ways that become natural and nearly invisible, part of the expected landscape of familiar technologies benefitting billions of people who may not even be aware that they are using these advanced technologies. Just as users assume there are computer chips embedded in many devices, they will assume that AI algorithms and well-designed HCAI supertools, tele-bots, and active appliances will work as they expect. They will think more about what they want to do, rather than the technologies they are using.

Boosting Citizen Science

Environmental issues are especially relevant to those who call themselves citizen scientists. Ordinary and some extraordinary people who live anywhere can contribute to research projects, partly motivated by a desire to learn and partly motivated by contributing to their community and a cause that is greater than themselves. The projects that they contribute to are many and varied, from nature, to biochemistry, to history, to anthropology—you name it and there is probably a citizen science project with that focus. Typically the projects are organized by scientists or other professionals and citizens who volunteer to help collect and analyze data. Increasingly, citizen scientists participate in planning and managing projects and in writing public reports and academic papers.[6]

There are thousands of citizen science projects. Some stand out for their size and longevity such as eBird, a Cornell University project that has more than 100 million reports about bird sightings, behavior, and migrations.[7] The Oxford University Zooniverse effort supports more than 100 projects.[8] Zooniverse began with the Galaxy Zoo project to label 150,000 images of spiral and globular cluster galaxies. Three master's degree students, Nate Agrin, Jessica Kline, and Ken-ichi Ueda, from the School of Information at the University of California-Berkeley started the iNaturalist project in 2008 to collect biodiversity data.[9] Their efforts blossomed as a joint initiative with the California Academy of Sciences and the National Geographic Society, so that by February 2021, iNaturalist boasts of 60 million reports on more than 320,000 species collected by more than 3 million community members. Each of these three major efforts have led to hundreds of peer-reviewed scientific papers and numerous stories in popular media. As of June 2021, the US federal government and its agencies support 491 citizen science projects, through diverse agencies such as the National Park Service, National Oceanic and Atmospheric Administration, NASA, and Library of Congress.[10] Their tag line is "Helping federal agencies accelerate innovation through public participation."

Dealing with the large volumes of data produced by citizen science projects is a challenge even in the age of low-cost, powerful computers. So, how do these projects ensure high-quality, reliable data while at the same time offering enriching experiences to the hundreds and thousands of citizen scientists and scientists who donate their time and energy? One answer to this question lies in bringing the skills of the citizens together with the power of AI.[11] Of course, this is already happening in some projects that use computer vision and deep learning methods to identify animal species in camera trap photos, count the number of birds flying overhead, and identify trees from photos of individual leaves.[12] Even more specific tasks are to identify individual zebras by their distinctive black and white stripes or whales by their barnacles, dorsal fins, fluke shapes, and tail-marking patterns.[13] These innovative successes are promising, but turning research prototypes into supertools that can be used reliably by the vast number of citizen scientists in different contexts remains to be done.

Acoustic recognition is a steadily growing technology that enables bird calls and songs to be used to identify the species and maybe understand what their meanings are. Similarly, whale and dolphin whistles can be used to track movements of specific individuals and pods of these remarkable mammals. A natural next step would be to build on the initial efforts to understand the language and dialog within pods of dolphins, and then engage with them through AI-generated whistles. Talking to animals seems like an excellent grand challenge. We would learn so much about the natural world, possibly giving us a clearer understanding of human abilities and limitations. A related goal would be to understand how dog trainers and *horse whisperers* (sometimes called natural horsemanship) have learned to be so effective in developing rapport in working with animals.

The Seek app for mobile devices is designed to inspire kids to look at the plants and creatures with which they share their world, identify them, and learn more about them (Figure 24.1).[14] It's a kid's version of the widely used

Fig 24.1 Citizen science application Seek by iNaturalist identifies plants, fungi, and animals using computer vision techniques. This fungus was identified as being in the Class Agaricomycetes.

Source: help+seek@inaturalist.org

iNaturalist app and website, but unlike iNaturalist, registration is not required and data are not collected about users, so kids are safe from predation and unwanted attention. Seek was designed by doctoral student Grant Van Horn, an adjunct scientist at iNaturalist, who developed the AI algorithms to power Seek. These AI algorithms use iNaturalist's huge database of crowdsourced, classified species data to predict the organism that the child focuses on with a smartphone camera, based on image analysis, geographical location, and time of year.[15] Often Seek suggests several alternatives inviting the child to compare with the plant, fungus, or animal they see to select possible matches. Sometimes the matches only get as far as a genus but at other times only a single correct image is offered.

Researchers who study citizen science projects want to understand what gets different groups of people—old/young, men/women, wealthy/poor—to not only join a project but become active in it for months and years. The iNaturalist leaderboard shows that some participants have contributed more than 6000 observations in a year and some experts who review the observations had identified more than 40,000 posts in a year.[16] The intense devotion of citizen scientists shows how much they value these projects. Similarly, the Wikipedia community engages tens of thousands of editors to write, improve, and sometimes delete articles for the benefit of more than a billion readers. Data analysis from these and other large projects will clarify how better AI and HCAI design could help tap the vast potential for participation in these and other grand challenge projects.

Some citizen science activities are evolving into more than massive research teams that publish academic papers.[17] Many citizen scientists are concerned about the loss of biodiversity through extinctions and the dramatic reduction in animal populations, especially during the past thirty years. Insects, such as honey bees, have suffered widespread colony collapses, and African elephant populations have dropped from 10 million in 1930 to under 400,000 today. The efforts to reverse these losses is helped by HCAI systems using machine learning, sensor data analysis, and image recognition. These techniques allow citizen scientists to track animal movements, monitor environmental pollutants, and prevent poaching. Restoring habitats or *rewilding* will take even more concerted efforts, energized by social media influencers who are devoted to these environmental issues.

Imagine that citizen science efforts grow by a factor of ten in the next decade, educating many people, engaging them to contribute to research, and turning some of them into activists who organize to fight for clean water, clean air, biodiversity, and environmental restoration. What forms of HCAI applications could help them find collaborators, organize lobbying efforts to change national policies, and influence investors to support corporations whose business models preserve the environment?

Stopping Misinformation

One of the perils of social media use is the widespread dissemination of misinformation and related problems like conspiracy theories, hate speech, and bullying. The process of slowing or stopping misinformation is often called content moderation, but it is a daunting task since billions of posts are made daily. Compelling misinformation and related stories during the COVID-19 crisis contributed to the resistance and unwillingness of many people to follow scientific guidance about social distancing, mask use, and vaccines. Misinformation is often engaging and therefore social media users spread it more rapidly than accurate reporting from government health officials or respected news media.[18] Novel algorithms generate *deep fakes*, fabricated images, voices, and videos of well-known figures inserted into protest rallies, making spurious statements, can be spread by vast robotic *bot farms* with millions of computers posting and sharing billions of messages.

While misinformation in its many forms may be spread by individuals and fringe organizations, there are also concerted efforts from governments, such as the thirty-year efforts of Russian intelligence agencies: the Federal Security Service (FSB), the Foreign Intelligence Service (SVR), and the Main Intelligence Directorate (GRU).[19] Orchestrated by Vladimir Putin using a carefully constructed plan called *active measures*, tens of thousands of agents developed compelling false stories that contained an element of truth or support from respected individuals. These were spread through low-profile publications around the world, and then amplified to propagate inflammatory stories such as that the HIV AIDS virus was created by the US military at Fort Detrick, Maryland and that Hilary Clinton's staff was running a child sex-trafficking operation in the basement of the Comet Pizza restaurant in Washington, DC. Active measures also used more than 50,000 fake social media accounts to provoke conspiracy theories, influence elections, launch anti-vaccination campaigns, and incite racial hatred online and at in-person protests.

Social media platforms, like Facebook, Instagram, YouTube, Reddit, and Twitter, struggle to identify and stop misinformation, but their efforts may be slowed by the fact that they benefit from the increased engagement that misinformation elicits. The AI algorithms used in Facebook News Feed and other platforms feature posts that have high numbers of likes or shares, spreading them even faster. While critics lobby the social media platforms to increase their content moderation efforts, government pressure has been weak. The challenge in setting these policies is to balance free expression with the desire to keep the platform safe.

The European Union's (EU) Code of Practice on Disinformation from 2018 defines misinformation as "verifiably false or misleading information" designed for economic gain, deception, or "threats to democratic political and policy-making processes as well as public goods such as the protection of EU citizens' health, the environment or security."[20]

Facebook works with the independent International Fact-Checking Network and other organizations to do the difficult task of deciding whether a social media post is misinformation or simply a protected opinion. Alon Halevy and his team at Facebook describe the many problems they face, including incitement to violence, fake news, hate speech, sexual solicitation, intellectual property violations, and dozens of others.[21] When dangerous misinformation is posted, the social media platforms remove it or demote it (reducing its spread) as rapidly as possible, but when billions of posts are issued daily this is a difficult task. The task is made even more difficult because malicious actors and some governments actively spread misinformation, using tens of thousands of faked accounts to re-post the misinformation in minutes.

Halevy's team writes: "Letting violating content stay on the network can have very severe consequences to individuals and to society. Hence, machine learning for integrity must err on the side of increasing recall and then use content reviewers to make the final decisions."[22] This combined approach of algorithms and human decision-making is very much in the spirit of HCAI. Detecting and removing these fake accounts help slow the misinformation, but the ever-growing resources of those who spread misinformation counters the progress that the platforms make.

Facebook has established an Oversight Board with forty prestigious international members to help guide the company in their difficult decisions about balancing free speech with the need to stop hate speech, bullying, incitement of violence, and harmful misinformation.[23] While Facebook gave this board its own funds and the authority to decide what content is removed, skeptics question its independence because Facebook selected the members.

Social media misinformation was alleged to have been a component of election interference by Cambridge Analytica in India, Brazil, the United

Kingdom, and the United States in 2016. When Facebook's chief executive Mark Zuckerberg testified before the US Congress in 2018 he promised that AI was "going to be the scalable way to identify and root out most of this harmful content,"[24] but the problems remain. Facebook's twice-yearly Community Standards and Enforcement reports describe how often content was removed, fact-checked, or demoted, how many appeals there were, and how many appeals led to restoring content.[25] This is helpful, but Facebook resists pressure to be more vigorous in reducing misinformation and anonymous bot accounts.

While removing every offensive post is impossible, reducing their prominence and stopping anonymous bot accounts are worthy endeavors. However, questions remain about how much effort social media platforms need to spend and what regulatory pressures would get Facebook to change its business model. Twitter Rules[26] and the YouTube Community Guidelines[27] are further examples of the efforts that social media platforms are making to prevent misinformation in its multiple forms. Twitter's decision to stop taking political ads was a positive step in reducing election interference.

Two positive examples of stopping misinformation suggest that progress is possible. Google fought a war with those who sought to game their search engine algorithms so as to promote restaurants, stores, or products to the top of Google search results page. A simple strategy used by devious businesses is to repeat the company or product name dozens of times invisibly on a website, while more complex strategies are to hire bot farms to leave positive reviews and link to the website, making it seem more popular than it is. Google assigned more than 3000 employees and developed sophisticated algorithms to counter these commercial deceptions, but Google had a strong motivation to make sure their search results were trusted. A second positive example is about Facebook's team in Germany, where hate speech laws are strongly enforced. Initially, Facebook did poorly in stopping hateful posts, leading to a €2 million fine, which is a tiny fraction of Facebook's revenues. However, the bad publicity and threats of much larger fines pushed Facebook to hire more than 1000 content checkers who used increasingly sophisticated AI algorithms to detect hate speech.

Other hate speech incitements to violence occurred in Myanmar, Ethiopia, India, and other countries around the world. Hate speech and misinformation played major roles in fomenting the January 6, 2021 insurrection at the US Capitol. Falsehoods about President Donald Trump's loss of the election, claiming fraudulent voting, rigged voting machines, and lost ballots stirred up violent protesters who stormed the Capitol to stop the election certification process, resulting in five deaths.

The belief that the Internet, the World Wide Web, and social media would give marginalized voices a greater say has been realized, but when malicious actors use this right, their efforts can harm individuals, be deadly to whole communities, and threaten formerly stable governments. More effective algorithms and better human control are necessary to ensure safe public discussions. While anonymity was always a valued principle for Internet services, it is tempered by requirements, such as Facebook's rule that users must register with "the name they go by in everyday life" and they can only have one identity.[28] These rules are often violated, so stricter enforcement and greater individual responsibility may help to reduce misuse.

If social media platforms are held responsible and liable for the harmful and illegal activity promoted on their sites, then these platforms could become more reliable, safe, and trustworthy. The magnitude and importance of this problem is huge, threatening established governments, corporations, and individuals. Stopping misinformation will require substantial investment and creative contributions from AI researchers and HCAI developers, as well as from government and business leaders.

Finding New Treatments and Vaccines for Major Diseases

The COVID-19 crisis of 2020–2021 raised worldwide attention to the problem of finding treatments for those who were infected and creating vaccines to prevent infections. Underlying both problems is the need to understand how DNA sequences of amino acid chains lead to proteins with distinctive 3-D structures. The proteins are fabricated in a linear way and then fold up in unpredictable ways based on attraction and repulsion among the hundreds or thousands of amino acids. Within milliseconds they fold into coils, sheets, and other structures, which determine the biological function of each protein.

DeepMind, a Google subsidiary in London, developed AlphaFold and the much improved AlphaFold 2 to predict how linear chains of hundreds or thousands of amino acids fold into 3-D protein structures. This has been a grand challenge for more than fifty years, but AlphaFold 2 has exceeded performance of other approaches in an annual contest called Critical Assessment of Techniques for Protein Structure Prediction (CASP). AlphaFold 2's deep learning program is trained on a database of 170,000 proteins. By November 2020, AlphaFold 2 had reliable predictions for two-thirds of the proteins that were in the

CASP contest, beating other competitors on eighty-eight of the ninety-seven targets. Responses to this success have been enthusiastic, with Nobel Prize-winning structural biologist Venki Ramakrishnan calling AlphaFold 2's success "a stunning advance on the protein folding problem."[29]

The implications are still emerging as biomedical researchers push to understand how the molecular structures influence biological processes, such as a virus's invasion of a cell membrane. Accurate protein folding results are one step in a larger process to develop treatments or vaccines. This is an important success for AI deep learning algorithms, but the next steps will be for biomedical researchers and drug developers to explore how known medications will react with virus molecules.

Finding candidate treatments and vaccines is an important first step, but HCAI methods and visualization tools are needed to analyze the data from randomized clinical trials with human subjects. Data analysis is move effective when statistical methods are combined with visualization to find data quality errors, unusual patterns, and important anomalies. These randomized clinical trials assess the effectiveness and safety with diverse people at different stages of life who have other conditions that could trigger deadly side effects. Interaction effects with other medications and the special needs of pregnant women or young children need to be understood to make successful treatments and vaccines.

As a greater fraction of the world's population come to expect better healthcare that increases life expectancy, the expectation and demand will grow for prevention and treatment of diseases, including cancer, heart–lung problems, and all forms of bacterial and viral infections. Raising the standard of living and medical care for the poorest regions will require creative low-cost and easily implementable preventions and treatments. Solving these problems will also take creative approaches to educating and informing people in their own languages, while being attentive to cultural differences. By combining the lessons about increasing citizen science and reducing misinformation, it may be possible to increase awareness of how individuals, communities, and regional leaders can adopt practices that improve health to prevent diseases.

Newer grand challenges will be raised regularly as problems and expectations rise. There will always be frontiers for researchers to push past and opportunities for innovative entrepreneurs. Some people believe that allowing researchers to pursue their curiosity freely lays the foundation for big breakthroughs decades later. This is certainly true in some circumstances, but an increasingly appreciated alternative is that when researchers work with practitioners on real problems, big breakthroughs in foundational research happen more often. This idea was popularized by Princeton University political scientist Donald Stokes in his book *Pasteur's Quadrant: Basic Science and Technological Innovation*.[30] Stokes describes how Louis Pasteur's efforts to help dairy farmers preserve freshness led to pasteurization and how his work with vintners to prevent wine from turning into vinegar led to sterilization methods to kill the harmful bacteria. These practical successes laid the basis for the big breakthrough of the germ theory of disease and an understanding of the powerful role bacteria played in health. They also laid the basis for the remarkable idea of vaccinations to prevent diseases.

Many others have since refined the methods and developed the evidence that working with practitioners has a higher chance of leading to big breakthroughs than solitary work in a laboratory.[31] The idea of working with practitioners on real problems is also tied to the empirical methods of HCAI.

Research Groups and Courses

HCAI research groups are sprouting up in many universities, companies, and beyond. Stanford University's Institute for Human-Centered AI[32] was an early, well-funded effort that brought together 140 faculty members. They run seminars and symposia that attract thousands of people in person and virtually. Hundreds of universities around the world have opened up research groups devoted to HCAI and variant themes, such as human-compatible AI, responsible AI, ethical AI, and humane AI (see partial list in Chapter 21, pp. 203–4).

Academic course instructors who cover the technical and programming aspects of machine and deep learning algorithms are expanding to include discussions of ethics. The University of Toronto's Centre for Ethics offers a course with an interdisciplinary set of guest speakers followed by group discussions. Many campuses are adding ethics courses, which are likely to have the strongest effect if they are inside computer science courses, thereby reaching those who are likely to do research and development for HCAI systems.[33] Business schools, like MIT's Sloan School of Management, promote the idea the ethics analyses and ethical design of HCAI systems is a competitive advantage.

HCAI methods are gradually being added to AI courses to address design of user interfaces for control panels and evaluation methods based on usability testing, observation, and interviews. However, more vigorous activity comes from human–computer interaction course instructors who now cover AI methods to meet the strong demand for the combined skills. In the United

States, Carnegie Mellon University has an admirable set of courses on HCAI from several units, as do the University of Illinois, Virginia Tech, and other US campuses. In the UK, Imperial University, University College London, Oxford, Cambridge, and many others are expanding their efforts on HCAI topics. In Denmark, Germany, Italy, France, the Netherlands, and many European countries these topics are often designed to align with the European General Data Protection Regulation (GDPR) requirements of explainability for AI systems. Other efforts in China, India, South Korea, and Japan add to the worldwide interest.

Professional training courses are also moving to integrate ethical issues and now usability methods. An online course from Coursera, "Artificial Intelligence Ethics in Action," uses project-oriented techniques to analyze ethical AI issues,[34] while edX offers "Ethics in AI and Big Data," teaching ethical frameworks for "technology and business initiatives to add transparency, build trust, and drive adoption."[35] These business-oriented courses make the case that ethical approaches should increase the appeal of products and services.

Conferences and Journals

As research and education grows, so too do the publications on HCAI at conferences and in journals. Traditional AI conferences, such as the Association for the Advancement of AI (AAAI), International Joint Conference on AI (IJCAI), and the Neural Information Processing Systems Conference (NeurIPS), draw more than 10,000 attendees each year, often reaching the capacity of their conference venues. The ACM's Computer–Human Interaction conference and the HCI International Conference draw several thousand attendees each year. Specialized topic conferences are held around the world, now including HCAI themes. Conferences in almost every discipline now include papers on AI and HCAI. The rise in popularity of these topics is astonishing.

These conferences are rapidly adding ethical and human-centered design topics to their calls for papers. The NeurIPS conference is admirable for requiring paper authors to add a section on "the broader impact of their work, including possible societal consequences—both positive and negative."[36] Even strong technical papers that are flagged for ethical lapses have been rejected. However, the community of organizers, reviewers, and authors is still struggling to agree on how to assess the broader impacts of foundational research and even for application research.[37]

Microsoft's AI researcher Hanna Wallach gave a keynote talk at the NeurIPS workshop on broader impact in which she criticized some in the AI community who promoted a "culture of immodesty where overselling is the norm and talking about limitations and negative results are discouraged." She called for greater awareness of broader impacts and the dangers of some research.[38] Other speakers and many authors are shifting to discuss ethical issues, responsible AI, and human values in AI systems, which move them closer to HCAI aspirations.

A model for HCAI conference organizers to follow is the US National Institute of Standards and Technology (NIST) Text REtrieval Conference (TREC) that dramatically improved information retrieval research over a thirty-year period as it matured into the widely used search engines.[39] TREC was distinctive in that participants had to contribute to at least one of the tracks to attend, making it an engaging workshop. Donna Harman initiated TREC and Ellen Voorhees has continued to run these annual conferences. They built on a long tradition of developing reusable data sets and metrics, such as precision and recall, to evaluate the quality of search systems. A ground truth data set consists of queries, search results, and relevance judgments for each result. Precision (0–100%) indicates the percentage of documents retrieved that are relevant for a searcher's query. A 70% precision means that if fifty documents are retrieved, then thirty-five of them are relevant and fifteen are not. Recall (0–100%) indicates the percentage of all documents in a collection relevant for a user's query that are retrieved. A 70% recall means that if thirty-five relevant documents are retrieved, then there are another fifteen in the data set that are also relevant, but were not retrieved.

Precision and recall measures require documents in a data set to be marked for relevance to each query that is tested, which requires a great deal of effort, making it prohibitive for web-scale collections. However, the development of new sample-based evaluation methods made it possible for the TREC organizers to run five to twelve search tasks each year that covered health, legal, web pages, social media, and other data sets. The competition tracks also addressed different tasks, such as interactive retrieval, filtering, recommendation, summarization, question answering, and data augmentation. As the conference grew, more than 100 people from dozens of research groups participated each year, leading to hundreds of papers that accelerated research and commercial development. The annual cost was about $1 million, but the payoffs were estimated to be hundreds of millions of dollars in commercial system successes.

An annual TRUstworthiness Conference, maybe called TRUC, could advance HCAI by developing standard challenges with trustworthiness measures that might be based on precision and recall. Numeric measures of trustworthiness have been done for some topics, such as facial recognition accuracy, which is similar to an information retrieval task, but other HCAI attributes (Chapter 25) will require new measures and ground truth data to compare algorithms as Joy Buolamwini and Timnit Gebru did so successfully to show racial and gender bias for facial recognition algorithms.[40] Within the AI research community the conference on Empirical Methods in Natural Language Processing is devoted to rigorous studies of algorithms on large data sets and evolved to include user performance. Other HCAI conferences with user studies are emerging from discourse and dialog studies,[41] machine translation,[42] and computational linguistics.[43]

Journal editors are also being challenged about their publication of some AI papers which have been seen as irresponsible or unethical, for example suggesting that facial recognition algorithms could identify criminal intent, personality, or political leanings. These revivals of discredited phrenology theories, which assume that head and skull shape determine behavior and attitude, are generally considered irresponsible, leading to inappropriate use by police. But the attraction to controversial articles with grand promises has seduced even highly respected journals.

The rise of concern about impact on society is a step forward, but many researchers feel that this is outside their range of knowledge or concern. This controversy is reflected in increasing public discussions about responsible research and papers in venues such as the *Journal of Responsible Innovation*.[44] While some foundational researchers feel that they should be free to follow their interests and curiosity, there is a growing awareness that working with off-campus partners on genuine problems leads to validated practical solutions and stronger foundational research.

Dozens of existing journals add special issues on ethics and HCAI topics, while new journals are being started to serve the growing interest and need. The growth in journal papers and online archives such as arXiv has transformed publishing. Open access strategies are becoming more common each year to allow free access to readers around the world. Since arXiv does no reviewing, publications are made available overnight, which speeds work in the hot topics of AI and HCAI.

Journals and professional societies have codes of ethics to cover their work, but a more focused approach might be a checklist for AI and HCAI papers that covers issues such as: are the research questions reasonable? Is the training data unbiased? Have proper programming and testing methods been used, and are the claims in harmony with the work? Additionally, there might be a writing style guide to limit what Hanna Wallach called "immodesty" and "overselling," while ensuring that limitations, conflicts of interest, and broader impacts are discussed adequately. A further problem is the difficulty of ensuring a research tradition of reproducibility, which means that other researchers can carry out the same study to verify that they get the same results. Many papers depend on large proprietary programs, huge data sets, and specialized hardware, which make it difficult for other groups, especially academic groups, to reproduce the results.

A final difficulty with research quality is the growing recognition that research results may not transfer when applied to real problems in different contexts. A stunning paper published on arXiv by thirty-three Google employees and seven others labeled the problem as *underspecification*, which the authors describe as the failure of their programs to perform well once they were deployed.[45] They warn that "underspecification is ubiquitous in modern applications of [machine learning] ML, and has substantial practical implications," but they recommend improved methods and testing as research directions. This paper focuses on algorithmic implementation issues, but there is some chance that HCAI methods and data visualization tools could help detect these problems in the algorithms and training data earlier and offer greater protection during deployment. Awareness of these problems has encouraged large technology companies to develop more careful techniques to document their algorithms and training data (Chapter 19).

Research Funding

Government research funding groups such as the US National Science Foundation (NSF), UK Engineering and Physical Sciences Research Council (EPSRC), European Research Council (ERC), National Natural Science Foundation of China (NSFC), and others are all increasing their funding of AI research. The expansion to include HCAI is especially apparent in the European, Japanese, and Canadian funding of AI ethics issues. The US NSF's National AI Research Institutes includes "Human–AI Interaction and Collaboration" (discussed in Chapter 22), which supports work on "ethics, fairness, privacy, lack of deception, explainability, protection of vulnerable and protected populations, and participatory and inclusive design."[46]

Corporate research groups have also come to deal with HCAI issues, setting up groups like Google's People and AI Research or Microsoft's Office of Responsible AI. Big tech companies such as Amazon, Facebook, Google, IBM, and Microsoft have teamed up to support the Partnership on AI with substantial funding and more than 100 other organizations who seek to "bring together diverse, global voices to realize the promise of artificial intelligence."[47]

The Japanese AI Research Center (AIRC) is also a partnership, which "aims to promote the implementation of AI in manufacturing, service, healthcare/caregiving, and security, and to strengthen Japan's competitiveness in the manufacturing and service sectors."[48] Other regional research groups are forming around the world.

The journey from ethics to practice is already underway, but the trip will be made smoother by a better foundation and by clarity about what the destination is. Chapter 25 has a list of thirty desirable attributes for HCAI whose definitions may evolve to make them measurable in objective ways. Meanwhile subjective surveys and qualitative evaluations can support comparisons of alternative systems and testing to see how well design ideas increase or decrease the evaluations. My proposed twelve-item questionnaire for assessing trustworthiness is a starting point.

Clarity about the destination is necessary for most projects. An often proposed project is to provide technology support for older adults. The HCAI approach is first to understand user needs, which is what Chapter 26 describes for older adults. It offers three examples of how technology could be used, emphasizing how technology could help older adults to help themselves and advancing the ideas that technology can also help others to learn from older adults. The desire for independent living, self-efficacy, and mentoring others is strong with many older adults. They want to be able to accomplish the activities of daily life and to reach out to help others in their communities. For this challenge and many others, social solutions are likely to complement or amplify technology solutions. Chapter 27 summarizes and offers suggestions about how to overcome the dangers skeptics point out.

CHAPTER 25

Assessing Trustworthiness

The scientific instrument-makers of the eighteenth and nineteenth centuries dramatically advanced the human ability to measure size, duration, temperature, and weight, leading to rapid advances in many disciplines. Their twentieth-century disciples went still further, broadening access to precision measurement for surveyors, physicians, carpenters, cooks, and many others. Lord Kelvin promoted measurement with his memorable statement: "If you cannot measure it, you cannot improve it."

Lord Kelvin's admonition is taught to business school students with the variation that "if you can't measure it, you can't manage it." However, success of business processes, capabilities of job candidates, and safety of manufacturing processes are not as easy to measure as a patient's temperature or a pumpkin's weight.

Equally challenging are evaluations of social systems, psychological attitudes, educational theories, wine vintages, and theatrical performances. In fact, for all our vast abilities to measure physical properties, our methods are limited when it comes to assessing, ranking, or comparing attributes of processes and systems.

The current challenge is to assess the attributes of HCAI systems. There is a great deal of discussion of ethical principles and attributes such as the attributes in Table 25.1, but very few suggestions about how to assess these attributes.[1] As described in Part 2, this book focuses on reliable, safe, and trustworthy attributes by describing how they might be achieved. This chapter focuses on trustworthiness, which is a stronger notion than trust, since trustworthiness emphasizes that the HCAI system deserves the trust that stakeholders grant it. However, trustworthiness is difficult to assess because it varies across applications contexts and over time as algorithms and training data sets are

Table 25.1 *Frequently mentioned attributes of HCAI systems organized into five categories*

General virtues of the system itself

Trustworthy:	Can users trust the system to perform correctly?
Responsible/humane:	Has the system been designed, developed, and tested in a responsible way?
Ethical design:	Were stakeholders involved in the design?
Ethical data:	Were the data collected in an ethical manner?
Ethical use:	Will the system's outcome be used in an ethical manner?
Well-being/benevolence:	Does the system support human health, comfort, and values?
Secure:	How vulnerable is the system to attack?
Private:	Does the system protect a person's identity and data?

Performs well in practice

Robust/agile:	Does the system perform well when inputs change?
Reliable/dependable:	Does the system do the right thing?
Available:	Is the system running when needed?
Resilient/adaptive:	Can the system recover from disruptions?
Testable/verifiable/ validatable/certifiable:	Can the system be tested to verify adherence to requirements?
Safe:	Does the system have a history of safe use?

Clarity to stakeholders

Accurate:	Does the system deliver correct results on test cases and real world cases?
Fair/unbiased:	Are the system's biases understood and reported?
Accountable/liable:	Who or what is responsible for the system's outcome?
Transparent:	Is it clear to an external observer how the system's outcome was produced?
Interpretable/explainable/ intelligible/explicable:	Can the system explain the outcome?
Usable:	Can a human use it easily?

Continued

Table 25.1 *Continued*

Enables independent oversight

Auditable:	Can the system be audited by others for retrospective forensic analysis of failures?
Trackable:	Does the system display status and next steps so human intervention is possible?
Traceable:	Is the system designed to allow tracing back from an outcome to the root cause?
Redressable:	Is there a process for those harmed to request review and compensation?
Insurable:	Does the design permit insurance companies to offer policies?
Recorded:	Does the system record activity for retrospective forensic review?
Open:	Are code and data publicly available for others to review?
Certifiable:	Can it be certified and approved for use?

Complies with accepted practices

Compliant with standards:	Does the system comply with relevant standards, e.g. IEEE P7000 series?
Compliant with accepted software engineering workflows:	Was a trusted process used?

updated. Recognizing that HCAI systems can never be 100% trustworthy should inspire humility among those who develop, manage, and use them.[2]

A recent hike gave me a good lesson about the difference between trusted and trustworthy. At the trailhead a professionally drawn map with detailed elevation data showed the trail going straight up to a scenic viewpoint. I trusted this professional map, but a half-hour into the hike, I came upon an unexpected split in the trail that was not shown on the professional map. A hand-drawn map at the split suggested I should turn left to reach the scenic viewpoint. Since I trusted the professional map, I went straight ahead, but it was not trustworthy. The hand-drawn map turned out to be the trustworthy one. Appearances can be deceiving, so validations of trustworthiness are needed.

Parts 3 and 4 of this book offer design metaphors and governance structures that support other attributes, such as traceability, auditability, explainability, and fairness, but researchers and developers are still struggling to assess how well an HCAI system scores on these attributes. This chapter focuses on assessing trustworthiness. Other scales are needed for the other attributes.

It would be useful to be able to compare two HCAI systems to guide designers by letting them know which changes would do the most to improve the ratings on these attributes. A useful approach would be a form of nutrition label for all the attributes, as is common on food packages, so that consumers can compare products, which is the goal of IBM's Factsheets, Microsoft's Datasheets, and Google's Model Cards.

System tests to validate and verify performance are helpful in identifying errors, but do not assess how reliable, safe, or trustworthy an HCAI system will be when it is put in diverse real-world contexts. Bias testing for the training data and usability testing for user interfaces are also positive steps for identifying problems, but they do not yield measures or complete system assessments or scores. Something like ratings of consumer products or rankings of universities, flawed as they are, would be helpful to decision-makers.

Some research proposals address particular attributes; for example, human factors experts Robert Hoffman and Peter Hancock offer an approach to measuring resilience by way of twenty-seven development procedures, such as tracking anomalies and evaluating data quality.[3] Similar proposals have been made for reliability, availability, and some other attributes, but they all need refinement to gain wide acceptance.

For some attributes, scoring can be accomplished by objective assessment or by subjective assessments of components. Beyond these methods, social processes and independent oversight could become useful for assessing the many attributes of HCAI systems. Table 25.1 has a list of more than thirty frequently mentioned attributes which I compiled and organized into five categories. The categories roughly indicate attributes of the system, how it performs in practice, how the stakeholders perceive it, how aligned it is with independent oversight, and how compliant it is with accepted practices. This chapter concludes with my proposal for an HCAI trustworthiness scale based on subjective judgments.

There are many approaches to evaluation but this chapter focuses on objective measurement, scoring by components, and assessment by social processes. The goal is to find evaluation approaches which are widely accepted, repeatable, and useful.

Objective Measurement

Many researchers take for granted that it is possible to get accurate, objective measures of physical properties, such as size, duration, temperature, and weight. To ensure objective measurement, the rules for measuring have to be agreed on; for example, are patients weighed with clothes on or naked, before

	5	4	3	2	1
Appearance	Clear, appropriate color, brilliance, no off colors			Cloudy, off colors	
Aroma	Complex, many detectable aromas, intense			Little or no aroma, off aromas	
Body	Perfect texture & weight feel in the mouth			Too little or too much texture or weight feel in the mouth	
Taste	Good balance, structure, several flavors detectable			Little balance & structure, few flavors	
Finish	Flavors linger after swallowing, smooth & rich aftertaste			Taste and flavors end abruptly, no after taste	

Fig 25.1 Wine tasting scoring scheme with five qualities: appearance, aroma, body, taste, and finish.

Source: https://winecountrygetaways.com/

breakfast or after daily meals? Is blood pressure measured standing, seated, or lying, and is there a two- or ten-minute quiet period before measurement? Some objective assessments are ordinal, such as gas, liquid, or solid. Others are binary, such as pregnancy and COVID-19 tests, which yield YES or NO answers, although there may be false negatives and false positives. The HCAI attributes cannot be objectively measured, yet.

Scoring by Components

Some attributes like wine quality are subjectively scored by human judges. The goal of subjective scores for something like wine quality would be useful when comparing two wines to decide which bottle to buy. There is no wine-o-meter that gives a numeric value for wine quality, but there are scoring systems such as that used by the magazine *Wine Spectator* that ranges from 50 to 100. In their scoring system, above 90 is "Outstanding: a wine of superior character and style," while above 80 is "Good: a solid, well-made wine." These scores originate from the subjective judgments of wine experts who give ratings to twenty or more wines in a day, without knowing which wine they are tasting. These ratings have large impacts on marketing, but they are less than scientific.

Other wine scoring schemes, meant to be used by everyday drinkers, may have five qualities such as appearance, aroma, body, taste, and finish, where each quality is given 1 to 5 points, for a maximum score of 25 points (Figure 25.1).[4]

More nuanced ratings or rubrics come from wine research centers, such as the University of California-Davis, located near the Napa Valley wine country. Their more rigorous rating scale has ten components, each getting 1, 2, or 4 points, but each is a subjective rating that comes from a human judgment.[5] The components include clarity, color, bouquet, acidity, flavor, sweetness, and body. Each component has a guide to rating, such as for flavor of the grape variety: complex (2.0), simple (1.5), agreeable (1.0), and non-descript (0.5).

Other complex scoring or rating systems use groups of raters. For example, the Code of Points was developed for Olympic figure skating, diving, boxing, and gymnastics. A panel of judges rate performance by components on a numeric scale, with the combined score determining the gold, silver, and bronze medal winners. This subjective judging is very different from events such as track or skiing, where speed is objectively assessed and turned into numeric scores.

One final example of scoring by components is the widely used APGAR scale for newborn health, created by Dr. Virginia Apgar in 1952.[6] Each of the five components (carefully chosen to spell APGAR) is rated at 0, 1, or 2, giving a 0 to 10 scale:

- Appearance (skin color: blue to pink)
- Pulse (absent to $\geq$100 bpm)
- Grimace (reflex irritability: no response to cry on stimulation)
- Activity (muscle tone: none to flexed arms and legs that resist extension)
- Respiration (absent to strong, robust cry)

These relatively simple examples of wine quality and newborn health may be helpful in developing scoring methods for assessing job candidates, retail store location choices, or software package purchase decisions. These are consequential decisions, but more challenging are life-critical decisions such as medical treatments, military options, or aircraft certification. These decisions raise the importance of improving the reliability of a scoring, ranking, or comparison. A good scoring method will have high *inter-rater reliability*, which means that different judges come up with fairly similar scores. Another expectation is that a scoring method will be repeatable, which means that when a judge is called on to rate a component they choose similar values.

Most scoring by components strategies depend on individual judgments, sometimes aggregated to form the final judgment, such as by a panel of Olympic judges or a hiring committee. Other strategies rely on social processes that in-volve discussion among panels or committee members, possibly followed by revision of individual scores or a joint assessment.

More elaborate versions of scoring by components include detailed ques-tionnaires with more than 100 items, using semantically anchored Likert-like scales that may range from 0 to 10 or from strongly agree to strongly disagree. Usability questionnaires have become widely used in human–computer inter-action research and product evaluations.[7] These questionnaires form a kind of checklist that also guides designers and developers in reviewing their own work. HCAI attributes might be scored by components, which is the basis for the HCAI trustworthiness scale proposed at the end of this chapter.

Assessment by Social Processes

Because consequential and life-critical decisions are so important, these deci-sions are often made by group processes, which bring together experts, as with most National Transportation Safety Board reviews or non-experts, as in a jury trial of peers of the defendant. These social processes may complement scoring by components with qualitative methods and social processes, such as struc-tured discussions, two or more rounds of voting, and adversarial debates with rules of evidence and cross-examinations of witnesses. HCAI systems could benefit from social processes incorporated into internal reviews and external independent oversight methods.

Familiar uses of social processes for assessment are hiring committees, which use scoring methods to review the many applicants, selecting a shortlist of candidates to interview more carefully, and requesting reference letters from independent reviewers. Then there may be a group discussion, often with vot-ing to rank the remaining candidates. In academic environments, papers and grant proposals are reviewed, typically with written comments, followed by a group discussion which yields an accept or reject decision. Sometimes con-ference committees, journal editorial boards, or grant agency managers alter the decisions to satisfy diversity requirements, policy restrictions, or budgetary limitations.

Corporate boards of directors or state legislatures are further forms of mak-ing complex decisions where objective measures and scoring by components is supplemented by ample deliberation to generate a consensus or force a decision by voting.

Some organizations apply structured processes, such as the Delphi method, that have multiple rounds of discussion, often led by a professional facilitator who impartially elicits positions, even if they are far from the normal ones. Another popular method of assessment is the SWOT analysis that focuses on the strengths, weaknesses, opportunities, and threats of an idea, plan, or organization. This simple four-way structure helps participants think through some of the qualities of what they are assessing.

The research funding bodies in the United Kingdom developed a research excellence framework (REF) to assess the impact of university research projects. Instead of using only quantitative measures such as numbers of papers published, students graduated, or citations received, the REF convened thirty-four expert panels in different research areas. Two controversial aspects were how strongly research should be assessed by academic outputs or societal impacts and how well the expert panels represented the wide range of universities. Although an important goal was to encourage self-reflection among academics so as to improve future research, the evidence was used by newspapers and other organizations to rank universities.

Another inspiration might be river or forest environmental reports, which describe components, such as water, soil, or air quality, and/or recent activities, such as restoration efforts. These reports can be produced internally or by an external panel of experts. These assessments can make comparisons to previous years, highlight innovative efforts, and caution about emerging threats. Assessment reports often give grades from F for failing to A for excellent, to recognize successful efforts or highlight where greater effort is needed.

Rather than a panel of experts, the US Conference Board conducts a monthly Consumer Confidence survey of 5000 people.[8] The University of Michigan Consumer Sentiment Index conducts a similar monthly consumer confidence index.[9] The index is normalized to have a value of 100 in December 1966. Each month at least 500 telephone interviews ask fifty core questions to a random sample across the contiguous United States sample.

Independent oversight is among the social processes for assessing consequential business, academic, and government systems (Chapter 19). Independence suggests that the reviewers are unbiased by past history or current affiliations with those who developed the systems. Corporations are required to have annual audits by internal committees as well as external audits, typically by respected accounting firms, such as Price Waterhouse Coopers, KPMG, Ernst and Young, and Deloitte. These firms, and many small ones, are prohibited from serving as consultants to the corporations at the same time as they are the independent auditors. Of course, independent oversight is imperfect as the Enron and other failures have shown. Independent oversight can also be conducted by insurance companies, consumer groups, journalists, and non-governmental organizations.

As Chapter 19 describes, there are three common forms of independent oversight:

1. **Planning oversight**: proposals for new systems or major upgrades are presented for review in advance so that feedback and discussion can influence the plans.

2. **Continuous monitoring**: this is an expensive approach, but continuous or period reviews ensure that even if context shifts, there will be a review to ensure quality.

3. **Retrospective analysis of disasters**: when disasters occur, a knowledgeable independent oversight review can give public assurance that the problems that led to the failure are being addressed.

Skeptics point to failures of independent oversight methods, sometimes tied to a lack of sufficient independence, but the value of these methods is widely appreciated.

Independent oversight boards are intended to provide careful reviews of documents and interviews with key personnel to produce well-documented reports whose assessments are respected by all stakeholders. In most cases these reports have recommendations for short- and long-term remedies for identified problems or serious accidents, with some provision to verify that the recommendations were followed in three, six, or twelve months. The goal is performance improvement. Since board members have experience in doing multiple reviews, they transfer knowledge across organizations and sometimes across industries, while providing information that guides design of future systems and becomes included in educational curricula.

Assessing HCAI Trustworthiness

Applying the scoring and assessment methods to HCAI systems will require innovative approaches to enable transparency and better define the desirable qualities. A growing circle of researchers, developers, managers, and policy-makers has proposed strong ethical foundations to ensure responsible or trustworthy AI, seeking fairness, accountability, transparency, explainability, and interpretability. Many more attributes have been proposed, such as those listed in Table 25.1, but measures, scoring methods, or assessment processes are yet to be agreed.

It's alarming that consequential systems have been fielded with few means to assess them. The pressure for innovation is enormous, with bold claims of success, but when research systems come out of the lab to be applied in real world contexts, failures often result. Past failures are widely known, such as the misleading predictions of Google Flu Trends, financial flash crashes, facial recognition bias, and offensive chatbots. These problems continue, as described by a group of thirty-three Google employees and seven external researchers who put out a troubling, yet refreshingly honest, report about how machine learning "models often exhibit unexpectedly poor behavior when they are deployed in real-world domains."[10] Their openness is a positive sign, since it encourages more attention to assessing the trustworthiness and other attributes of HCAI systems.

Many of the HCAI system attributes are closely related. Responsible, safe, secure, accurate, and fair are all faces of a multiheaded creature. Similarly, transparent, explainable, and usable seem to describe the same attribute, yet each term has a devoted community who use these terms. At least four steps need to be taken to develop a credible assessment process: definitions, methods, assessors, and audience (Table 25.2). All of these steps will take time for consensus to emerge, but that is the challenge for researchers and developers.

Advocates of formal methods and proofs of correctness during development believe these methods could improve trustworthiness for a complex HCAI system. Similarly, advocates of static analysis and testing methods believe they would be helpful, but assessment of the trustworthiness of a system is probably only credible if the system's performance is shown to be safe and effective in repeated use over periods of months and years. While early faults are tolerated, these problems should taper off over time, so that stakeholders come to see what becomes known as a trustworthy mature system.

Will Griffin, a Harvard-trained lawyer and Chief Ethics Officer of Hyper-Giant, suggested during a phone interview that the viable measure of trustworthiness is the degree of transparency of an HCAI system.[11] Griffin makes the point that adding ethics should bring a competitive advantage for companies. He sees an analogy to nuclear non-proliferation reviews, in which trust is tied to the degree which a country is transparent about its nuclear efforts. The countries that allow inspections of their nuclear facilities are trusted. Support for

Table 25.2 *HCAI trustworthiness assessment process*

1) **Definitions**	Agree on a smaller set of terms with clear definitions that could be assessed, possibly with scoring by components.
2) **Methods**	Consider how to do assessments with at least these methods: • Static analysis of the code itself and the machine learning training data • Performance of the system in benchmark testing • Performance of the system in practice • Subjective perceptions of stakeholders • Reviews by internal or external experts
3) **Assessors**	Decide who does the assessment and how many are needed in each group. Candidate assessors include those capable of contributing to an assessment: • Developers of the system, although they are likely to have preconceived beliefs • Knowledgeable developers of similar systems who were not involved • Managers of projects that use the system • Users of the system who are affected by its actions or predictions • Independent oversight reviewers who are familiar with similar applications
4) **Audience**	Decide who the audience is for the assessment. Candidates include stakeholders who might benefit from an assessment: • Developers of the system, who might be able to improve it • Knowledgeable developers of similar systems who might benefit from lessons learned • Managers of projects that use the system who might revise their usage process • Users of the system who are affected by its actions or predictions, or their representatives

this idea comes from the committee developing the IEEE Standard P7001 for Transparency in Autonomous Systems.[12]

The general principle behind the P7001 standard is that "it should always be possible to understand why and how an autonomous system made a particular decision."[13] This principle is refined by having five stakeholder audiences that might review a system: users, general public, certifying agencies, incident investigators, and lawyers. For each audience there is a 1 to 5 rating scale for transparency with detailed descriptions of what each rating means, accompanied by examples. This is a useful first effort, which could be developed into a practical assessment tool.

Table 25.3 *Proposed HCAI trustworthiness scale*

Up to 1 point for openly available thorough report
Up to 1 point if report has positive results

---

1) Internal independent review prior to implementation
2) Audit trail has been implemented
3) Training data was collected and assessed (e.g. Microsoft's Datasheets)
4) Software was verified and validated
5) Fairness was tested
6) Explainability was implemented and tested
7) Performance in first two months of usage
8) Performance in first six months of usage
9) Stakeholders make suggestions, raise questions, and report on incidents, near misses, and failures
10) Internal review process for incidents with redress for failures
11) Continuous reviews to support refinements
12) External review by an independent oversight body

One final inspirational example is the AI Social Contract Index from the Dukakis Center for AI and Digital Policy.[14] The index rates twenty-five nations as to how strongly their national policies support democratic values. The twelve attributes, each rated on a 0 to 1 scale, record whether the government has endorsed and implemented foundational documents such as the OECD's AI Principles and the UN's Universal Declaration of Human Rights. Then the index gives points for algorithmic transparency, accountability, public participation in forming policy, and public documents describing policies. In the 382-page report, Germany comes out on top with 10.5 out of a possible 12 points. Nine countries were in the second tier with scores from 8.5 to 9.5.

I propose a scoring method with twelve factors to produce an HCAI trustworthiness scale for assessors to give up to one point if there is an openly available thorough report and up to one more point if the report has positive results. That makes for a scale of 0 to 24 points for consequential large applications (not research or prototype systems) (Table 25.3). Issues such as the criteria for each item, expertise level of assessors, and number of assessors from each of the assessor groups will have to be described.

This proposed HCAI trustworthiness scale, which offers a subjective rating approach that scores by components, will require testing and refinement. Other items could be added to expand the scope. The scale emphasizes transparency by way of reports for each item, which will require organizations to provide more information to stakeholders. The process fits the safety culture approach of getting organizations to develop consistent processes to conduct reviews and make reports.

The European Union commissions, US National Institute of Standards and Technology (NIST), and many companies are working to develop assessments for HCAI trustworthiness.[15]

In summary, assessing attributes of HCAI systems would be a strong stimulus for rapid improvement. Current discussions of important attributes like ethical, responsible, explainable, or fair will deepen if rating scales become widely accepted. The HCAI trustworthiness scale is a proposal to move these discussions forward.

CHAPTER 26

Caring for and Learning from Older Adults

Caring for older adult parents, grandparents, family members, and friends is a virtue that can be an enriching experience for all. However, it requires a serious commitment if the older adult needs help to maintain independent living, which often leads to the older adult moving to a facility that will provide support for the activities of daily life. Historically, many cultures had multigenerational households in which respected older adults participated actively, shared their wisdom, and received care when they needed it. Now, in many countries, less than 10% of the households are multigenerational, with the vast majority of older adults living independently, in assisted living residences, or in nursing homes if they need more regular care.[1]

Caregivers need to arrange their schedules, commit the time, and remain flexible when emergencies arise. Caring for an older adult is a long-term effort, which can be emotionally enriching for all involved, or challenging when chronic illnesses and dementia require more intense care. Caregivers need care too, with family support and backup helpers when the demands are greater. Organizations such as the AARP provide guidance and resources about caring for older adults.[2]

But what do caregivers gain from caring for others? Philosopher Shannon Vallor, formerly a Google ethicist now at the University of Edinburgh, writes that care can "be understood as an activity of personally meeting another's need . . . Caring for people well is not easy. We must learn how to care in the right ways, at the right times and places."[3] She focuses on the virtues and benefits of giving care because it teaches the "meaning and importance of reciprocity . . . we learn through being there for others to trust that someday someone will be there for us. . ... Caregiving practices also foster . . . empathy, the emotional connection that moves us to 'take trouble' for others."[4]

Vallor is open to the possibility of social robots, which she calls *carebots*, to provide some services to older adults, but raises questions about their limits and the loss of connections between the older adult and family, friends, and professional caregivers if they are no longer needed. However, there are other technology support options beyond carebots—better designs could enable older adults to do more by themselves. Well-designed devices increase self-efficacy, provide mental stimulation, and let time with caregivers be more about emotional needs or richer experiences. Many design guides for older adults focus on mobile device and web applications, but the growing possibilities for HCAI for physical devices open up new possibilities.[5]

Caring for older adults is only half of the story. The other half is how others can learn from older adults, whose experiences, knowledge, and skills are an attraction for many adults, young adults, and children. Mentoring, teaching, and partnering is appealing for older adults who want connections with other people. The combination of old and young abilities can make formidable teams. Just as gig economy services, like Lyft, Uber, TaskRabbit, and Fiverr, match up people who need work done with people who can do the work, older adults could be matched up by HCAI recommender services with individuals and community groups that provide needed services. The AI recommender algorithms would be tuned to the age, health, interests, and personal history of older adults and the interests of those seeking to learn from them.

For older adults to partner with younger people means they have to be in good enough health and be reliable as a partner. This means that older adults have to manage the activities of daily life as part of an intergenerational household or in independent living arrangements. Older adults seek to live in place or *age in place* as long as possible to preserve familiar surroundings, keep community friends and services, and satisfy their desire to be in charge of their lives. The US Centers for Disease Control and Prevention describes ageing in place as "[t]he ability to live in one's own home and community safely, independently, and comfortably, regardless of age, income, or ability level."[6] Group homes, small communities, and apartment buildings with onsite staff to assist with tasks and call for help when needed offer diverse options that preserve the desire for independence. Older adults and people with disabilities want their independence, so they can make choices for their needs, but with support from family, friends, social/medical services, and home care workers. They also want access to appropriate technology.

The central question here is: what is appropriate technology? The HCAI approach begins by asking two basic questions:

Who are the users? The term older adults covers a wide range of diverse users:

- Energetic 60-year olds, capable 70-year olds, vigorous 80-year olds, slower 90-year olds, and a growing number of people who are 100+.

- Different levels of technology skill, physical mobility, mental agility, language capacity, medical problems, mood disorders, and disabilities.

- Healthy independent living older adults, couples or friends living together, frail residents in assisted living residences, and those in greater need in nursing homes or clinics.

- Varied ethnic, racial, religious, and cultural backgrounds, with a wide range of financial resources, living conditions, and attitudes.

Attitudes about older adults are often shaped by notions of coping with age-related decline, deficits, and infirmities, but many authors are shifting their language to appreciate that healthy ageing, emotional maturity, and pleasurable activities are possible.[7] Some older adults may need to be cared for, but they can also care for others and offer their insights to younger people who are open to hearing from them.

What are the tasks? The tasks for older adults are unusually broad, covering many requirements, so a technology-centered approach might suggest a broad solution such as a fully functioning human-like robot that could satisfy many needs. Its dexterous hands could open medication bottles, its mobility would enable it to clean up dinner dishes, and its flexibility would make it an excellent yoga instructor. Maybe it would also have the strength to carry an infirm older adult up a flight of stairs or from a wheelchair onto a bed. Helen Petrie and Jenny Darzentas of the University of York, UK caution against a technology-centered approach: "All too often the interventions are driven by technological developments not by the needs and wishes of older adults and an understanding of their living situations."[8]

Rather than think of what technologies might be appropriate, an HCAI approach begins by understanding how older adults differ from younger adults and children.[9] HCAI researchers study user needs through observations, interviews, and surveys to identify primary and secondary needs, while ranking frequent and rare needs. Abraham Maslow's hierarchy of human needs has remained a prominent model since he introduced it in the 1940s. Maslow's hierarchy has a wide base of physiological and safety needs, middle levels with psychological needs for belonging, intimacy, and esteem, and the top layer with self-actualization to be creative and achieve a person's full potential. More recent lists cover basic survival needs such as food, water, shelter, and sleep, plus social needs for connection and touch that release hormones, such as oxytocin, and the desire for novelty which delivers dopamine.[10] These are good guides, but a detailed list of user needs would be helpful, such as the eighteen categories in Table 26.1. This list will vary across cultures, economic, social, and other communities.

Beyond these daily tasks that an older adult might need to carry out or have done for them, there are long duration plans that need to be made, including financial planning, legal necessities such as preparing a will and health directives, and civic responsibilities such as voting and paying taxes. For older adults, medical services such as getting a check-up and going for lab tests can take a large portion of their time, especially if they are dealing with chronic conditions or depression, suffer injuries, or become ill. Medical care is a primary need, as it governs quality of life and survival itself, but working within government care programs takes time and skill. Another primary need is housing, which requires resources to provide housing to those who need it and then design or redesign houses and apartments to accommodate the needs of older adults, such as single-level designs (no steps), remodeled bathrooms, wheelchair accessibility, and appropriate security. Vacation trips and visits to family members and friends may also be important for many older adults.

As populations age, governments, corporations, and families devote more time, energy, and expense to caring for adults. Government policies around social security, healthcare, and other services are increasingly focused on serving older adults and those with disabilities.[11] Similarly, regulations for group, assisted living residences, and nursing homes are increasingly important, made more urgent by the tragic and numerous deaths from COVID-19 in these facilities.

Advocates of older adult carebots cite statistics about the growing number of older adults and the declining number of young people to care for them. Through tens of thousands of academic papers and millions of websites, they focus on designing older adult care robots, usually in humanoid forms, which

Table 26.1 *Informal list of older adult needs and examples of tasks with devices that serve those needs*

Older adult needs	Example tasks with devices that serve needs
Mobility	Use canes, walkers, powered wheelchairs, public transportation, car driving, taxi services
Food preparation, cooking, and cleaning	Use simple/safe preparation tools, cooking appliances, clearing tables, cleaning dishes
Personal care	Wash, bath, care for teeth, mouth, and skin, brush hair, dress/undress, manage personal appearance
Medical care	Ensure medication adherence; use medical devices, insulin pumps, pacemakers, prosthetics; telehealth appointments
Medical monitoring	Use and record results from weight scale, thermometer, oximeter, blood pressure, heart rate, insulin testing, ECG, EEG
Wellness and emotional support	Record nutrition, sleep, exercise, yoga, mood, social contacts, perceptual, cognitive, and motor capacities
Shopping	Order food, bathroom items, medications, clothes, durable supplies; receive and store deliveries
Finances	Track income and expenses, prepare taxes, pay bills, management assets
Information and education	Access web-based information on medical, legal, and financial services, and educational opportunities
News and entertainment	Access news (local, national, international), sports, music, photos, movies, hobbies, games, books
Communication and human connection	Use email, text messaging, writing, groupware, calendar, digital photography, video conferencing, social media
Security	Protect home with intrusion detection, monitoring devices, fire alarms; request help when needed.
House cleaning	Operate vacuuming, mopping, dusting, bathroom cleaning devices, garbage disposal
House maintenance	Maintain and replace appliances, furniture, plumbing, electrical supply, heating, ventilation, and air-conditioning
Gardening and pet care	Maintain outdoor spaces, watering, weeding, flowers, vegetable gardens; pet care chores, dog walking
Mentoring	Guide younger family members, tutor children, lecture to groups, mentor professionals
Contributing	Help with local volunteer efforts, community organizing, religious groups, citizen science, writing memoirs and histories
Creative projects	Writing, music, craft work, painting, photography, gardening, cooking, community or family history projects

can navigate in existing homes designed for human activity. These social robotic scenarios are modeled on what a live-in home care workers would do, repeating the questionable notion that human behavior is the appropriate model for technology design. Social robots for older adults are discussed in Chapter 16. The large number of research and entrepreneurial efforts developing social robots seek to find technologies that serve older adults. An Israeli team, which interviewed thirty healthy older adults of average age 78.5 years who were living independently, reported: "In sum, our findings suggest that most participants were open for social interaction with a robot. However, when the social interaction was the robot's main function, participants expressed a strong rejection. . . . [they] believed the robot should have a clear function that can enhance their quality of life."[12]

Another finding was that their participants required authenticity, while rejecting "devices that pretend to be something they are not" and worried that "a robot's proactivity and mobility may threaten . . . [their] need for control and independence." Social robotics researchers may find it useful to take in these concerns and consider how their designs provide services that contribute to human autonomy, independence, and self-efficacy.

Alternative HCAI approaches to assisting older adults emphasize technology supports for independent living that raise self-efficacy and increase participation of family, friends, community volunteers, and other caregivers.[13] Even small design improvements can be valuable: such as stoves that turn off automatically to prevent food from burning, reminders older adults can set to alert them if they have been too sedentary, or recommenders that point to events in their neighborhood or online related to their interests.[14] Games for older adults can be for fun and they can provide mental stimulation to preserve fluid thinking, exercise memory, and teach new skills.

A more challenging design would be a medication device, programmed by scanning the prescription drug bottle, to let older adults set up the kinds of gentle notifications they like or firmer alerts when they are overdue to take their pills. The dispenser would have to be sophisticated enough to provide multiple pills at different times of day, while keeping a record of compliance. Every design should be reviewed to ensure that older adults can be in control as much as they like and that their privacy is protected. Monitoring devices can protect against dangers and track performance, but if older adults are involved in the decisions about who receives the information, they are more likely to accept its use. Security is another consideration to increase protection from criminals, intruders, and scammers.

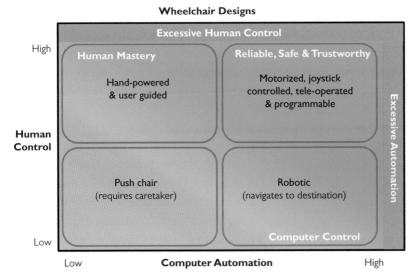

Fig 26.1 HCAI framework shows possible wheelchair designs.

Three more elaborate examples of design possibilities suggest other opportunities:

Example 1: Wheelchairs The HCAI framework (Chapter 8) shows how human control and computer automation guide designers to consider alternatives for needs such as wheelchair mobility. The older wheelchairs were heavy push chairs that required a caretaker to move the seated user around (Figure 26.1, lower left quadrant). Newer, lighter wheelchairs were hand-powered, giving users independence, control, and exercise, which spawned wheelchair races and basketball games (upper left quadrant). A powered wheelchair could be operated by joystick or voice controls. Higher levels of automation could be built into wheelchairs, automatically selecting destinations and paths, bringing users to meals or to other parts of their home on a schedule (lower right quadrant). Wheelchairs are now regularly used outside with automated navigation guiding the chair automatically across neighborhoods, made possible by curbcuts and ramps. Public transportation busses and trains have lifts for wheelchair users, enabling longer distance trips. The desired high level of human control and high level of automation in the upper right quadrant might be a powered wheelchair that used AI algorithms to avoid obstacles, people, and precipices, and was programmable to get to frequent destinations along favored paths. Voice controlled wheelchairs are available for those who need them.[15] A computer vision system with voice guidance was built to help users of powered wheelchairs with navigation and collision avoidance. User studies of six older adults with cognitive impairments showed more accurate movement and fewer collisions in a large indoor test maze.[16] Older adults and users with disabilities found later versions helpful in getting through narrow doorways or elevators, backing up into desired locations and crowded areas, and onto public transport.[17]

Further refinements would allow monitoring, if agreed to by the older adult, to report that all is well and permit tele-operation by trusted family or caregivers. If problems occur, the wheelchair user could summon assistance. If the user is incapacitated or the chair knocked over, automated designs could summon assistance. Aggregate data over time and across multiple wheelchairs could be used in machine learning algorithms to determine when preventive maintenance or design improvements were needed. Sensors could also reveal which sidewalks had bumps, potholes, or pools of water that could turn to ice. Wireless reports could feed machine learning algorithms that guide city officials to where repairs would bring the largest benefits to the largest number of users by identifying routes that were most frequently used. However, some human intervention may be needed to ensure that badly broken sidewalks that were avoided by wheelchair riders were repaired. Wheelchair rider reports would complement the data provided by crowdsourced approaches like Project Sidewalk.[18]

Following a central principle of users with disabilities, "Nothing about us without us!", wheelchair users should be invited to participate in discussions about improving wheelchair designs.

Example 2: Dishwasher in a dinner table The HCAI framework could help imagine designs for other needs such as dinner table clearing and dishwashing. Instead of home robots that clear dinner tables to fill traditional dishwashers, a small dishwasher could be built into, under, or beside a dinner table so that an older adult or couple could simply put their plates, bowls, cups, and cutlery into the dishwasher, washing them to make them readily available for the next meal. There are small dishwashers for camper vans and countertops that hold dishes for a family of four, and even a patent on a dining table with a built-in dishwasher for four people. However, a still smaller dishwasher for one or two people would need to hold just two plates, two bowls, two cups, and eight utensils (Figure 26.2). This approach enhances an older adult's self-efficacy rather than waiting for a mobile robot to carry off the dishes to the kitchen and bring them back when requested.

(a)   (b)

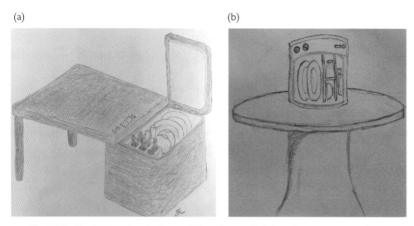

Fig 26.2 Design sketches by Samuel Turin for small dishwasher in a rectangular or circular dinner table for one or two people.

Similar solutions for food preparation are possible, to enable older adults to prepare their own food with easy-to-open containers and safe cooking devices that are accessible to someone in a wheelchair, maybe even plates and bowls that would heat food and drink containers or dispensers designed for easy and safe use.

Human-centered AI thinking would also promote community-based social solutions for some problems. For older adults and people living with disabilities, the Meals on Wheels programs that deliver prepared meals are much appreciated, not only for the food, but for the social contact with the delivery person who may bring the food in, check on the recipient, and maybe clear the table.[19] Those who deliver the meals not only learn from and gain satisfaction in helping those in need, but the stories of successful connections might be celebrated in their communities. AI algorithms could play a useful role in scheduling routes efficiently, as is done for many delivery services. In addition, recommender algorithms could match the older adult's interests and personalities with the delivery person. Meals on Wheels programs, which began in the United Kingdom during World War II, have local branches and international efforts in many countries.

Appreciation for professional caretakers, family members, and helpful friends could increase their pride and satisfaction for taking compassionate care of homebound individuals. Smartphone applications could weave together networks of professional caregivers with income-earning strategies that give workers a better deal than existing gig-economy schemes. However, the special needs of older adults and people with disabilities would prioritize long-term commitments that build relationships, and opportunities for care recipients to rate the caregivers, possibly with public comments of praise, would raise caregivers' status.

Example 3: Yoga instruction   There are hundreds of yoga apps in the Apple and Google Play portfolios, but one of the most popular is Down Dog Yoga from Buddhi.[20] Its thoughtful design, which offers a high degree of user control, has earned more than 300,000 5-star ratings on Apple and Android platforms ("best yoga app I've used," "transformative," "absolutely perfect").

Down Dog Yoga app uses an AI strategy called constraint solving to ensure safe sequences of poses and a consistent combination of standing, bending, and lying down. The app benefits from applying user experience design principles to accommodate older adults with gentle sessions that can be set for four to sixty minutes. It has ten types of yoga, such as Vinyasa, "a gentle warmup, a mix of standing poses, and a cool down on the floor focused on deep stretching," and more vigorous versions, which range from beginner to advanced. Users can choose from twenty boosts, such as aerobic and standing balances and different musical accompaniments. Other choices are from five levels of pace from slowest to fastest and for the level of spoken instruction from full explanation to least explanation plus silence (just the pose name). Users can also choose the image resolution based on their available bandwidth from high definition to low definition and no video. There is a beginner's instruction, a prenatal version, a choice of ten languages, and a set of community features.

Everyday there is a slightly different version balancing familiar with new poses. The voice narration is precise, engaging, and poetic ("windmill your arms," "blossom into warrior two"), with suggestions of variations to let users choose easier or more difficult poses. The sequence follows a consistent path from easy sitting or lying, then more challenging lunges, to standing poses, balances, twists, and floor poses, so as to always make a comprehensive set of stretches of ankles, knees, hips, shoulders, and wrists. The constraint solving algorithm always makes it fit the exact number of minutes users select.

From personal experience with Down Dog Yoga, I appreciate its value. My wife and I have been doing thirty minutes of yoga most mornings for more than four years because the ever-changing sessions and choices keep us engaged. The improvements in muscle strength and range of motion (flexibility) are clear, with benefits likely to mood, stress, sleep, and general health. Certain poses were too hard for us to do initially, but now we do them regularly. More advanced HCAI ideas would be to include social features that allow sharing with others or match users with others whose practice is similar, who live nearby, or who share some history. Another useful feature would be personalized feedback at the end of each session from computer vision algorithms that gauge style, to give guidance about which boosts would be helpful or whether users were ready to move up to a higher level.

For those building a personal health record, sometimes called quantified self, the results of each session could be included with other data, such as step counts, sleep, weight, heart rate, and blood pressure, so that evolutions in health could be tracked. Personal trainers also measure muscle strength and range of motion to track progress, but computer vision algorithms and sensors could provide some of these data.

This well-designed Down Dog Yoga app offers greater variety and user control than videos, which repeat the same poses. Going to an exercise studio to join classes or have personal instruction has its attractions, but the ease of doing exercise at home at the time users choose has value for many. Research includes questions about the relationship between exercise, physical health, mood, stress, and cognitive abilities, which is being done in the HealthKit project tied to the Apple Watch,[21] in Google Health's efforts with Fitbit,[22] and in many other business, academic, and government research groups.

The emerging possibility is that people will be able to assemble data-rich personal health records, which provide more detailed information than the electronic health records that healthcare providers assemble with lab tests, treatments, and physician notes. HCAI-driven analysis of patient- and provider-generated health data could yield valuable insights about the benefits and side effects of treatments, diets, exercise, and lifestyle changes, as well as guidance for individuals about what they can do to improve their health. The ultimate effect is that every person is in multiple clinical trials on a daily basis, getting excellent care and novel treatments. The development of novel data analysis methods, based on machine learning, statistics, and interactive visualization, would take advantage of the best features of the controlled, randomized clinical trial strategies and long-term observational data. The early stages of these ideas, in focused efforts to collect data from individuals coping with a disease, such as PatientsLikeMe,[23] and massive government efforts to collect genetic and other data for millions of people, such as All of Us,[24] are already yielding useful results.

Older adults are increasingly active, leading to World Masters Games and Senior Olympics for dozens of sports. Just as in typical sports competitions, only a small percentage of the population can be competitors, but seeing older adults in track and field events, competitive games like tennis, and skills like skiing or figure skating inspires many to take up sports and maybe compete in local or regional competitions. HCAI technologies, based on computer vision and sensor data, could be helpful in tailoring training for individual older adults and monitoring performance to protect against falls or other injuries. AI-driven ski coaches use sensors in boots and trackers on legs to provide voice guidance through headphones.

While monitoring daily physical activity, such as step counts or heart rates, and detecting falls are important, designs that give older adults choices of what activities to engage in and what to monitor build their sense of initiative and ownership over wearable devices.[25] When older adults can set their own goals and share their performance with others, they tend to increase their use of tracking devices. These design refinements come naturally when design teams include older adults and wearable device testing is done with older adults.

Beyond health and wellness, older adults are volunteers, fund raisers, board members, or leaders in community, political, consumer, and cultural groups. They bring their experience and skills, teaching younger people what they know and helping with meaningful projects that bring purpose to their daily lives. In the United Kingdom during the COVID-19 crisis, World War II veteran Captain Tom Moore used his walker to do 100 laps around his garden for his 100th birthday, raising more than $40 million for the National Health Service Charities. The donations from more than a million people brought Capt. Moore worldwide celebrity, inspiring many and leading to his knighthood from Queen Elizabeth II. To continue his work, supporters launched the Captain Tom Foundation.[26] For older adults looking to find a project in their area that could benefit from their skills, web search engines are a good start, but HCAI recommender systems could provide better control panels to facilitate exploration.

Partnerships between eighty-five-year olds and twenty-year olds for political, environmental, or community activities is a growing trend. They join forces to work on neighborhood flower or vegetable gardens that build community spirit or provide food boxes for needy families. For those seriously into nature, citizen science projects could be an attraction to collect data on birds, wildlife, insects, and plants. These projects have millions of contributors whose efforts results in influential scientific papers. The ninety-five-year old English natural history filmmaker David Attenborough continues to write and present successful programs viewed by hundreds of millions of people. His films show the beauty of nature and have strongly worded statements about the need to address the climate crisis. Also ninety-five years old, Britain's Queen Elizabeth II became head of the Commonwealth in 1952, making her the longest reigning monarch that historians record. Despite controversies and incidents which disappointed her followers, she remains popular in the UK and around the world.

Entrepreneurial activities by older adults might also grow, since they have business skills and may recognize needs that could be served. Martha Stewart at age eighty continues to be an innovative entrepreneur and magazine publisher, offering cooking, fashion, and household advice, products, and services. More modest business successes among older adults can come from e-commerce or craft sales on websites such as Etsy.com. *Forbes* business magazine asked: "Are Older Entrepreneurs the Best Entrepreneurs?"[27] Business projects are a goal of the Older Adults Technology Service, which launched the Senior Planet website that "harnesses technology to change the way we age."[28]

Exceptional stories like Capt. Moore and Martha Stewart are inspirational, but many older adults live with chronic illnesses, dementia, or perceptual, cognitive, and motor disabilities that limit what they can do. Substantial investment in these cases and end-of-life care are necessary to build societies in which we are proud to live.

In summary, the range of older adult needs suggests many possible benefits from HCAI efforts. This chapter touched on three examples that show how human control and computer automation can be productively applied to support independent living, self-efficacy, and physical and mental health. But caring for and learning from older adults comes from more than excellent technology design. Older adults need social engagement that comes from family, friends, social/medical services, and home care workers, whose efforts should be valued and appreciated. They also seek meaningful projects that give purpose to their lives by sharing their knowledge and contributing their skills.

CHAPTER 27

Summary and Skeptic's Corner

Trust is the foundation of society. Where there is no truth, there can be no trust, and where there is no trust, there can be no society. Where there is society, there is trust, and where there is trust, there is something upon which it is supported.

Frederick Douglass, *"Our Composite Nationality"* (December 7, 1869), Boston, MA

E arly in the book, I promised to deliver a guidebook to hope and a roadmap to realistic policies. The guidebook calls for human-centered thinking that integrates disciplines, such as science, engineering, design, art, social sciences, and humanities. Combining disciplines will speed the creation of technologies that respect human values of rights, justice, and dignity, while supporting individual goals of self-efficacy, creativity, responsibility, and social connections (Figure 1.2).

The design aspirations are for reliable, safe, and trustworthy systems that support progress in racial justice, greater income equality, and environmental preservation. Working together, we may be able to follow the roadmap to reach worthy destinations such as healthcare/well-being, economic growth, broad education, food safety, and the other UN Sustainable Development Goals.

While one eye should be on the admirable values, goals, and aspirations for the many stakeholders who are affected by HCAI systems, the other eye should be alert to the threats from malicious actors, bias, and flawed software. External threats from criminals, hate groups, terrorists, and oppressive politicians deserve attention from researchers, developers, managers, and policy-makers, but equally important is awareness of the dangers of biased data, unconscious biases that emerge in critical decisions, and flawed software. Assets in making a safe journey are an attitude of humility about our abilities, openness about the possibility of failure, and readiness to take in fresh ideas.

Other assets will be the courage to do the right thing when the going gets rough, while balancing the desire to be bold with the need to be cautious. The journey may be helped by faster, better technologies, but the destination is human welfare and environmental preservation.

These many goals at different levels of specificity leave room for wide participation and many opportunities to contribute. Skeptics may question whether researchers and technology innovators will revise their efforts to support HCAI ideas and methods. This is a legitimate concern, but the growing interest in HCAI is a positive indicator. Researchers are coming to recognize that they must consider the positive and negative impacts of their work. Conference program committees and journal editorial boards are increasingly evaluating papers from an ethical point of view. Controversies in technology companies and liability for damages are forcing a growing awareness among business leaders that ethical practices and trustworthiness are competitive advantages. Government bodies around the world are stepping up their efforts to make business responsible for their systems moving towards regulatory approaches and independent oversight. Maybe my call to action needs blaring trumpets or even a whole brass band, but I hope it can gain attention with an orchestral synthesis of the gentler violins of realistic policies and rhythmic drumbeats of actionable agendas.

Personal Epilogue: How I Became Passionate about Human-Centered Approaches

You can't use up creativity. The more you use, the more you have.

Maya Angelou

As an increasing number of academics adopt an HCAI approach, there is still resistance and lack of interest from many researchers and practitioners. They wonder why I am so eager to expand AI research and development to include HCAI? Why do I think there is an alternative to the dominant themes so widely accepted by researchers, practitioners, business leaders, and policy-makers? I am eager to see changes in these broad communities, which would recognize the need for and benefits from a human-centered attitude. These changes reflect my own shifts in thinking that began in my early days.

As an undergraduate math and physics major, I wrote enthusiastically about the possibilities of artificial intelligence and neural networks for the City College of New York engineering magazine. My plans to take a generous fellowship for doctoral study with AI leaders Allen Newell and Herbert Simon at Carnegie Mellon University were thwarted by the Vietnam War. Instead, my national service for three years was teaching data processing at a two-year community college—the State University of New York (SUNY) at Farmingdale on New York's Long Island. This led me to graduate study on optimization of data structures for the emerging topic of database systems, becoming the first PhD in computer science at SUNY Stony Brook in 1973.

My rationalist side was strong at this time of my life, even though I was increasingly influenced by thinkers like English professor Marshall McLuhan, whose books, especially *Understanding Media: The Extensions of Man*,[1] had a profound effect on me. His descriptions of a global electronic village foresaw the World Wide Web and his sometimes puzzling discussions of hot and cold media led me to think more deeply about the impact of technologies on human experiences. McLuhan's theories explained how the linearity of text, in which each word follows in an orderly way, led to privacy and specialization. This idea stoked my rebellion against choosing a major, preferring broader multidisciplinary approaches. My eclectic interests led me to study psychology, photography, sociology, and other disciplines beyond science and engineering.

As an assistant professor at Indiana University, I broke from traditional computer science by partnering with a young psychology colleague, Richard Mayer, who trained me in experimental methods and statistics. I began by studying programmer performance, so as to improve design of programming languages and tools. After three satisfying years in Bloomington, Indiana, I moved to the University of Maryland where I developed close cooperations with psychologists, like Nancy Anderson and Kent Norman. While still teaching programming and database systems, I committed to research on designing technologies to empower people, just as personal computers were emerging—helping to create the new field of human–computer interaction.

My exotic ideas led to a forward-looking book *Software Psychology: Human Factors in Computer and Information Systems*.[2] To my delight, it was chosen as a featured selection by both of the computer science book-of-the-month clubs, quickly bringing attention to this new topic. My pride was even greater when one of my heroes, AI research leader Allen Newell, gave a 1985 keynote talk that featured *Software Psychology* as an inspiration for his shift towards human–computer interaction research.

Another inspiration for me was my chance to host J. C. R Licklider on his visit to the University of Maryland. His 1960 article on "Man–Computer Symbiosis" was seen by many as supporting the idea that computers would become our partners and equals, but Licklider was clear in the distinction between humans and computers:

In the anticipated symbiotic partnership, men [and women] will set the goals, formulate the hypotheses, determine the criteria, and perform the evaluations. Computing machines will do the routinizable work that must be done to prepare the way for insights and decisions in technical and scientific thinking.[3]

Licklider understood that computers would do different tasks than humans, who he saw as directing the effort, gaining insights, and making decisions. He hosted me on a visit to speak at MIT and, in his calm gentle way, encouraged me to pursue the psychological studies of user interface design.

Another hero was Doug Engelbart, whose work in the 1960s on augmenting human abilities led him to invent many fundamental ideas, such as the mouse for moving a cursor on a screen. His ideas grew into modern graphical user interfaces and collaborative computing. Engelbart's human-centered approaches challenged AI leaders, who he believed had a role in stopping his funding. Fearing that his work was ignored, he was very moved, nearly in tears, when he received the ACM Special Interest Group on Computer–Human Interaction (SIGCHI)[4] Award for Lifetime Achievement in 1998. The passions over these issues have a long history.

The importance of human values in technology received further support from Joseph Weizenbaum's *Computer Power and Human Reason: From Judgment to Calculation*, which reiterated the distinctions between computers and people.[5] While Weizenbaum's chatbot ELIZA provoked great interest in the mid-1960s, he was appalled that some people saw this demonstration as a step towards computer-based psychotherapy and human-like conversation. Weizenbaum showed that computers could be programmed to respond in natural language, yet he forcefully contended that people had distinctive capabilities for reasoning, were deeply social, and were driven by intense passions that were very different from what computers could ever be.

Weizenbaum's criticism of his AI colleagues encouraged me to question AI ideas and systems in *Software Psychology*. I was especially hard on the natural language understanding research presented by Terry Winograd in his influential 1972 MIT PhD dissertation. His SHRDLU robot responded to a narrow range of commands involving a few nouns and verbs, such as "PICK UP THE RED BLOCK," but his work was seen as a big breakthrough. For me, the very title of his dissertation, "Understanding Natural Language," was an annoying exaggeration.

When Winograd's book with Fernando Flores, *Understanding Computers and Cognition*,[6] reported that "computers can't understand natural language," I was pleased. They also wrote that "in designing tools we are designing ways of being" and that among the important questions was how to make "machines that are suited to human purposes." I phoned Winograd to discuss his work. My apprehension about what he would say dissipated when he reported recommending my SHRDLU critique to his students. Our positions were in closer harmony than I had expected. From then on, we developed a warm, collegial relationship. He inspired me through his work on software design and his advocacy of technology policy issues through his leadership of the Computer Professionals for Social Responsibility. Winograd is also celebrated for mentoring Sergei Brin and Larry Page as they co-authored the 1998 paper that laid the algorithmic foundation for Google's hugely successful search tools.

Winograd's shift from AI researcher to human–computer interaction thought leader indicated that a shift to human-centered thinking was possible, but many technology-focused researchers remained devoted to AI, even as multidisciplinary human-centered approaches gained strength. To accelerate the movement, I led an effort to bring together 200–300 psychology, human factors, and computer science researchers at a conference at the National Institutes for Standards and Technology (then the National Bureau of Standards) in spring 1982. To our amazement, 906 people showed up, helping to accelerate research on human–computer interaction. Encouraged by this astonishing success, we and others formed a professional group, the ACM SIGCHI, which has continued to host a conference that now draws 4000 people a year and more than thirty subsidiary conferences around the world.

Conferences, journals, and courses on human–computer interaction grew steadily, encouraged by the arrival of personal computers that had to be human-centered. In 1981, I developed the idea of direct manipulation user interfaces in which users click, drag, and drop objects on their screens to do their work.[7] I later learned that Ivan Sutherland showed some examples in 1963, but I was influenced by air-traffic control systems, certain games, and especially Italian educator Maria Montessori's and Swiss psychologist Jean Piaget's ideas of teaching children by using manipulatives. Direct manipulation describes and explains current successes, giving terminology and psychological foundations for visual metaphors, manipulated with hand–eye coordination based on Engelbart's mouse or touchscreens. Direct manipulation was the guiding concept that led me to develop the highlighted selectable link, which was a key idea in the Hyperties commercial product and a component in Tim Berners-Lee's 1989 manifesto for the World Wide Web. It also led to our work on tiny touchscreen keyboards and the patent on tagging photos.

Professor Azriel Rosenfeld, a University of Maryland leader in computer vision research, gave me a boost by inviting me to form the Human–Computer Interaction Lab in 1983. Our lab took an early lead in promoting user interface design, theories, guidelines, and empirical studies, described in the 1986 first edition of *Designing the User Interface: Strategies for Effective Human–Computer Interaction*.[8] Steve Jobs, whose Apple computers invigorated the field, saw his human-centered position as "technology married with liberal arts, married with the humanities that yields us the results that make our heart sing." His October 1988 visit to our University of Maryland lab was memorable, leading to my consulting for Apple for five years. That story and others are in my photo-history of human–computer interaction: *Encounters with HCI Pioneers: A Personal History and Photo Journal.*[9]

Even though human–computer interaction was a growing research area, AI gained even more momentum as industry forces believed that AI agents and robots would soon become widespread. The controversies grew, leading to several public debates, culminating in the now legendary1997 encounters in which Pattie Maes and I laid out our cases for AI and human–computer interaction.[10] Pattie Maes was a respected MIT Media Lab professor who was counted in *Time Magazine*'s Cyber-Elite and also in *People Magazine*'s 50 Most Beautiful People in the World. My dark bearded face led some to label our debates as a contest between Beauty and the Beast.

The debates generated interest and clarified two views of future technologies, which I describe in Chapter 14. Maes argued for agents that knew your habits and took initiative to give you what you wanted, even before you realized you wanted it. I argued for human initiative and the capacity to do it yourself through clicking, dragging, and dropping objects on a display. I worried that her approach might be annoying when it made mistakes; she thought my approach was too tedious, requiring users to do everything on their own.

In a twentieth anniversary replay, we met again at the 2017 SIGCHI conference, each wiser from the passing events, willing to admit our missteps. I saw hope for broader changes in that Maes became a founder of the Augmented Human Conference and her MIT Software Agents Lab morphed into the Fluid Interfaces Lab, suggesting that she too saw value in the human-centered approach.

As my research on user interfaces and user experience design matured, I came to value visual user interfaces that presented data, relationships, patterns, and processes. John Tukey's famed book on *Exploratory Data Analysis* claimed that fast computers and high-resolution displays had made interactive exploration of data easier.[11] Inspired by the potential of improving human capacity to understand the world around us, I turned my efforts to supporting interactive visual data exploration, now called information visualization. Even our early examples led to valuable insights about missing, incorrect, or anomalous data, encouraging us to enable users to gather insights about their data. Our group soon saw how excited users became as they discovered previously hidden patterns such as clusters, gaps, relationships, and outliers.

For a hastily prepared conference keynote I announced a compact information visualization mantra: "overview first, zoom and filter, then details on demand."[12] That phrase suggested that visual interfaces should start by showing all the data, even if there were billions of data items, then allow the users to zoom in on what they wanted, filter out what they didn't want, and then click to get details on demand. The mantra was a compact guideline derived from my observation of what brought enthusiasm from users. Even though the paper describing the mantra appeared in a second tier conference, it has received more than 7000 citations, an astonishing number for a simple guideline that did not have research results to back it up. I think what drives its success is the assumption that overviews help orient users, inviting users to operate the control panel to rapidly explore in previously impossible ways.

Visual user interfaces have become powerful telescopes for understanding the complexities of HCAI systems, starting with developers who are probing the intricacies of their deep learning algorithms. Visual user interfaces are also a gift for the consumers who want comprehensible recommender systems and for business leaders who are called on to make consequential decisions. Furthermore, visual user interfaces also give operators better control of robotic systems for manufacturing, transportation, and medical care. The adoption of visual user interfaces is increasingly a part of the movement to HCAI systems.

Another lesson has been the strong desire that people have to communicate with other people to exchange messages, share photos, tell stories, or assemble and coordinate teams. The boom in Zoom video conferencing and related systems during the COVID-19 crisis accelerated the development of these tools. However, the backlash because of fatigue at staring at small rectangles showing faces led to even more innovative social designs such as Gather.town, Kumospace, and their competitors that built on game-like spatial environments. These systems will be woven into future HCAI systems to facilitate the principle: humans in the group, computers in the loop.

Creative researchers and developers will apply HCAI designs to advance human values of protection of rights, access to justice, and support for dignity. Innovators know that by bolstering self-efficacy, creativity, responsibility, and social connections they will gain devoted users who benefit from their designs. They also know that they must be vigilant to reduce ever-present threats from malicious actors, unconscious and conscious bias, and flawed software. Other challenges include overcoming racial injustice, shrinking income inequality, and restoring damaged environments, which are all part of the UN's Sustainable Development Goals. I have great satisfaction in seeing the progress that has been made, imperfect as it will always be, during the past four decades. Of course, there's much work to be done, but I remain optimistic that the best is yet to come and I am ready to do my share.

NOTES

CHAPTER 1

1. Dubber, M. D., Pasquale, F. and Das, S., eds. (2020). *The Oxford Handbook of Ethics of AI*. New York: Oxford University Press; Braunschweig, B. and Ghallab, M., eds. (2021). *Reflections on Artificial Intelligence for Humanity*. New York: Springer.

2. AI for Good. Get Involved. Accessed June 9, 2021. https://ai4good.org/.

3. DataKind. Accessed June 9, 2021. https://www.datakind.org/.

4. IBM Watson AI XPRIZE Foundation. AI to Solve Global Issues. Accessed June 9, 2021. https://www.xprize.org/prizes/artificial-intelligence.

5. AI for Good. About Us. Accessed June 9, 2021. https://aiforgood.itu.int/about-us/.

6. United Nations, Department of Economic and Social Affairs, Sustainable Development. The 17 Goals. Accessed June 9, 2021. https://sdgs.un.org/goals.

7. United Nations. Department of Economic and Social Affairs. The Sustainable Development Goals Report 2020. Accessed June 9, 2021. https://unstats.un.org/sdgs/report/2020/.

8. Schiff, D., Ayesh, A., Musikanski, L., and Havens, J. C. (October 2020). IEEE 7010: A New Standard for Assessing the Well-Being Implications of Artificial Intelligence. In *2020 IEEE International Conference on Systems, Man, and Cybernetics (SMC)*. IEEE, 2746–53. https://ieeexplore.ieee.org/abstract/document/9283454/.

9. AI Incident Database. Welcome to the Artificial Intelligence Incident Database. Accessed June 9, 2021. https://incidentdatabase.ai/.

10. McGregor, S. (2021). Preventing Repeated Real World AI Failures by Cataloging Incidents: The AI Incident Database. *Proc. Thirty-Third Annual Conference on Innovative Applications of Artificial Intelligence (IAAI-21)*, 35(17). Virtual conference. https://ojs.aaai.org/index.php/AAAI/article/view/17817.

11. US National Research Council (2008). *Protecting Individual Privacy in the Struggle Against Terrorists: A Framework for Program Assessment*. Washington, DC: National Academies Press.

12. Bostrom, N. (2014). *Superintelligence: Paths, Dangers, Strategies*. Oxford University Press; Russell, S. and Norvig, P. (2020). *Artificial Intelligence: A Modern Approach*, 4th ed. New York: Pearson.

CHAPTER 2

1. Klein, G., Shneiderman, B., Hoffman, R. R., and Wears, R. L. (2019). The "War" on Expertise. In Ward, P., Schraagen, J. M., Gore, J. and Roth, E. M., eds. *The Oxford Handbook of Expertise*. Oxford University Press.

2. Pearl, J. and Mackenzie, D. (2018). *The Book of Why: The New Science of Cause and Effect*. New York: Basic Books.

3. Waldrop, M. M. (2019). News Feature: What Are the Limits of Deep Learning? *Proceedings of the National Academy of Sciences*, 116(4): 1074–7. https://www.pnas.org/content/116/4/1074.short.

4. Future of Life Institute. Lethal Autonomous Weapons Systems. Accessed June 21, 2021. https://futureoflife.org/lethal-autonomous-weapons-systems/.

5. Santoni de Sio, F. and Van den Hoven, J. (2018). Meaningful Human Control over Autonomous Systems: A Philosophical Account. *Frontiers in Robotics and AI*, 5: 15. https://www.frontiersin.org/articles/10.3389/frobt.2018.00015/full.

6. OpenFDA. FDA Adverse Event Reporting System. Accessed June 21, 2021. https://open.fda.gov/data/faers/.

7. Aviation Safety Reporting System. Accessed June 21, 2021. https://asrs.arc.nasa.gov/.

CHAPTER 3

1. Stanford University (2016). Artificial Intelligence and Life in 2030: One Hundred Year Study on Artificial Intelligence. https://ai100.stanford.edu/sites/g/files/sbiybj9861/f/ai100report10032016fnl_singles.pdf.

2. Lanier, J. (2010). *You Are Not a Gadget*. New York: Knopf Doubleday Publishing Group; Smith, B. C. (2019). *The Promise of Artificial Intelligence: Reckoning and Judgment*. Cambridge, MA: MIT Press.

3. Paul Ekman Group. Universal Emotions. Accessed June 21, 2021. https://www.paulekman.com/universal-emotions/.

4. Feldman-Barrett, L. (2017). *How Emotions are Made: The Secret Life of the Brain*. New York: Houghton Mifflin Harcourt.

5. Crawford, K. (2021). *The Atlas of AI*. New Haven, CT: Yale University Press.

6. Natale, S. (2021). Deceitful Media: Artificial Intelligence and Social Life after the Turing Test. New York: Oxford University Press.

7. Paul Brown. Accessed June 21, 2021. http://www.paul-brown.com/.

8. Ernest Edmonds. Accessed June 21, 2021. http://www.ernestedmonds.com/.

9. AIArtists.org. Alexander Mordvintsev. Accessed June 21, 2021. https://aiartists. org/alexander-mordvintsev.

10. Alexander Mordvintsev. Accessed June 21, 2021. https://znah.net/.

11. Sarid, D. (November 23,#2020). Email message to author.

CHAPTER 4

1. Ford, M. (2015). *Rise of the Robots: Technology and the Threat of a Jobless Future.* New York: Basic Books.

2. Frey, C. B. and Osborne, M. (2013). The Future of Employment: How Suscepti- ble Are Jobs to Computerisation? Oxford Martin School, University of Oxford, UK. http://www.oxfordmartin.ox.ac.uk/downloads/academic/The_Future_of_Employ- ment.pdf.

3. Ovide, S. (June 16, 2021). Amazon Is Brilliant. Why Not at H.R.? *The New York Times.* https://www.nytimes.com/2021/06/16/technology/amazon-work-force. html.

4. Toffler, A. (1970). *Future Shock.* New York: Bantam Publishers.

5. Autor, D. H., Mindell, D. A. and Reynolds, E. B. (2020). The Work of the Fu- ture: Building Better Jobs in an Age of Intelligent Machines, 3. MIT Work of the Future. https://workofthefuture.mit.edu/wp-content/uploads/2021/01/2020- Final-Report4.pdf.

6. Autor et al. (2020), 5.

7. Autor et al. (2020), 4.

8. Autor et al. (2020), 10.

CHAPTER 5

1. Creative Destruction Lab (November 24, 2016). Geoff Hinton: On Radiology. YouTube video, 1:24. https://youtu.be/2HMPRXstSvQ.

CHAPTER 6

1. Harambam, J., Bountouridis, D., Makhortykh, M. and Van Hoboken, J. (September 2019). Designing for the Better by Taking Users into Account: A Qual- itative Evaluation of User Control Mechanisms in (News) Recommender Systems. *Proc. 13th ACM Conference on Recommender Systems,* 69–77. https://dl.acm.org/doi/abs/10.1145/3298689.3347014.

2. Kunkel, J., Schwenger, C. and Ziegler, J. (July 2020). NewsViz: Depicting and Con- trolling Preference Profiles Using Interactive Treemaps in News Recommender Systems. *Proc. 28th ACM Conference on User Modeling, Adaptation and Person- alization,* 126–135. https://dl.acm.org/doi/abs/10.1145/3340631.3394869.

3. Sheridan, T. B. and Verplank, W. L. (1978). Human and Computer Control of Undersea Teleoperators. Technical report. Massachusetts Institute of Technology Cambridge Man-Machine Systems Lab. https://apps.dtic.mil/sti/citations/ADA057655.

4. Parasuraman, R., Sheridan, T. B. and Wickens, C. D. (2000). A Model for Types and Levels of Human Interaction with Automation. *IEEE Transactions on Systems, Man and Cybernetics-Part A: Systems and Humans*, 30: 286–97.

5. Parasuraman et al. (2000).

6. Sheridan, T. B. (2000). Function Allocation: Algorithm, Alchemy or Apostasy? *International Journal of Human-Computer Studies*, 52(2): 203–16. https://www.sciencedirect.com/science/article/pii/S1071581999902859.

7. Hoffman, R. R. and Johnson, M. (2019). The quest for alternatives to "Levels of Automation" and "Task Allocation." In M. Mouloua and P. A. Hancock, eds., *Human Performance in Automated and Autonomous Systems*. Boca Raton, FL: CRC Press, 43–68.

8. Society of Automotive Engineers (SAE) (2014). Taxonomy and Definitions for Terms Related to On-Road Motor Vehicle Automated Driving Systems. SAE Report J3016. https://www.sae.org/standards/content/j3016_201401/; Brooks, R. (July 27, 2017). The Big Problem with Self-driving Cars Is People. *IEEE Spectrum*. https://spectrum.ieee.org/transportation/self-driving/the-big-problem-with-selfdriving-cars-is-people.

9. SAE (2014).

10. Bainbridge, L. (1983). Ironies of Automation. *Automatica*, 19(6): 775–9.

11. Mindell, D. (2015). *Our Robots, Ourselves: Robotics and the Myths of Autonomy*. New York: Viking Press.

12. Endsley, M. R. (2017). From Here to Autonomy: Lessons Learned from Human–Automation Research. *Human Factors*, 59(1): 5–27.

13. Hancock, P. A. (2017). Imposing Limits on Autonomous Systems. *Ergonomics*, 60(2): 284–91.

14. Bradshaw, J. M., Hoffman, R. R., Woods, D. D. and Johnson, M. (2013). The Seven Deadly Myths of Autonomous Systems. *IEEE Intelligent Systems*, 28(3): 54–61. https://ieeexplore.ieee.org/abstract/document/6588858/.

15 Bradshaw et al. (2013).

16. Murphy, R. and Shields, J. (July 2012). The Role of Autonomy in DoD Systems. Defense Science Board Task Force Report. Washington, DC.

17. Defense Science Board (2016). Summer Study on Autonomy. Washington, DC: Office of the Undersecretary for Defense for Acquisition, Technology and Logistics, Department of Defense.

18. Hoffman, R. R., Cullen, T. M. and Hawley, J. K. (2016). The Myths and Costs of Autonomous Weapon Systems. *Bulletin of the Atomic Scientists*, 72(4): 247–55. https://www.tandfonline.com/doi/abs/10.1080/00963402.2016.1194619.

19. Blackhurst, J. L., Gresham, J. S. and Stone, M. O. (2011). The Autonomy Paradox. *Armed Forces Journal,* 20–40.

20. Nicas, J., Kitroeff, N., Gelles, D. and Glanz, J. (June 6, 2019). Boeing Built Deadly Assumptions into 737 Max, Blind to a Late Design Change. *The New York Times.* https://www.nytimes.com/2019/06/01/business/boeing-737-max-crash.html

21. Blackhurst et al. (2011); Strauch, B. (2017). Ironies of Automation: Still Unresolved after All These Years. *IEEE Transactions on Human-Machine Systems,* 48(5): 419–33. https://ieeexplore.ieee.org/abstract/document/8013079/.

22. Woods, D. D., Tittle, J., Feil, M. and Roesler, A. (2004). Envisioning Human–Robot Coordination in Future Operations. *IEEE Transactions on Systems, Man, and Cybernetics, Part C (Applications and Reviews),* 34(2): 210–18. https://ieeexplore.ieee.org/abstract/document/1291668/.

23. Li, F.-F. (March 7, 2018). How to Make A.I. That's Good for People. *The New York Times.* https://www.nytimes.com/2018/03/07/opinion/artificial-intelligence-human.html.

24. Stanford University Human-Centered Artificial Intelligence. Letter from the Denning Co-Directors. Accessed June 22, 2021. https://hai.stanford.edu/welcome.

25. Jordan, M. I. (2018). Artificial Intelligence—The Revolution Hasn't Happened Yet. https://medium.com/@mijordan3/artificial-intelligence-the-revolution-hasnt-happened-yet-5e1d5812e1e7.

26. Jordan (2018).

CHAPTER 7

1. Modarres, M., Kaminskiy, M. P. and Krivtsov, V. (2016). *Reliability Engineering and Risk Analysis: A Practical Guide.* Boca Raton, FL: CRC Press.

2. Guldenmund, F. W. (2000). The Nature of Safety Culture: A Review of Theory and Research. *Safety Science,* 34(1–3): 215–57. https://www.sciencedirect.com/science/article/pii/S092575350000014X; Berry, J. C., Davis, J. T., Bartman, T., Hafer, C. C., Lieb, L. M., Khan, N. and Brilli, R. J. (January 7, 2020). Improved Safety Culture and Teamwork Climate Are Associated with Decreases in Patient Harm and Hospital Mortality across a Hospital System. *Journal of Patient Safety,* 16(2): 130–6. http://www.ncbi.nlm.nih.gov/pubmed/26741790.

3. Fraser, P., Moultrie, J. and Gregory, M. (2002). The use of maturity models/grids as a tool in assessing product development capability. *Proc. IEEE International Engineering Management Conference,* 1: 244–9; Lacerda, T. C. and von Wangenheim, C. G. (2018). Systematic Literature Review of Usability Capability/Maturity Models. *Computer Standards and Interfaces,* 55: 95–105.

4. Fukuyama, F. (1995). *Trust: The Social Virtues and the Creation of Prosperity.* New York: Free Press.

5. Edmonds, E. A. and Candy, L. (2002). Creativity, Art Practice and Knowledge. *Communications of the ACM* Special Section on Creativity and Interface, 45(10):

91–5. https://dl.acm.org/doi/fullHtml/10.1145/570907.570939; Giuliani, M., Lenz, C., Müller, T., Rickert, M. and Knoll, A. (2010). Design Principles for Safety in Human–Robot Interaction. *International Journal of Social Robotics*, 2(3): 253–74; Woods, D. D. (2017). Essential Characteristics of Resilience. In Hollnagel, E., Woods, D. D. and Leveson, N. eds., *Resilience Engineering: Concepts and Precepts*. Farnham, UK: Ashgate Publishing, 21–34; Candy, L. (2019). Creating with the Digital: Tool, Medium, Mediator, Partner. In Brooks, A. L. and Sylla, C., eds., *Interactivity, Game Creation, Design, Learning, and Innovation*. Cham, Switzerland: Springer. https://link.springer.com/chapter/10.1007/978-3-030-53294-9_2.

CHAPTER 8

1. Martin, C. D. (1993). The Myth of the Awesome Thinking Machine, *Communications of the ACM*, 36(4): 120–33. https://dl.acm.org/doi/abs/10.1145/255950.153587.

2. Konstan, J. A. and Riedl, J. (2012). Recommender Systems: From Algorithms Tommen Reco User Experience. *User Modeling and User-Adapted Interaction*, 22(1–2): 101–23. https://link.springer.com/article/10.1007/s11257-011-9112-x.

3. Heer, J. (2019). Agency Plus Automation: Designing Artificial Intelligence into Interactive Systems, *Proc. National Academy of Sciences*, 116(6): 1844–50. https://www.pnas.org/content/116/6/1844

4. Heer (2019), 1845.

5. Lazer, D., Kennedy, R., King, G. and Vespignani, A. (March 14, 2014). The Parable of Google Flu: Traps in the Big Data Analysis. *Science* 343: 1203–5.

6. Shneiderman, B. (1987). *Designing the User Interface: Strategies for Effective Human-Computer Interaction*. Boston, MA: Addison-Wesley.

7. Calvo, R. A., Peters, D., Vold, V. and Ryan, R. M. (2020). Supporting Human Autonomy in AI systems: A Framework for Ethical Enquiry. In Burr, C. and Floridi, L., eds., *Ethics of Digital Well-Being: A Multidisciplinary Approach*. New York: Springer Open.

8. IBM Design for AI. Fundamentals. Accessed June 22, 2021. https://www.ibm.com/design/ai/fundamentals/.

9. Thimbleby, H. (2020). *Fix IT: Stories from Healthcare IT*. Oxford University Press.

10. US National Transportation Safety Board (2017). Collision between a Car Operating with Automated Vehicle Control Systems and a Tractor-Semitrailer Truck near Williston, Florida, May 7, 2016. Accident Report NTSB/HAR-17/02, PB2017-102600. Available at: https://www.ntsb.gov/investigations/accidentreports/pages/har1702.aspx.

11. Tesla. Future of Driving. Accessed June 22, 2021. https://www.tesla.com/autopilot.

12. Insurance Institute for Highway Safety, Highway Loss Data Institute (IIHS-HLDI). Acessed July 7, 2021. https://www.iihs.org/.

13. Mueller, A. S., Reagan, I. J. and Cicchino, J. B. (2021). Addressing Driver Disengagement and Proper System Use: Human Factors Recommendations for Level 2 Driving Automation Design. *Journal of Cognitive Engineering and Decision Making,* 15(1): 3–27.

14. Brooks, C. and Szafir, D. (March 2019). Balanced Information Gathering and Goal-Oriented Actions in Shared Autonomy. *2019 14th ACM/IEEE International Conference on Human-Robot Interaction (HRI),* 85–94. https://ieeexplore.ieee.org/abstract/document/8673192/; Brooks, C. and Szafir, D. (2020). Visualization of Intended Assistance for Acceptance of Shared Control. arXiv preprint. https://arxiv.org/abs/2008.10759.

15. Waymo. Accessed June 22, 2021. http://www.waymo.com.

16. Let's Talk Autonomous Driving. Safety. Accessed June 22, 2021. https://ltad.com/about/safety.html.

17. Let's Talk Autonomous Driving. Passengers. Accessed June 22, 2021. https://www.ltad.com/about/passengers.html.

18. Macintyre, P. E. (2001). Safety and Efficacy of Patient-Controlled Analgesia. *British Journal of Anaesthesia,* 87(1): 36–46. https://bjanaesthesia.org/article/S0007-0912(17)36342-0/fulltext.

19. Wang, R., Wang, S., Duan, N. and Wang, Q. (2020). From Patient-Controlled Analgesia to Artificial Intelligence-Assisted Patient-Controlled Analgesia: Practices and Perspectives. *Frontiers in Medicine,* 7: 145. https://www.frontiersin.org/articles/10.3389/fmed.2020.00145/full.

20. Desmet, P. and Fokkinga, S. (2020). Beyond Maslow's Pyramid: Introducing a Typology of Thirteen Fundamental Needs for Human-Centered Design. *Multimodal Technologies and Interaction,* 4(3): 38.

CHAPTER 9

1. Markoff, J. (2016). *Machines of Loving Grace: The Quest for Common Ground between Humans and Robots.* New York: HarperCollins.

2. People + AI Guidebook. Accessed June 22, 2021. https://pair.withgoogle.com/guidebook.

3. Google AI. Responsible AI Practices. Accessed June 28, 2021. https://ai.google/responsibilities/responsible-ai-practices/.

4. Horvitz, E. (1999). Principles of Mixed-Initiative User Interfaces. *CHI '99: Proceedings of the SIGCHI Conference on Human Factors in Computing Systems.* ACM, 159–66. https://dl.acm.org/doi/abs/10.1145/302979.303030.

5. Microsoft. Guidelines for Human–AI Interaction. Accessed June 22, 2021. https://www.microsoft.com/en-us/research/project/guidelines-for-human-ai-interaction.

6. Amershi, S., Weld, D., Vorvoreanu, M., Fourney, A., Nushi, B., Collisson, P., . . . and Horvitz, E. (2019b). Guidelines for Human-AI Interaction. *CHI '19: Proceedings of the 2019 CHI Conference on Human Factors in Computing Systems,* Paper 3, 1–13. ACM. https://dl.acm.org/doi/abs/10.1145/3290605.3300233.

7. IBM Design for AI. Fundamentals. Accessed June 22, 2021. https://www.ibm. com/design/ai/fundamentals/.

8. Endsley, M. R. (March 2018). Level of Automation Forms a Key Aspect of Autonomy Design. *Journal of Cognitive Engineering and Decision Making*, 12(1): 29–34. https://journals.sagepub.com/doi/abs/10.1177/1555343417723432.

9. Dudley, J. J. and Kristensson, P. O. (2018). A Review of User Interface Design for Interactive Machine Learning. *ACM Transactions on Interactive Intelligent Systems (TIIS)*, 8(2): 8. https://dl.acm.org/doi/abs/10.1145/3185517.

10. Shneiderman, B., Plaisant, C., Cohen, M., Jacobs, S. and Elmqvist, N. (2016). *Designing the User Interface: Strategies for Effective Human–Computer Interaction*. 6th ed. New York: Pearson.

11. Shneiderman, B. The Eight Golden Rules of Interface Design. Accessed June 22, 2021. https://www.cs.umd.edu/~ben/goldenrules.html.

12. Shneiderman, B. The Eight Golden Rules of Interface Design.

13. Wong, E. (2020). Shneiderman's Eight Golden Rules Will Help You Design Better Interfaces. Interaction Design Foundation. https://www.interaction-design. org/literature/article/shneiderman-s-eight-golden-rules-will-help-you-design-better-interfaces.

14. Fischer, G. (2018). Design Trade-offs for Quality of Life. *ACM Interactions*, 25(1): 26–33. https://dl.acm.org/doi/fullHtml/10.1145/3170706.

15. Apple Developer (2019). Human Interface Guidelines. https://developer.apple. com/design/human-interface-guidelines/ios/overview/themes/

16. Shneiderman et al. (2016).

CHAPTER 10

1. IEEE Global Initiative on Ethics of Autonomous and Intelligent Systems (2019). *Ethically Aligned Design: A Vision for Prioritizing Human Well-being with Autonomous and Intelligent Systems*. IEEE. https://standards.ieee.org/content/ieee-standards/en/industry-connections/ec/autonomous-systems.html.

PART 3

1. Poole, D. and Mackworth, A. (2017). *Artificial Intelligence: Foundations of Computational Agents*, 2nd ed. Cambridge University Press.

2. Poole and Mackworth (2017).

CHAPTER 11

1. Turing, A. M. (1950). Computing Machinery and Intelligence. *Mind*, 49: 433–460.

2. Russell, S. (2019). *Human Compatible: Artificial Intelligence and the Problem of Control*. New York: Penguin Group.

3. Russell (2019).

4. Hsu, F.-h. (2002). *Behind Deep Blue: Building the Computer that Defeated the World Chess Champion*. Princeton University Press.

5. Laborie, P., Rogerie, J., Shaw, P. and Vilím, P. (2018). IBM ILOG CP Optimizer for Scheduling. *Constraints*, 23(2): 210–50.

6. Lobosco, K. (March 12, 2015). Talking Barbie Is Too Creepy for Some Parents. CNN Business. https://money.cnn.com/2015/03/11/news/companies/creepy-hello-barbie/; Haibe-Kains, B., Adam, G. A., Hosny, A., Khodakarami, F., MAQC Society Board of Directors, Waldron, L., . . . and Aerts, H. J. W. L. (October 15, 2020). Transparency and Reproducibility in Artificial Intelligence. *Nature*, 586: E14–E16. https://doi.org/10.1038/s41586-020-2766-y.

7. Marcus, G. and Davis, E. (2019). *Rebooting AI: Building Artificial Intelligence We Can Trust*. New York: Pantheon.

8. Waldrop, M. M. (2019). News Feature: What Are the Limits of Deep Learning? *Proceedings of the National Academy of Sciences*, 116(4): 1074–7. https://www.pnas.org/content/116/4/1074.short.

9. Shneiderman, B. (2020). Human-Centered Artificial Intelligence: Reliable, Safe & Trustworthy, *International Journal of Human–Computer Interaction*, 36(6): 495–504. https://doi.org/10.1080/10447318.2020.1741118.

CHAPTER 12

1. Russell, S. and Norvig, P. (2009). *Artificial Intelligence: A Modern Approach*. Englewood Cliffs, NJ: Prentice Hall.

2. Poole, D. and Mackworth, A. (2017). *Artificial Intelligence: Foundations of Computational Agents*, 2nd ed. Cambridge University Press.

3. Poole and Mackworth (2017); Marcus, G. and Davis, E. (2019). *Rebooting AI: Building Artificial Intelligence We Can Trust*. New York: Pantheon; Russell, S. (2019). *Human Compatible: Artificial Intelligence and the Problem of Control*. New York: Penguin Group.

4. Stanford University (2016). Artificial Intelligence and Life in 2030: One Hundred Year Study on Artificial Intelligence, https://ai100.stanford.edu/2016-report.

5. Broadbent, E. (2017). Interactions with Robots: The Truths We Reveal about Ourselves. *Annual Review of Psychology*, 68: 627–52.

6. Marcus and Davis (2019).

7. Bryson, J. J., Diamantis, M. E. and Grant, T. D. (2017). Of, for, and by the People: The Legal Lacuna of Synthetic Persons. *Artificial Intelligence and Law*, 25: 273–91. https://doi.org/10.1007/s10506-017-9214-9.

8. Friedman, B. and Hendry, D. G. (2019). *Value Sensitive Design: Shaping Technology with Moral Imagination*. Cambridge, MA: MIT Press.

9. O'Neil, C. (2016). *Weapons of Math Destruction: How Big Data Increases Inequality and Threatens Democracy*. New York: Crown Publishers.

10. Shneiderman, B. (2007). Human Responsibility for Autonomous Agents. *IEEE Intelligent Systems*, 22(2): 60–1.

11. Ammari, T., Kaye, J., Tsai, J. Y. and Bentley, F. (2019). Music, Search, and IoT: How People (Really) Use Voice Assistants. *ACM Transactions on Computer-Human Interaction (TOCHI)*, 26(3): 1–28. http://web.mit.edu/bentley/www/papers/iot.pdf.

12. Murphy, R. R. (2014). *Disaster Robotics*. Cambridge, MA: MIT Press.

13. Mumford, L. (1934). *Technics and Civilization*. University of Chicago Press.

14. Mumford (1934).

CHAPTER 13

1. Martin, C. D. (1993). The Myth of the Awesome Thinking Machine. *Communications of the ACM*, 36(4): 120–33. https://dl.acm.org/doi/abs/10.1145/-255950.153587.

2. Turing, Alan M. (1950). Computing Machinery and Intelligence. *Mind*, 49: 433–460.

3. The Loebner Prize. Accessed June 24, 2021. https://www.ocf.berkeley.edu/~arihuang/academic/research/loebner.html.

4. Marcus, G., Rossi, F. and Veloso, M., eds. (2016). Beyond the Turing Test. *AI Magazine*, 37(1): 3–4. https://doi.org/10.1609/aimag.v37i1.2650.

5. Natale, S. (2021). *Deceitful Media: Artificial Intelligence and Social Life after the Turing Test*. New York: Oxford University Press.

6. Licklider, J. C. R. (1960). Man-Computer Symbiosis. *Transactions on Human Factors in Electronics*, HFE-1: 4–11.

7. Sukis, J. (March 13, 2020). Email message to author.

8. People and AI Research. Accessed June 24, 2021. https://pair.withgoogle.com/.

9. Sundar, S. S., Waddell, T. F. and Jung, E. H. (2016). The Hollywood Robot Syndrome Media Effects on Older Adults' Attitudes toward Robots and Adoption Intentions. *Proc. 11th ACM/IEEE International Conference on Human-Robot Interaction (HRI)*. IEEE, 343–50.

10. Smith, B. C. (2019). The Promise of Artificial Intelligence: Reckoning and Judgment. Cambridge, MA: MIT Press.

11. Martin, C. D. (1995). ENIAC: Press Conference That Shook the World. *IEEE Technology and Society Magazine*, 14(4): 3–10. https://ieeexplore.ieee.org/abstract/document/476631.

12. Toews, R. (December 13, 2020). 8 Leading Women in the Field of AI. Forbes. https://www.forbes.com/sites/robtoews/2020/12/13/8-leading-women-in-the-field-of-ai/.

13. Engelbart, D. C. (1962). Augmenting Human Intellect: A Conceptual Framework. Reprinted in Packer, R. and Jordan, K., eds. (2001). *Multimedia: From Wagner to Virtual Reality*. New York: W. W. Norton, 64–90.

14. Engelbart, D. C. and English, W. K. (1968). A Research Center for Augmenting Human Intellect. *Proc. 1968 Fall Joint Computer Conference*, Part I, 395–410.

15. Markoff, J. (2016). *Machines of Loving Grace: The Quest for Common Ground between Humans and Robots*. New York: HarperCollins.

16. Shneiderman, B. and Maes, P. (1997). Direct Manipulation vs. Interface Agents. *ACM interactions*, 4(6): 42–61.

17. Shneiderman, B. (1982). The Future of Interactive Systems and the Emergence of Direct Manipulation, *Behaviour and Information Technology*, 1(3): 237–56; Shneiderman, B. (August 1983). Direct Manipulation: A Step beyond Programming Languages, *IEEE Computer*, 16(8): 57–69.

18. Shneiderman (1982).

19. Apple Developer (2019). Human Interface Guidelines. https://developer.apple.com/design/human-interface-guidelines/ios/overview/themes/.

20. Usability.gov. Accessed June 24, 2021. http://www.usability.gov.

21. Augmented Humans. Augmented Humans 2021: Online, 22–24 February 2021. Accessed June 24, 2021. https://augmented-humans.org/.

22. SIGCHI. Accessed June 24, 2021. http://www.sigchi.org.

23. UXPA International. Accessed June 24, 2021. https://uxpa.org/about-uxpa-international/.

24. World Usability Day. Accessed June 24, 2021. https://worldusabilityday.org/.

25. ACM IUI 2022. Accessed June 24, 2021. https://iui.acm.org/.

26. Heer, J. (2019). Agency Plus Automation: Designing Artificial Intelligence into Interactive Systems. *Proceedings of the National Academy Sciences*, 116(6): 1844–50. https://www.pnas.org/content/116/6/1844.

27. Koch, J., Lucero, A., Hegemann, L. and Oulasvirta, A. (May 2019). May AI? Design Ideation with Cooperative Contextual Bandits. *Proc. 2019 CHI Conference on Human Factors in Computing Systems*. ACM, 1–12. https://dl.acm.org/doi/abs/10.1145/3290605.3300863; Koch, J., Taffin, N., Beaudouin-Lafon, M., Laine, M., Lucero, A. and Mackay, W. E. (2020). ImageSense: An Intelligent Collaborative Ideation Tool to Support Diverse Human-Computer Partnerships. *Proc. ACM on Human-Computer Interaction*, 4(CSCW1): 1–27. https://dl.acm.org/doi/abs/10.1145/3392850.

CHAPTER 14

1. Kahn, P. H., Freier, N. G., Kanda, T., Ishiguro, H., Ruckert, J. H., Severson, R. L. and Kane, S. K. (March 2008). Design Patterns for Sociality in Human-Robot Interaction. *Proc. 3rd ACM/IEEE International Conference on Human Robot Interaction.* ACM, 97–104; Krämer, N. C., von der Pütten, A. and Eimler, S. (2012). Human-Agent and Human-Robot Interaction Theory: Similarities to and Differences from Human-Human Interaction. In: Zacarias, M. and de Oliveira, J. V., eds., *Human-Computer Interaction: The Agency Perspective.* Heidelberg/Berlin: Springer, 215–40. http://dx.doi.org/10.1007/978-3-642-25691-2_9.

2. You, S. and Robert, L. P. (2018). Emotional Attachment, Performance, and Viability in Teams Collaborating with Embodied Physical Action (EPA) Robots. *Journal of the Association for Information Systems*, 19(5): 377–407. doi: 10.17705/1jais.00496.

3. Reeves, B. and Nass, C. (1996). *How People Treat Computers, Television, and New Media Like Real People and Places.* Cambridge, MA: MIT Press; Nass, C. and Moon, Y. (2000). Machines and Mindlessness: Social Responses to Computers. *Journal of Social Issues*, 56(1): 81–103.

4. Groom, V. and Nass, C. (2007). Can Robots Be Teammates?: Benchmarks in Human–Robot Teams. *Interaction Studies*, 8(3): 483–500. https://www.jbe-platform.com/content/journals/10.1075/is.8.3.10gro.

5. Robert, L. (2017). The Growing Problem of Humanizing Robots. *International Robotics and Automation Journal*, 3(1): 247–8. https://papers.ssrn.com/sol3/papers.cfm?abstract_id=3027628.

6. Wang, W. and Siau, K. (2019). Artificial Intelligence, Machine Learning, Automation, Robotics, Future of Work and Future of Humanity: A Review and Research Agenda. *Journal of Database Management*, 30(1): 61–79.

7. Sebo, S., Stoll, B., Scassellati, B., and Jung, M. F. (2020). Robots in Groups and Teams: A Literature Review. *Proc. ACM on Human-Computer Interaction*, 4(CSCW2): 1–36. https://dl.acm.org/doi/abs/10.1145/3415247; Traeger, M. L., Sebo, S. S., Jung, M., Scassellati, B. and Christakis, N. A. (2020). Vulnerable Robots Positively Shape Human Conversational Dynamics in a Human–Robot Team. *Proc. National Academy of Sciences,* 117(12), 6370–5. https://www.pnas.org/content/117/12/6370.

8. Klein, G., Woods, D. D., Bradshaw, J. M., Hoffman, R. R. and Feltovich, P. J. (2004). Ten Challenges for Making Automation a "Team Player" in Joint Human-Agent Activity. *IEEE Intelligent Systems*, 6: 91–5. https://ieeexplore.ieee.org/abstract/document/1363742/.

9. Natale, S. (2021). *Deceitful Media: Artificial Intelligence and Social Life after the Turing Test.* Oxford University Press.

10. Boden, M., Bryson, J., Caldwell, D., Dautenhahn, K., Edwards, L., Kember, S., . . . and Winfield, A. F. (2017). Principles of Robotics: Regulating Robots in the Real World. *Connection Science*, 29(2): 124–9.

11. Boden et al. (2017).

12. Shneiderman, B. (2007). Human Responsibility for Autonomous Agents. *IEEE Intelligent Systems*, 22(2): 60–1.

13. Canadian Government (2019). Knowledge Requirements for Pilots of Remotely Piloted Aircraft Systems 250 g up to and including 25 kg, Operating within Visual Line-of-Sight (VLOS). TP 15263. https://www.tc.gc.ca/en/services/aviation/publications/tp-15263.html.

14. Calo, R. (2016). Robots in American Law. University of Washington School of Law Research Paper, 2016–04. https://papers.ssrn.com/sol3/papers.cfm?abstract_id=2737598.

15. Mumford, L. (1934). *Technics and Civilization*. University of Chicago Press.

16. Intuitive for Patients. Accessed June 24, 2021. https://www.davincisurgery.com/.

CHAPTER 15

1. US Defense Science Board (June 2016). *Summer Study on Autonomy*. Washington, DC: US Department of Defense.

2. US Defense Science Board Task Force (July 2012). *The Role of Autonomy in DoD Systems*. Washington, DC: US Department of Defense.

3. Blackhurst, J. L., Gresham, J. S. and Stone, M. O. (2011). The Autonomy Paradox. *Armed Forces Journal*, 20–40.

4. US National Transportation Safety Board (2017). Collision between a Car Operating with Automated Vehicle Control Systems and a Tractor-Semitrailer Truck Near Williston, Florida, May 7, 2016. Accident Report NTSB/HAR-17/02, PB2017-102600. Available at: https://www.ntsb.gov/investigations/accidentreports/pages/har1702.aspx.

5. Nicas, J., Kitroeff, N., Gelles, D. and Glanz, J. (June 6, 2019). Boeing Built Deadly Assumptions into 737 Max, Blind to a Late Design Change. *The New York Times*. https://www.nytimes.com/2019/06/01/business/boeing-737-max-crash.html.

6. Woods, D. D., Tittle, J., Feil, M. and Roesler, A. (2004). Envisioning Human-Robot Coordination in Future Operations. *IEEE Transactions on Systems, Man, and Cybernetics, Part C (Applications and Reviews)*, 34(2): 210–18. https://doi.org/10.1109/TSMCC.2004.826272.

7. Bainbridge, L. (1983). Ironies of Automation. *Automatica*, 19(6): 775–9.

8. Blackhurst et al. (2011); Mindell, D. (2015). *Our Robots, Ourselves: Robotics and the Myths of Autonomy*. New York: Viking Press; Hancock, P. A. (2017). Imposing Limits on Autonomous Systems. *Ergonomics*, 60(2): 284–91.

9. Strauch, B. (2017). Ironies of Automation: Still Unresolved After All These Years. *IEEE Transactions on Human-Machine Systems*, 48(5): 419–33. https://ieeexplore.ieee.org/abstract/document/8013079/.

10. Bradshaw, J. M., Hoffman, R. R., Woods, D. D. and Johnson, M. (2013). The Seven Deadly Myths of Autonomous Systems. *IEEE Intelligent Systems*, 28(3): 54–61. https://ieeexplore.ieee.org/abstract/document/6588858/.

11. Endsley, M. R. (2017). From Here to Autonomy: Lessons Learned from Human–Automation Research. *Human Factors*, 59(1): 5–27.

12. Hancock, P. (2022). Avoiding Adverse Autonomous Agent Actions. *Human-Computer Interaction Journal* (forthcoming).

13. Lethal Autonomous Weapons. Accessed June 24, 2021. https://autonomous-weapons.org/.

14. Hoffman, R. R., Cullen, T. M. and Hawley, J. K. (2016). The Myths and Costs of Autonomous Weapon Systems. *Bulletin of the Atomic Scientists*, 72(4): 247–55. https://doi.org/10.1080/00963402.2016.1194619.

15. Topcu, U., Bliss, N., Cooke, N., Cummings, M., Llorens, A., Shrobe, H. and Zuck, L. (2020). Assured Autonomy: Path Toward Living with Autonomous Systems We Can Trust. arXiv preprint. https://arxiv.org/abs/2010.14443.

16. Johns Hopkins Institute for Assured Autonomy. Accessed June 24, 2021. https://iaa.jhu.edu/.

17. UKRI Trustworthy Autonomous Systems Hub. Accessed July 2, 2021. https://www.tas.ac.uk/.

18. Sheridan, T. B. (1992). *Telerobotics, Automation, and Human Supervisory Control.* Cambridge, MA: MIT Press.

19. Schwarting, W., Alonso-Mora, J., Pauli, L., Karaman, S. and Rus, D. (May 2017). Parallel Autonomy in Automated Vehicles: Safe Motion Generation with Minimal Intervention. *Proc. 2017 IEEE International Conference on Robotics and Automation (ICRA).* IEEE, 1928–35. https://ieeexplore.ieee.org/abstract/document/7989224/.

CHAPTER 16

1. Mou, Y., Shi, C., Shen, T. and Xu, K. (2020). A Systematic Review of the Personality of Robot: Mapping Its Conceptualization, Operationalization, Contextualization and Effects, *International Journal of Human–Computer Interaction*, 36(6): 591–605. https://doi.org/10.1080/10447318.2019.1663008; Prescott, T. J. and Robillard, J. (2021). Are Friends Electric? The Benefits and Risks of Human-Robot Relationships. *iScience*, 24(1), 101993. https://www.sciencedirect.com/science/article/pii/S2589004220311901.

2. Michael, K., Bowman, D., Jones, M. L. and Pringle, R. (2018). Robots and Socio-ethical Implications. *IEEE Technology and Society Magazine*, 37(1): 19–21.

3. McAllister, B. (September 21, 1993). "Postal Buddy" Gets an *unfriendly push*. *Washington Post*. https://www.washingtonpost.com/archive/politics/1993/09/21/postal-buddy-gets-an-unfriendly-push/66554041-0218-44d0-b6d7-92a89b1da5e6/.

4. Kuo, L. (November 9, 2018). World's First AI News Anchor Unveiled in China, *The Guardian*. https://www.theguardian.com/world/2018/nov/09/worlds-first-ai-news-anchor-unveiled-in-china.

5. Honda (2019). Asimo: The World's Most Advanced Humanoid Robot. Accessed May 15, 2020. https://asimo.honda.com/.

6. Hanson Social Robotics (September 24, 2018). Meet Sophia, the Robot That Looks Human. https://www.hansonrobotics.com/news-meet-sophia-the-robot-that-looks-almost-human/.

7. Breazeal, C. L. (2002). *Designing Sociable Robots*. Cambridge, MA: MIT Press.

8. Hoffman, G. (May 1, 2019). Anki, Jibo, and Kuri: What We Can Learn from Social Robots That Didn't Make It. *IEEE Spectrum*. https://spectrum.ieee.org/automaton/robotics/home-robots/anki-jibo-and-kuri-what-we-can-learn-from-social-robotics-failures.

9. Hoffman (2019).

10. Jung, M. (December 15, 2020). Email message to author.

11. Boston Dynamics. Accessed June 25, 2021. https://www.bostondynamics.com.

12. SoftBank Robotics. Pepper. Accessed June 25, 2021. https://www.softbankrobotics.com/emea/en/pepper.

13. Pandey, A. K. and Gelin, R. (2018). A Mass-Produced Sociable Humanoid Robot: Pepper: The First Machine of Its Kind. *IEEE Robotics and Automation Magazine*, 25(3): 40–8. https://ieeexplore.ieee.org/abstract/document/8409927/.

14. Carros, F., Meurer, J., Löffler, D., Unbehaun, D., Matthies, S., Koch, I., . . . and Wulf, V. (April 2020). Exploring Human-Robot Interaction with the Elderly: Results from a Ten-Week Case Study in a Care Home. *Proc. 2020 CHI Conference on Human Factors in Computing Systems*. ACM, 1–12. https://dl.acm.org/doi/abs/10.1145/3313831.3376402.

15. Gale, A. and Mochizuki, T. (January 14, 2019). Robot Hotel Loses Love for Robots. *Wall Street Journal*. https://www.wsj.com/articles/robot-hotel-loses-love-for-robots-11547484628.

16. Richardson, K., Coeckelbergh, M., Wakunuma, K., Billing, E., Ziemke, T., Gomez, P., . . . and Belpaeme, T. (2018). Robot Enhanced Therapy for Children with Autism (DREAM): A Social Model of Autism. *IEEE Technology and Society Magazine*, 37(1): 30–9.

17. McBride, N. (2020). Robot Enhanced Therapy for Autistic Children: An Ethical Analysis. *IEEE Technology and Society Magazine*, 39(1): 51–60.

18. Watson, D. (2019). The Rhetoric and Reality of Anthropomorphism in Artificial Intelligence. *Minds and Machines*, 29(3): 417–40.

19. Watson (2019).

20. Prescott and Robillard (2021).

21. PARO. Accessed June 25, 2021. http://www.parorobots.com.

22. Hung, L., Gregorio, M., Mann, J., Wallsworth, C., Horne, N., Berndt, A., . . . and Chaudhury, H. (2019). Exploring the Perceptions of People with Dementia about the Social Robot PARO in a Hospital Setting. *Dementia*, 20(2): 485–504. https://doi.org/10.1177/1471301219894141.

23. National Geographic. In Japan, a Funeral Service for Robot Dogs. Video. Accessed June 25, 2021. https://www.nationalgeographic.com/travel/destinations/asia/japan/in-japan–a-buddhist-funeral-service-for-robot-dogs/.

24. Aibo. Accessed June 25, 2021. https://us.aibo.com/feature/feature1.html.

25. Joy for All. Companion Pet Pup. Accessed June 25, 2021. https://joyforall.com/products/companion-pet-golden-pup.

26. Tombot. Accessed June 25, 2021. http://www.tombot.com.

27. Brownlee, M. (2020). Dope Tech: Boston Dynamics Robot Dog! YouTube video. Accessed June 25, 2021. https://www.youtube.com/watch?v=s6_azdBnAlU; Pro Robots (2020). Evolution of Boston Dynamics. YouTube video. Accessed June 25, 2021. https://www.youtube.com/watch?v=xH9sXhYA3nE; Boston Dynamics. Spot. Accessed June 25, 2021. https://www.bostondynamics.com/spot.

28. Lambert, A., Norouzi, N., Bruder, G. and Welch, G. (2020). A Systematic Review of Ten Years of Research on Human Interaction with Social Robots. *International Journal of Human–Computer Interaction*, 36(19): 1804–17. https://doi.org/10.1080/10447318.2020.1801172.

29. Mishra, K. (February 24, 2020). How AI-powered Devices Are Remodeling the Consumer Electronics Industry. https://www.pathpartnertech.com/how-ai-powered-devices-are-remodeling-the-consumer-electronics-industry/.

30. iRobot. Accessed June 25, 2021. http://www.irobot.com.

31. Honig, S. and Oron-Gilad, T. (2018). Understanding and Resolving Failures in Human-Robot Interaction: Literature Review and Model Development. *Frontiers in Psychology*, 9(861): 1–21. https://www.frontiersin.org/articles/10.3389/fpsyg.2018.00861/full.

32. Honig, S., Bartal, A. and Oron-Gilad, T. (March 2020). Using Customers' Online Reviews to Identify and Classify Human Robot Interaction Failures in Domestic Robots. In *Companion of the 2020 ACM/IEEE International Conference on Human-Robot Interaction*. ACM, 251–3.

33. Sciuto, A., Saini, A., Forlizzi, J., and Hong, J. I. (2018). Hey Alexa, What's Up?: A Mixed-Methods Studies of In-home Conversational Agent Usage. *Proc. Designing Interactive Systems Conference 2018*. ACM, 857–68. https://dl.acm.org/doi/abs/10.1145/3196709.3196772; López G., Quesada L. and Guerrero L.A. (2018). Alexa vs. Siri vs. Cortana vs. Google Assistant: A Comparison of Speech-based Natural User Interfaces. In Nunes, I. (ed.). *Advances in Human Factors and Systems Interaction*. AHFE 2017. Advances in Intelligent Systems and Computing, vol. 592. New York: Springer;

Lopatovska, I., Rink, K., Knight, I., Raines, K., Cosenza, K., Williams, H., ... and Martinez, A. (2019). Talk to Me: Exploring User Interactions with the Amazon Alexa. *Journal of Librarianship and Information Science*, 51(4): 984–97. https://journals.sagepub.com/doi/abs/10.1177/0961000618759414; Lopatovska, I., Griffin, A. L., Gallagher, K., Ballingall, C., Rock, C. and Velazquez, M. (2020). User Recommendations for Intelligent Personal Assistants. *Journal of Librarianship and Information Science*, 52(2): 577–91. https://journals.sagepub.com/doi/abs/10.1177/0961000619841107; Natale, S. (2020). To Believe in Siri: A Critical Analysis of AI Voice Assistants. Communicative Figurations, Working Paper 32, 1–17. https://www.uni-bremen.de/fileadmin/user_upload/fachbereiche/fb9/zemki/media/photos/publikationen/working-papers/2020/CoFi_EWP_No-32_Simone-Natale.pdf.

34. Ammari, T., Kaye, J., Tsai, J. Y. and Bentley, F. (2019). Music, Search, and IoT: How People (Really) Use Voice Assistants. *ACM Transactions on Computer-Human Interaction (TOCHI)*, 26(3): 1–28. http://web.mit.edu/bentley/www/papers/iot.pdf.

35. Pearl, C. (2016). *Designing Voice User Interfaces: Principles of Conversational Experiences*. Sebastapol, CA: O'Reilly Media.

36. Shneiderman, B. (2000). The Limits of Speech Recognition. *Communications of the ACM*, 43(9): 63–5. https://dl.acm.org/doi/fullHtml/10.1145/348941.348990.

37. Lobosco, K. (March 12, 2015). Talking Barbie Is Too Creepy for Some Parents. CNN Business. https://money.cnn.com/2015/03/11/news/companies/creepy-hello-barbie/.

38. Replika. Accessed June 25, 2021. https://replika.ai/.

39. Woebot Health. Accessed June 25, 2021. https://woebothealth.com/.

40. Sheehan, B., Jin, H. S. and Gottlieb, U. (2020). Customer Service Chatbots: Anthropomorphism and Adoption. *Journal of Business Research*, 115: 14–24. https://www.sciencedirect.com/science/article/pii/S0148296320302484.

41. Adam, M., Wessel, M. and Benlian, A. (2020). AI-Based Chatbots in Customer Service and Their Effects on User Compliance. *Electronic Markets*, 1–19. https://link.springer.com/content/pdf/10.1007/s12525-020-00414-7.pdf; Khadpe, P., Krishna, R., Fei-Fei, L., Hancock, J. T. and Bernstein, M. S. (2020). Conceptual Metaphors Impact Perceptions of Human-AI Collaboration. *Proc. ACM on Human-Computer Interaction*, 4(CSCW2): Article 163, 1–26. https://dl.acm.org/doi/abs/10.1145/3415234.

42. Broadbent, E. (2017). Interactions with Robots: The Truths We Reveal about Ourselves. *Annual Review of Psychology*, 68: 627–52.

43. Sprinkle, T. (2017). Robophobia: Bridging the Uncanny Valley. American Society of Mechanical Engineers. https://www.asme.org/topics-resources/content/robophobia-bridging-the-uncanny-valley.

44. Liang, Y. and Lee, S. A. (2017). Fear of Autonomous Robots and Artificial Intelligence: Evidence from National Representative Data with Probability Sampling. *International Journal of Social Robotics*, 9(3): 379–84.

45. Strait, M. K., Aguillon, C., Contreras, V. and Garcia, N. (2017). The Public's Perception of Humanlike Robots: Online Social Commentary Reflects an Appearance-Based Uncanny Valley, a General Fear of a "Technology Takeover", and the Unabashed Sexualization of Female-Gendered Robots. *Proc. 26th IEEE International Symposium on Robot and Human Interactive Communication (RO-MAN)*. IEEE, 1418–23.

46. Reeves, B. and Nass, C. (1996). *How People Treat Computers, Television, and New Media Like Real People and Places*. Cambridge, MA: MIT Press.

47. Apple Developer (2019). Human Interface Guidelines. https://developer.apple.com/design/human-interface-guidelines/ios/overview/themes/.

48. Russell, S. (2019). *Human Compatible: Artificial Intelligence and the Problem of Control*. New York: Penguin Group.

49. Murphy, R. R. (2014). *Disaster Robotics*. Cambridge, MA: MIT Press.

50. Amazon Robotics. Accessed June 25, 2021. https://www.amazonrobotics.com.

CHAPTER 18

1. Shneiderman, B. (2016). Opinion: The Dangers of Faulty, Biased, or Malicious Algorithms Requires Independent Oversight. *Proceedings of the National Academy of Sciences*, 113(48), 13538–40. http://www.pnas.org/content/113/48/13538.full; Xu, W. (2019). Toward Human-Centered AI: A Perspective from Human-Computer Interaction. *ACM Interactions*, 26(4): 42–6. doi.org/10.1145/3328485.

2. Shneiderman, B. (2020a). Human-Centered Artificial Intelligence: Reliable, Safe & Trustworthy, *International Journal of Human–Computer Interaction*, 36(6): 495–504. https://doi.org/10.1080/10447318.2020.1741118; Shneiderman, B. (2020b). Design lessons from AI's two grand goals: Human emulation and useful applications, *IEEE Transactions on Technology and Society*, 1(2): 73–82. https://ieeexplore.ieee.org/document/9088114; Dignum, V. (2019). *Responsible Artificial Intelligence: How to Develop and Use AI in a Responsible Way*. New York: Springer Nature; Brundage, M., Avin, S., Wang, J., Belfield, H., Krueger, G., Hadfield, G., . . . and Maharaj, T. (2020). Toward Trustworthy AI Development: Mechanisms for Supporting Verifiable Claims. arXiv preprint. https://arxiv.org/abs/2004.07213.

3. Stanford University. Human-Centered Artificial Intelligence. Accessed June 25, 2021. http://hai.stanford.edu

4. Santoni de Sio, F., and Van den Hoven, J. (2018). Meaningful Human Control over Autonomous Systems: A Philosophical Account. *Frontiers in Robotics and AI*, 5: 15.

5. Rosenberg, F., and Dustdar, S. (2005). Design and Implementation of a Service-Oriented Business Rules Broker. *Seventh IEEE International Conference on E-Commerce Technology Workshops*. IEEE, 55–63.

6. Fjeld, J., Achten, N., Hilligoss, H., Nagy, A. and Srikumar, M. (2020). Principled Artificial Intelligence: Mapping Consensus in Ethical And Rights-Based Approaches to Principles for AI. Berkman Klein Center Research Publication. https://cyber.harvard.edu/publication/2020/principled-ai.

7. IEEE Ethics in Action in Autonomous and Intelligent Systems. Accessed June 25, 2021. https://ethicsinaction.ieee.org/; IEEE Global Initiative on Ethics of Autonomous and Intelligent Systems (2019). *Ethically Aligned Design: A Vision for Prioritizing Human Well-being with Autonomous and Intelligent Systems*. IEEE. https://standards.ieee.org/content/ieee-standards/en/industry-connections/ec/autonomous-systems.html.

8. Winfield, A. F., and Jirotka, M. (2018). Ethical Governance Is Essential to Building Trust in Robotics and Artificial Intelligence Systems. *Philosophical Transactions of the Royal Society A: Mathematical, Physical and Engineering Sciences*, 376(2133): 20180085.

9. Kalluri, P. (2020). Don't Ask If Artificial Intelligence Is Good or Fair, Ask How It Shifts Power. *Nature*, 583(7815): 169.

10. Leveson, N. (2011). *Engineering a Safer World: Systems Thinking Applied to Safety*. Cambridge, MA: MIT Press; Wenskovitch, J., Zhou, M. X., Collins, C., Chang, R., Dowling, M., Endert, A. and Xu, K. (2020). Putting the "I" in Interaction: Interactive Interfaces Personalized to Individuals. *IEEE Computer Graphics and Applications*, 40(3): 73–82.

11. Heilweil, R. (June 11, 2020). Big Tech Companies Back away from Selling Facial Recognition to Police. That's Progress. *Vox News*. https://www.vox.com/recode/2020/6/10/21287194/amazon-microsoft-ibm-facial-recognition-moratorium-police.

12. Falco, G., Shneiderman, B., Badger, J., Carrier, R., Dahbura, A., Danks, D., . . . and Yeong, Z. K. (2021). Governing AI Safety through Independent Audits. *Nature Machine Intelligence*, 3(7): 566–71. https://doi.org/10.1038/s42256-021-00370-7.

CHAPTER 19

1. Mittelstadt, B., Russell, C. and Wachter, S. (2019). Explaining Explanations in AI. *Proc. Conference on Fairness, Accountability, and Transparency*. ACM, 279–88. https://doi.org/10.1145/3287560.3287574; Amershi, S., Begel, A., Bird, C., DeLine, R., Gall, H., Kamar, E., . . . and Zimmermann, T. (2019a). Software Engineering for Machine Learning: A Case Study. *Proc. IEEE/ACM 41st International Conference on Software Engineering: Software Engineering in Practice (ICSE-SEIP)*. IEEE, 291–300.

2. Canadian Government (2019). Responsible Use of Artificial Intelligence (AI). https://www.canada.ca/en/government/system/digital-government/modern-emer-ging-technologies/responsible-use-ai.html.

3. Grossi, D. R. (May 1999). Aviation Recorder Overview. *Proc. International Symposium On Transportation Recorders.* Arlington, VA, 153–64; Campbell, N. (2007). The evolution of flight Data Analysis. *Proceedings of Australian Society of Air Safety Investigators.* https://asasi.org/papers/2007/The_Evolution_of_Flight_Data_Analysis_Neil_Campbell.pdf; Kavi, K. M. (2010). Beyond the Black Box. *IEEE Spectrum,* 47(8): 46–51; Bonsor, K. and Chandler, N. (2020). How Black Boxes Work. https://science.howstuffworks.com/transport/flight/modern/black-box.htm.

4. Pettersson, O. (2005). Execution Monitoring in Robotics: A Survey. *Robotics and Autonomous Systems,* 53(2): 73–88; Theodorou, A., Wortham, R. H. and Bryson, J. J. (2017). Designing and Implementing Transparency for Real Time Inspection of Autonomous Robots. *Connection Science,* 29(3): 230–41. https://doi.org/10.1080/09540091.2017.1310182; Winfield, A. F., and Jirotka, M. (2017, July). The Case for an Ethical Black Box. In *Annual Conference Towards Autonomous Robotic Systems.* New York: Springer, 262–73. https://link.springer.com/chapter/10.1007/978-3-319-64107-2_21; Mitrevski, A., Thoduka, S., Sáinz, A. O., Schöbel, M., Nagel, P., Plöger, P. G. and Prassler, E. (2018). Deploying Robots in Everyday Environments: towards Dependable and Practical Robotic Systems. In *29th International Workshop Principles of Diagnosis DX,* Vol. 18. http://www.ropod.org/downloads/dx18.pdf.

5. Siegel, G. (2014). *Forensic Media: Reconstructing Accidents in Accelerated Modernity.* Durham, NC: Duke University Press; Elbaum, S., and Munson, J. C. (October 2000). Software Black Box: An Alternative Mechanism for Failure Analysis. *Proc. 11th International Symposium on Software Reliability Engineering. ISSRE 2000.* IEEE, 365–76. https://ieeexplore.ieee.org/abstract/document/885887.

6. Pérez, A., García, M. I., Nieto, M., Pedraza, J. L., Rodríguez, S. and Zamorano, J. (2010). Argos: An Advanced in-vehicle Data Recorder on a Massively Sensorized Vehicle for Car Driver Behavior Experimentation. *IEEE Transactions on Intelligent Transportation Systems,* 11(2): 463–73; Yao, Y. and Atkins, E. (2020). The Smart Black Box: A Value-Driven High-Bandwidth Automotive Event Data R. https://ieeexplore.ieee.org/document/8995510.

7. A3 Robotics. Accessed June 29, 2021. https://www.automate.org/robotics.

8. Seddon, J. J. and Currie, W. L. (2017). A Model for Unpacking Big Data Analytics in High-Frequency Trading. *Journal of Business Research,* 70: 300–7; Vishnia, G. R. and Peters, G. W. (2020). AuditChain: A Trading Audit Platform over Blockchain. *Frontiers in Blockchain,* 3: 9.

9. Amershi, S. et al. (2019a).

10. Zhang, J. M., Harman, M., Ma, L. and Liu, Y. (2020). Machine Learning Testing: Survey, Landscapes and Horizons. *IEEE Transactions on Software Engineering.* https://ieeexplore.ieee.org/abstract/document/9000651.

11. Shneiderman, B., Plaisant, C., Cohen, M., Jacobs, S. and Elmqvist, N. (2016). *Designing the User Interface: Strategies for Effective Human-Computer Interaction*, 6th ed. New York: Pearson; Sharp, H., Preece, J. and Rogers, Y. (2019). *Interaction Design: Beyond Human-Computer Interaction*, 5th ed. New York: Wiley.

12. Wickramasinghe, C. S., Marino, D. L., Grandio, J. and Manic, M. (June 2020). Trustworthy AI Development Guidelines for Human System Interaction. *Proc. 2020 13th International Conference on Human System Interaction (HSI).* IEEE, 130–6. https://ieeexplore.ieee.org/abstract/document/9142644/.

13. Appugliese, C., Nathan, P. Roberts, W. S. (2020). *Agile AI: A Practical Guide to Building AI Applications and Teams.* Sebastopol, CA: O'Reilly Media.

14. Principles behind the Agile Manifesto. Accessed June 28, 2021. http://agilemanifesto.org/principles.html.

15. Appugliese et al. (2020).

16. Amershi et al. (2019a).

17. Amershi et al. (2019a), 298.

18. US National Security Commission on Artificial Intelligence (2019). Interim Report. https://epic.org/foia/epic-v-ai-commission/AI-Commission-Interim-Report-Nov-2019.pdf.

19. Zhang et al. (2020).

20. Couzin-Frankel, J. (2019). Medicine Contends with How to Use Artificial Intelligence. *Science*, 354(6446): 1119–20. https://science.sciencemag.org/content/364/6446/1119.summary.

21. GitHub. Accessed June 26, 2021. https://github.com/.

22. Liang, X., Shetty, S., Tosh, D., Kamhoua, C., Kwiat, K. and Njilla, L. (2017). Provchain: A Blockchain-based Data Provenance Architecture in Cloud Environment with Enhanced Privacy and Availability. *Proc. 2017 17th IEEE/ACM International Symposium on Cluster, Cloud and Grid Computing (CCGRID)*, 468–477.

23. Ebert, C. and Weyrich, M. (2019). Validation of Autonomous Systems. *IEEE Software*, 36(5): 15–23. https://ieeexplore.ieee.org/abstract/document/8802868/.

24. Brundage, M., Avin, S., Wang, J., Belfield, H., Krueger, G., Hadfield, G., ... and Maharaj, T. (2020). Toward Trustworthy AI Development: Mechanisms for Supporting Verifiable Claims. arXiv preprint. https://arxiv.org/abs/2004.07213.

25. MITRE ATT&CK. Accessed June 28, 2021. https://attack.mitre.org/.

26. MITRE Partnership Network. AI Fails and How We Learn from Them. Accessed July 5, 2021. https://sites.mitre.org/aifails/.

27. Breck, E., Polyzotis, N., Roy, S., Whang, S. E. and Zinkevich, M. (2019). Data Validation for Machine Learning. In *Conference on Systems and Machine Learning (SysML)*. https://www.sysml.cc/doc/2019/167.pdf; Zhang et al. (2020).

28. Gebru, T., Morgenstern, J., Vecchione, B., Vaughan, J. W., Wallach, H., Daumé III, H. and Crawford, K. (2018). Datasheets for Datasets. arXiv preprint. https://arxiv.org/abs/1803.09010.

29. Mitchell, M., Wu, S., Zaldivar, A., Barnes, P., Vasserman, L., Hutchinson, B., ... and Gebru, T. (January 2019). Model Cards for Model Reporting. *Proc. Conference on Fairness, Accountability, and Transparency*. ACM, 220–9. https://dl.acm.org/doi/abs/10.1145/3287560.3287596.

30. Herschel, M., Diestelkämper, R. and Lahmar, H. B. (2017). A Survey on Provenance: What for? What Form? What from? *The VLDB Journal*, 26(6): 881–906.

31. Ragan, E. D., Endert, A., Sanyal, J. and Chen, J. (2015). Characterizing Provenance in Visualization and Data Analysis: An Organizational Framework of Provenance Types and Purposes. *IEEE Transactions on Visualization and Computer Graphics*, 22(1): 31–40.

32. Bostelman, R., Hong, T. and Marvel, J. (2016). Survey of Research for Performance Measurement of Mobile Manipulators. *Journal of Research of the National Institute of Standards and Technology*, 121(3): 342–66.

33. O'Neil, C. (2016). *Weapons of Math Destruction: How Big Data Increases Inequality and Threatens Democracy*. New York: Crown Publishers.

34. ACM Conference on Fairness, Accountability, and Transparency (ACM FAccT). Accessed June 28, 2021. https://facctconference.org/.

35. Holstein, K., Wortman Vaughan, J., Daumé III, H., Dudik, M. and Wallach, H. (May 2019). Improving Fairness in Machine Learning Systems: What Do Industry Practitioners Need? In *Proc. 2019 CHI Conference on Human Factors in Computing Systems*. ACM, 1–16. https://doi.org/10.1145/3290605.3300830.

36. Perez, C. C. (2019). *Invisible Women: Exposing Data Bias in a World Designed for Men*. New York: Random House.

37. Friedman, B. and Nissenbaum, H. (1996). Bias in Computer Systems. *ACM Transactions on Information Systems (TOIS)*, 14(3): 330–47.

38. Baeza-Yates, R. (2018). Bias on the Web. *Communications of the ACM*, 61(6): 54–61.

39. Mehrabi, N., Morstatter, F., Saxena, N., Lerman, K. and Galstyan, A. (2019). A Survey on Bias and Fairness in Machine Learning. arXiv preprint. https://arxiv.org/abs/1908.09635.

40. Morris, M. R. (2020). AI and Accessibility: A Discussion of Ethical Considerations. *Communications of the ACM*, 63(6): 35–7.

41. Obermeyer, Z., Powers, B., Vogeli, C. and Mullainathan, S. (2019). Dissecting of Racial Bias in an Algorithm Used to Manage the Health of Populations. Science, 366(6464): 447–53. https://science.sciencemag.org/content/366/6464/447.

42. Brundage et al. (2020); Schiff, D., Rakova, B., Ayesh, A., Fanti, A. and Lennon, M. (2021). Principles to practices for responsible AI: Closing the gap. *IEEE Technology and Society Magazine*.

43. Friedler, S. A., Scheidegger, C., Venkatasubramanian, S., Choudhary, S., Hamilton, E. P., and Roth, D. (January 2019). A Comparative Study of Fairness-Enhancing Interventions in Machine Learning. *Proc. Conference on Fairness, Accountability, and Transparency*. ACM, 329–38. https://doi.org/10.1145/3287560.3287589.

44. Bellamy, R. K., Dey, K., Hind, M., Hoffman, S. C., Houde, S., Kannan, K., . . . and Nagar, S. (2019). AI Fairness 360: An Extensible Toolkit for Detecting and Mitigating Algorithmic Bias. *IBM Journal of Research and Development*, 63(4/5): 4:1–4:15.

45. Pasquale, F. (2015). *The Black Box Society: The Secret Algorithms that Control Money and Information*. Cambridge, MA: Harvard University Press; Pasquale, F. (2018). When Machine Learning Is Facially Invalid. *Communications of the ACM*, 61(9): 25–7. https://dl.acm.org/doi/fullHtml/10.1145/3241367.

46. Buolamwini, J. and Gebru, T. (January 2018). Gender Shades: Intersectional Accuracy Disparities in Commercial Gender Classification. *Proc. 1st Conference on Fairness, Accountability, and Transparency*, PMLR, 81: 77–91. http://proceedings.mlr.press/v81/buolamwini18a.html.

47. Buolamwini and Gebru (2018).

48. Marks, P. (2021). Can the Biases in Facial Recognition Be Fixed; Also Should They? *Communications of the ACM*, 64(3): 20–2. https://cacm.acm.org/magazines/2021/3/250698-can-the-biases-in-facial-recognition-be-fixed-also-should-they/fulltext.

49. Coded Bias. Accessed July 5, 2021. https://www.codedbias.com/.

50. Benjamin, R. (2019). *Race after Technology: Abolitionist Tools for the New Jim Code*. Boston: Polity Press; Noble, S. U. (2018). *Algorithms of Oppression: How Search Engines Reinforce Racism*. NYU Press.

51. Lewis, J. E., ed. (2020). *Indigenous Protocol and Artificial Intelligence Position Paper*. Honolulu, HI: The Initiative for Indigenous Futures and the Canadian Institute for Advanced Research (CIFAR). https://spectrum.library.concordia.ca/986506.

52. Harrell, D. F. (2013). *Phantasmal media: An Approach to Imagination, Computation, and Expression*. Cambridge, MA: MIT Press.

53. Goodman, B. and Flaxman, S. (2017). European Union Regulations on Algorithmic Decision-Making and a "Right to Explanation". *AI Magazine*, 38(3): 50–7; Wachter, S., Mittelstadt, B. and Russell, C. (2017). Counterfactual Explanations without Opening the Black Box: Automated Decisions and the GDPR. *Harvard Journal of Law and Technology*, 31: 841–87.

54. Biran, O. and Cotton, C. (August 2017). Explanation and Justification in Machine Learning: A Survey. *IJCAI-17 Workshop on Explainable AI (XAI)*, 8(1);

Hoffman, R. R. and Klein, G. (2017). Explaining Explanation, Part 1: Theoretical Foundations. *IEEE Intelligent Systems*, 32(3): 68–73. https://ieeexplore.ieee.org/abstract/document/7933919/; Hoffman, R. R., Mueller, S. T., and Klein, G. (2017). Explaining Explanation, Part 2: Empirical Foundations. *IEEE Intelligent Systems*, 32(4): 78–86. https://ieeexplore.ieee.org/abstract/document/8012316/; Theodorou et al. (2017); Abdul, A., Vermeulen, J., Wang, D., Lim, B. Y. and Kankanhalli, M. (April 2018). Trends and Trajectories for Explainable, Accountable and Intelligible Systems: An HCI Research Agenda. *Proc. 2018 CHI Conference on Human Factors in Computing Systems*. ACM, 1–18. https://dl.acm.org/doi/10.1145/3173574.3174156; Wang, D., Yang, Q., Abdul, A., and Lim, B. Y. (2019). Designing Theory-Driven User-Centric Explainable AI. *Proc. 2019 CHI Conference on Human Factors in Computing Systems*. ACM, 1–15. https://doi.org/10.1145/3290605.3300831; Mittelstadt et al. (2019); Liao, Q. V., Gruen, D., and Miller, S. (2020). Questioning the AI: Informing Design Practices for Explainable AI User Experiences. *Proc. 2020 ACM CHI Conference on Human Factors in Computing Systems*. ACM, 1–15.

55. Information Commissioner's Office and Alan Turing Institute (2019). Explaining Decisions Made with AI. https://ico.org.uk/about-the-ico/ico-and-stakeholder-consultations/ico-and-the-turing-consultation-on-explaining-ai-decisions-guid -ance/.

56. Information Commissioner's Office and Alan Turing Institute (2019). Explaining Decisions Made with AI. Part 1: The Basics of Explaining AI. https://ico.org.uk/media/about-the-ico/consultations/2616434/explaining-ai-deci -sions-part-1.pdf.

57. Weld, D. S. and Bansal, G. (2019). The Challenge of Crafting Intelligible Intelligence. *Communications of the ACM*, 62(6): 70–9.

58. Hong, S., Hullman, J., and Bertini, E. (2020). Human Factors in Model Interpretability: Industry Practices, Challenges, and Needs. *Proc. ACM on Human-Computer Interaction*, 4(CSCW1): 1–26. https://dl.acm.org/doi/pdf/10.1145/3392878.

59. Ehsan, U., Liao, Q. V., Muller, M., Riedl, M. O. and Weisz, J. D. (2021). Expanding Explainability: Towards Social Transparency in AI systems. *Proc. 2021 CHI Conference on Human Factors in Computing Systems*, ACM, Article 82, 1–19. https://doi.org/10.1145/3411764.3445188.

60. Miller, T. (2019). Explanation in Artificial Intelligence: Insights from the *social sciences*. *Artificial Intelligence*, 267: 1–38. https://doi.org/10.1016/j.artint.2018.07.007.

61. Arya, V., Bellamy, R. K., Chen, P. Y., Dhurandhar, A., Hind, M., Hoffman, S. C., . . . and Zhang, Y. (2020). AI Explainability 360: An Extensible Toolkit for Understanding Data and Machine Learning Models. *Journal of Machine Learning Research*, 21(130): 1–6. https://www.jmlr.org/papers/volume21/19-1035/19-1035.pdf.

62. Hind, M. (2019). Explaining Explainable AI. XRDS: Crossroads, The *ACM Magazine for Students*, 25(3): 16–19. https://dl.acm.org/doi/abs/10.1145/3313096;

Mojsilovic, A. (August 8, 2019). Introduction AI Explainability 360. IBM Research Blog. https://www.ibm.com/blogs/research/2019/08/ai-explainability-360/.

63. Du, M., Liu, N. and Hu, X. (2020). Techniques for Interpretable Machine Learning. *Communications of the ACM*, 63(1): 68–77. https://dl.acm.org/doi/fullHtml/10.1145/3359786; Letham, B., Rudin, C., McCormick, T. H., and Madigan, D. (2015). Interpretable Classifiers Using Rules and Bayesian Analysis: Building a Better Stroke Prediction Model. *Annals of Applied Statistics*, 9(3): 1350–71; Doshi-Velez, F. and Kim, B. (2017). Towards a Rigorous Science of Interpretable Machine Learning. arXiv preprint. https://arxiv.org/abs/1702.08608.

64. Rathi, S. (2019). Generating Counterfactual and Contrastive Explanations Using SHAP. arXiv preprint. https://arxiv.org/abs/1906.09293.

65. Kulesza, T., Burnett, M., Wong, W. K. and Stumpf, S. (2015). Principles of Explanatory Debugging to Personalize Interactive Machine Learning. *Proc. 20th International Conference on Intelligent User Interfaces*. ACM, 126–37. https://dl.acm.org/doi/abs/10.1145/2678025.2701399.

66. Rudin, C. (2019). Stop Explaining Black Box Machine Learning Models for High Stakes Decisions and Use Interpretable Models Instead. *Nature Machine Intelligence*, 1(5): 206–15.

67. Buchanan, B. G. and Shortliffe, E. H., eds. (1985). *Rule-based Expert Systems: The MYCIN Experiments of the Stanford Heuristic Programming Project*. Boston: Addison-Wesley.

68. Clancey, W. J. (1986). From GUIDON to NEOMYCIN and HERACLES in Twenty Short Lessons. *AI Magazine*, 7(3): 40–60.

69. Hull, R., Kumar, B., Lieuwen, D., Patel-Schneider, P. F., Sahuguet, A., Varadarajan, S. and Vyas, A. (2003). "Everything Personal, Not Just Business": Improving User Experience through Rule-Based Service Customization. *International Conference on Service-Oriented Computing*, Berlin: Springer, 149–64. https://link.springer.com/chapter/10.1007/978-3-540-24593-3_11; Rosenberg, F. and Dustdar, S. (2005). Design and Implementation of a Service-Oriented Business Rules Broker. *Seventh IEEE International Conference on E-Commerce Technology Workshops*. IEEE, 55–63.

70. Shneiderman et al. (2016).

71. Brooks, C. and Szafir, D. (March 2019). Balanced Information Gathering and Goal-Oriented Actions in Shared Autonomy. *Proc. 2019 14th ACM/IEEE International Conference on Human-Robot Interaction (HRI)*. IEEE, 85–94. https://ieeexplore.ieee.org/abstract/document/8673192/; Brooks, C. and Szafir, D. (2020). Visualization of Intended Assistance for Acceptance of Shared Control. *Proc. 2020 IEEE/RSJ International Conference on Intelligent Robots and Systems (IROS)*. IEEE, 11425–30. https://ieeexplore.ieee.org/document/9340964; Szafir, D. and Szafir, D. (2021). Connecting Human-Robot Interaction with Data Visualization. *Proc. 2021 ACM/IEEE International Conference on Human-Robot Interaction*. IEEE.

72. Nourashrafeddin, S., Sherkat, E., Minghim, R. and Milios, E. E. (2018). A Visual Approach for Interactive Keyterm-Based Clustering. *ACM Transactions on Interactive Intelligent Systems (TIIS)*: 8(1): 1–35. https://dl.acm.org/doi/abs/10.1145/3181669; Du, F., Plaisant, C., Spring, N., Crowley, K. and Shneiderman, B. (2019). EventAction: A Visual Analytics Approach to Explainable Recommendation for Event Sequences. *ACM Transactions on Interactive Intelligent Systems*, 9(4): 1–31. https://dl.acm.org/doi/10.1145/3301402; Cheng, H. F., Wang, R., Zhang, Z., O'Connell, F., Gray, T., Harper, F. M. and Zhu, H. (2019). Explaining Decision-Making Algorithms through UI: Strategies to Help Non-expert Stakeholders. *Proc. 2019 CHI Conference on Human Factors in Computing Systems.* ACM, 1–12. https://dl.acm.org/doi/abs/10.1145/3290605.3300789; Naveed, S., and Ziegler, J. (2019). Feature-Driven Interactive Recommendations and Explanations with Collaborative Filtering Approach. *Proc. ComplexRec@ RecSys*, 10–15. http://ceur-ws.org/Vol-2449/paper2.pdf.

73. Zhou, M. X., Mark, G., Li, J. and Yang, H. (2019). Trusting Virtual Agents: The Effect of Personality. *ACM Transactions on Interactive Intelligent Systems (TIIS)*, 9(2–3): 1–36. https://dl.acm.org/doi/abs/10.1145/3232077; Wenskovitch, J., Zhou, M. X., Collins, C., Chang, R., Dowling, M., Endert, A. and Xu, K. (2020). Putting the "I" in Interaction: Interactive Interfaces Personalized to Individuals. *IEEE Computer Graphics and Applications*, 40(3): 73–82.

74. Hohman, F., Head, A., Caruana, R., DeLine, R. and Drucker, S. M. (2019). Gamut: A Design Probe to Understand How Data Scientists Understand Machine Learning Models. *Proc. 2019 CHI Conference on Human Factors in Computing Systems.* ACM, 1–13. https://dl.acm.org/doi/abs/10.1145/3290605.3300809.

75. Hohman, F., Park, H., Robinson, C., and Chau, D. H. P. (2019). SUMMIT: Scaling Deep Learning Interpretability by Visualizing Activation and Attribution Summarizations. *IEEE Transactions on Visualization and Computer Graphics*, 26(1): 1096–1106. https://fredhohman.com/papers/19-summit-vast.pdf.

76. Cai, C. J., Reif, E., Hegde, N., Hipp, J., Kim, B., Smilkov, D., . . . and Terry, M. (May 2019). Human-Centered Tools for Coping with Imperfect Algorithms during Medical Decision-Making. *Proc. 2019 CHI Conference on Human Factors in Computing Systems.* ACM, 1–14. https://dl.acm.org/doi/10.1145/3290605.3300234.

77. Weld and Bansal (2019).

78. Koenemann, J. and Belkin, N. J. (April 1996). A Case for Interaction: A Study of Interactive Information Retrieval Behavior and Effectiveness. *Proc. SIGCHI Conference on Human Factors in Computing Systems.* ACM, 205–12. https://dl.acm.org/doi/fullHtml/10.1145/238386.238487.

79. Harambam, J., Bountouridis, D., Makhortykh, M., and Van Hoboken, J. (September 2019). Designing for the Better by Taking Users into Account: A Qualitative Evaluation of User Control Mechanisms in (News) Recommender Systems. *Proc. 13th ACM Conference on Recommender Systems,* 69–77. https://dl.acm.org/doi/abs/10.1145/3298689.3347014.

80. Chen, L., Yan, D. and Wang, F. (December 2019). User Evaluations on Sentiment-Based Recommendation Explanations. *ACM Transactions on Interactive Intelligent Systems*, 9(4): Article 20, 1–38. https://doi.org/10.1145/3282878; Zhu, D. and Lee, S. (2020). Autonomous Readers: The Impact of News Customisation on Audiences' Psychological and Behavioural Outcomes. *Communication Research and Practice*, 6(2): 125–42. https://www.tandfonline.com/doi/abs/10.1080/22041451.2019.1644586.

81. Du et al. (2020).

82. Vought, R. T. (November 17, 2020). Guidance for Regulation of Artificial Intelligence Applications, Washington, DC: U.S. White House. https://www.whitehouse.gov/wp-content/uploads/2020/11/M-21-06.pdf.

83. Du et al. (2019).

84. Du et al. (2019).

85. He, C., Parra, D. and Verbert, K. (2016). Interactive Recommender Systems: A Survey of the State of the Art and Future Research Challenges and Opportunities. *Expert Systems with Applications*, 56: 9–27. https://www.sciencedirect.com/science/article/pii/S0957417416300367.

86. Jin, Y., Cardoso, B. and Verbert, K. (2017). How Do Different Levels of User Control Affect Cognitive Load and Acceptance of Recommendations?. *Proc. CEUR Workshop*, 1884: 35–42. https://lirias.kuleuven.be/1633445; Jin, Y., Tintarev, N. and Verbert, K. (September 2018). Effects of Personal Characteristics on Music Recommender Systems with Different Levels of Controllability. *Proc. 12th ACM Conference on Recommender Systems*. ACM, 13–21. https://dl.acm.org/doi/abs/10.1145/3240323.3240358; Charleer, S., Gutiérrez, F. and Verbert, K. (March 2019). Supporting Job Mediator and Job Seeker through an Actionable Dashboard. In *Proceedings of the 24th International Conference on Intelligent User Interfaces*, 121–31. https://dl.acm.org/doi/abs/10.1145/3301275.3302312.

87. Millecamp, M., Htun, N. N., Jin, Y. and Verbert, K. (July 2018). Controlling Spotify Recommendations: Effects of Personal Characteristics on Music Recommender User Interfaces. *Proc. 26th Conference on User Modeling, Adaptation and Personalization*. ACM, 101–9. https://dl.acm.org/doi/abs/10.1145/3209219.3209223.

88. OECD Better Life Index. Accessed June 29, 2021. http://www.oecdbetterlifeindex.org/

89. Whichbook. Accessed June 28, 2021. https://www.whichbook.net/.

90. Hsu, S., Vaccaro, K., Yue, Y., Rickman, A. and Karahalios, K. (2020). Awareness, Navigation, and Use of Feed Control Settings Online. *Proc. 2020 CHI Conference on Human Factors in Computing Systems*. ACM, 1–13. https://dl.acm.org/doi/abs/10.1145/3313831.3376583.

91. Stray, J. (2020). Aligning AI optimization to community well-being. *International Journal of Community Well-Being*, 3: 443–63. https://link.springer.com/

article/10.1007/s42413-020-00086-3; Stray, J., Adler, S. and Hadfield-Menell, D. (2020). What Are You Optimizing for? Aligning Recommender Systems with Human Values. Participatory Approaches to Machine Learning Workshop, *International Conference on Machine Learning (ICML)*. https://participatoryml.github.io/papers/2020/42.pdf.

CHAPTER 20

1. Perrow, C. (2011). *Normal Accidents: Living with High Risk Technologies-Updated edition*. Princeton University Press.

2. Klein, G. A. (2017). *Sources of Power: How People Make Decisions*. Cambridge, MA: MIT Press; Hopkins, A. (1999). The Limits of Normal Accident Theory. *Safety Science*, 32(2): 93–102. https://www.sciencedirect.com/science/article/pii/S0925753599000156/pdf.

3. La Porte, T. R. (1996). High Reliability Organizations: Unlikely, Demanding and at Risk. *Journal of Contingencies and Crisis Management*, 4(2): 60–71; Dietterich, T.G. (2019). Robust Artificial Intelligence and Robust Human Organizations. *Frontiers of Computer Science*, 13: 1–3. https://doi.org/10.1007/s11704-018-8900-4.

4. Brown, H. (2018). Keeping the Lights On: A Comparison of Normal Accidents and High Reliability Organizations. *IEEE Technology and Society Magazine*, 37(2): 62–70.

5. Haavik, T. K., Antonsen, S., Rosness, R. and Hale, A. (2019). HRO and RE: A Pragmatic Perspective. *Safety Science*, 117: 479–89.

6. Woods, D. D. (2017). Essential Characteristics of Resilience. In Hollnagel, E., Woods, D. D. and Leveson, N., eds., *Resilience Engineering: Concepts and Precepts*. Farnham, UK: Ashgate Publishing, 21–34.

7. Guldenmund, F. W. (2000). The Nature of Safety Culture: A Review of Theory and Research. *Safety Science*, 34(1–3): 215–57; Berry, J. C., Davis, J. T., Bartman, T., Hafer, C. C., Lieb, L. M., Khan, N. and Brilli, R. J. (2020). Improved Safety Culture and Teamwork Climate Are Associated with Decreases in Patient Harm and Hospital Mortality across a Hospital System. *Journal of Patient Safety*, 16(2): 130–6. http://www.ncbi.nlm.nih.gov/pubmed/26741790.

8. Erickson, S. M., Wolcott, J., Corrigan, J. M. and Aspden, P., eds. (2004). *Patient Safety: Achieving a New Standard for Care*. Washington, DC: National Academies Press.

9. Leveson, N. (2011). *Engineering a Safer World: Systems Thinking Applied to Safety*. Cambridge, MA: MIT Press.

10. Landon, P., Weaver, P. and Fitch, J. P. (2016). Tracking Minor and Near-Miss Events and Sharing Lessons Learned as a Way to Prevent Accidents. *Applied Biosafety*, 21(2): 61–5. https://journals.sagepub.com/doi/abs/10.1177/1535676016646642.

11. Weick, K. E., Sutcliffe, K. M. and Obstfeld D. (1999). Organizing for High Relia-bility: Processes of Collective Mindfulness. In Sutton, R. S. and Staw, B. M., eds., *Research in Organizational Behavior*, Vol. 1. Stanford, CA: JAI Press, 81–123.

12. Berry et al. (2020).

13. Challen, R., Denny, J., Pitt, M., Gompels, L., Edwards, T. and Tsaneva-Atanasova, K. (2019). Artificial Intelligence, Bias and Clinical Safety. *BMJ Quality and Safety*, 28(3): 231–7; Tamboli, A. (2019) *Keeping Your AI Under Control: A Pragmatic Guide to Identifying, Evaluating, and Quantifying Risks*. Berkeley, CA: Apress. https://doi.org/10.1007/978-1-4842-5467-7; Reddy, S., Allan, S., Coghlan, S. and Cooper, P. (2020). A Governance Model for the Application of AI in Health Care. *Journal of the American Medical Informatics Association*, 27(3): 491–7.

14. Amodei, D., Olah, C., Steinhardt, J., Christiano, P., Schulman, J. and Mané, D. (2016). Concrete Problems in AI Safety. arXiv preprint. https://arxiv.org/abs/1606.06565; Leike, J., Martic, M., Krakovna, V., Ortega, P. A., Everitt, T., Lefrancq, A., Orseau, L., and Legg, S. (2017). AI Safety Gridworlds. arXiv preprint. https://arxiv.org/abs/1711.09883.

15. Apple Developer (2019). Human Interface Guidelines. https://developer.apple.com/design/human-interface-guidelines/ios/overview/themes/.

16. People and AI Research. Accessed June 26, 2021. https://pair.withgoogle.com/.

17. Microsoft. Guidelines for Human–AI Interaction. Accessed June 26, 2021. https://www.microsoft.com/en-us/research/project/guidelines-for-human-ai-interaction/.

18. IBM Design for AI. Fundamentals. Accessed June 26, 2021. https://www.ibm.com/design/ai/fundamentals/.

19. Shneiderman, B., Plaisant, C., Cohen, M., Jacobs, S. and Elmqvist, N. (2016). *Designing the User Interface: Strategies for Effective Human-Computer Interaction*, 6th ed. New York: Pearson; Sharp, H., Preece, J. and Rogers, Y. (2019). *Interaction Design: Beyond Human-Computer Interaction*, 5th edn. New York: Wiley.

20. Dudley, J. J. and Kristensson, P. O. (2018). A Review of User Interface Design for Interactive Machine Learning. *ACM Transactions on Interactive Intelligent Systems (TiiS)*, 8(2): article 8, 1–37. https://dl.acm.org/doi/abs/10.1145/3185517; Amershi, S., Weld, D., Vorvoreanu, M., Fourney, A., Nushi, B., Collisson, P., . . . and Horvitz, E. (2019b). Guidelines for Human-AI Interaction. *Proc. 2019 CHI Conference on Human Factors in Computing Systems*. ACM, Paper 3, 1–13; Shneiderman, Ben (2020b). Design Lessons from AI's Two Grand Goals: Human Emulation and Useful Applications. *IEEE Transactions on Technology and Society*, 1(2): 73–82. https://ieeexplore.ieee.org/document/9088114.

21. Daugherty, P. R. and Wilson, H. J. (2018). *Human+ Machine: Reimagining Work in the Age of AI*. Cambridge, MA: Harvard Business Press.

22. Erickson et al. (2004).

23. National Safety Council. Accessed June 26, 2021. http://www.nsc.org.

24. Federal Aviation Administration. Accessed June 26, 2021. https://hotline.faa.gov/

25. Aviation Safety Reporting System. Accessed June 26, 2021. https://asrs.arc. nasa.gov/.

26. US Food and Drug Administration. MedWatch: The FDA Safety Information and Adverse Event Reporting Program. Accessed June 26, 2021. https:// www.fda.gov/safety/medwatch-fda-safety-information-and-adverse-event-repor -ting-program.

27. US Food and Drug Administration. MedWatch Online Voluntary Reporting Form. Accessed June 26, 2021. https://www.accessdata.fda.gov/ scripts/medwatch/index.cfm.

28. Alemzadeh, H., Raman, J., Leveson, N., Kalbarczyk, Z. and Iyer, R. K. (2016). Adverse Events in Robotic Surgery: A Retrospective Study of 14 Years of FDA Data. *PloS One*, 11(4): e0151470. https://doi.org/10.1371/journal.pone.0151470.

29. CVE. Accessed June 26, 2021. https://cve.mitre.org/.

30. National Institute of Standards and Technology. National Vulnerability Database. Accessed June 26, 2021. https://nvd.nist.gov/vuln.

31. GitHub. Accessed June 26, 2021. https://github.com/.

32. Bugzilla. About Bugzilla. Accessed June 26, 2021. https://www.bugzilla.org/about/.

33. Rubinovitz, J. B. (2018). Bias Bounty Programs as a Method of Combatting Bias in AI. https://rubinovitz.com/2018/08/01/bias-bounty-programs-as-a-method-of-combatting/; Brundage, M., Avin, S., Wang, J., Belfield, H., Krueger, G., Hadfield, G., . . . and Maharaj, T. (2020). Toward Trustworthy AI Development: Mechanisms for Supporting Verifiable Claims. arXiv preprint. https://arxiv.org/abs/2004. 07213.

34. HackerOne. Accessed June 26, 2021. https://www.hackerone.com/.

35. BugCrowd. Accessed June 26, 2021. https://www.bugcrowd.com/.

36. Magazinius, A., Mellegård, N. N. and Olsson, L. (August 2019). Bug Bounty Programs—A Mapping Study. *Proc. 2019 45th Euromicro Conference on Software Engineering and Advanced Applications (SEAA)*. IEEE, 412–15. https:// ieeexplore.ieee.org/abstract/document/8906758/; Breidenbach, L., Daian, P., Tramèr, F. and Juels, A. (2018). Enter the Hydra: Towards Principled Bug Bounties and Exploit-Resistant Smart Contracts. *Proc. 27th USENIX Security Symposium*. IEEE, 1335–52. https://www.usenix.org/conference /usenixsecurity18/presentation/breindenbach.

37. Mai, T., Khanna, R., Dodge, J., Irvine, J., Lam, K. H., Lin, Z., . . . and Fern, A. (2020). Keeping It "Organized and Logical" After-action Review for AI (AAR/AI). *Proc. 25th International Conference on Intelligent User Interfaces*. ACM, 465–76.

38. Yampolskiy, R. V. (2019). Predicting Future AI Failures from Historic Examples. *Foresight*, 21(1): 138–52. https://www.emerald.com/insight/content/doi/10.1108/FS-04-2018-0034/full/html.

39. McGregor, S. (2020). Preventing Repeated Real World AI Failures by Cataloging Incidents: The AI Incident Database. arXiv preprint. https://arxiv.org/abs/2011.08512; Incident Database. Accessed June 26, 2021. https://incidentdatabase.ai/.

40. Tesla Deaths. Accessed June 26, 2021. https://www.tesladeaths.com/.

41. Motor Vehicle Death Petition to Recall All Tesla Vehicles due to Sudden Unintended Acceleration. Accessed June 26, 2021. https://static.nhtsa.gov/odi/inv/2020/INBC-DP20001-3494.pdf.

42. Tesla. There is No "Unintended" Acceleration in Tesla Vehicles. Accessed June 26, 2021. https://www.tesla.com/blog/no-unintended-acceleration-tesla-vehicles.

43. Brundage et al. (2020).

44. Agency for Healthcare Research and Quality. Surveys on Patient Safety Culture. Accessed June 26, 2021. https://www.ahrq.gov/sops/index.html.

45. Bell, S. K., Smulowitz, P. B., Woodward, A. C., Mello, M. M., Duva, A. M., Boothman, R. C. and Sands, K. (2012). Disclosure, Apology, and Offer Programs: Stakeholders' Views of Barriers to and Strategies for Broad Implementation. *The Milbank Quarterly*, 90(4): 682–705.

46. Bell et al. (2012).

47. Raji, I. D., Smart, A., White, R. N., Mitchell, M., Gebru, T., Hutchinson, B., . . . and Barnes, P. (2020). Closing the AI Accountability Gap: Defining an End-to-End Framework for Internal Algorithmic Auditing. *Proc. 2020 Conference on Fairness, Accountability, and Transparency (FAT* '20).* ACM, 33–44. https://doi.org/10.1145/3351095.3372873.

48. Facebook. Welcoming the Oversight Board. Accessed June 26, 2021. https://about.fb.com/news/2020/05/welcoming-the-oversight-board/.

49. Microsoft. Our Approach to Responsible AI at Microsoft. Accessed June 26, 2021. https://www.microsoft.com/en-us/ai/our-approach.

50. A3 Robotics. Accessed June 26, 2021. https://www.automate.org/robotics.

51. American National Standards Institute. Accessed June 26, 2021. https://www.ansi.org.

52. ISO/TC 299. About ISO/TC 299 Robotics. Accessed June 26, 2021. https://committee.iso.org/home/tc299.

53. Open Community for Ethics in Autonomous and Intelligent Systems. IEEE P7000 Projects. Accessed June 26, 2021. https://ethicsstandards.org/p7000/.

54. Open Community for Ethics in Autonomous and Intelligent Systems. Accessed June 26, 2021. https://ethicsstandards.org/.

55. Web Content Accessibility Guidelines (WCAG) 2.1 Accessed June 26, 2021. https://www.w3.org/TR/WCAG21/.

56. Digital.gov. An Introduction to Accessibility. Accessed June 26, 2021. https://digital.gov/resources/introduction-accessibility/.

57. Humphrey, W. S. (1988). Characterizing the Software Process: A Maturity Framework. *IEEE Software*, 5(2): 73–9. https://ieeexplore.ieee.org/document/2014.

58. Paulk, M. C., Curtis, B., Chrissis, M. B. and Weber, C. V. (1993). Capability Maturity Model, Version 1.1. *IEEE Software*, 10(4): 18–27; von Wangenheim, C. G., Hauck, J. C. R., Zoucas, A., Salviano, C. F., McCaffery, F. and Shull, F. (2010). Creating Software Process Capability/Maturity Models. *IEEE Software*, 27(4): 92–4.

59. Fraser, P., Moultrie, J. and Gregory, M. (2002). The Use of Maturity Models/Grids as a Tool in Assessing Product Development Capability. *Proc. IEEE International Engineering Management Conference*, 1: 244–9; Lacerda, T. C. and von Wangenheim, C. G. (2018). Systematic Literature Review of Usability Capability/Maturity Models. *Computer Standards & Interfaces*, 55: 95–105.

60. Alsheibani, S., Messom, C. and Cheung, Y. (2019). Towards an Artificial Intelligence Maturity Model: From Science Fiction to Business Facts. *Proc. 23rd Pacific Asia Conference on Information Systems*, Xian, China, Association for Information Systems. https://www.semanticscholar.org/paper/Towards-An-Artificial-Intelligence-Maturity-Model%3A-Alsheibani-Cheung/1d0b75dce15e26779db0a3f82a307f9682280b55; Carvalho, J. V., Rocha, Á., Vasconcelos, J. and Abreu, A. (2019). A Health Data Analytics Maturity Model for Hospitals Information Systems. *International Journal of Information Management*, 46: 278–85; Office of the Under Secretary of Defense for Acquisition and Sustainment Cybersecurity Maturity Model Certification. Accessed June 26, 2021. https://www.acq.osd.mil/cmmc/.

61. The Institue for Ethical AI and Machine Learning. The Machine Learning Maturity Model. Accessed June 26, 2021. https://ethical.institute/mlmm.html.

62. Brundage et al. (2020).

63. Gebru, T., Morgenstern, J., Vecchione, B., Vaughan, J. W., Wallach, H., Daumé III, H., and Crawford, K. (2018). Datasheets for Datasets. arXiv preprint. https://arxiv.org/abs/1803.09010.

64. Piorkowski, D., González, D., Richards, J., and Houde, S. (2020). Towards Evaluating and Eliciting High-Quality Documentation for Intelligent Systems. arXiv preprint. https://arxiv.org/abs/2011.08774.

65. IBM Research: FactSheets 360. Accessed June 26, 2021. https://aifs360.mybluemix.net/

66. Sokol, K. and Flach, P. (January 2020). Explainability Fact Sheets: A Framework for Systematic Assessment of Explainable Approaches. *Proc. 2020 Conference on Fairness, Accountability, and Transparency*, 56–67.

CHAPTER 21

1. US National Research Council (2008). *Protecting Individual Privacy in the Struggle Against Terrorists: A Framework for Program Assessment.* Washington, DC: National Academies Press. http://www.nap.edu/catalog.php?record_id=12452; Shneiderman, B. (2016). Opinion: The Dangers of Faulty, Biased, or Malicious Algorithms Requires Independent Oversight. *Proceedings of the National Academy of Sciences*, 113(48), 13538–40. http://www.pnas.org/content/113/48/13538.full; Brundage, M., Avin, S., Wang, J., Belfield, H., Krueger, G., Hadfield, G., . . . and Maharaj, T. (2020). Toward Trustworthy AI Development: Claims. arXiv preprint. https://arxiv.org/abs/2004.07213.

2. IEEE Global Initiative on Ethics of Autonomous and Intelligent Systems (2019). *Ethically Aligned Design: A Vision for Prioritizing Human Well-being with Autonomous and Intelligent Systems.* IEEE. https://standards.ieee.org/content/ieee-standards/en/industry-connections/ec/autonomous-systems.html; Fjeld, J., Achten, N., Hilligoss, H., Nagy, A. and Srikumar, M. (2020). Principled Artificial Intelligence: Mapping Consensus in Ethical and Rights-Based Approaches to Principles for AI. Berkman Klein Center Research Publication. https://cyber.harvard.edu/publication/2020/principled-ai.

3. Pasquale, F. (2017). Toward a Fourth Law of Robotics: Preserving Attribution, Responsibility, and Explainability in an Algorithmic Society. *Ohio State Law Journal*, 78: 1243–55.

4. European Union Expert Group on Liability and New Technologies (2019). Liability for Artificial Intelligence and other Emerging Digital Technologies. https://www.europarl.europa.eu/meetdocs/2014_2019/plmrep/COMMITTEES/JURI/DV/2020/01-09/AI-report_EN.pdf.

5. Garfinkel, S., Matthews, J., Shapiro, S. S. and Smith, J. M. (2017). Toward Algorithmic Transparency and Accountability. *Communications of the ACM*, 60(9): 5.

6. IEEE Global Initiative on Ethics of Autonomous and Intelligent Systems (2019).

7. Fjeld et al. (2020).

8. Calo, R. (2016). Robots in American Law. University of Washington School of Law Research Paper, 2016–04. https://papers.ssrn.com/sol3/papers.cfm?abstract_id=2737598.

9. Birnbaum, E. (March 28, 2019). HUD Charges Facebook with Enabling House Discrimination. *The Hill.* https://thehill.com/policy/technology/436209-hud-charges-facebook-with-housing-discrimination-over-its-targeted.

10. US National Research Council (2008).

11. Shneiderman (2016).

12. Reisman, D., Schultz, J., Crawford, K., and Whittaker, M. (2018). *Algorithmic Impact Assessments: A Practical Framework for Public Agency Accountability*. AI Now Institute, 1–22. https://ainowinstitute.org/aiareport2018.pdf.

13. PWC. Accessed June 26, 2021. https://www.pwc.com/gx/en/issues/data-and-analytics/artificial-intelligence.html.

14. Deloitte. Accessed June 26, 2021. https://www2.deloitte.com/us/en/pages/deloitte-analytics/solutions/analytics-ai.html.

15. EY. Accessed June 26, 2021. https://www.ey.com/en_us/ai.

16. KPMG. Accessed June 26, 2021. https://advisory.kpmg.us/services/data-analytics/artificial-intelligence.html.

17. ForHumanity. Taxonomy: AI Audit, Assurance, and Assessment. Accessed July 5, 2021. https://forhumanity.center/contact-tracing-audit.

18. COSO. Accessed June 26, 2021. https://www.coso.org.

19. Landwehr, C.E. (2013). A Building Code for Building Code: Putting What We Know Works to Work. *Proc. 29th Ann. Computer Security Applications Conf. (ACSAC),* 139–147; http://www.landwehr.org/2013-12-cl-acsac-essay-bc.pdf; Landwehr, C. (2015). We Need a Building Code for Building Code. *Communications of the ACM*, 58(2): 24–6.

20. Calo (2016); Pasquale (2017).

21. Travelers Institute. Insuring Autonomy: How Auto Insurance Can Adapt to Changing Risks. Accessed June 26, 2021. https://www.travelers.com/iw-documents/travelers-institute/Final-Digital-2018-AV-White-Paper.pdf.

22. Koopman, P., Kane, A., and Black, J. (February 2019). Credible Autonomy Safety Argumentation. *Proc. 27th Safety-Critical Systems Symposium*, 1–27. http://users.ece.cmu.edu/~koopman/pubs/Koopman19_SSS_CredibleSafetyArgumentation.pdf.

23. Metz, C. (May 24, 2021). The Costly Pursuit of Self-Driving Cars Continues On. And On. And On. *The New York Times.* https://www.nytimes.com/2021/05/24/technology/self-driving-cars-wait.html.

24. Open Community for Ethics in Autonomous and Intelligent Systems. IEEE P7000 Projects. Accessed June 27, 2021. https://ethicsstandards.org/p7000/.

25. IEEE Standards Association. The Ethics Certification Program for Autonomous and Intelligent Systems (ECPAIS). Accessed June 26, 2021. https://standards.ieee.org/industry-connections/ecpais.html.

26. Nadella, S. (June 28, 2016). The Partnership of the Future. *Slate.* https://slate.com/technology/2016/06/microsoft-ceo-satya-nadella-humans-and-a-i-can-work-together-to-solve-societys-challenges.html.

27. Pichai, S. (June 7, 2018). AI at Google: Our Principles. https://www.blog.google/technology/ai/ai-principles/.

28. Raji, I. D., Smart, A., White, R. N., Mitchell, M., Gebru, T., Hutchinson, B., ... and Barnes, P. (2020). Closing the AI Accountability Gap: Defining an End-to-End Framework for Internal Algorithmic Auditing. *Proc. 2020 Conference on Fairness, Accountability, and Transparency (FAT* '20)*. ACM, 33–44. https://doi.org/10.1145/3351095.3372873.

29. UL. Our Mission. Accessed June 26, 2021. https://www.ul.com/about/mission.

30. Brookings Institution. Artificial Intelligence and Emergine Technology Initiative. Accessed June 26, 2021. https://www.brookings.edu/project/artificial-intelligence-and-emerging-technology-initiative/.

31. Epic.org. Accessed June 26, 2021. http://epic.org.

32. Algorithmic Justice League. Accessed June 26, 2021. https://www.ajlunited.org.

33. AI Now Institute. Accessed June 26, 2021. https://ainowinstitute.org.

34. Data and Society. Accessed June 26, 2021. https://datasociety.net.

35. Responsible Robotics. Accessed June 26, 2021. https://responsiblerobotics.org.

36. AI4ALL. Accessed June 26, 2021. http://ai-4-all.org.

37. ForHumanity. Accessed June 26, 2021. https://www.forhumanity.center/.

38. Future of Life Institute. Accessed June 26, 2021. https://futureoflife.org.

39. Center for AI and Digital Policy. Accessed July 5, 2021. https://www.caidp.org/.

40. Wikipedia. Category: Artificial Intelligence Associations. Accessed June 26, 2021. https://en.wikipedia.org/wiki/Category:Artificial_intelligence_associations.

41. IEEE Standards Association. The IEEEE Global Initiative on Ethics of Autonomous and Intelligent Systems. Accessed June 26, 2021. https://standards.ieee.org/industry-connections/ec/autonomous-systems.html.

42. IEEE Global Initiative on Ethics of Autonomous and Intelligent Systems (2019); IEEE Ethics in Action in Autonomous and Intelligent Systems. Accessed June 26, 2021. https://ethicsinaction.ieee.org/.

43. Garfinkel et al. (2017); Association for Computing Machinery. Accessed June 26, 2021. https://www.acm.org/.

44. Association for the Advancement of Artificial Intelligence. Accessed June 26, 2021. https://www.aaai.org/.

45. OECD.AI. Accessed June 26, 2021. https://oecd.ai/about.

46. A3 Robotics. Accessed June 26, 2021. https://www.automate.org/robotics.

47. Machine Intelligence Research Institute. Accessed June 26, 2021. https://intelligence.org.

48. OpenAI. Accessed June 26, 2021. https://openai.com.

49. Partnership on AI. Accessed June 26, 2021. https://www.partnershiponai.org.

50. Montreal AI Ethics Institute. Accessed June 26, 2021. https://montrealethics.ai/.

CHAPTER 22

1. Roberts, H., Cowls, J., Morley, J., Taddeo, M., Wang, V. and Floridi, L. (2020). The Chinese Approach to Artificial Intelligence: An Analysis of Policy, Ethics, and Regulation. *AI and Society*, 1–19.

2. Lee, K.-F. (September 22, 2018). What China can teach the U.S. about artificial intelligence. *The New York Times*. https://www.nytimes.com/2018/09/22/opinion/sunday/ai-china-united-states.html.

3. US National Science and Technology Council (June 2019). The National Artificial Intelligence Research and Development Strategic Plan: 2019 Update. Executive Office of the President. https://www.nitrd.gov/pubs/National-AI-RD-Strategy-2019.pdf.

4. West, D. M. and Allen, J. R. (2020). *Turning Point: Policymaking in the Era of Artificial Intelligence*. Washington, DC: Brookings Institution Press.

5. National Science Foundation. National Artificial Intelligence (AI) Research Institutes. NSF 20-604. Accessed June 28, 2021. https://www.nsf.gov/pubs/2020/nsf20604/nsf20604.htm.

6. Pielke Jr, R. (2020). A "Sedative" for Science Policy. *Issues in Science and Technology*, 37(1): 41–7. https://issues.org/endless-frontier-sedative-for-science-policy-pielke/.

7. Advancing Research Impact in Society. Accessed June 28, 2021. https://www.researchinsociety.org/about-us/aris.

8. The HIBAR Research Alliance. Accessed June 28, 2021. https://hibar-research.org/.

9. UIDP. Accessed June 28, 2021. http://www.uidp.org.

10. Shneiderman, B. (2018). Twin-Win Model: A Human-Centered Approach to Research Success. *Proceedings of the National Academy of Sciences*, 115(50): 12590–4. https://www.pnas.org/content/115/50/12590.

11. National Science Foundation. National AI Research Institutes. NSF 20-604.

12. Government of Canada. Responsible Use of Artificial Intelligence (AI). Accessed June 28, 2021. https://www.canada.ca/en/government/system/digital-government/digital-government-innovations/responsible-use-ai.html.

13. Goodman, B. and Flaxman, S. (2017). European Union Regulations on Algorithmic Decision-Making and a "Right to Explanation". *AI Magazine*, 38(3): 50–7; Wachter, S., Mittelstadt, B., and Russell, C. (2017). Counterfactual Explanations without Opening the Black Box: Automated Decisions and the GDPR. *Harvard Journal of Law and Technology*, 31: 841–87.

14. Royal Society (April 2017). *Machine Learning: The Power and Promise of Computers That Learn by Example*. London: Royal Society.

15. Information Commissioner's Office and Alan Turing Institute (2019). ICO and the Turing Consultation on Explaining AI Decisions Guidance. https://ico.org.uk/about-the-ico/ico-and-stakeholder-consultations/ico-and-the-turing-consultation-on-explaining-ai-decisions-guidance/.

16. European Commission (2020a). White Paper on Artificial Intelligence—A European Approach to Excellence and Trust, Brussels. https://ec.europa.eu/info/sites/info/files/commission-white-paper-artificial-intelligence-feb2020_en.pdf.

17. European Commission (2020b). The Assessment List for Trustworthy Artificial Intelligence (ALTAI) for Self-Assessment, Independent High-Level Expert Group on Artificial Intelligence, Brussels. https://ec.europa.eu/digital-single-market/en/news/assessment-list-trustworthy-artificial-intelligence-altai-self-assessment.

18. OECD. Artificial Intelligence. Accessed June 28, 2021. https://www.oecd.org/going-digital/ai/.

19. OECD.AI. OECD AI Principles Overview. Accessed June 28, 2021. https://oecd.ai/ai-principles.

20. AI for Good. Accessed June 28, 2021. https://aiforgood.itu.int/.

21. UN Sustainable Development. Accessed June 28, 2021. https://sdgs.un.org/.

22. Engstrom, D. E., Ho. D. E., Sharkey, C. M. and Cuellar, M.-F. (2020). Government by Algorithm: Artificial Intelligence in Federal Administrative Agencies, Administrative Conference of the United States https://www-cdn.law.stanford.edu/wp-content/uploads/2020/02/ACUS-AI-Report.pdf; Rotenberg, M. (2020a). The AI Policy Sourcebook 2020. Washington, DC: Electronic Privacy Information Center.

23. US National Transportation Safety Board (2017). Collision between a Car Operating with Automated Vehicle Control Systems and a Tractor-Semitrailer Truck Near Williston, Florida May 7, 2016. Report HAR1702. https://www.ntsb.gov/investigations/AccidentReports/Reports/HAR1702.pdf.

24. Bryson, J. J. (2020). The Artificial Intelligence of the Ethics of Artificial Intelligence: An Introductory Overview for Law and Regulation. In Dubber, M. D., Pasquale, F. and Das, S., eds., The Oxford Handbook of Ethics of AI. New York: Oxford University Press.

25. Shneiderman, B. (2016). Opinion: The Dangers of Faulty, Biased, or Malicious Algorithms Requires Independent Oversight. Proceedings of the National Academy of Sciences, 113(48): 13538–40. http://www.pnas.org/content/113/48/13538.full.

26. US Food and Drug Administration (April 2, 2019). Proposed Regulatory Framework for Modifications to Artificial Intelligence/Machine Learning (AI/ML)-Based Software as a Medical Device (SaMD). US FDA Artificial Intelligence and Machine Learning Discussion Paper. https://www.fda.gov/media/122535/download.

27. EASA. Artificial Intelligence Roadmap. Accessed June 28, 2021. https://www.easa.europa.eu/ai.

28. NIST. Artificial Intelligence. Accessed June 28, 2021. https://www.nist.gov/artificial-intelligence.

29. US National Security Commission on Artificial Intelligence (2021). Final Report. Washington, DC. https://www.nscai.gov/2021-final-report/.

30. Federal Trade Commission (April 8, 2020). Using Artificial Intelligence and Algorithms. https://www.ftc.gov/news-events/blogs/business-blog/2020/04/using-artificial-intelligence-algorithms.

31. Zuboff, S. (2019). *The Age of Surveillance Capitalism: The Fight for a Human Future at the New Frontier of Power*. New York: PublicAffairs.

32. Vought, R. T. (February 11, 2019). Guidance for Regulation of Artificial Intelligence Applications. US White House Announcement, Washington, DC. https://www.whitehouse.gov/wp-content/uploads/2020/01/Draft-OMB-Memo-on-Regulation-of-AI-1-7-19.pdf.

33. US White House (2020). American Artificial Intelligence Initiative: Year One Annual Report. Office of Science and Technology Policy. https://www.nitrd.gov/nitrdgroups/images/c/c1/American-AI-Initiative-One-Year-Annual-Report.pdf.

34. Vought, R. T. (November 17, 2020). Guidance for Regulation of Artificial Intelligence Applications. Washington, DC: US White House. https://www.whitehouse.gov/wp-content/uploads/2020/11/M-21-06.pdf.

35. Lee, N. T., Resnick, P. and Barton, G. (2019). Algorithmic Bias Detection and Mitigation: Best Practices and Policies to Reduce Consumer Harms. Center for Technology Innovation, Brookings. https://www.brookings.edu/research/algorithmic-bias-detection-and-mitigation-best-practices-and-policies-to-reduce-consumer-harms/.

CHAPTER 23

1. Miller, T. (2019). Explanation in Artificial Intelligence: Insights from the Social Sciences. *Artificial Intelligence*, 267: 1–38. https://doi.org/10.1016/j.artint.2018.07.007; Falco, G., Eling, M., Jablanski, D., Weber, M., Miller, V., Gordon, L. A., . . . and Lin, H. (2019). Cyber Risk Research Impeded by Disciplinary Barriers. *Science*, 366(6469): 1066–9.

2. UN Sustainable Development. Accessed June 28, 2021. https://sdgs.un.org/.

3. Rotenberg, M., ed. (2020b). *Artificial Intelligence and Democratic Values: An AI Social Contract Index-2020*. Dukakis Center for AI and Digital Policy. https://dukakis.org/center-for-ai-and-digital-policy/caidp-publishes-artificial-intelligence-and-democratic-values/.

4. Crawford, K. (2021). *The Atlas of AI*. New Haven, CT: Yale University Press.

CHAPTER 24

1. UN Sustainable Development. Accessed June 28, 2021. https://sdgs.un.org/.

2. National Academy of Engineering. 14 Grand Challenges for Engineering in the 21st Century. Accessed June 29, 2021. http://www.engineeringchallenges. org/challenges.aspx.

3. GOV.UK. The Grand Challenges. Accessed June 29, 2021. https://www.gov.uk/ government/publications/industrial-strategy-the-grand-challenges/industrial-strategy-the-grand-challenges.

4. Bill and Melinda Gates Foundation. Accessed June 29, 2021. https://www. gatesfoundation.org/.

5. XPRIZE. Accessed June 29, 2021. https://www.xprize.org/.

6. Preece, J. (2016). Citizen Science: New Research Challenges for Human–Computer Interaction. *International Journal of Human–Computer Interaction*, 32(8): 585–612. https://www.tandfonline.com/doi/abs/10.1080/10447318.2016.1194153.

7. eBird. Accessed June 29, 2021. https://ebird.org/home.

8. Zooniverse. Accessed June 29, 2021. https://www.zooniverse.org/.

9. iNaturalist. Accessed June 29, 2021. https://www.inaturalist.org/.

10. CitizenScience.gov. Accessed July 6, 2021. https://www.citizenscience.gov/.

11. Ceccaroni, L., Bibby, J., Roger, E., Flemons, P., Michael, K., Fagan, L. and Oliver, J. L. (2019). Opportunities and Risks for Citizen Science in the Age of Artificial Intelligence. *Citizen Science: Theory and Practice*, 4(1): article 29, 1–14. https:// par.nsf.gov/servlets/purl/10175492.

12. Green, S. E., Rees, J. P., Stephens, P. A., Hill, R. A. and Giordano, A. J. (2020). Innovations in Camera Trapping Technology and Approaches: The Integration of Citizen Science and Artificial Intelligence. *Animals*, 10(1), 132. https://www.mdpi.com/2076-2615/10/1/132; Kumar, N., Belhumeur, P. N., Biswas, A., Jacobs, D. W., Kress, W. J., Lopez, I. C. and Soares, J. V. (October 2012). Leafsnap: A Computer Vision System for Automatic Plant Species Iden- tification. *Proc. 2012 European Conference on Computer Vision*. Berlin: Springer, 502–16. https://link.springer.com/chapter/10.1007/978-3-642-33709-3_36.

13. Flukebook. Accessed June 29, 2021. https://www.flukebook.org/.

14. Seek by iNaturalist. Accessed June 29, 2021. https://www.inaturalist.org/ pages/seek_app.

15. Aristeidou, M., Herodotou, C., Ballard, H. L., Young, A. N., Miller, A. E., Higgins, L. and Johnson, R. F. (2021). Exploring the Participation of Young Citizen Scientists in Scientific Research: The Case of iNaturalist. *PLOS ONE*, 16(1), e0245682. https://journals.plos.org/plosone/article?id=10.1371/journal.pone.0245682.

16. The People of iNaturalist. Accessed June 29, 2021. https://www.inaturalist. org/people.

17. Citizen Science Association. Citizen Science: Theory and Practice. Accessed July 6, 2021. https://theoryandpractice.citizenscienceassociation.org/.

18. Haughey, M. M., Muralikumar, M. D., Wood, C. A. and Starbird, K. (2020). On the Misinformation Beat: Understanding the Work of Investigative Journalists Reporting on Problematic Information Online. *Proc. ACM on Human-Computer Interaction*, 4(CSCW2): 1–22. https://dl.acm.org/doi/abs/10.1145/3415204; Singh V. K., Ghosh, I. and Sonagara, D. (2021). Detecting Fake News Stories via Multimodal Analysis. *Journal of the Association for Information Science and Technology*, 72: 3–17. https://doi.org/10.1002/asi.24359.

19. Ellick, A. and Westbrook, A. (November 12, 2018). Operation Infektion: Russian Disinformation from Cold War to Kanye. *The New York Times*. https://www.nytimes.com/2018/11/12/opinion/russia-meddling-disinformation-fake-news-elections.html.

20. European Commission. Code of Practice on Disinformation. Accessed June 29, 2021. https://ec.europa.eu/digital-single-market/en/code-practice-disinform ation.

21. Halevy, A., Ferrer, C. C., Ma, H., Ozertem, U., Pantel, P., Saeidi, M., Silvestri, F., and Stoyanov, V. (2020). Preserving Integrity in Online Social Networks. arXiv preprint. https://arxiv.org/abs/2009.10311.

22. Halevy et al. (2020).

23. Oversight Board. Accessed June 29, 2021. https://oversightboard.com/.

24. Bloomberg Government (April 11, 2018). Transcript of Mark Zuckerberg's Senate Hearing. The Washington Post. https://www.washingtonpost.com/news/the-switch/wp/2018/04/10/transcript-of-mark-zuckerbergs-senate-hearing/.

25. Facebook Transparency Center. Transparenty Reports. Accessed June 29, 2021. https://transparency.facebook.com/.

26. Twitter. Help Center. The Twitter Rules. Accessed June 29, 2021. https://help.twitter.com/en/rules-and-policies/twitter-rules.

27. YouTube. Community Guidelines. Accessed June 29, 2021. https://www.youtube.com/intl/ALL_ca/howyoutubeworks/policies/community-guidelines/.

28. Facebook Help Center. What Names Are Allowed on Facebook? Accessed June 29, 2021. https://www.facebook.com/help/112146705538576.

29. DeepMind (November 30, 2020). AlphaFold: A Solution a Fifty-Year-Old Grand Challenge in Biology. https://deepmind.com/blog/article/alphafold-a-solution-to-a-50-year-old-grand-challenge-in-biology.

30. Stokes, D. E. (1997). *Pasteur's Quadrant: Basic Science and Technological Innovation*. Washington, DC: Brookings Institution Press.

31. Shneiderman, B. (2016). *The New ABCs of Research: Achieving Breakthrough Collaborations*. Oxford University Press; Shneiderman, B. (2018). Twin-Win Model: A Human-Centered Approach to Research Success. *Proc. National Academy of Sciences*, 115(50): 12590–94. https://www.pnas.org/content/115/50/12590.short;

The HIBAR Research Alliance. Accessed June 29, 2021. https://hibar-research.org/; Advancing Research Impact in Society. Accessed June 29, 2021. https://www.researchinsociety.org/.

32. Stanford University. Human-Centered Artificial Intelligence. Accessed June 25, 2021. http://hai.stanford.edu.

33. Fiesler, C., Garrett, N., and Beard, N. (February 2020). What Do We Teach When We Teach Tech Ethics? A Syllabi Analysis. *Proc. 51st ACM Technical Symposium on Computer Science Education*, 289–95. https://dl.acm.org/doi/abs/10.1145/3328778.3366825; Garrett, N., Beard, N. and Fiesler, C. (February 2020). More Than "If Time Allows": The Role of Ethics in AI Education. *Proc. AAAI/ACM Conference on AI, Ethics, and Society*, 272–8. https://dl.acm.org/doi/abs/10.1145/3375627.3375868; Saltz, J., Skirpan, M., Fiesler, C., Gorelick, M., Yeh, T., Heckman, R., Dewar, N., and Beard, N. (2019). Integrating Ethics within Machine Learning Courses. *ACM Transactions on Computing Education (TOCE)*, 19(4): 1–26. https://dl.acm.org/doi/abs/10.1145/3341164.

34. Coursera. Artificial Intelligence Ethics in Action. Accessed June 29, 2021. https://www.coursera.org/learn/ai-ethics-analysis.

35. edX. Ethics in AI and Big Data. Accessed June 29, 2021. https://www.edx.org/course/ethics-in-ai-and-big-data.

36. NeurIPS 2020. Call for Papers. Accessed June 29, 2021. https://nips.cc/Conferences/2020/CallForPapers.

37. Boyarskaya, M., Olteanu, A., and Crawford, K. (2020). Overcoming "Failures of Imagination" in AI Infused System Development and Deployment. arXiv preprint. https://arxiv.org/abs/2011.13416; Campbell, R. (January 28, 2021). Navigating the Broader Impacts of AI Research: Workshop at NeurIPS 2020. Partnership on AI. https://www.partnershiponai.org/navigating-the-broader-impacts-of-ai-research-workshop-at-neurips-2020/.

38. Wallach, H. NeurIPS Keynote. Video. Accessed June 29, 2021. https://www.partnershiponai.org/navigating-the-broader-impacts-of-ai-research-workshop-at-neurips-2020/.

39. Text Retrieval Conference. Accessed June 29, 2021. https://trec.nist.gov/.

40. Buolamwini, J. and Gebru, T. (January 2018). Gender Shades: Intersectional Accuracy Disparities in Commercial Gender Classification. *Proc. 1st Conference on Fairness, Accountability, and Transparency*, PMLR, 81: 77–91. http://proceedings.mlr.press/v81/buolamwini18a.html.

41. Special Interest Group on Discourse and Dialogue. Accessed June 29, 2021. https://sigdial.org/.

42. AMTA. Accessed June 29, 2021. https://amtaweb.org/.

43. HCI + NLP Workshop. Accessed June 29, 2021. https://sites.google.com/view/hciandnlp.

44. *Journal of Responsible Innovation.* Accessed June 29, 2021. https://www.tandfonline.com/loi/tjri20.

45. D'Amour, A., Heller, K., Moldovan, D., Adlam, B., Alipanahi, B., Beutel, A., ... and Sculley, D. (November 6, 2020). Underspecification Presents Challenges for Credibility in Modern Machine Learning. arXiv preprint. https://arxiv.org/abs/2011.03395.

46. National Science Foundation. National Artificial Intelligence (AI) Research Institutes. NSF 20-604. Accessed June 28, 2021. https://www.nsf.gov/pubs/2020/nsf20604/nsf20604.htm.

47. Partnership on AI. Accessed June 29, 2021. https://www.partnershiponai.org/.

48. AIRC. About AIRC. Accessed June 29, 2021. https://www.airc.aist.go.jp/en/intro/.

CHAPTER 25

1. Fjeld, J., Achten, N., Hilligoss, H., Nagy, A., and Srikumar, M. (2020). Principled Artificial Intelligence: Mapping Consensus in Ethical and Rights-Based Approaches to Principles for AI. Berkman Klein Center Research. https://cyber.harvard.edu/publication/2020/principled-ai; IEEE Global Initiative on Ethics of Autonomous and Intelligent Systems (2019). *Ethically Aligned Design: A Vision for Prioritizing Human Well-being with Autonomous and Intelligent Systems*, 1st ed. IEEE. https://standards.ieee.org/content/ieee-standards/en/industry-connections/ec/autonomous-systems.html; Floridi, L., Cowls, J., Beltrametti, M., Chatila, R., Chazerand, P., Dignum, V., ... and Vayena, E. (2018). AI4People—An Ethical Framework for a Good AI Society: Opportunities, Risks, Principles, and Recommendations. *Minds and Machines*, 28(4): 689–707. https://doi.org/10.1007/s11023-018-9482-5; Thiebes, S., Lins, S. and Sunyaev, A. (2020). Trustworthy Artificial Intelligence. *Electronic Markets*, 1–18. https://link.springer.com/article/10.1007/s12525-020-00441-4.

2. Hoffman, R. R. (2017). A Taxonomy of Emergent Trusting in the Human-Machine Relationship. In Smith, P. and Hoffman, R. R., eds., *Cognitive Systems Engineering: The Future for a Changing World*, 137–64. Boca Raton, FL: Taylor and Francis.

3. Hoffman, R. R. and Hancock, P. A. (2017). Measuring Resilience. *Human Factors*, 59(4): 564–81.

4. Wine Country Getaways. Wine Scoring Sheets, Wine Tasting Forms, Wine Scorecards. Accessed June 29, 2021. https://winecountrygetaways.com/wine-enjoyment-guide/hosting-a-wine-tasting/wine-scoring-sheets-wine-tasting-forms-wine-scorecards.

5. University of California-Davis. UC David 20 Point System. Accessed June 29, 2021. http://www.musingsonthevine.com/MusingsUCDavisForm.pdf.

6. Wikipedia. Apgar Score. Accessed June 29, 2021. https://en.wikipedia.org/wiki/Apgar_score.

7. ScienceDirect. Usability Questionnaire. Accessed June 29, 2021. https://www. sciencedirect.com/topics/computer-science/usability-questionnaire; Lewis, J. R. (2014). Usability: Lessons Learned . . . and Yet to be Learned. *International Journal of Human–Computer Interaction*, 30(9): 663–84.

8. The Conference Board. Consumer Confidence Survey. Accessed June 29, 2021. https://conference-board.org/data/consumerconfidence.cfm.

9. University of Michigan. Surveys of Consumers. Accessed June 29, 2021. http:// www.sca.isr.umich.edu/.

10. D'Amour, A., Heller, K., Moldovan, D., Adlam, B., Alipanahi, B., Beutel, A., . . . and Sculley, D. (November 6, 2020). Underspecification Presents Challenges for Credibility in Modern Machine Learning. arXiv preprint. https:// arxiv.org/abs/2011.03395.

11. Griffin, W. (January 5, 2021). Phone interview with the author.

12. IEEE Standards Association. IEEE P7001—IEEE Draft Standard for Transparency of Autonomous Systems. Accessed June 29, 2021. https://standards. ieee.org/project/7001.html.

13. Engineering 360. IEEE P7001 Draft: Draft Standard for Transparency of Autonomous Systems. Accessed June 30, 2021. https://standards.globalspec. com/std/14328511/P7001/D1.

14. Rotenberg, M., ed. (2020). *Artificial Intelligence and Democratic Values: An AI Social Contract Index-2020.* Dukakis Center for AI and Digital Policy. https://dukakis.org/center-for-ai-and-digital-policy/caidp-publishes-artificial-intelligence-and-democratic-values/.

15. Cho, J. H., Xu, S., Hurley, P. M., Mackay, M., Benjamin, T. and Beaumont, M. (2019). Stram: Measuring the Trustworthiness of Computer-Based Systems. *ACM Computing Surveys (CSUR)*, 51(6): 1–47; Brundage, M., Avin, S., Wang, J., Belfield, H., Krueger, G., Hadfield, G., . . . and Anderljung, M. (2020). Toward Trustworthy AI Development: Mechanisms for Supporting Verifiable Claims. arXiv preprint. https://arxiv.org/abs/2004.07213.

CHAPTER 26

1. Van Wynsberghe, A. (2013). Designing Robots for Care: Care Centered Value-Sensitive Design. *Science and Engineering Ethics*, 19(2): 407–33. https://www.ncbi.nlm.nih.gov/pmc/articles/PMC3662860/; Czaja, S. J., Boot, W. R., Charness, N. and Rogers, W. A. (2019). *Designing for Older Adults: Principles and Creative Human Factors Approaches*, 3rd ed. Boca Raton, FL: CRC Press.

2. Family Caregiving: Care at Home. Accessed June 29, 2021. https://www.aarp. org/caregiving/home-care/.

3. Vallor, S. (2016). *Technology and the Virtues: A Philosophical Guide to a Future Worth Wanting*. Oxford University Press.

4. Vallor (2016).

5. Czaja et al. (2019); Johnson, J. and Finn, K. (2017). *Designing User Interfaces for an Aging Population: Towards Universal Design.* Burlington, MA: Morgan Kaufmann; Lazar, J., Goldstein, D. F. and Taylor, A. (2015). *Ensuring Digital Accessibility through Process and Policy.* Waltham, MA: Elsevier/Morgan Kaufmann; Interaction Design Foundation. Accessibility. Accessed June 29, 2021. https://www.interaction-design.org/literature/topics/accessibility.

6. Centers for Disease Control and Prevention. Healthy Places Terminology. Accessed June 29, 2021. https://www.cdc.gov/healthyplaces/terminology.htm.

7. Vines, J., Pritchard, G., Wright, P., Olivier, P. and Brittain, K. (2015). An Age-Old Problem: Examining the Discourses of Ageing in HCI and Strategies for Future Research. *ACM Transactions on Computer-Human Interaction (TOCHI)*, 22(1): 1–27. https://dl.acm.org/doi/abs/10.1145/2696867; Gerling, K., Ray, M., Abeele, V. V. and Evans, A. B. (2020). Critical Reflections on Technology to Support Physical Activity among Older Adults: An Exploration of Leading HCI Venues. *ACM Transactions on Accessible Computing (TACCESS)*, 13(1): 1–23. https://dl.acm.org/doi/abs/10.1145/3374660.

8. Petrie, H. and Darzentas, J. (June 2017). Older People and Robotic Technologies in the Home: Perspectives from Recent Research Literature. *Proc. 10th International Conference on Pervasive Technologies Related to Assistive Environments (PETRA)*. ACM, 29–36. https://dl.acm.org/doi/abs/10.1145/3056540.3056553.

9. Mahmud, S., Alvina, J., Chilana, P. K., Bunt, A. and McGrenere, J. (2020). Learning through Exploration: How Children, Adults, and Older Adults Interact with a New Feature-Rich Application. *Proc. 2020 CHI Conference on Human Factors in Computing Systems.* ACM, 1–14. https://dl.acm.org/doi/abs/10.1145/3313831.3376414.

10. Kaufman, S. B. (2020). *Transcend: The New Science of Self-Actualization.* New York: TarcherPerigree Books.

11. Lazar et al. (2015).

12. Zuckerman, O., Walker, D., Grishko, A., Moran, T., Levy, C., Lisak, B., Wald, I. Y. and Erel, H. (April 2020). Companionship Is Not a Function: The Effect of a Novel Robotic Object on Healthy Older Adults' Feelings of "Being-Seen". *Proc. 2020 CHI Conference on Human Factors in Computing Systems.* ACM, 1–14. https://dl.acm.org/doi/abs/10.1145/3313831.3376411.

13. Astell, A. J., Bouranis, N., Hoey, J., Lindauer, A., Mihailidis, A., Nugent, C. and Robillard, J. M. (2019). Technology and Dementia: The Future is Now. *Dementia and Geriatric Cognitive Disorders*, 47(3): 131–9. https://www.karger.com/Article/Abstract/497800; Xie, B., Tao, C., Li, J., Hilsabeck, R. C. and Aguirre, A. (2020). Artificial Intelligence for Caregivers of Persons with Alzheimer's Disease and Related Dementias: Systematic Literature Review. *JMIR Medical Informatics*, 8(8), e18189. https://medinform.jmir.org/2020/8/e18189/.

14. Choi, Y. K., Lazar, A., Demiris, G. and Thompson, H. J. (2019). Emerging Smart Home Technologies to Facilitate Engaging with Aging. *Journal of Gerontological Nursing*, 45(12): 41–8.

15. Smith, E. M., Mortenson, W. B., Mihailidis, A. and Miller, W. C. (2020). Understanding the Task Demands for Powered Wheelchair Driving: A Think-Aloud Task Analysis. Disability and Rehabilitation: Assistive Technology, 1–8. https://www.tandfonline.com/doi/abs/10.1080/17483107.2020.1810335.

16. Viswanathan, P., Little, J. J., Mackworth, A. K. and Mihailidis, A. (October 2012). An Intelligent Powered Wheelchair for Users with Dementia: Case Studies with NOAH (Navigation and Obstacle Avoidance Help). *Proc. 2012 AAAI Fall Symposium.* https://www.cs.ubc.ca/~mack/Publications/ViswanathanAAAI2012.pdf; Viswanathan, P., Little, J. J., Mackworth, A. K., How, T. V., Wang, R. H. and Mihailidis, A. (2013). Intelligent Wheelchairs for Cognitively-Impaired Older Adults in Long-Term Care: A Review. *Proc. Rehabilitation Engineering and Assistive Technology Society of North America 2013 Annual Conference.* http://www.resna.org/sites/default/files/legacy/conference/proceedings/2013/Wheeled%20Mobility/Viswanathan.html.

17. Braze Mobility. Accessed June 29, 2021. https://brazemobility.com/.

18. Project Sidewalk. Accessed June 29, 2021. https://sidewalk-sea.cs.washington.edu/.

19. Meals on Wheels America. Accessed June 29, 2021. https://www.mealsonwheelsamerica.org/.

20. Down Dog. Accessed June 29, 2021. https://www.downdogapp.com/.

21. Apple Developer. Health and Fitness. Accessed June 29, 2021. https://developer.apple.com/health-fitness.

22. Fitbit. Accessed June 29, 2021. https://www.fitbit.com/.

23. PatientsLikeMe. Accessed June 29, 2021. https://www.patientslikeme.com/.

24. National Institutes of Health. All of Us Research Program. Accessed June 29, 2021. https://allofus.nih.gov/.

25. Vargemidis, D., Gerling, K., Spiel, K., Abeele, V. V., and Geurts, L. (2020). Wearable Physical Activity Tracking Systems for Older Adults—A Systematic Review. *ACM Transactions on Computing for Healthcare*, 1(4): 1–37. https://dl.acm.org/doi/abs/10.1145/3402523.

26. The Captain Tom Foundation. Accessed June 29, 2021. https://captaintom.org/.

27. Gaskell, A. (December 11, 2019). Are Older Entrepreneurs the Best Entrepreneurs? *Forbes.* https://www.forbes.com/sites/adigaskell/2019/12/11/are-older-entrepreneurs-the-best-entrepreneurs/.

28. Senior Planet. Our Purpose. Accessed June 29, 2021. https://seniorplanet.org/about/our-purpose/.

CHAPTER 27

1. McLuhan, M. (1964). *Understanding Media: The Extensions of Man.* Cambridge, MA: MIT Press.

2. Shneiderman, B. (1980). *Software Psychology: Human Factors in Computer and Information Systems.* New York: Winthrop Publishers.

3. Licklider, J. C. R. (1960). Man-Computer Symbiosis. *IRE Transactions on Human Factors in Electronics*, 1: 4–11.

4. SIGCHI. Accessed June 29, 2021. https://sigchi.org.

5. Weizenbaum, J. (1976). *Computer Power and Human Reason: From Judgment to Calculation.* New York: W H Freeman.

6. Winograd, T. and Flores, F. (1986). *Understanding Computers and Cognition: A New Foundation for Design.* Bristol, UK: Intellect Books.

7. Shneiderman, B. (1983). Direct Manipulation: A Step beyond Programming Languages. *IEEE Computer*, 16(8): 57–69.

8. Shneiderman, B. (1986). *Designing the User Interface: Strategies for Effective Human-Computer Interaction.* Boston, MA: Addison Wesley; Shneiderman, B., Plaisant, C., Cohen, M., Jacobs, S. and Elmqvist, N. (2016). *Designing the User Interface: Strategies for Effective Human-Computer Interaction*, 6th ed. New York: Pearson.

9. Shneiderman, B. (2019). *Encounters with HCI Pioneers: A Personal History and Photo Journal.* Synthesis Lectures on Human-Centered Informatics. San Rafael, CA: Morgan & Claypool. https://www.morganclaypool.com/doi/abs/10.2200/S00889ED1V01Y201812HCI041.

10. Shneiderman, B. and Maes, P. (1997). Direct Manipulation vs. Interface Agents. *ACM interactions*, 4(6): 42–61.

11. Tukey, J. W. (1977). *Exploratory Data Analysis.* New York: Pearson.

12. Shneiderman, B. (1996). The Eyes Have It: A Task by Data Type Taxonomy for Information Visualizations. *Proc. 1996 IEEE Symposium on Visual Languages.* IEEE, 336–43.

BIBLIOGRAPHY

Abdul, A., Vermeulen, J., Wang, D., Lim, B. Y. and Kankanhalli, M. (April 2018). Trends and Trajectories for Explainable, Accountable and Intelligible Systems: An HCI Research Agenda. *Proc. 2018 CHI Conference on Human Factors in Computing Systems.* ACM, 1–18.

Adam, M., Wessel, M. and Benlian, A. (2020). AI-Based Chatbots in Customer Service and Their Effects on User Compliance. *Electronic Markets*, 1–19. https://link.springer.com/content/pdf/10.1007/s12525-020-00414-7.pdf.

Alemzadeh, H., Raman, J., Leveson, N., Kalbarczyk, Z. and Iyer, R. K. (2016). Adverse Events in Robotic Surgery: A Retrospective Study of 14 Years of FDA Data. *PloS One*, 11(4): e0151470. https://doi.org/10.1371/journal.pone.0151470.

Alsheibani, S., Messom, C. and Cheung, Y. (2019). Towards an Artificial Intelligence Maturity Model: From Science Fiction to Business Facts. *Proc. 23rd Pacific Asia Conference on Information Systems*, Xian, China, Association for Information Systems. https://www.semanticscholar.org/paper/Towards-An-Artificial-Intelligence-Maturity-Model%3A-Alsheibani-Cheung/1d0b75dce15e26779db0a3f82a307f9682280b55.

Amershi, S., Begel, A., Bird, C., DeLine, R., Gall, H., Kamar, E., . . . and Zimmermann, T. (2019a). Software Engineering for Machine Learning: A Case Study. *Proc. IEEE/ACM 41st International Conference on Software Engineering: Software Engineering in Practice (ICSE-SEIP)*. IEEE, 291–300.

Amershi, S., Weld, D., Vorvoreanu, M., Fourney, A., Nushi, B., Collisson, P., . . . and Horvitz, E. (2019b). Guidelines for Human-AI Interaction. *Proc. ACM 2019 CHI Conference on Human Factors in Computing Systems*, Paper 3, 1–13. ACM. https://dl.acm.org/doi/abs/10.1145/3290605.3300233.

Ammari, T., Kaye, J., Tsai, J. Y. and Bentley, F. (2019). Music, Search, and IoT: How People (Really) Use Voice Assistants. *ACM Transactions on Computer-Human Interaction (TOCHI)*, 26(3): 1–28. http://web.mit.edu/bentley/www/papers/iot.pdf.

Amodei, D., Olah, C., Steinhardt, J., Christiano, P., Schulman, J. and Mané, D. (2016). Concrete Problems in AI Safety. arXiv preprint. https://arxiv.org/abs/1606.06565.

Apple Developer (2019). Human Interface Guidelines. https://developer.apple.com/design/human-interface-guidelines/ios/overview/themes/.

Appugliese, C., Nathan, P. Roberts, W. S. (2020). *Agile AI: A Practical Guide to Building AI Applications and Teams*. Sebastopol, CA: O'Reilly Media.

Aristeidou, M., Herodotou, C., Ballard, H. L., Young, A. N., Miller, A. E., Higgins, L. and Johnson, R. F. (2021). Exploring the Participation of Young Citizen Scientists in Scientific Research: The Case of iNaturalist. *PLOS ONE*, 16(1): e0245682. https://journals.plos.org/plosone/article?id=10.1371/journal.pone.0245682.

Arya, V., Bellamy, R. K., Chen, P. Y., Dhurandhar, A., Hind, M., Hoffman, S. C., . . . and Zhang, Y. (2020). AI Explainability 360: An Extensible Toolkit for Understanding Data and Machine Learning Models. *Journal of Machine Learning Research*, 21(130): 1–6. https://www.jmlr.org/papers/volume21/19-1035/19-1035.pdf.

Astell, A. J., Bouranis, N., Hoey, J., Lindauer, A., Mihailidis, A., Nugent, C. and Robillard, J. M. (2019). Technology and Dementia: The Future is Now. *Dementia and Geriatric Cognitive Disorders*, 47(3): 131–9. https://www.karger.com/Article/Abstract/497800.

Autor, D. H., Mindell, D. A. and Reynolds, E. B. (2020). *The Work of the Future: Building Better Jobs in an Age of Intelligent Machines*. MIT Work of the Future. https://workofthefuture.mit.edu/wp-content/uploads/2021/01/2020-Final-Report4.pdf.

Baeza-Yates, R. (2018). Bias on the Web. *Communications of the ACM*, 61(6): 54–61.

Bainbridge, L. (1983). Ironies of Automation. *Automatica*, 19(6): 775–9.

Bell, S. K., Smulowitz, P. B., Woodward, A. C., Mello, M. M., Duva, A. M., Boothman, R. C., and Sands, K. (2012). Disclosure, Apology, and Offer Programs: Stakeholders' Views of Barriers to and Strategies for Broad Implementation. *The Milbank Quarterly*, 90(4): 682–705.

Bellamy, R. K., Dey, K., Hind, M., Hoffman, S. C., Houde, S., Kannan, K., . . . and Nagar, S. (2019). AI Fairness 360: An Extensible Toolkit for Detecting and Mitigating Algorithmic Bias. *IBM Journal of Research and Development*, 63(4/5): 4:1–4:15.

Benjamin, R. (2019). *Race after Technology: Abolitionist Tools for the New Jim Code*. Boston: Polity Press.

Berry, J. C., Davis, J. T., Bartman, T., Hafer, C. C., Lieb, L. M., Khan, N. and Brilli, R. J. (June 2020). Improved Safety Culture and Teamwork Climate Are Associated with Decreases in Patient Harm and Hospital Mortality across a Hospital System. *Journal of Patient Safety*, 16(2): 130–6. http://www.ncbi.nlm.nih.gov/pubmed/26741790.

Biran, O. and Cotton, C. (August 2017). Explanation and Justification in Machine Learning: A Survey. *IJCAI-17 Workshop on Explainable AI (XAI)*, 8(1). http://www.cs.columbia.edu/~orb/papers/xai_survey_paper_2017.pdf

Birnbaum, E. (March 28, 2019). HUD Charges Facebook with Enabling House Discrimination. *The Hill*. https://thehill.com/policy/technology/436209-hud-charges-facebook-with-housing-discrimination-over-its-targeted.

Blackhurst, J. L., Gresham, J. S. and Stone, M. O. (2011). The Autonomy Paradox. *Armed Forces Journal*, 20–40.

Bloomberg Government (April 11, 2018). Transcript of Mark Zuckerberg's Senate Hearing. *The Washington Post*. https://www.washingtonpost.com/news/the-switch/wp/2018/04/10/transcript-of-mark-zuckerbergs-senate-hearing/.

Boden, M., Bryson, J., Caldwell, D., Dautenhahn, K., Edwards, L., Kember, S., . . . and Winfield, A. F. (2017). Principles of Robotics: Regulating Robots in the Real World. *Connection Science*, 29(2): 124–9.

Bonsor, K. and Chandler, N. (2020). How Black Boxes Work. https://science.howstuffworks.com/transport/flight/modern/black-box.htm.

Bostelman, R., Hong, T. and Marvel, J. (2016). Survey of Research for Performance Measurement of Mobile Manipulators. *Journal of Research of the National Institute of Standards and Technology*, 121(3): 342–66.

Bostrom, N. (2014). *Superintelligence: Paths, Dangers, Strategies*. Oxford University Press.

Boyarskaya, M., Olteanu, A. and Crawford, K. (2020). Overcoming "Failures of Imagination" in AI Infused System Development and Deployment. arXiv preprint. https://arxiv.org/abs/2011.13416.

Bradshaw, J. M., Hoffman, R. R., Woods, D. D. and Johnson, M. (2013). The Seven Deadly Myths of Autonomous Systems. *IEEE Intelligent Systems*, 28(3): 54–61. https://ieeexplore.ieee.org/abstract/document/6588858/.

Braunschweig, B. and Ghallab, M., eds. (2021). *Reflections on Artificial Intelligence for Humanity*. New York: Springer.

Breazeal, C. L. (2002). *Designing Sociable Robots*. Cambridge, MA: MIT Press.

Breck, E., Polyzotis, N., Roy, S., Whang, S. E. and Zinkevich, M. (2019). Data Validation for Machine Learning. In *Conference on Systems and Machine Learning (SysML)*. https://www.sysml.cc/doc/2019/167.pdf.

Breidenbach, L., Daian, P., Tramèr, F. and Juels, A. (2018). Enter the Hydra: Towards Principled Bug Bounties and Exploit-Resistant Smart Contracts. *Proc. 27th USENIX Security Symposium*. IEEE, 1335–52. https://www.usenix.org/conference /usenixsecurity18/presentation/breindenbach.

Broadbent, E. (2017). Interactions with Robots: The Truths We Reveal about Ourselves. *Annual Review of Psychology*, 68: 627–52.

Brooks, C. and Szafir, D. (March 2019). Balanced Information Gathering and Goal-Oriented Actions in Shared Autonomy. *2019 14th ACM/IEEE International Conference on Human-Robot Interaction (HRI)*, 85–94. https://ieeexplore. ieee.org/abstract/document/8673192/.

Brooks, C. and Szafir, D. (2020). Visualization of Intended Assistance for Acceptance of Shared Control. arXiv preprint. https://arxiv.org/abs/2008.10759.

Brooks, R. (July 27, 2017). The Big Problem with Self-driving Cars Is People. *IEEE Spectrum*. https://spectrum.ieee.org/transportation/self-driving/the-big -problem-with-selfdriving-cars-is-people.

Brown, H. (2018). Keeping the Lights On: A Comparison of Normal Accidents and High Reliability Organizations. *IEEE Technology and Society Magazine*, 37(2): 62–70.

Brundage, M., Avin, S., Wang, J., Belfield, H., Krueger, G., Hadfield, G., . . . and Maharaj, T. (2020). Toward Trustworthy AI Development: Mechanisms for Supporting Verifiable Claims. arXiv preprint. https://arxiv.org/abs/2004. 07213.

Bryson, J. J. (2020). The Artificial Intelligence of the Ethics of Artificial Intelligence: An Introductory Overview for Law and Regulation. In Dubber, M. D., Pasquale, F. and Das, S., eds., *The Oxford Handbook of Ethics of AI*. New York: Oxford University Press.

Bryson, J. J., Diamantis, M. E. and Grant, T. D. (2017). Of, for, and by the People: The Legal Lacuna of Synthetic Persons. *Artificial Intelligence and Law*, 25: 273–91. https://doi.org/10.1007/s10506-017-9214-9.

Buchanan, B. G. and Shortliffe, E. H., eds. (1985). *Rule-based Expert Systems: The MYCIN Experiments of the Stanford Heuristic Programming Project*. Boston: Addison-Wesley.

Buolamwini, J. and Gebru, T. (January 2018). Gender Shades: Intersectional Accuracy Disparities in Commercial Gender Classification. *Proc. 1st Conference on Fairness, Accountability, and Transparency*, PMLR, 81: 77–91. http://proceedings.mlr.press/v81/buolamwini18a.html.

Cai, C. J., Reif, E., Hegde, N., Hipp, J., Kim, B., Smilkov, D., . . . and Terry, M. (May 2019). Human-Centered Tools for Coping with Imperfect Algorithms during Medical Decision-Making. *Proc. 2019 CHI Conference on Human Factors in Computing Systems*. ACM, 1–14. https://dl.acm.org/doi/10.1145/3290605.3300234.

Calo, R. (2016). Robots in American Law. University of Washington School of Law Research Paper, 2016–04. https://papers.ssrn.com/sol3/papers.cfm?abstract_id=2737598.

Calvo, R. A., Peters, D., Vold, V. and Ryan, R. M. (2020). Supporting Human Autonomy in AI systems: A Framework for Ethical Enquiry. In Burr, C. and Floridi, L., eds., *Ethics of Digital Well-Being: A Multidisciplinary Approach*. New York: Springer Open.

Campbell, N. (2007). The Evolution of Flight Data Analysis. *Proceedings of Australian Society of Air Safety Investigators*. https://asasi.org/papers/2007/The_Evolution_of_Flight_Data_Analysis_Neil_Campbell.pdf.

Campbell, R. (January 28, 2021). Navigating the Broader Impacts of AI Research: Workshop at NeurIPS 2020. Partnership on AI. https://www.partnershiponai.org/navigating-the-broader-impacts-of-ai-research-workshop-at-neurips-2020/.

Canadian Government (2019). Knowledge Requirements for Pilots of Remotely Piloted Aircraft Systems 250 g up to and including 25 kg, Operating within Visual Line-of-Sight (VLOS). TP 15263. https://www.tc.gc.ca/en/services/aviation/publications/tp-15263.html.

Canadian Government (2019b). Responsible Use of Artificial Intelligence (AI). https://www.canada.ca/en/government/system/digital-government/modern-emerging-technologies/responsible-use-ai.html.

Candy, L. (2019). Creating with the Digital: Tool, Medium, Mediator, Partner. In Brooks, A. L. and Sylla, C., eds., *Interactivity, Game Creation, Design, Learning, and Innovation*. Cham, Switzerland: Springer. https://link.springer.com/chapter/10.1007/978-3-030-53294-9_2.

Carros, F., Meurer, J., Löffler, D., Unbehaun, D., Matthies, S., Koch, I., . . . and Wulf, V. (April 2020). Exploring Human-Robot Interaction with the Elderly: Results from a Ten-Week Case Study in a Care Home. *Proc. 2020 CHI Conference on Human Factors in Computing Systems*. ACM, 1–12. https://dl.acm.org/doi/abs/10.1145/3313831.3376402.

Carvalho, J. V., Rocha, Á., Vasconcelos, J. and Abreu, A. (2019). A Health Data Analytics Maturity Model for Hospitals Information Systems. *International Journal of Information Management*, 46: 278–85.

Ceccaroni, L., Bibby, J., Roger, E., Flemons, P., Michael, K., Fagan, L. and Oliver, J. L. (2019). Opportunities and Risks for Citizen Science in the Age of Artificial Intelligence. *Citizen Science: Theory and Practice*, 4(1): article 29, 1–14. https://par.nsf.gov/servlets/purl/10175492.

Challen, R., Denny, J., Pitt, M., Gompels, L., Edwards, T. and Tsaneva-Atanasova, K. (2019). Artificial Intelligence, Bias and Clinical Safety. *BMJ Quality and Safety*, 28(3): 231–7.

Charleer, S., Gutiérrez, F. and Verbert, K. (March 2019). Supporting Job Mediator and Job Seeker through an Actionable Dashboard. In *Proc. ACM 24th International*

Conference on Intelligent User Interfaces, 121–31. https://dl.acm.org/doi/abs /10.1145/3301275.3302312.

Chen, L., Yan, D. and Wang, F. (December 2019). User Evaluations on Sentiment-Based Recommendation Explanations. *ACM Transactions on Interactive Intelligent Systems*, 9(4): Article 20, 1–38. https://doi.org/10.1145/3282878.

Cheng, H. F., Wang, R., Zhang, Z., O'Connell, F., Gray, T., Harper, F. M. and Zhu, H. (2019). Explaining Decision-Making Algorithms through UI: Strategies to Help Non-expert Stakeholders. *Proc. 2019 CHI Conference on Human Factors in Computing Systems*. ACM, 1–12. https://dl.acm.org/doi/abs/10.1145/3290605. 3300789.

Cho, J. H., Xu, S., Hurley, P. M., Mackay, M., Benjamin, T. and Beaumont, M. (2019). Stram: Measuring the Trustworthiness of Computer-Based Systems. *ACM Computing Surveys (CSUR)*, 51(6): 1–47.

Choi, Y. K., Lazar, A., Demiris, G. and Thompson, H. J. (2019). Emerging Smart Home Technologies to Facilitate Engaging with Aging. *Journal of Gerontological Nursing*, 45(12): 41–8.

Clancey, W. J. (1986). From GUIDON to NEOMYCIN and HERACLES in Twenty Short Lessons. *AI Magazine*, 7(3): 40–60.

Couzin-Frankel, J. (2019). Medicine Contends with How to Use Artificial Intelligence. *Science*, 354(6446): 1119–20. https://science.sciencemag.org/content/364 /6446/1119.summary.

Crawford, K. (2021). *The Atlas of AI*. New Haven, CT: Yale University Press.

Czaja, S. J., Boot, W. R., Charness, N. and Rogers, W. A. (2019). *Designing for Older Adults: Principles and Creative Human Factors Approaches*, 3rd ed. Boca Raton, FL: CRC Press.

D'Amour, A., Heller, K., Moldovan, D., Adlam, B., Alipanahi, B., Beutel, A., . . . and Sculley, D. (November 6, 2020). Underspecification Presents Challenges for Credibility in Modern Machine Learning. arXiv preprint. https://arxiv.org/abs/2011. 03395.

Daugherty, P. R. and Wilson, H. J. (2018). *Human+ Machine: Reimagining Work in the Age of AI*. Cambridge, MA: Harvard Business Press.

DeepMind (November 30, 2020). AlphaFold: A Solution a Fifty-Year-Old Grand Challenge in Biology. https://deepmind.com/blog/article/alphafold-a-solution-to-a-50 -year-old-grand-challenge-in-biology.

Defense Science Board (2016). *Summer Study on Autonomy*. Washington, DC: Office of the Undersecretary for Defense for Acquisition, Technology and Logistics, Department of Defense.

Desmet, P. and Fokkinga, S. (2020). Beyond Maslow's Pyramid: Introducing a Typology of Thirteen Fundamental Needs for Human-Centered Design. *Multimodal Technologies and Interaction*, 4(3): 38.

Dietterich, T. G. (2019). Robust Artificial Intelligence and Robust Human Organizations. *Frontiers of Computer Science*, 13: 1–3. https://doi.org/10.1007/s11704-018 -8900-4.

Dignum, V. (2019). *Responsible Artificial Intelligence: How to Develop and Use AI in a Responsible Way*. New York: Springer Nature.

Doshi-Velez, F. and Kim, B. (2017). Towards a Rigorous Science of Interpretable Machine Learning. arXiv preprint. https://arxiv.org/abs/1702.08608.

Du, F., Plaisant, C., Spring, N., Crowley, K. and Shneiderman, B. (2019). EventAction: A Visual Analytics Approach to Explainable Recommendation for Event Sequences. *ACM Transactions on Interactive Intelligent Systems*, 9(4): 1–31. https://dl.acm.org/doi/10.1145/3301402.

Du, M., Liu, N. and Hu, X. (2020). Techniques for Interpretable Machine Learning. *Communications of the ACM*, 63(1): 68–77. https://dl.acm.org/doi/fullHtml/10.1145/3359786.

Dubber, M. D., Pasquale, F. and Das, S., eds. (2020). *The Oxford Handbook of Ethics of AI*. New York: Oxford University Press.

Dudley, J. J. and Kristensson, P. O. (2018). A Review of User Interface Design for Interactive Machine Learning. *ACM Transactions on Interactive Intelligent Systems (TIIS)*, 8(2): 8. https://dl.acm.org/doi/abs/10.1145/3185517.

Ebert, C. and Weyrich, M. (2019). Validation of Autonomous Systems. *IEEE Software*, 36(5): 15–23. https://ieeexplore.ieee.org/abstract/document/8802868/.

Edmonds, E. A. and Candy, L. (2002). Creativity, Art Practice and Knowledge. *Communications of the ACM*, Special Section on Creativity and Interface, 45(10): 91–5. https://dl.acm.org/doi/fullHtml/10.1145/570907.570939.

Ehsan, U., Liao, Q. V., Muller, M., Riedl, M. O. and Weisz, J. D. (2021). Expanding Explainability: Towards Social Transparency in AI Systems. *Proc. 2021 CHI Conference on Human Factors in Computing Systems*. ACM, Article 82, 1–19. https://doi.org/10.1145/3411764.3445188.

Elbaum, S. and Munson, J. C. (October 2000). Software Black Box: An Alternative Mechanism for Failure Analysis. *Proc. 11th International Symposium on Software Reliability Engineering. ISSRE 2000*. IEEE, 365–76. https://ieeexplore.ieee.org/abstract/document/885887.

Ellick, A. and Westbrook, A. (November 12, 2018). Operation Infektion: Russian Disinformation from Cold War to Kanye. *The New York Times*. https://www.nytimes.com/2018/11/12/opinion/russia-meddling-disinformation-fake-news-elections.html.

Endsley, M. R. (2017). From Here to Autonomy: Lessons Learned from Human–Automation Research. *Human Factors*, 59(1): 5–27.

Endsley, M. R. (March 2018). Level of Automation Forms a Key Aspect of Autonomy Design. *Journal of Cognitive Engineering and Decision Making*, 12(1): 29–34. https://journals.sagepub.com/doi/abs/10.1177/1555343417723432.

Engelbart, D. C. (1962). Augmenting human intellect: a conceptual framework. Reprinted in Packer, R. and Jordan, K., eds. (2001). *Multimedia: From Wagner to Virtual Reality*. New York: W. W. Norton, 64–90.

Engelbart, D. C. and English, W. K. (1968). A Research Center for Augmenting Human Intellect. *Proc. 1968 Fall Joint Computer Conference*, part I, 395–410.

Engstrom, D. E., Ho. D. E., Sharkey, C. M. and Cuellar, M.-F. (2020). Government by Algorithm: Artificial Intelligence in Federal Administrative Agencies, Administrative Conference of the United States. https://www-cdn.law.stanford.edu/wp-content/uploads/2020/02/ACUS-AI-Report.pdf.

Erickson, S. M., Wolcott, J., Corrigan, J. M. and Aspden, P., eds. (2004). *Patient Safety: Achieving a New Standard for Care*. Washington, DC: National Academies Press.

European Commission (2020a). White Paper on Artificial Intelligence—A European Approach to Excellence and Trust, Brussels. https://ec.europa.eu/info/sites/info/files/commission-white-paper-artificial-intelligence-feb2020_en.pdf.

European Commission (2020b). The Assessment List for Trustworthy Artificial Intelligence (ALTAI) for Self-Assessment, Independent High-Level Expert Group on Artificial Intelligence, Brussels. https://ec.europa.eu/digital-single-market/en/news/assessment-list-trustworthy-artificial-intelligence-altai-self-assessment.

European Union Expert Group on Liability and New Technologies (2019). Liability for Artificial Intelligence and other Emerging Digital Technologies. https://www.europarl.europa.eu/meetdocs/2014_2019/plmrep/COMMITTEES/JURI/DV/2020/01-09/AI-report_EN.pdf.

Federal Trade Commission (April 8, 2020). Using Artificial Intelligence and Algorithms. https://www.ftc.gov/news-events/blogs/business-blog/2020/04/using-artificial-intelligence-algorithms.

Falco, G., Eling, M., Jablanski, D., Weber, M., Miller, V., Gordon, L. A., . . . and Lin, H. (2019). Cyber Risk Research Impeded by Disciplinary Barriers. *Science*, 366(6469): 1066–9.

Falco, G., Shneiderman, B., Badger, J., Carrier, R., Dahbura, A., Danks, D., . . . and Yeong, Z. K. (2017). Governing AI Safety through Independent Audits. *Nature Machine Intelligence*, 566–71. https://doi.org/10.1038/s42256-021-00370-7.

Feldman-Barrett, L. (2017). *How Emotions are Made: The Secret Life of the Brain.* New York: Houghton Mifflin Harcourt.

Fiesler, C., Garrett, N. and Beard, N. (February 2020). What Do We Teach When We Teach Tech Ethics? A Syllabi Analysis. *Proc. 51st ACM Technical Symposium on Computer Science Education*, 289–95. https://dl.acm.org/doi/abs/10.1145/3328778.3366825.

Fischer, G. (2018). Design Trade-offs for Quality of Life. *ACM Interactions*, 25(1): 26–33. https://dl.acm.org/doi/fullHtml/10.1145/3170706.

Fjeld, J., Achten, N., Hilligoss, H., Nagy, A. and Srikumar, M. (2020). *Principled Artificial Intelligence: Mapping Consensus in Ethical And Rights-Based Approaches to Principles for AI.* Berkman Klein Center Research Publication. https://cyber.harvard.edu/publication/2020/principled-ai.

Floridi, L., Cowls, J., Beltrametti, M., Chatila, R., Chazerand, P., Dignum, V., . . . and Vayena, E. (2018). AI4People—An Ethical Framework for a Good AI Society: Opportunities, Risks, Principles, and Recommendations. *Minds and Machines*, 28(4): 689–707. https://doi.org/10.1007/s11023-018-9482-5.

Ford, M. (2015). *Rise of the Robots: Technology and the Threat of a Jobless Future.* New York: Basic Books.

Fraser, P., Moultrie, J. and Gregory, M. (2002). The Use of Maturity Models/Grids as a Tool in Assessing Product Development Capability. *Proc. IEEE International Engineering Management Conference*, 1: 244–9.

Frey, C. B. and Osborne, M. (2013). *The Future of Employment: How Susceptible Are Jobs to Computerisation?* Oxford Martin School, University of Oxford. http://www.oxfordmartin.ox.ac.uk/downloads/academic/The_Future_of_Employment.pdf.

Friedler, S. A., Scheidegger, C., Venkatasubramanian, S., Choudhary, S., Hamilton, E. P. and Roth, D. (January 2019). A Comparative Study of Fairness-Enhancing Interventions in Machine Learning. *Proceedings of the*

Conference on Fairness, Accountability, and Transparency. ACM, 329–38. https://doi.org/10.1145/3287560.3287589.

Friedman, B. and Hendry, D. G. (2019). *Value Sensitive Design: Shaping Technology with Moral Imagination*. Cambridge, MA: MIT Press.

Friedman, B. and Nissenbaum, H. (1996). Bias in Computer Systems. *ACM Transactions on Information Systems (TOIS)*, 14(3): 330–47.

Fukuyama, F. (1995). *Trust: The Social Virtues and the Creation of Prosperity*. New York: Free Press.

Gale, A. and Mochizuki, T. (January 14, 2019). Robot Hotel Loses Love for Robots. *Wall Street Journal*. https://www.wsj.com/articles/robot-hotel-loses-love-for-robots-11547484628.

Garfinkel, S., Matthews, J., Shapiro, S. S. and Smith, J. M. (2017). Toward Algorithmic Transparency and Accountability. *Communications of the ACM*, 60(9): 5.

Garrett, N., Beard, N. and Fiesler, C. (February 2020). More Than "If Time Allows": The Role of Ethics in AI Education. *Proc. AAAI/ACM Conference on AI, Ethics, and Society*, 272–8. https://dl.acm.org/doi/abs/10.1145/3375627.3375868.

Gaskell, A. (December 11, 2019). Are Older Entrepreneurs the Best Entrepreneurs? *Forbes*.https://www.forbes.com/sites/adigaskell/2019/12/11/are-older-entrepreneurs-the-best-entrepreneurs/.

Gebru, T., Morgenstern, J., Vecchione, B., Vaughan, J. W., Wallach, H., Daumé III, H. and Crawford, K. (2018). Datasheets for Datasets. arXiv preprint. https://arxiv.org/abs/1803.09010.

Gerling, K., Ray, M., Abeele, V. V. and Evans, A. B. (2020). Critical Reflections on Technology to Support Physical Activity among Older Adults: An Exploration of Leading HCI Venues. *ACM Transactions on Accessible Computing (TACCESS)*, 13(1): 1–23. https://dl.acm.org/doi/abs/10.1145/3374660.

Giuliani, M., Lenz, C., Müller, T., Rickert, M. and Knoll, A. (2010). Design Principles for Safety in Human–Robot Interaction. *International Journal of Social Robotics*, 2(3): 253–74.

Goodman, B. and Flaxman, S. (2017). European Union Regulations on Algorithmic Decision-Making and a "Right to Explanation". *AI Magazine*, 38(3): 50–7.

Green, S. E., Rees, J. P., Stephens, P. A., Hill, R. A. and Giordano, A. J. (2020). Innovations in Camera Trapping Technology and Approaches: The Integration of Citizen Science and Artificial Intelligence. *Animals*, 10(1), 132. https://www.mdpi.com/2076-2615/10/1/132.

Groom, V. and Nass, C. (2007). Can Robots Be Teammates?: Benchmarks in Human–Robot Teams. *Interaction Studies*, 8(3): 483–500. https://www.jbe-platform.com/content/journals/10.1075/is.8.3.10gro.

Grossi, D. R. (May 1999). Aviation Recorder Overview. *Proc. International Symposium on Transportation Recorders*. Arlington, VA, 153–64.

Guldenmund, F. W. (2000). The Nature of Safety Culture: A Review of Theory and Research. *Safety Science*, 34(1–3): 215–57. https://www.sciencedirect.com/science/article/pii/S092575350000014X.

Haavik, T. K., Antonsen, S., Rosness, R. and Hale, A. (2019). HRO and RE: A Pragmatic Perspective. *Safety Science*, 117: 479–89.

Haibe-Kains, B., Adam, G. A., Hosny, A., Khodakarami, F., MAQC Society Board of Directors, Waldron, L., ... and Aerts, H. J. W. L. (October 15, 2020). Transparency and Reproducibility in Artificial Intelligence. *Nature*, 586: E14–E16. https://doi.org/10.1038/s41586-020-2766-y.

Halevy, A., Ferrer, C. C., Ma, H., Ozertem, U., Pantel, P., Saeidi, M., Silvestri, F., and Stoyanov, V. (2020). Preserving Integrity in Online Social Networks. arXiv preprint. https://arxiv.org/abs/2009.10311.

Hancock, P. A. (2017). Imposing Limits on Autonomous Systems. *Ergonomics*, 60(2): 284–91.

Hancock, P. (2022). Avoiding Adverse Autonomous Agent Actions. *Human-Computer Interaction Journal* (forthcoming).

Hanson Social Robotics (September 24, 2018). Meet Sophia, the Robot That Looks Human. https://www.hansonrobotics.com/news-meet-sophia-the-robot-that-looks-almost-human/.

Harambam, J., Bountouridis, D., Makhortykh, M. and Van Hoboken, J. (September 2019). Designing for the Better by Taking Users into Account: A Qualitative Evaluation of User Control Mechanisms in (News) Recommender Systems. *Proc. 13th ACM Conference on Recommender Systems*, 69–77. https://dl.acm.org/doi/abs/10.1145/3298689.3347014.

Harrell, D. F. (2013). *Phantasmal Media: An Approach to Imagination, Computation, and Expression*. Cambridge, MA: MIT Press.

Haughey, M. M., Muralikumar, M. D., Wood, C. A. and Starbird, K. (2020). On the Misinformation Beat: Understanding the Work of Investigative Journalists Reporting on Problematic Information Online. *Proc. ACM on Human-Computer Interaction*, 4(CSCW2): 1–22. https://dl.acm.org/doi/abs/10.1145/3415204.

He, C., Parra, D. and Verbert, K. (2016). Interactive Recommender Systems: A Survey of the State of the Art and Future Research Challenges and Opportunities. *Expert Systems with Applications*, 56: 9–27. https://www.sciencedirect.com/science/article/pii/S0957417416300367.

Heer, J. (2019). Agency Plus Automation: Designing Artificial Intelligence into Interactive Systems. *Proceedings of the National Academy Sciences*, 116(6): 1844–50. https://www.pnas.org/content/116/6/1844.

Heilweil, R. (June 11, 2020). Big Tech Companies Back away from Selling Facial Recognition to Police. That's Progress. *Vox News*. https://www.vox.com/recode/2020/6/10/21287194/amazon-microsoft-ibm-facial-recognition-moratorium-police.

Herschel, M., Diestelkämper, R. and Lahmar, H. B. (2017). A Survey on Provenance: What for? What Form? What from? *The VLDB Journal*, 26(6): 881–906.

Hind, M. (2019). Explaining Explainable AI. XRDS: Crossroads, The *ACM Magazine for Students*, 25(3): 16–19. https://dl.acm.org/doi/abs/10.1145/3313096.

Hoffman, G. (May 1, 2019). Anki, Jibo, and Kuri: What We Can Learn From Social Robots That Didn't Make It. *IEEE Spectrum*. https://spectrum.ieee.org/automaton/robotics/home-robots/anki-jibo-and-kuri-what-we-can-learn-from-social-robotics-failures.

Hoffman, R. R. (2017). A Taxonomy of Emergent Trusting in the Human-Machine Relationship. In Smith, P. and Hoffman, R. R., eds., *Cognitive Systems Engineering: The Future for a Changing World*, 137–64. Boca Raton, FL: Taylor and Francis.

Hoffman, R. R., Cullen, T. M. and Hawley, J. K. (2016). The Myths and Costs of Autonomous Weapon Systems. *Bulletin of the Atomic Scientists*, 72(4): 247–55. https://doi.org/10.1080/00963402.2016.1194619.

Hoffman, R. R. and Hancock, P. A. (2017). Measuring Resilience. *Human Factors*, 59(4): 564–81.

Hoffman, R. R. and Johnson, M. (2019). The Quest for Alternatives to "Levels of Automation" and "Task Allocation." In Mouloua, M., and Hancock, P. A., eds., *Human Performance in Automated and Autonomous Systems*. Boca Raton, FL: CRC Press, 43–68.

Hoffman, R. R. and Klein, G. (2017). Explaining Explanation, Part 1: Theoretical Foundations. *IEEE Intelligent Systems*, 32(3): 68–73. https://ieeexplore.ieee.org/abstract/document/7933919/.

Hoffman, R. R., Mueller, S. T. and Klein, G. (2017). Explaining Explanation, Part 2: Empirical Foundations. *IEEE Intelligent Systems*, 32(4): 78–86. https://ieeexplore.ieee.org/abstract/document/8012316.

Hohman, F., Head, A., Caruana, R., DeLine, R. and Drucker, S. M. (2019). Gamut: A Design Probe to Understand How Data Scientists Understand Machine Learning Models. *Proc. 2019 CHI Conference on Human Factors in Computing Systems*. ACM, 1–13. https://dl.acm.org/doi/abs/10.1145/3290605.3300809.

Hohman, F., Park, H., Robinson, C. and Chau, D. H. P. (2019). SUMMIT: Scaling Deep Learning Interpretability by Visualizing Activation and Attribution Summarizations. *IEEE Transactions on Visualization and Computer Graphics*, 26(1): 1096–106. https://fredhohman.com/papers/19-summit-vast.pdf.

Holstein, K., Wortman Vaughan, J., Daumé III, H., Dudik, M. and Wallach, H. (May 2019). Improving Fairness in Machine Learning Systems: What Do Industry Practitioners Need? In *Proc. 2019 CHI Conference on Human Factors in Computing Systems*. ACM, 1–16. https://doi.org/10.1145/3290605.3300830.

Hong, S., Hullman, J. and Bertini, E. (2020). Human Factors in Model Interpretability: Industry Practices, Challenges, and Needs. *Proc. ACM on Human-Computer Interaction*, 4(CSCW1): 1–26. https://dl.acm.org/doi/pdf/10.1145/3392878.

Honig, S., Bartal, A. and Oron-Gilad, T. (March 2020). Using Customers' Online Reviews to Identify and Classify Human Robot Interaction Failures in Domestic Robots. In *Companion of the 2020 ACM/IEEE International Conference on Human-Robot Interaction*. ACM, 251–3.

Honig, S. and Oron-Gilad, T. (2018). Understanding and Resolving Failures in Human-Robot Interaction: Literature Review and Model Development. *Frontiers in Psychology*, 9(861): 1–21. https://www.frontiersin.org/articles/10.3389/fpsyg.2018.00861/full.

Hopkins, A. (1999). The Limits of Normal Accident Theory. *Safety Science*, 32(2): 93–102. https://www.sciencedirect.com/science/article/pii/S0925753599000156/pdf.

Horvitz, E. (1999). Principles of Mixed-Initiative User Interfaces. *Proc. ACM SIGCHI Conference on Human Factors in Computing Systems*. ACM, 159–66. https://dl.acm.org/doi/abs/10.1145/302979.303030.

Hsu, F.-h. (2002). *Behind Deep Blue: Building the Computer that Defeated the World Chess Champion*. Princeton University Press.

Hsu, S., Vaccaro, K., Yue, Y., Rickman, A. and Karahalios, K. (2020). Awareness, Navigation, and Use of Feed Control Settings Online. *Proc. 2020 CHI Conference on Human Factors in Computing Systems.* ACM, 1–13. https://dl.acm.org /doi/abs/10.1145/3313831.3376583.

Hull, R., Kumar, B., Lieuwen, D., Patel-Schneider, P. F., Sahuguet, A., Varadarajan, S. and Vyas, A. (2003). "Everything Personal, Not Just Business": Improving User Experience through Rule-Based Service Customization. *International Conference on Service-Oriented Computing.* Berlin: Springer, 149–64. https://link.springer.com/chapter/10.1007/978-3-540-24593-3_11.

Humphrey, W. S. (1988). Characterizing the Software Process: A Maturity Framework. *IEEE Software,* 5(2): 73–9. https://ieeexplore.ieee.org/document /2014.

Hung, L., Gregorio, M., Mann, J., Wallsworth, C., Horne, N., Berndt, A., . . . and Chaudhury, H. (2019). Exploring the Perceptions of People with Dementia about the Social Robot PARO in a Hospital Setting. *Dementia,* 20(2): 485–504. https://doi.org/10.1177/1471301219894141.

IEEE Global Initiative on Ethics of Autonomous and Intelligent Systems (2019). *Ethically Aligned Design: A Vision for Prioritizing Human Well-being with Autonomous and Intelligent Systems.* IEEE. https://standards.ieee.org/content/ieee-standards/en/industry-connections/ec/autonomous-systems.html.

Information Commissioner's Office and Alan Turing Institute (2019). Explaining Decisions Made with AI. https://ico.org.uk/about-the-ico/ico-and-stakeholder-consultations/ico-and-the-turing-consultation-on-explaining-ai-decisions-guidance/.

Jin, Y., Cardoso, B. and Verbert, K. (2017). How Do Different Levels of User Control Affect Cognitive Load and Acceptance of Recommendations?. *Proc. CEUR Workshop,* 1884: 35–42. https://lirias.kuleuven.be/1633445.

Jin, Y., Tintarev, N. and Verbert, K. (September 2018). Effects of Personal Characteristics on Music Recommender Systems with Different Levels of Controllability. *Proc. 12th ACM Conference on Recommender Systems.* ACM, 13–21. https://dl.acm.org/doi/abs/10.1145/3240323.3240358.

Johnson, J. and Finn, K. (2017). *Designing User Interfaces for an Aging Population: Towards Universal Design.* Burlington, MA: Morgan Kaufmann.

Jordan, M. I. (2018). Artificial Intelligence—The Revolution Hasn't Happened Yet. https://medium.com/@mijordan3/artificial-intelligence-the-revolution-hasnt-happened-yet-5e1d5812e1e7.

Kahn, P. H., Freier, N. G., Kanda, T., Ishiguro, H., Ruckert, J. H., Severson, R. L. and Kane, S. K. (March 2008). Design Patterns for Sociality in Human-Robot Interaction. *Proc. 3rd ACM/IEEE International Conference on Human Robot Interaction.* ACM, 97–104.

Kalluri, P. (2020). Don't Ask If Artificial Intelligence Is Good or Fair, Ask How It Shifts Power. *Nature,* 583(7815): 169.

Kaufman, S. B. (2020). *Transcend: The New Science of Self-Actualization.* New York: TarcherPerigree Books.

Kavi, K. M. (2010). Beyond the Black Box. *IEEE Spectrum,* 47(8): 46–51.

Khadpe, P., Krishna, R., Fei-Fei, L., Hancock, J. T. and Bernstein, M. S. (2020). Conceptual Metaphors Impact Perceptions of Human-AI Collaboration. *Proc. ACM* on *Human-Computer Interaction*, 4(CSCW2): Article 163, 1–26. https://dl.acm.org/doi/abs/10.1145/3415234.

Klein, G. A. (2017). *Sources of Power: How People Make Decisions.* Cambridge, MA: MIT Press.

Klein, G., Shneiderman, B., Hoffman, R. R. and Wears, R. L. (2019). The "War" on Expertise. In Ward, P., Schraagen, J. M., Gore, J. and Roth, E. M., eds., *The Oxford Handbook of Expertise.* Oxford University Press.

Klein, G., Woods, D. D., Bradshaw, J. M., Hoffman, R. R. and Feltovich, P. J. (2004). Ten Challenges for Making Automation a "Team Player" in Joint Human-Agent Activity. *IEEE Intelligent Systems*, 6: 91–5. https://ieeexplore.ieee.org/abstract/document/1363742/.

Koch, J., Lucero, A., Hegemann, L. and Oulasvirta, A. (May 2019). May AI? Design Ideation with Cooperative Contextual Bandits. *Proc. 2019 CHI Conference on Human Factors in Computing Systems.* ACM, 1–12. https://dl.acm.org/doi/abs/10.1145/3290605.3300863.

Koch, J., Taffin, N., Beaudouin-Lafon, M., Laine, M., Lucero, A. and Mackay, W. E. (2020). ImageSense: An Intelligent Collaborative Ideation Tool to Support Diverse Human-Computer Partnerships. *Proc. ACM on Human-Computer Interaction*, 4(CSCW1): 1–27. https://dl.acm.org/doi/abs/10.1145/3392850.

Koenemann, J. and Belkin, N. J. (April 1996). A Case for Interaction: A Study of Interactive Information Retrieval Behavior and Effectiveness. *Proc. SIGCHI Conference on Human Factors in Computing Systems.* ACM, 205–12. https://dl.acm.org/doi/fullHtml/10.1145/238386.238487.

Konstan, J. A. and Riedl, J. (2012). Recommender Systems: From Algorithms Tommen Reco User Experience. *User Modeling and User-Adapted Interaction*, 22(1–2): 101–23. https://link.springer.com/article/10.1007/s11257-011-9112-x.

Koopman, P., Kane, A. and Black, J. (February 2019). Credible Autonomy Safety Argumentation. *Proc. 27th Safety-Critical Systems Symposium*, 1–27. http://users.ece.cmu.edu/~koopman/pubs/Koopman19_SSS_CredibleSafetyArgumentation.pdf.

Krämer, N. C., von der Pütten, A. and Eimler, S. (2012). Human-Agent and Human-Robot Interaction Theory: Similarities to and Differences from Human-Human Interaction. In: Zacarias, M. and de Oliveira, J. V., eds., *Human-Computer Interaction: The Agency Perspective.* Heidelberg/Berlin: Springer, 215–40. http://dx.doi.org/10.1007/978-3-642-25691-2_9.

Kulesza, T., Burnett, M., Wong, W. K. and Stumpf, S. (2015). Principles of Explanatory Debugging to Personalize Interactive Machine Learning. *Proc. 20th International Conference on Intelligent User Interfaces.* ACM, 126–37. https://dl.acm.org/doi/abs/10.1145/2678025.2701399.

Kumar, N., Belhumeur, P. N., Biswas, A., Jacobs, D. W., Kress, W. J., Lopez, I. C. and Soares, J. V. (October 2012). Leafsnap: A Computer Vision System for Automatic Plant Species Identification. *Proc. 2012 European Conference on Computer Vision.* Berlin: Springer, 502–16. https://link.springer.com/chapter/10.1007/978-3-642-33709-3_36.

Kunkel, J., Schwenger, C. and Ziegler, J. (July 2020). NewsViz: Depicting and Controlling Preference Profiles Using Interactive Treemaps in News Recommender Systems. *Proc. 28th ACM Conference on User Modeling, Adaptation and Personalization*, 126–35. https://dl.acm.org/doi/abs/10.1145/3340631.3394869.

Kuo, L. (November 9, 2018). World's First AI News Anchor Unveiled in China, *The Guardian*. https://www.theguardian.com/world/2018/nov/09/worlds-first-ai-news-anchor-unveiled-in-china.

Laborie, P., Rogerie, J., Shaw, P. and Vilím, P. (2018). IBM ILOG CP Optimizer for Scheduling. *Constraints*, 23(2): 210–50.

Lacerda, T. C. and von Wangenheim, C. G. (2018). Systematic Literature Review of Usability Capability/Maturity Models. *Computer Standards and Interfaces*, 55: 95–105.

Lambert, A., Norouzi, N., Bruder, G. and Welch, G. (2020). A Systematic Review of Ten Years of Research on Human Interaction with Social Robots. *International Journal of Human–Computer Interaction*, 36(19): 1804–17. https://doi.org/10.1080/10447318.2020.1801172.

Landon, P., Weaver, P. and Fitch, J. P. (2016). Tracking Minor and Near-miss Events and Sharing Lessons Learned as a Way to Prevent Accidents. *Applied Biosafety*, 21(2): 61–5. https://journals.sagepub.com/doi/abs/10.1177/1535676016646642.

Landwehr, C.E. (2013). A Building Code for Building Code: Putting What We Know Works to Work. *Proc. 29th Ann. Computer Security Applications Conf. (ACSAC)*, 139–47. http://www.landwehr.org/2013-12-cl-acsac-essay-bc.pdf.

Landwehr, C. (2015). We Need a Building Code for Building Code. *Communications of the ACM*, 58(2): 24–6.

Lanier, J. (2010). *You Are Not a Gadget*. New York: Knopf Doubleday.

La Porte, T. R. (1996). High Reliability Organizations: Unlikely, Demanding and at Risk. *Journal of Contingencies and Crisis Management*, 4(2): 60–71.

Lazar, J., Goldstein, D. F. and Taylor, A. (2015). *Ensuring Digital Accessibility through Process and Policy*. Waltham, MA: Elsevier/Morgan Kaufmann.

Lazer, D., Kennedy, R., King, G. and Vespignani, A. (March 14, 2014). The Parable of Google Flu: Traps in the Big Data Analysis. *Science* 343: 1203–5.

Lee, K.-F. (September 22, 2018). What China Can Teach the U.S. about Artificial Intelligence. *The New York Times*. https://www.nytimes.com/2018/09/22/opinion/sunday/ai-china-united-states.html.

Lee, N. T., Resnick, P. and Barton, G. (2019). Algorithmic Bias Detection and Mitigation: Best Practices and Policies to Reduce Consumer Harms. Center for Technology Innovation, Brookings. https://www.brookings.edu/research/algorithmic-bias-detection-and-mitigation-best-practices-and-policies-to-reduce-consumer-harms/.

Leike, J., Martic, M., Krakovna, V., Ortega, P. A., Everitt, T., Lefrancq, A., Orseau, L., and Legg, S. (2017). AI Safety Gridworlds. arXiv preprint. https://arxiv.org/abs/1711.09883.

Letham, B., Rudin, C., McCormick, T. H. and Madigan, D. (2015). Interpretable Classifiers Using Rules and Bayesian Analysis: Building a Better Stroke Prediction Model. *Annals of Applied Statistics*, 9(3): 1350–71.

Leveson, N. (2011). *Engineering a Safer World: Systems Thinking Applied to Safety*. Cambridge, MA: MIT Press.

Lewis, J. E., ed. (2020). *Indigenous Protocol and Artificial Intelligence Position Paper*. Honolulu, HI: The Initiative for Indigenous Futures and the Canadian Institute for Advanced Research (CIFAR). https://spectrum.library.concordia.ca/986506.

Lewis, J. R. (2014). Usability: Lessons Learned . . . and Yet to be Learned. *International Journal of Human–Computer Interaction*, 30(9): 663–84.

Li, F.-F. (March 7, 2018). How to Make A.I. That's Good for People. *The New York Times*. https://www.nytimes.com/2018/03/07/opinion/artificial-intelligence-human.html.

Liang, Y. and Lee, S. A. (2017). Fear of Autonomous Robots and Artificial Intelligence: Evidence from National Representative Data with Probability Sampling. *International Journal of Social Robotics*, 9(3): 379–84.

Liang, X., Shetty, S., Tosh, D., Kamhoua, C., Kwiat, K. and Njilla, L. (2017). Provchain: A Blockchain-based Data Provenance Architecture in Cloud Environment with Enhanced Privacy and Availability. *Proc. 2017 17th IEEE/ACM International Symposium on Cluster, Cloud and Grid Computing (CCGRID)*, IEEE/ACM, 468–77.

Liao, Q. V., Gruen, D. and Miller, S. (2020). Questioning the AI: Informing Design Practices for Explainable AI User Experiences. *Proc. 2020 ACM CHI Conference on Human Factors in Computing Systems*. ACM, 1–15.

Licklider, J. C. R. (1960). Man-Computer Symbiosis. *Transactions on Human Factors in Electronics*, HFE-1: 4–11.

Lobosco, K. (March 12, 2015). Talking Barbie Is Too Creepy for Some Parents. *CNN Business*. https://money.cnn.com/2015/03/11/news/companies/creepy-hello-barbie/.

Lopatovska, I., Rink, K., Knight, I., Raines, K., Cosenza, K., Williams, H., ... and Martinez, A. (2019). Talk to Me: Exploring User Interactions with the Amazon Alexa. *Journal of Librarianship and Information Science*, 51(4): 984–97. https://journals.sagepub.com/doi/abs/10.1177/0961000618759414.

Lopatovska, I., Griffin, A. L., Gallagher, K., Ballingall, C., Rock, C. and Velazquez, M. (2020). User Recommendations for Intelligent Personal Assistants. *Journal of Librarianship and Information Science*, 52(2): 577–91. https://journals.sagepub.com/doi/abs/10.1177/0961000619841107.

López G., Quesada L. and Guerrero L.A. (2018). Alexa vs. Siri vs. Cortana vs. Google Assistant: A Comparison of Speech-based Natural User Interfaces. In Nunes, I., ed., *Advances in Human Factors and Systems Interaction, AHFE 2017. Advances in Intelligent Systems and Computing*, vol. 592. New York: Springer.

McAllister, B. (September 21, 1993). "Postal Buddy" Gets an unfriendly push. *Washington Post*. https://www.washingtonpost.com/archive/politics/1993/09/21/postal-buddy-gets-an-unfriendly-push/66554041-0218-44d0-b6d7-92a89b1da5e6/.

McBride, N. (2020). Robot Enhanced Therapy for Autistic Children: An Ethical Analysis. *IEEE Technology and Society Magazine*, 39(1): 51–60.

McGregor, S. (2021). Preventing Repeated Real World AI Failures by Cataloging Incidents: The AI Incident Database. *Proc. Thirty-Third Annual Conference on Innovative Applications of Artificial Intelligence (IAAI-21)*, 35(17). Virtual conference. https://ojs.aaai.org/index.php/AAAI/article/view/17817.

McLuhan, M. (1964). *Understanding Media: The Extensions of Man*. Cambridge, MA: MIT Press.

Macintyre, P. E. (2001). Safety and Efficacy of Patient-Controlled Analgesia. *British Journal of Anaesthesia*, 87(1): 36–46. https://bjanaesthesia.org/article/S0007-0912(17)36342-0/fulltext.

Magazinius, A., Mellegård, N. N. and Olsson, L. (August 2019). Bug Bounty Programs—A Mapping Study. *Proc. 2019 45th Euromicro Conference on Software Engineering and Advanced Applications (SEAA)*. IEEE, 412–15. https://ieeexplore.ieee.org/abstract/document/8906758.

Mahmud, S., Alvina, J., Chilana, P. K., Bunt, A. and McGrenere, J. (2020). Learning through Exploration: How Children, Adults, and Older Adults Interact with a New Feature-Rich Application. *Proc. 2020 CHI Conference on Human Factors in Computing Systems*. ACM, 1–14. https://dl.acm.org/doi/abs/10.1145/3313831. 3376414.

Mai, T., Khanna, R., Dodge, J., Irvine, J., Lam, K. H., Lin, Z., . . . and Fern, A. (2020). Keeping It "Organized and Logical" After-action Review for AI (AAR/AI). *Proc. 25th International Conference on Intelligent User Interfaces*. ACM, 465–76.

Marcus, G. and Davis, E. (2019). *Rebooting AI: Building Artificial Intelligence We Can Trust*. New York: Pantheon.

Marcus, G., Rossi, F. and Veloso, M., eds. (2016). Beyond the Turing Test. *AI Magazine*, 37(1): 3–4. https://doi.org/10.1609/aimag.v37i1.2650.

Markoff, J. (2016). *Machines of Loving Grace: The Quest for Common Ground between Humans and Robots*. New York: HarperCollins.

Marks, P. (2021). Can the Biases in Facial Recognition Be Fixed; Also Should They? *Communications of the ACM*, 64(3): 20–2. https://cacm.acm.org/magazines/2021/3/250698-can-the-biases-in-facial-recognition-be-fixed-also-should-they/fulltext.

Martin, C. D. (1993). The Myth of the Awesome Thinking Machine. *Communications of the ACM*, 36(4): 120–33. https://dl.acm.org/doi/abs/10.1145/255950. 153587.

Martin, C. D. (1995). ENIAC: Press Conference That Shook the World. *IEEE Technology and Society Magazine*, 14(4): 3–10. https://ieeexplore.ieee.org/abstract/document/476631.

Mehrabi, N., Morstatter, F., Saxena, N., Lerman, K. and Galstyan, A. (2019). A Survey on Bias and Fairness in Machine Learning. arXiv preprint. https://arxiv.org/abs/1908.09635.

Metz, C. (May 24, 2021). The Costly Pursuit of Self-Driving Cars Continues On. And On. And On. *The New York Times*. https://www.nytimes.com/2021/05/24/technology/self-driving-cars-wait.html.

Michael, K., Bowman, D., Jones, M. L. and Pringle, R. (2018). Robots and Socio-ethical Implications. *IEEE Technology and Society Magazine*, 37(1): 19–21.

Millecamp, M., Htun, N. N., Jin, Y. and Verbert, K. (July 2018). Controlling Spotify Recommendations: Effects of Personal Characteristics on Music Recommender User Interfaces. *Proc. 26th Conference on User Modeling, Adaptation and Personalization*. ACM, 101–9. https://dl.acm.org/doi/abs/10.1145/3209219.3209223.

Miller, T. (2019). Explanation in Artificial Intelligence: Insights from the *social sciences*. *Artificial Intelligence*, 267: 1–38. https://doi.org/10.1016/j.artint.2018.07.007.

Mindell, D. (2015). *Our Robots, Ourselves: Robotics and the Myths of Autonomy*. New York: Viking Press.

Mishra, K. (February 24, 2020). How AI-powered Devices Are Remodeling the Consumer Electronics Industry. https://www.pathpartnertech.com/how-ai-powered-devices-are-remodeling-the-consumer-electronics-industry/.

Mitchell, M., Wu, S., Zaldivar, A., Barnes, P., Vasserman, L., Hutchinson, B., . . . and Gebru, T. (January 2019). Model Cards for Model Reporting. *Proc. Conference on Fairness, Accountability, and Transparency*. ACM, 220–9. https://dl.acm.org/doi/abs/10.1145/3287560.3287596.

Mitrevski, A., Thoduka, S., Sáinz, A. O., Schöbel, M., Nagel, P., Plöger, P. G. and Prassler, E. (2018). Deploying Robots in Everyday Environments: Towards Dependable and Practical Robotic Systems. In *29th International Workshop Principles of Diagnosis DX*, vol. 18. http://www.ropod.org/downloads/dx18.pdf.

Mittelstadt, B., Russell, C. and Wachter, S. (2019). Explaining Explanations in AI. *Proc. Conference on Fairness, Accountability, and Transparency*. ACM, 279–88. https://doi.org/10.1145/3287560.3287574.

Modarres, M., Kaminskiy, M. P. and Krivtsov, V. (2016). *Reliability Engineering and Risk Analysis: A Practical Guide*. Boca Raton, FL: CRC Press.

Morris, M. R. (2020). AI and Accessibility: A Discussion of Ethical Considerations. *Communications of the ACM*, 63(6): 35–7.

Mojsilovic, A. (August 8, 2019). Introduction AI Explainability 360. IBM Research Blog. https://www.ibm.com/blogs/research/2019/08/ai-explainability-360/.

Mou, Y., Shi, C., Shen, T. and Xu, K. (2020). A Systematic Review of the Personality of Robot: Mapping Its Conceptualization, Operationalization, Contextualization and Effects, *International Journal of Human–Computer Interaction*, 36(6): 591–605. https://doi.org/10.1080/10447318.2019.1663008;

Mueller, A. S., Reagan, I. J. and Cicchino, J. B. (2021). Addressing Driver Disengagement and Proper System Use: Human Factors Recommendations for Level 2 Driving Automation Design. *Journal of Cognitive Engineering and Decision Making*, 15(1): 3–27.

Mumford, L. (1934). *Technics and Civilization*. University of Chicago Press

Murphy, R. and Shields, J. (July 2012). The Role of Autonomy in DoD Systems. Defense Science Board Task Force Report. Washington, DC.

Murphy, R. R. (2014). *Disaster Robotics*. Cambridge, MA: MIT Press.

Nadella, S. (June 28, 2016). The Partnership of the Future. *Slate*. https://slate.com/technology/2016/06/microsoft-ceo-satya-nadella-humans-and-a-i-can-work-together-to-solve-societys-challenges.html.

Nass, C. and Moon, Y. (2000). Machines and Mindlessness: Social Responses to Computers. *Journal of Social Issues*, 56(1): 81–103.

Natale, S. (2020). To Believe in Siri: A Critical Analysis of AI Voice Assistants. Communicative Figurations, Working Paper 32, 1–17. https://www.uni-bremen.de/fileadmin/user_upload/fachbereiche/fb9/zemki/media/photos/publikationen/working-papers/2020/CoFi_EWP_No-32_Simone-Natale.pdf.

Natale, S. (2021). *Deceitful Media: Artificial Intelligence and Social Life after the Turing Test*. New York: Oxford University Press.

Naveed, S. and Ziegler, J. (2019). Feature-Driven Interactive Recommendations and Explanations with Collaborative Filtering Approach. *Proc. ComplexRec@ RecSys*, 10–15. http://ceur-ws.org/Vol-2449/paper2.pdf.

Nicas, J., Kitroeff, N., Gelles, D. and Glanz, J. (June 6, 2019). Boeing Built Deadly Assumptions into 737 Max, Blind to a Late Design Change. *The New York Times*. https://www.nytimes.com/2019/06/01/business/boeing-737-max-crash.html.

Noble, S. U. (2018). *Algorithms of Oppression: How Search Engines Reinforce Racism*. New York University Press.

Nourashrafeddin, S., Sherkat, E., Minghim, R. and Milios, E. E. (2018). A Visual Approach for Interactive Keyterm-Based Clustering. *ACM Transactions on Interactive Intelligent Systems (TIIS)*, 8(1): 1–35. https://dl.acm.org/doi/abs/10.1145/3181669.

Obermeyer, Z., Powers, B., Vogeli, C. and Mullainathan, S. (2019). Dissecting of Racial Bias in an Algorithm Used to Manage the Health of Populations. *Science*, 366(6464): 447–53. https://science.sciencemag.org/content/366/6464/447.

O'Neil, C. (2016). *Weapons of Math Destruction: How Big Data Increases Inequality and Threatens Democracy*. New York: Crown Publishers.

Ovide, S. (June 16, 2021). Amazon Is Brilliant. Why Not at H.R.? *The New York Times*. https://www.nytimes.com/2021/06/16/technology/amazon-work-force.html.

Pandey, A. K. and Gelin, R. (2018). A Mass-Produced Sociable Humanoid Robot: Pepper: The First Machine of Its Kind. *IEEE Robotics and Automation Magazine*, 25(3): 40–8. https://ieeexplore.ieee.org/abstract/document/8409927/.

Parasuraman, R., Sheridan, T. B. and Wickens, C. D. (2000). A Model for Types and Levels of Human Interaction with Automation. *IEEE Transactions on Systems, Man and Cybernetics—Part A: Systems and Humans*, 30: 286–97.

Pasquale, F. (2015). *The Black Box Society: The Secret Algorithms that Control Money and Information*. Cambridge, MA: Harvard University Press.

Pasquale, F. (2017). Toward a Fourth Law of Robotics: Preserving Attribution, Responsibility, and Explainability in an Algorithmic Society. *Ohio State Law Journal*, 78: 1243–55.

Pasquale, F. (2018). When Machine Learning Is Facially Invalid. *Communications of the ACM*, 61(9): 25–7. https://dl.acm.org/doi/fullHtml/10.1145/3241367.

Paulk, M. C., Curtis, B., Chrissis, M. B. and Weber, C. V. (1993). Capability Maturity Model, Version 1.1. *IEEE Software*, 10(4): 18–27.

Pearl, C. (2016). *Designing Voice User Interfaces: Principles of Conversational Experiences*. Sebastopol, CA: O'Reilly Media.

Pearl, J. and Mackenzie, D. (2018). *The Book of Why: The New Science of Cause and Effect*. New York: Basic Books.

Pérez, A., García, M. I., Nieto, M., Pedraza, J. L., Rodríguez, S. and Zamorano, J. (2010). Argos: An Advanced In-vehicle Data Recorder on a Massively Sensorized Vehicle for Car Driver Behavior Experimentation. *IEEE Transactions on Intelligent Transportation Systems*, 11(2): 463–73.

Perez, C. C. (2019). *Invisible Women: Exposing Data Bias in a World Designed for Men*. New York: Random House.

Perrow, C. (2011). *Normal Accidents: Living with High Risk Technologies*, updated edition. Princeton University Press.

Petrie, H. and Darzentas, J. (June 2017). Older People and Robotic Technologies in the Home: Perspectives from Recent Research Literature. *Proc.10th International Conference on Pervasive Technologies Related to Assistive Environments (PETRA)*. ACM, 29–36. https://dl.acm.org/doi/abs/10.1145/3056540.3056553.

Pettersson, O. (2005). Execution Monitoring in Robotics: A Survey. *Robotics and Autonomous Systems*, 53(2): 73–88.

Pichai, S. (June 7, 2018). AI at Google: Our Principles. https://www.blog.google/technology/ai/ai-principles/.

Pielke Jr, R. (2020). A "Sedative" for Science Policy. *Issues in Science and Technology*, 37(1): 41–7. https://issues.org/endless-frontier-sedative-for-science-policy-pielke/.

Piorkowski, D., González, D., Richards, J. and Houde, S. (2020). Towards Evaluating and Eliciting High-Quality Documentation for Intelligent Systems. arXiv preprint. https://arxiv.org/abs/2011.08774.

Poole, D. and Mackworth, A. (2017). *Artificial Intelligence: Foundations of Computational Agents*, 2nd ed. Cambridge University Press.

Preece, J. (2016). Citizen Science: New Research Challenges for Human–Computer Interaction. *International Journal of Human–Computer Interaction*, 32(8): 585–612. https://www.tandfonline.com/doi/abs/10.1080/10447318.2016.1194153.

Prescott, T. J. and Robillard, J. (2021). Are Friends Electric? The Benefits and Risks of Human-Robot Relationships. *iScience*, 24(1), 101993. https://www.sciencedirect.com/science/article/pii/S2589004220311901.

Ragan, E. D., Endert, A., Sanyal, J. and Chen, J. (2015). Characterizing Provenance in Visualization and Data Analysis: An Organizational Framework of Provenance Types and Purposes. *IEEE Transactions on Visualization and Computer Graphics*, 22(1): 31–40.

Raji, I. D., Smart, A., White, R. N., Mitchell, M., Gebru, T., Hutchinson, B., ... and Barnes, P. (2020). Closing the AI Accountability Gap: Defining an End-to-End Framework for Internal Algorithmic Auditing. *Proc. 2020 Conference on Fairness, Accountability, and Transparency (FAT* '20)*. ACM, 33–44. https://doi.org/10.1145/3351095.3372873.

Reddy, S., Allan, S., Coghlan, S. and Cooper, P. (2020). A Governance Model for the Application of AI in Health Care. *Journal of the American Medical Informatics Association*, 27(3): 491–7.

Reeves, B. and Nass, C. (1996). *How People Treat Computers, Television, and New Media Like Real People and Places*. Cambridge, MA: MIT Press.

Reisman, D., Schultz, J., Crawford, K. and Whittaker, M. (2018). *Algorithmic Impact Assessments: A Practical Framework for Public Agency Accountability*. AI Now Institute, 1–22. https://ainowinstitute.org/aiareport2018.pdf.

Richardson, K., Coeckelbergh, M., Wakunuma, K., Billing, E., Ziemke, T., Gomez, P., ... and Belpaeme, T. (2018). Robot Enhanced Therapy for Children with Autism (DREAM): A Social Model of Autism. *IEEE Technology and Society Magazine*, 37(1): 30–9.

Robert, L. (2017). The Growing Problem of Humanizing Robots. *International Robotics and Automation Journal*, 3(1): 247–8. https://papers.ssrn.com/sol3/papers.cfm?abstract_id=3027628.

Roberts, H., Cowls, J., Morley, J., Taddeo, M., Wang, V. and Floridi, L. (2020). The Chinese Approach to Artificial Intelligence: An Analysis of Policy, Ethics, and Regulation. *AI and Society*, 1–19.

Rosenberg, F. and Dustdar, S. (2005). Design and Implementation of a Service-Oriented Business Rules Broker. *Seventh IEEE International Conference on E-Commerce Technology Workshops*. IEEE, 55–63.

Rotenberg, M. (2020a). *The AI Policy Sourcebook 2020*. Washington, DC: Electronic Privacy Information Center

Rotenberg, M., ed. (2020b). *Artificial Intelligence and Democratic Values: An AI Social Contract Index-2020*. Dukakis Center for AI and Digital Policy. https://dukakis.org/center-for-ai-and-digital-policy/caidp-publishes-artificial-intelligence-and-democratic-values/.

Royal Society (April 2017). *Machine Learning: The Power and Promise of Computers That Learn by Example*. London: Royal Society.

Rubinovitz, J. B. (2018). Bias Bounty Programs as a Method of Combatting Bias in AI. https://rubinovitz.com/2018/08/01/bias-bounty-programs-as-a-method-of-combatting/.

Rudin, C. (2019). Stop Explaining Black Box Machine Learning Models for High Stakes Decisions and Use Interpretable Models Instead. *Nature Machine Intelligence*, 1(5): 206–15.

Russell, S. (2019). *Human Compatible: Artificial Intelligence and the Problem of Control*. New York: Penguin Group.

Russell, S. and Norvig, P. (2009). *Artificial Intelligence: A Modern Approach*. Englewood Cliffs, NJ: Prentice Hall.

Saltz, J., Skirpan, M., Fiesler, C., Gorelick, M., Yeh, T., Heckman, R., Dewar, N., and Beard, N. (2019). Integrating Ethics within Machine Learning Courses. *ACM Transactions on Computing Education (TOCE)*, 19(4): 1–26. https://dl.acm.org/doi/abs/10.1145/3341164.

Santoni de Sio, F. and Van den Hoven, J. (2018). Meaningful Human Control over Autonomous Systems: A Philosophical Account. *Frontiers in Robotics and AI*, 5: 15. https://www.frontiersin.org/articles/10.3389/frobt.2018.00015/full.

Schiff, D., Ayesh, A., Musikanski, L. and Havens, J. C. (October 2020). IEEE 7010: A New Standard for Assessing the Well-Being Implications of Artificial Intelligence. In *2020 IEEE International Conference on Systems, Man, and Cybernetics (SMC)*. IEEE, 2746–53. https://ieeexplore.ieee.org/abstract/document/9283454/.

Schiff, D., Rakova, B., Ayesh, A., Fanti, A. and Lennon, M. (2021). Principles to practices for responsible AI: Closing the gap. *IEEE Technology and Society Magazine*.

Schwarting, W., Alonso-Mora, J., Pauli, L., Karaman, S. and Rus, D. (May 2017). Parallel Autonomy in Automated Vehicles: Safe Motion Generation with Minimal Intervention. *Proc. 2017 IEEE International Conference on Robotics and Automation (ICRA)*. IEEE, 1928–35. https://ieeexplore.ieee.org/abstract/document/7989224/.

Sciuto, A., Saini, A., Forlizzi, J. and Hong, J. I. (2018). Hey Alexa, What's Up?: A Mixed-Methods Studies of In-home Conversational Agent Usage. *Proc. Designing Interactive Systems Conference 2018*. ACM, 857–68. https://dl.acm.org/doi/abs/10.1145/3196709.3196772.

Sebo, S., Stoll, B., Scassellati, B. and Jung, M. F. (2020). Robots in Groups and Teams: A Literature Review. *Proc. ACM on Human-Computer Interaction*, 4(CSCW2): 1–36. https://dl.acm.org/doi/abs/10.1145/3415247.

Seddon, J. J. and Currie, W. L. (2017). A Model for Unpacking Big Data Analytics in High-Frequency Trading. *Journal of Business Research*, 70: 300–7.

Sharp, H., Preece, J. and Rogers, Y. (2019). *Interaction Design: Beyond Human-Computer Interaction*, 5th ed. New York Wiley.

Sheehan, B., Jin, H. S. and Gottlieb, U. (2020). Customer Service Chatbots: Anthropomorphism and Adoption. *Journal of Business Research*, 115: 14–24. https://www.sciencedirect.com/science/article/pii/S0148296320302484.

Sheridan, T. B. (1992). *Telerobotics, Automation, and Human Supervisory Control*. Cambridge, MA: MIT Press.

Sheridan, T. B. (2000). Function Allocation: Algorithm, Alchemy or Apostasy? *International Journal of Human-Computer Studies*, 52(2): 203–16. https://www.sciencedirect.com/science/article/pii/S1071581999902859.

Sheridan, T. B. and Verplank, W. L. (1978). Human and Computer Control of Undersea Teleoperators. Technical report. Massachusetts Institute of Technology Cambridge Man-Machine Systems Lab. https://apps.dtic.mil/sti/citations/ADA057655.

Shneiderman, B. (1980). *Software Psychology: Human Factors in Computer and Information Systems*. New York: Winthrop Publishers.

Shneiderman, B. (1982). The Future of Interactive Systems and the Emergence of Direct Manipulation, *Behaviour and Information Technology*, 1(3): 237–56.

Shneiderman, B. (August 1983). Direct Manipulation: A Step Beyond Programming Languages, *IEEE Computer*, 16(8): 57–69.

Shneiderman, B. (1987). *Designing the User Interface: Strategies for Effective Human-Computer Interaction*. Boston, MA: Addison-Wesley.

Shneiderman, B. (1996). The Eyes Have It: A Task by Data Type Taxonomy for Information Visualizations. *Proc. 1996 IEEE Symposium on Visual Languages*. IEEE, 336–43.

Shneiderman, B. (2000). The Limits of Speech Recognition. *Communications of the ACM*, 43(9): 63–5. https://dl.acm.org/doi/fullHtml/10.1145/348941.348990.

Shneiderman, B. (2007). Human Responsibility for Autonomous Agents. *IEEE Intelligent Systems*, 22(2): 60–1.

Shneiderman, B. (2016a). Opinion: The Dangers of Faulty, Biased, or Malicious Algorithms Requires Independent Oversight. *Proceedings of the National Academy of Sciences*, 113(48), 13538–40. http://www.pnas.org/content/113/48/13538.full.

Shneiderman, B. (2016b). *The New ABCs of Research: Achieving Breakthrough Collaborations*. Oxford University Press.

Shneiderman, B. (2018). Twin-Win Model: A Human-Centered Approach to Research Success. *Proceedings of the National Academy of Sciences*, 115(50): 12590–4. https://www.pnas.org/content/115/50/12590.

Shneiderman, B. (2019). *Encounters with HCI Pioneers: A Personal History and Photo Journal*. Synthesis Lectures on Human-Centered Informatics. San Rafael, CA: Morgan and Claypool. https://www.morganclaypool.com/doi/abs/10.2200/S00889ED1V01Y201812HCI041.

Shneiderman, B. (2020a). Human-Centered Artificial Intelligence: Reliable, Safe and Trustworthy. *International Journal of Human–Computer Interaction*, 36(6): 495–504. https://doi.org/10.1080/10447318.2020.1741118.

Shneiderman, B. (2020b). Design Lessons from AI's Two Grand Goals: Human Emulation and Useful Applications. *IEEE Transactions on Technology and Society*, 1(2): 73–82. https://ieeexplore.ieee.org/document/9088114.

Shneiderman, B. and Maes, P. (1997). Direct Manipulation vs. Interface Agents. *ACM Interactions*, 4(6): 42–61.

Shneiderman, B., Plaisant, C., Cohen, M., Jacobs, S. and Elmqvist, N. (2016). *Designing the User Interface: Strategies for Effective Human-Computer Interaction*, 6th ed. New York: Pearson..

Siegel, G. (2014). *Forensic Media: Reconstructing Accidents in Accelerated Modernity*. Durham, NC: Duke University Press.

Singh V. K., Ghosh, I. and Sonagara, D. (2021). Detecting Fake News Stories via Multimodal Analysis. *Journal of the Association for Information Science and Technology*, 72: 3–17. https://doi.org/10.1002/asi.24359.

Smith, B. C. (2019). *The Promise of Artificial Intelligence: Reckoning and Judgment*. Cambridge, MA: MIT Press.

Smith, E. M., Mortenson, W. B., Mihailidis, A. and Miller, W. C. (2020). Understanding the Task Demands for Powered Wheelchair Driving: A Think-Aloud Task Analysis. *Disability and Rehabilitation: Assistive Technology*, 1–8. https://www.tandfonline.com/doi/abs/10.1080/17483107.2020.1810335.

Society of Automotive Engineers (SAE) (2014). Taxonomy and Definitions for Terms Related to On-Road Motor Vehicle Automated Driving Systems. SAE Report J3016. https://www.sae.org/standards/content/j3016_201401/.

Sokol, K. and Flach, P. (January 2020). Explainability Fact Sheets: A Framework for Systematic Assessment of Explainable Approaches. *Proc. 2020 Conference on Fairness, Accountability, and Transparency (FAT* '20)*. ACM, 56–67.

Sprinkle, T. (2017). Robophobia: Bridging the Uncanny Valley. *American Society of Mechanical Engineers*. https://www.asme.org/topics-resources/content/robophobia-bridging-the-uncanny-valley.

Stanford University (2016). Artificial Intelligence and Life in 2030: One Hundred Year Study on Artificial Intelligence. https://ai100.stanford.edu/2016-report.

Stokes, D. E. (1997). *Pasteur's Quadrant: Basic Science and Technological Innovation*. Washington, DC: Brookings Institution Press.

Strait, M. K., Aguillon, C., Contreras, V. and Garcia, N. (2017). The Public's Perception of Humanlike Robots: Online Social Commentary Reflects an Appearance-Based Uncanny Valley, a General Fear of a "Technology Takeover", and the Unabashed Sexualization of Female-Gendered Robots. *Proc. 26th IEEE International Symposium on Robot and Human Interactive Communication (RO-MAN)*. IEEE, 1418–23.

Strauch, B. (2017). Ironies of Automation: Still Unresolved After All These Years. *IEEE Transactions on Human-Machine Systems*, 48(5): 419–33. https://ieeexplore.ieee.org/abstract/document/8013079/.

Stray, J. (2020). Aligning AI Optimization to Community Well-being. *International Journal of Community Well-Being*, 3: 443–63. https://link.springer.com/article/10.1007/s42413-020-00086-3.

Stray, J., Adler, S. and Hadfield-Menell, D. (2020). What Are You Optimizing for? Aligning Recommender Systems with Human Values. *Participatory Approaches to Machine Learning Workshop, International Conference on Machine Learning (ICML)*. https://participatoryml.github.io/papers/2020/42.pdf.

Sundar, S. S., Waddell, T. F. and Jung, E. H. (March 2016). The Hollywood Robot Syndrome Media Effects on Older Adults' Attitudes toward Robots and Adoption Intentions. *Proc. 11th ACM/IEEE International Conference on Human-Robot Interaction (HRI)*. IEEE, 343–50.

Szafir, D. and Szafir, D. (2021). Connecting Human-Robot Interaction with Data Visualization. *Proc. 2021 ACM/IEEE International Conference on Human-Robot Interaction*. IEEE.

Tamboli, A. (2019) *Keeping Your AI Under Control: A Pragmatic Guide to Identifying, Evaluating, and Quantifying Risks*. Berkeley, CA: Apress. https://doi.org/10.1007/978-1-4842-5467-7.

Theodorou, A., Wortham, R. H. and Bryson, J. J. (2017). Designing and Implementing Transparency for Real Time Inspection of Autonomous Robots. *Connection Science*, 29(3): 230–41. https://doi.org/10.1080/09540091.2017.1310182.

Thiebes, S., Lins, S. and Sunyaev, A. (2020). Trustworthy Artificial Intelligence. *Electronic Markets*, 1–18. https://link.springer.com/article/10.1007/s12525-020-00441-4.

Thimbleby, H. (2020). *Fix IT: Stories from Healthcare IT*. Oxford University Press.

Toews, R. (December 13, 2020). 8 Leading Women in the Field of AI. *Forbes*. https://www.forbes.com/sites/robtoews/2020/12/13/8-leading-women-in-the-field-of-ai/.

Toffler, A. (1970). *Future Shock*. New York: Bantam Publishers.

Topcu, U., Bliss, N., Cooke, N., Cummings, M., Llorens, A., Shrobe, H. and Zuck, L. (2020). Assured Autonomy: Path Toward Living with Autonomous Systems We Can Trust. arXiv preprint. https://arxiv.org/abs/2010.14443.

Traeger, M. L., Sebo, S. S., Jung, M., Scassellati, B. and Christakis, N. A. (2020). Vulnerable Robots Positively Shape Human Conversational Dynamics in a Human–Robot Team. *Proc. National Academy of Sciences*, 117(12), 6370–5. https://www.pnas.org/content/117/12/6370.

Tukey, J. W. (1977). *Exploratory Data Analysis*. New York: Pearson.

Turing, A. M. (1950). Computing Machinery and Intelligence. *Mind*, 49: 433–60.

US Defense Science Board (June 2016). *Summer Study on Autonomy*. Washington, DC: US Department of Defense.

US Defense Science Board Task Force (July 2012). *The Role of Autonomy in DoD Systems*. Washington, DC: US Department of Defense.

US Food and Drug Administration (April 2, 2019). Proposed Regulatory Framework for Modifications to Artificial Intelligence/Machine Learning (AI/ML)-Based Software as a Medical Device (SaMD). US FDA Artificial Intelligence and Machine Learning Discussion Paper. https://www.fda.gov/media/122535/download.

US National Research Council (2008). *Protecting Individual Privacy in the Struggle against Terrorists: A Framework for Program Assessment*. Washington, DC: National Academies Press. http://www.nap.edu/catalog.php?record_id=12452.

US National Science and Technology Council (June 2019). The National Artificial Intelligence Research and Development Strategic Plan: 2019 Update. Executive Office of the President. https://www.nitrd.gov/pubs/National-AI-RD-Strategy-2019.pdf.

US National Security Commission on Artificial Intelligence (2019). Interim Report. https://epic.org/foia/epic-v-ai-commission/AI-Commission-Interim-Report-Nov-2019.pdf.

US National Security Commission on Artificial Intelligence (2021). Final Report. Washington, DC. https://www.nscai.gov/2021-final-report/.

US National Transportation Safety Board (2017). Collision between a Car Operating with Automated Vehicle Control Systems and a Tractor-Semitrailer Truck Near Williston, Florida, May 7, 2016. Accident Report NTSB/HAR-17/02, PB2017-102600. Available at: https://www.ntsb.gov/investigations/accidentreports/pages/har1702.aspx.

US White House (2020). American Artificial Intelligence Initiative: Year One Annual Report. Office of Science and Technology Policy. https://www.nitrd.gov/nitrdgroups/images/c/c1/American-AI-Initiative-One-Year-Annual-Report.pdf.

Vallor, S. (2016). *Technology and the Virtues: A Philosophical Guide to a Future Worth Wanting*. Oxford University Press.

Van Wynsberghe, A. (2013). Designing Robots for Care: Care Centered Value-Sensitive Design. *Science and Engineering Ethics*, 19(2): 407–33. https://www.ncbi.nlm.nih.gov/pmc/articles/PMC3662860/.

Vargemidis, D., Gerling, K., Spiel, K., Abeele, V. V. and Geurts, L. (2020). Wearable Physical Activity Tracking Systems for Older Adults—A Systematic Review. *ACM Transactions on Computing for Healthcare*, 1(4): 1–37. https://dl.acm.org/doi/abs/10.1145/3402523.

Vines, J., Pritchard, G., Wright, P., Olivier, P. and Brittain, K. (2015). An Age-Old Problem: Examining the Discourses of Ageing in HCI and Strategies for Future Research. *ACM Transactions on Computer-Human Interaction (TOCHI)*, 22(1): 1–27. https://dl.acm.org/doi/abs/10.1145/2696867.

Vishnia, G. R. and Peters, G. W. (2020). AuditChain: A Trading Audit Platform over Blockchain. *Frontiers in Blockchain*, 3: 9.

Viswanathan, P., Little, J. J., Mackworth, A. K. and Mihailidis, A. (October 2012). An Intelligent Powered Wheelchair for Users with Dementia: Case Studies with NOAH (Navigation and Obstacle Avoidance Help). *Proc. 2012 AAAI Fall Symposium*. https://www.cs.ubc.ca/~mack/Publications/ViswanathanAAAI2012.pdf.

Viswanathan, P., Little, J. J., Mackworth, A. K., How, T. V., Wang, R. H. and Mihailidis, A. (2013). Intelligent Wheelchairs for Cognitively-Impaired Older Adults in Long-Term Care: A Review. *Proc. Rehabilitation Engineering and Assistive Technology Society of North America 2013 Annual Conference*. http://www.resna.org/sites/default/files/legacy/conference/proceedings/2013/Wheeled%20Mobility/Viswanathan.html.

von Wangenheim, C. G., Hauck, J. C. R., Zoucas, A., Salviano, C. F., McCaffery, F. and Shull, F. (2010). Creating Software Process Capability/Maturity Models. *IEEE Software*, 27(4): 92–4.

Vought, R. T. (February 11, 2019). Guidance for Regulation of Artificial Intelligence Applications. Draft memorandum. Washington, DC: US White House. https://www.whitehouse.gov/wp-content/uploads/2020/01/Draft-OMB-Memo-on-Regulation-of-AI-1-7-19.pdf.

Vought, R. T. (November 17, 2020). Guidance for Regulation of Artificial Intelligence Applications. Memorandum for the Heads of Executive Departments and Agencies. Washington, DC: US White House. https://www.whitehouse.gov/wp-content/uploads/2020/11/M-21-06.pdf.

Wachter, S., Mittelstadt, B. and Russell, C. (2017). Counterfactual Explanations without Opening the Black Box: Automated Decisions and the GDPR. *Harvard Journal of Law and Technology*, 31: 841–87.

Waldrop, M. M. (2019). News Feature: What Are the Limits of Deep Learning? *Proceedings of the National Academy of Sciences*, 116(4): 1074–7. https://www.pnas.org/content/116/4/1074.short.

Wang, D., Yang, Q., Abdul, A. and Lim, B. Y. (2019). Designing Theory-Driven User-Centric Explainable AI. *Proc. 2019 CHI Conference on Human Factors in Computing Systems*. ACM, 1–15. https://doi.org/10.1145/3290605.3300831.

Wang, R., Wang, S., Duan, N. and Wang, Q. (2020). From Patient-Controlled Analgesia to Artificial Intelligence-Assisted Patient-Controlled Analgesia: Practices and Perspectives. *Frontiers in Medicine*, 7: 145. https://www.frontiersin.org/articles/10.3389/fmed.2020.00145/full.

Wang, W. and Siau, K. (2019). Artificial Intelligence, Machine Learning, Automation, Robotics, Future of Work and Future of Humanity: A Review and Research Agenda. *Journal of Database Management*, 30(1): 61–79.

Watson, D. (2019). The Rhetoric and Reality of Anthropomorphism in Artificial Intelligence. *Minds and Machines*, 29(3): 417–40.

Weick, K. E., Sutcliffe, K. M. and Obstfeld D. (1999). Organizing for High Reliability: Processes of Collective Mindfulness. In Sutton, R. S. and Staw, B. M., eds., *Research in Organizational Behavior*, vol. 1. Stanford, CA: JAI Press, 81–123.

Weizenbaum, J. (1976). *Computer Power and Human Reason: From Judgment to Calculation*. New York: W H Freeman.

Weld, D. S. and Bansal, G. (2019). The Challenge of Crafting Intelligible Intelligence. *Communications of the ACM*, 62(6): 70–9.

Wenskovitch, J., Zhou, M. X., Collins, C., Chang, R., Dowling, M., Endert, A. and Xu, K. (2020). Putting the "I" in Interaction: Interactive Interfaces Personalized to Individuals. *IEEE Computer Graphics and Applications*, 40(3): 73–82.

West, D. M. and Allen, J. R. (2020). *Turning Point: Policymaking in the Era of Artificial Intelligence*. Washington, DC: Brookings Institution Press.

Wickramasinghe, C. S., Marino, D. L., Grandio, J. and Manic, M. (June 2020). Trustworthy AI Development Guidelines for Human System Interaction. *Proc. 2020 13th International Conference on Human System Interaction (HSI)*. IEEE, 130–6. https://ieeexplore.ieee.org/abstract/document/9142644/.

Winfield, A. F. and Jirotka, M. (July 2017). The Case for an Ethical Black Box. In *Annual Conference towards Autonomous Robotic Systems*. New York: Springer, 262–73. https://link.springer.com/chapter/10.1007/978-3-319-64107-2_21.

Winfield, A. F. and Jirotka, M. (2018). Ethical Governance Is Essential to Building Trust in Robotics and Artificial Intelligence Systems. *Philosophical Transactions of the Royal Society A: Mathematical, Physical and Engineering Sciences*, 376(2133): 20180085.

Winograd, T. and Flores, F. (1986). *Understanding Computers and Cognition: A New Foundation for Design*. Bristol, UK: Intellect Books.

Wong, E. (2020). Shneiderman's Eight Golden Rules Will Help You Design Better Interfaces. Interaction Design Foundation. https://www.interaction-design.org /literature/article/shneiderman-s-eight-golden-rules-will-help-you-design-better-interfaces.

Woods, D. D. (2017). Essential Characteristics of Resilience. In Hollnagel, E., Woods, D. D. and Leveson, N. eds., *Resilience Engineering: Concepts and Precepts*. Farnham, UK: Ashgate Publishing, 21–34.

Woods, D. D., Tittle, J., Feil, M. and Roesler, A. (2004). Envisioning Human-Robot Coordination in Future Operations. *IEEE Transactions on Systems, Man, and Cybernetics, Part C (Applications and Reviews)*, 34(2): 210–18. https://doi.org /10.1109/TSMCC.2004.826272.

Xie, B., Tao, C., Li, J., Hilsabeck, R. C. and Aguirre, A. (2020). Artificial Intelligence for Caregivers of Persons with Alzheimer's Disease and Related Dementias: Systematic Literature Review. *JMIR Medical Informatics*, 8(8): e18189. https://medinform.jmir.org/2020/8/e18189/.

Xu, W. (2019). Toward Human-Centered AI: A Perspective from Human-Computer Interaction. *ACM Interactions*, 26(4): 42–6. doi.org/10.1145/3328485.

Yampolskiy, R. V. (2019). Predicting Future AI Failures from Historic Examples. *Foresight*, 21(1): 138–52. https://www.emerald.com/insight/content/doi/10.1108/FS-04-2018-0034/full/html.

Yao, Y. and Atkins, E. (2020). The Smart Black Box: A Value-Driven High-Bandwidth Automotive Event Data R. https://ieeexplore.ieee.org/document/8995510.

You, S. and Robert, L. P. (2018). Emotional Attachment, Performance, and Viability in Teams Collaborating with Embodied Physical Action (EPA) Robots. *Journal of the Association for Information Systems*, 19(5): 377–407. doi: 10.17705/1jais. 00496.

Zhang, J. M., Harman, M., Ma, L. and Liu, Y. (2020). Machine Learning Testing: Survey, Landscapes and Horizons. *IEEE Transactions on Software Engineering*. https://ieeexplore.ieee.org/abstract/document/9000651.

Zhou, M. X., Mark, G., Li, J. and Yang, H. (2019). Trusting Virtual Agents: The Effect of Personality. *ACM Transactions on Interactive Intelligent Systems (TIIS)*, 9(2–3): 1–36. https://dl.acm.org/doi/abs/10.1145/3232077.

Zhu, D. and Lee, S. (2020). Autonomous Readers: The Impact of News Customisation on Audiences' Psychological and Behavioural Outcomes. *Communication Research and Practice*, 6(2): 125–42. https://www.tandfonline.com /doi/abs/10.1080/22041451.2019.1644586.

Zuboff, S. (2019). *The Age of Surveillance Capitalism: The Fight for a Human Future at the New Frontier of Power*. New York: Public Affairs.

Zuckerman, O., Walker, D., Grishko, A., Moran, T., Levy, C., Lisak, B., Wald, I. Y., and Erel, H. (April 2020). Companionship Is Not a Function: The Effect of a Novel Robotic Object on Healthy Older Adults' Feelings of "Being-Seen". *Proc. 2020 CHI Conference on Human Factors in Computing Systems*. ACM, 1–14. https://dl.acm.org/doi/abs/10.1145/3313831.3376411.

WEBSITES

A3 Robotics. Accessed June 29, 2021. https://www.automate.org/robotics.

ACM Conference on Fairness, Accountability, and Transparency (ACM FAccT). Accessed June 28, 2021. https://facctconference.org/.

ACM IUI 2022. Accessed June 24, 2021. https://iui.acm.org/.

Advancing Research Impact in Society. Accessed June 28, 2021. https://www. researchinsociety.org/about-us/aris.

Agency for Healthcare Research and Quality. Surveys on Patient Safety Culture. Accessed June 26, 2021. https://www.ahrq.gov/sops/index.html.

AI4ALL. Accessed June 26, 2021. http://ai-4-all.org.

AIArtists.org. Alexander Mordvintsev. Accessed June 21, 2021. https://aiartists.org /alexander-mordvintsev.

Aibo. Accessed June 25, 2021. https://us.aibo.com/feature/feature1.html.

AI for Good. Accessed June 28, 2021. https://aiforgood.itu.int/.

AI for Good. Get Involved. Accessed June 9, 2021. https://ai4good.org/get-involved/.

AI Incident Database. Welcome to the Artificial Intelligence Incident Database. Accessed June 9, 2021. https://incidentdatabase.ai/.

AI Now Institute. Accessed June 26, 2021. https://ainowinstitute.org.

AIRC. About AIRC. Accessed June 29, 2021. https://www.airc.aist.go.jp/en/intro/.

Alexander Mordvintsev. Accessed June 21, 2021. https://znah.net/.

Algorithmic Justice League. Accessed June 26, 2021. https://www.ajlunited.org.

Amazon Robotics. Accessed June 25, 2021. https://www.amazonrobotics.com.

American National Standards Institute. Accessed June 26, 2021. https://www.ansi.org.

AMTA. Accessed June 29, 2021. https://amtaweb.org/.

Apple Developer. Health and Fitness. Accessed June 29, 2021. https://developer. apple.com/health-fitness.

Association for the Advancement of Artificial Intelligence. Accessed June 26, 2021. https://www.aaai.org/.

Association for Computing Machinery. Accessed June 26, 2021. https://www.acm.org/.

Augmented Humans. Augmented Humans 2021: Online, 22–24 February 2021. Accessed June 24, 2021. https://augmented-humans.org/.

Aviation Safety Reporting System. Accessed June 21, 2021. https://asrs.arc.nasa. gov/.

Bill and Melinda Gates Foundation. Accessed June 29, 2021. https://www.gatesfound ation.org/.

Boston Dynamics. Accessed June 25, 2021. https://www.bostondynamics.com.

Boston Dynamics. Spot. Accessed June 25, 2021. https://www.bostondynamics.com /spot.

Braze Mobility. Accessed June 29, 2021. https://brazemobility.com/.

Brookings Institution. Artificial Intelligence and Emergine Technology Initiative. Accessed June 26, 2021. https://www.brookings.edu/project/artificial-intelligence-and-emerging-technology-initiative/.

Brownlee, M. (2020). Dope Tech: Boston Dynamics Robot Dog! YouTube video, 15:09. Accessed June 25, 2021. https://www.youtube.com/watch?v=s6_azdBnAlU.

BugCrowd. Accessed June 26, 2021. https://www.bugcrowd.com/.

Bugzilla. About Bugzilla. Accessed June 26, 2021. https://www.bugzilla.org/about/.

The Captain Tom Foundation. Accessed June 29, 2021. https://captaintom.org/.

Center for AI and Digital Policy. Accessed July 5, 2021. https://www.caidp.org/.

Centers for Disease Control and Prevention. Healthy Places Terminology. Accessed June 29, 2021. https://www.cdc.gov/healthyplaces/terminology.htm.

Citizen Science Association. Citizen Science: Theory and Practice. Accessed July 6, 2021. https://theoryandpractice.citizenscienceassociation.org/.

CitizenScience.gov. Accessed July 6, 2021. https://www.citizenscience.gov/.

Coded Bias. Accessed July 5, 2021. https://www.codedbias.com/.

The Conference Board. Consumer Confidence Survey. Accessed June 29, 2021. https://conference-board.org/data/consumerconfidence.cfm.

COSO. Accessed June 26, 2021. https://www.coso.org.

Coursera. Artificial Intelligence Ethics in Action. Accessed June 29, 2021. https://www.coursera.org/learn/ai-ethics-analysis.

Creative Destruction Lab (November 24, 2016). Geoff Hinton: On Radiology. YouTube video, 1:24. https://youtu.be/2HMPRXstSvQ.

CVE. Accessed June 26, 2021. https://cve.mitre.org/.

Data and Society. Accessed June 26, 2021. https://datasociety.net.

DataKind. Accessed June 9, 2021. https://www.datakind.org/.

Deloitte. Accessed June 26, 2021. https://www2.deloitte.com/us/en/pages/deloitte-analytics/solutions/analytics-ai.html.

Digital.gov. An Introduction to Accessibility. Accessed June 26, 2021. https://digital.gov /resources/introduction-accessibility/.

Down Dog Yoga. Accessed June 29, 2021. https://www.downdogapp.com/.

EASA. Artificial Intelligence Roadmap. Accessed June 28, 2021. https://www.easa. europa.eu/ai.

eBird. Accessed June 29, 2021. https://ebird.org/home.

edX. Ethics in AI and Big Data. Accessed June 29, 2021. https://www.edx.org/course/ethics-in-ai-and-big-data.

Engineering 360. IEEE P7001 Draft: Draft Standard for Transparency of Autonomous Systems. Accessed June 30, 2021. https://standards.globalspec.com/std/14328511/P7001/D1.

Epic.org. Accessed June 26, 2021. http://epic.org.

Ernest Edmonds. Accessed June 21, 2021. http://www.ernestedmonds.com/.

European Commission. Code of Practice on Disinformation. Accessed June 29, 2021. https://ec.europa.eu/digital-single-market/en/code-practice-disinformation.

EY. Accessed June 26, 2021. https://www.ey.com/en_us/ai.

Facebook. Welcoming the Oversight Board. Accessed June 26, 2021. https://about.fb.com/news/2020/05/welcoming-the-oversight-board/.

Facebook Help Center. What Names Are Allowed on Facebook? Accessed June 29, 2021. https://www.facebook.com/help/112146705538576.

Facebook Transparency Center. Transparency Reports. Accessed June 29, 2021. https://transparency.facebook.com/.

Family Caregiving: Care at Home. Accessed June 29, 2021. https://www.aarp.org/caregiving/home-care/.

Federal Aviation Administration. Accessed June 26, 2021. https://hotline.faa.gov/.

Fitbit. Accessed June 29, 2021. https://www.fitbit.com/.

Flukebook. Accessed June 29, 2021. https://www.flukebook.org/.

ForHumanity. Accessed June 26, 2021. https://www.forhumanity.center/.

ForHumanity. Taxonomy: AI Audit, Assurance, and Assessment. Accessed July 5, 2021. https://forhumanity.center/contact-tracing-audit.

Future of Life Institute. Accessed June 26, 2021. https://futureoflife.org.

Future of Life Institute. Lethal Autonomous Weapons Systems. Accessed June 21, 2021. https://futureoflife.org/lethal-autonomous-weapons-systems/.

GitHub. Accessed June 26, 2021. https://github.com/.

Google AI. Responsible AI Practices. Accessed June 28, 2021. https://ai.google/responsibilities/responsible-ai-practices/.

Government of Canada. Responsible Use of Artificial Intelligence (AI). Accessed June 28, 2021. https://www.canada.ca/en/government/system/digital-government/digital-government-innovations/responsible-use-ai.html.

GOV.UK. The Grand Challenges. Accessed June 29, 2021. https://www.gov.uk/government/publications/industrial-strategy-the-grand-challenges/industrial-strategy-the-grand-challenges.

HackerOne. Accessed June 26, 2021. https://www.hackerone.com/.

HCI + NLP Workshop. Accessed June 29, 2021. https://sites.google.com/view/hciandnlp.

The HIBAR Research Alliance. Accessed June 28, 2021. https://hibar-research.org/.

Honda (2019). Asimo: The World's Most Advanced Humanoid Robot. Accessed May 15, 2020. https://asimo.honda.com/.

IBM Design for AI. Fundamentals. Accessed June 22, 2021. https://www.ibm.com/design/ai/fundamentals/.

IBM Research: FactSheets 360. Accessed June 26, 2021. https://aifs360.mybluemix.net/.

IBM Watson AI XPRIZE Foundation. AI to Solve Global Issues. Accessed June 9, 2021. https://www.xprize.org/prizes/artificial-intelligence.

IEEE Ethics in Action in Autonomous and Intelligent Systems. Accessed June 25, 2021. https://ethicsinaction.ieee.org/.

IEEE Standards Association. The IEEEE Global Initiative on Ethics of Autonomous and Intelligent Systems. Accessed June 26, 2021. https://standards.ieee.org/industry-connections/ec/autonomous-systems.html.

IEEE Standards Association. The Ethics Certification Program for Autonomous and Intelligent Systems (ECPAIS). Accessed June 26, 2021. https://standards.ieee.org/industry-connections/ecpais.html.

IEEE Standards Association. IEEE P7001—IEEE Draft Standard for Transparency of Autonomous Systems. Accessed June 29, 2021. https://standards.ieee.org/project/7001.html.

iNaturalist. Accessed June 29, 2021. https://www.inaturalist.org/.

Incident Database. Accessed June 26, 2021. https://incidentdatabase.ai/.

Institute for Ethical AI and Machine Learning. The Machine Learning Maturity Model. Accessed June 26, 2021. https://ethical.institute/mlmm.html.

Insurance Institute for Highway Safety, Highway Loss Data Institute (IIHS-HLDI). Accessed July 7, 2021. https://www.iihs.org/.

Interaction Design Foundation. Accessibility. Accessed June 29, 2021. https://www.interaction-design.org/literature/topics/accessibility.

Intuitive for Patients. Accessed June 24, 2021. https://www.davincisurgery.com/.

ISO/TC 299. About ISO/TC 299 Robotics. Accessed June 26, 2021. https://committee.iso.org/home/tc299.

Johns Hopkins Institute for Assured Autonomy. Accessed June 24, 2021. https://iaa.jhu.edu/.

Journal of Responsible Innovation. Accessed June 29, 2021. https://www.tandfonline.com/loi/tjri20.

Joy for All. Companion Pet Pup. Accessed June 25, 2021. https://joyforall.com/products/companion-pet-golden-pup.

KPMG. Accessed June 26, 2021. https://advisory.kpmg.us/services/data-analytics/artificial-intelligence.html.

Lethal Autonomous Weapons. Accessed June 24, 2021. https://autonomousweapons.org/.

Let's Talk Autonomous Driving. Safety. Accessed June 22, 2021. https://ltad.com/about/safety.html.

The Loebner Prize. Accessed June 24, 2021. https://www.ocf.berkeley.edu/~arihuang/academic/research/loebner.html.

Machine Intelligence Research Institute. Accessed June 26, 2021. https://intelligence.org.

Meals on Wheels America. Accessed June 29, 2021. https://www.mealsonwheelsamerica.org/.

Microsoft. Guidelines for Human–AI Interaction. Accessed June 22, 2021. https://www.microsoft.com/en-us/research/project/guidelines-for-human-ai-interaction/.

Microsoft. Our Approach to Responsible AI at Microsoft. Accessed June 26, 2021. https://www.microsoft.com/en-us/ai/our-approach.

MITRE ATT&CK. Accessed June 28, 2021. https://attack.mitre.org/.

MITRE Partnership Network. AI Fails and How We Learn from Them. Accessed July 5, 2021. https://sites.mitre.org/aifails/.

Montreal AI Ethics Institute. Accessed June 26, 2021. https://montrealethics.ai/.

Motor Vehicle Death Petition to Recall All Tesla Vehicles due to Sudden Unintended Acceleration. Accessed June 26, 2021. https://static.nhtsa.gov/odi/inv/2020/INBC-DP20001-3494.pdf.

National Academy of Engineering. 14 Grand Challenges for Engineering in the 21st Century. Accessed June 29, 2021. http://www.engineeringchallenges.org/challenges.aspx.

National Geographic. In Japan, a Funeral Service for Robot Dogs. Video, 3:04. Accessed June 25, 2021. https://www.nationalgeographic.com/travel/destinations/asia/japan/in-japan–a-buddhist-funeral-service-for-robot-dogs/.

National Institute of Standards and Technology. National Vulnerability Database. Accessed June 26, 2021. https://nvd.nist.gov/vuln.

National Institute of Standards and Technology. Artificial Intelligence. Accessed June 28, 2021. https://www.nist.gov/artificial-intelligence.

National Institutes of Health. All of Us Research Program. Accessed June 29, 2021. https://allofus.nih.gov/.

National Safety Council. Accessed June 26, 2021. http://www.nsc.org.

National Science Foundation. National Artificial Intelligence (AI) Research Institutes. NSF 20-604. Accessed June 28, 2021. https://www.nsf.gov/pubs/2020/nsf20604/nsf20604.htm.

NeurIPS 2020. Call for Papers. Accessed June 29, 2021. https://nips.cc/Conferences/2020/CallForPapers.

OECD.AI. Accessed June 26, 2021. https://oecd.ai/about.

OECD.AI. OECD AI Principles Overview. Accessed June 28, 2021. https://oecd.ai/ai-principles.

OECD. Artificial Intelligence. Accessed June 28, 2021. https://www.oecd.org/going-digital/ai/.

OECD Better Life Index. Accessed June 29, 2021. http://www.oecdbetterlifeindex.org/.

Office of the Under Secretary of Defense for Acquisition and Sustainment Cybersecurity Maturity Model Certification. Accessed June 26, 2021. https://www.acq.osd.mil/cmmc/.

OpenAI. Accessed June 26, 2021. https://openai.com.

Open Community for Ethics in Autonomous and Intelligent Systems. Accessed June 26, 2021. https://ethicsstandards.org/.

Open Community for Ethics in Autonomous and Intelligent Systems. IEEE P7000 Projects. Accessed June 26, 2021. https://ethicsstandards.org/p7000/.

OpenFDA. FDA Adverse Event Reporting System. Accessed June 21, 2021. https://open.fda.gov/data/faers/.

Oversight Board. Accessed June 29, 2021. https://oversightboard.com/.

PARO. Accessed June 25, 2021. http://www.parorobots.com.

Partnership on AI. Accessed June 26, 2021. https://www.partnershiponai.org.

PatientsLikeMe. Accessed June 29, 2021. https://www.patientslikeme.com/.

Paul Brown. Accessed June 21, 2021. http://www.paul-brown.com/.

Paul Ekman Group. Universal Emotions. Accessed June 21, 2021. https://www.paulekman.com/universal-emotions/.

People + AI Guidebook. Accessed June 22, 2021. https://pair.withgoogle.com/guidebook.

People and AI Research. Accessed June 24, 2021. https://pair.withgoogle.com/.

The People of iNaturalist. Accessed June 29, 2021. https://www.inaturalist.org/pe
-ople.

Principles behind the Agile Manifesto. Accessed June 28, 2021. http://agile
-manifesto.org/principles.html.

Project Sidewalk. Accessed June 29, 2021. https://sidewalk-sea.cs.washington.edu/.

Pro Robots (2020). Evolution of Boston Dynamics. YouTube video, 11:00. Accessed June
25, 2021. https://www.youtube.com/watch?v=xH9sXhYA3nE.

PWC. Accessed June 26, 2021. https://www.pwc.com/gx/en/issues/data-and-analytics
/artificial-intelligence.html.

Replika. Accessed June 25, 2021. https://replika.ai/.

Responsible Robotics. Accessed June 26, 2021. https://responsiblerobotics.org.

ScienceDirect. Usability Questionnaire. Accessed June 29, 2021. https://www.
sciencedirect.com/topics/computer-science/usability-questionnaire.

Seek by iNaturalist. Accessed June 29, 2021. https://www.inaturalist.org/pages/seek_
app.

Senior Planet. Our Purpose. Accessed June 29, 2021. https://seniorplanet.org/about
/our-purpose/.

Shneiderman, B. The Eight Golden Rules of Interface Design. Accessed June 22, 2021.
https://www.cs.umd.edu/~ben/goldenrules.html.

SIGCHI. Accessed June 24, 2021. http://www.sigchi.org.

SoftBank Robotics. Pepper. Accessed June 25, 2021. https://www.softbankrobotics.
com/emea/en/pepper.

Special Interest Group on Discourse and Dialogue. Accessed June 29, 2021. https://
sigdial.org/.

Stanford University Human-Centered Artificial Intelligence. Letter from the Denning
Co-Directors. Accessed June 22, 2021. https://hai.stanford.edu/welcome.

Tesla. Future of Driving. Accessed June 22, 2021. https://www.tesla.com/autopilot.

Tesla. There is No "Unintended" Acceleration in Tesla Vehicles. Accessed June 26, 2021.
https://www.tesla.com/blog/no-unintended-acceleration-tesla-vehicles.

Tesla Deaths. Accessed June 26, 2021. https://www.tesladeaths.com/.

Text Retrieval Conference. Accessed June 29, 2021. https://trec.nist.gov/.

Tombot. Accessed June 25, 2021. http://www.tombot.com.

Travelers Institute. Insuring Autonomy: How Auto Insurance Can Adapt to Changing
Risks. Accessed June 26, 2021. https://www.travelers.com/iw-documents/travelers-
institute/Final-Digital-2018-AV-White-Paper.pdf.

Twitter. Help Center. The Twitter Rules. Accessed June 29, 2021. https://help.twitter.
com/en/rules-and-policies/twitter-rules.

UIDP. Accessed June 28, 2021. http://www.uidp.org.

UKRI Trustworthy Autonomous Systems Hub. Accessed July 2, 2021. https://www.
tas.ac.uk/.

UL. Our Mission. Accessed June 26, 2021. https://www.ul.com/about/mission.

United Nations, Department of Economic and Social Affairs, Sustainable Development.
The 17 Goals Accessed June 9, 2021. https://sdgs.un.org/goals.

United Nations, Department of Economic and Social Affairs. The Sustainable Development Goals Report 2020. Accessed June 9, 2021. https://unstats.un.org/sdgs
/report/2020/.

UN Sustainable Development. Accessed June 28, 2021. https://sdgs.un.org/.

University of California-Davis. UC David 20 Point System. Accessed June 29, 2021. http://www.musingsonthevine.com/MusingsUCDavisForm.pdf.

University of Michigan. Surveys of Consumers. Accessed June 29, 2021. http://www.sca.isr.umich.edu/.

Usability.gov. Accessed June 24, 2021. http://www.usability.gov.

US Food and Drug Administration. MedWatch: The FDA Safety Information and Adverse Event Reporting Program. Accessed June 26, 2021. https://www.fda.gov/safety/medwatch-fda-safety-information-and-adverse-event-reporting-program.

US Food and Drug Administration. MedWatch Online Voluntary Reporting Form. Accessed June 26, 2021. https://www.accessdata.fda.gov/scripts/medwatch/index.cfm.

UXPA International. Accessed June 24, 2021. https://uxpa.org/about-uxpa-inter-national/.

Wallach, H. NeurIPS Keynote. Video, 28:04. Accessed June 29, 2021. https://www.partnershiponai.org/navigating-the-broader-impacts-of-ai-research-workshop-at-neurips-2020/.

Waymo. Accessed June 22, 2021. http://www.waymo.com.

Web Content Accessibility Guidelines (WCAG) 2.1 Accessed June 26, 2021. https://www.w3.org/TR/WCAG21/.

Whichbook. Accessed June 28, 2021. https://www.whichbook.net/.

Wikipedia. Apgar Score. Accessed June 29, 2021. https://en.wikipedia.org/wiki/Apgar_score.

Wikipedia. Category: Artificial Intelligence Associations. Accessed June 26, 2021. https://en.wikipedia.org/wiki/Category:Artificial_intelligence_associations.

Wine Country Getaways. Wine Scoring Sheets, Wine Tasting Forms, Wine Scorecards. Accessed June 29, 2021. https://winecountrygetaways.com/wine-enjoyment-guide/hosting-a-wine-tasting/wine-scoring-sheets-wine-tasting-forms-wine-scorec-ards.

Woebot Health. Accessed June 25, 2021. https://woebothealth.com/.

World Usability Day. Accessed June 24, 2021. https://worldusabilityday.org/.

XPRIZE. Accessed June 29, 2021. https://www.xprize.org/.

YouTube. Community Guidelines. Accessed June 29, 2021. https://www.youtube.com/intl/ALL_ca/howyoutubeworks/policies/community-guidelines/.

Zooniverse. Accessed June 29, 2021. https://www.zooniverse.org/.

NAME INDEX

Figures are indicated by an italic *f* following the page number.

Abdul, A. 304
Abeele, V. V. 324, 325
Abreu, A. 312
Achten, N. 299, 313, 322
Adam, G. A. 289
Adam, M. 297
Adlam, B. 322, 323
Adler, S. 308
Aerts, H. J. W. L. 289
Agrin, N. 232
Aguillon, C. 298
Aguirre, A. 324
Alemzadeh, H. 310
Alipanahi, B. 322, 323
Allan, S. 309
Allen, J. R. 214, 316
Alonso-Mora, J. 294
Alsheibani, S. 312
Alvina, J. 324
Amershi, S. 287, 299, 300,
    301, 309
Ammari, T. 290, 297
Amodei, D. 309
Anderljung, M. 323
Anderson, N. 276
Angelou, M. 275
Antonsen, S. 308
Apgar, V. 250
Appugliese, C. 301
Aristeidou, M. 319
Aristotle 17, 18
Armstrong, N. 107
Arya, V. 304
Aspden, P. 308
Astell, A. J. 324
Atkins, E. 300
Attenborough, D. 271

Autor, D. H. 36, 283
Avin, S. 298, 301, 310, 313,
    323
Ayesh, A. 281, 303

Badger, J. 299
Baeza-Yates, R. 161, 302
Bainbridge, L. 284, 293
Ballard, H. L. 319
Ballingall, C. 297
Bansal, G. 165, 170, 304, 306
Barnes, P. 302, 311, 315
Barry, J. C. 285
Bartal, A. 296
Bartman, T. 285, 308
Barton, G. 318
Beard, N. 321
Beaudouin-Lafon, M. 291
Beaumont, M. 323
Begel, A. 299
Belfield, H. 298, 301, 310,
    313, 323
Belhumeur, P. N. 319
Belkin, N. J. 171, 306
Bell, S. K. 311
Bellamy, R. K. 303, 304
Belpaeme, T. 295
Beltrametti, M. 322
Benjamin, R. 303
Benjamin, T. 323
Benlian, A. 297
Bentley, F. 290, 297
Berndt, A. 296
Berners-Lee, T. 4, 278
Bernstein, M. S. 297
Berry, J. C. 181, 308, 309
Bertini, E. 304

Beutel, A. 322, 323
Bibby, J. 319
Billing, E. 295
Biran, O. 303
Bird, C. 299
Birnbaum, E. 313
Biswas, A. 319
Black, J. 314
Blackhurst, J. L. 285, 293
Bliss, N. 294
Boden, M. 106, 292, 293
Bonsor, K. 300
Boot, W. R. 323
Boothman, R. C. 311
Bostelman, R. 302
Bostrom, N. 14, 282
Bountouridis, D. 283, 306
Bouranis, N. 324
Bowman, D. 294
Boyarskaya, M. 321
Bradshaw, J. M. 49–50,
    112–13, 284, 292, 294
Braunschweig, B. 281
Breazeal, C. L. 119, 295
Breck, E. 302
Breidenbach, L. 310
Brilli, R. J. 285, 308
Brin, S. 278
Brittain, K. 324
Broadbent, E. 94, 297, 298
Brooks, A. L. 286
Brooks, C. 64, 287, 305, 306
Brooks, R. 284
Brown, H. 180, 308
Brown, P. 30, 282
Brownlee, M. 296
Bruder, G. 296

Brundage, M. 298, 301, 303, 310, 311, 312, 313, 323
Bryson, J. J. 145, 289, 292, 300, 317
Buchanan, B. G. 305
Bunt, A. 324
Buolamwini, J. 163, 242, 303, 321
Burnett, M. 166, 305
Burr, C. 286
Bush, V. 215

Cai, C. J. 306
Caldwell, D. 292
Calo, R. 293, 313
Calvo, R. A. 286
Campbell, N. 300
Campbell, R. 321
Candy, L. 285
Cantwell Smith, B. 79, 100–1
Capek, K. 118
Cardoso, B. 307
Carrier, R. 299
Carros, F. 295
Caruana, R. 306
Carvalho, J. V. 312
Ceccaroni, L. 319
Challen, R. 309
Chandler, N. 300
Chang, R. 299, 306
Charleer, S. 307
Charness, N. 323
Chatila, R. 322
Chau, D. H. P. 306
Chazerand, P. 322
Chen, J. 302
Chen, L. 307
Chen, P. Y. 304
Cheng, H. F. 306
Cheung, Y. 312
Chilana, P. K. 324
Cho, J. 323
Choi, Y. K. 325
Choudhary, S. 303
Chrissis, M. B. 312
Christakis, N. A. 292
Christiano, P. 309
Cicchino, J. R. 63–4, 287
Clancey, W. J. 167–8, 305
Clinton, H. 234
Coeckelbergh, M. 295
Coghlan, S. 309
Cohen, H. 30, 31

Cohen, M. 288, 301, 309, 326
Collins, C. 299, 306
Collisson, P. 287, 309
Contreras, V. 298
Cooke, N. 294
Cooper, P. 309
Corrigan, J. M. 308
Cosenza, K. 297
Cotton, C. 303
Couzin-Frankel, J. 301
Cowls, J. 316, 322
Crawford, K. 224, 282, 302, 312, 314, 318, 321
Crowley, K. 306
Cuellar, M.-F. 317
Cullen, T. M. 284, 294
Cummings, M. 294
Currie, W. L. 300
Curtis, B. 312
Czaja, S. J. 323, 324

Daguerre, L. 35
Dahbura, A. 299
Daian, P. 310
D'Amour, A. 322, 323
Danks, D. 299
Darwin, C. 19
Darzentas, J. 261, 324
Das, S. 281, 317
Daugherty, P. R. 183, 309
Daumé III, H. 302, 312
Dautenhahn, K. 292
Davis, E. 89, 94, 289
Davis, J. T. 285, 308
de Oliveira, J. V. 292
Delaroche, L. 35
DeLine, R. 299, 306
Demiris, G. 325
Denny, J. 309
Descartes, R. 18
Desmet, P. 67–8, 287
Dey, K. 303
Dhuranandhar, A. 304
Diamantis, M. E. 289
Dietelkämper, R. 302
Dietterich, T. G. 308
Dignum, V. 87, 298, 322
Dodge, J. 310
Doshi-Velez, F. 305
Douglas, F. 273
Dowling, M. 306
Drucker, S. M. 306
Du, F. 172, 306

Du, M. 166, 172, 305, 307
Duan, N. 287
Dubber, M. D. 281, 317
Dudik, M. 302
Dudley, J. J. 288, 309
Dustdar, S. 299, 305
Duva, A. M. 311

Ebert, C. 301
Edison, T. 4, 133
Edmonds, E. A. 30, 282, 285
Edwards, L. 292
Edwards, T. 309
Ehsan, U. 304
Eimler, S. 292
Eirckson, S. M. 308
Ekman, P. 26, 26f, 27
Elbaum, S. 300
Eling, M. 318
Elizabeth II 270, 271
Ellick, A. 320
Elmqvist, N. 288, 301, 309, 326
Endert, A. 299, 302, 306
Endsley, M. R. 70, 113, 284, 288, 294
Engelbart, D. C. 101, 277, 291
English, W. K. 291
Engstrom, D. E. 317
Erel, H. 324
Erickson, S. M. 308, 309
Etchemendy, J. 51
Evans, A. B. 324
Everitt, T. 309

Fagan, L. 319
Falco, G. 299, 318
Fanti, A. 303
Fei-Fei, L. 297
Feil, M. 285, 293
Feldman-Barrett, L. 27–8, 282
Feltovich, P. J. 292
Fern, A. 310
Ferrer, C. C. 320
Fiesler, C. 321
Finn, K. 324
Fischer, G. 288
Fischer, T. 124
Fisher, R. 18
Fitch, J. P. 308
Fjeld, J. 299, 313, 322

Flach, P. 193, 312
Flaxman, S. 303, 316
Flemons, P. 319
Flores, F. 277, 326
Floridi, L. 286, 316, 322
Fokkinga, S. 67–8, 287
Ford, M. 33, 283
Forlizzi, J. 296
Fourney, A. 287, 309
Fraser, P. 285, 312
Freier, N. G. 292
Frey, C. B. 283
Friedler, S. A. 303
Friedman, B. 161, 290, 302
Fukuyama, F. 54, 285

Gale, A. 295
Galileo Galilei 19
Gall, H. 299
Gallagher, K. 297
Galstyan, A. 302
García, M. I. 300
Garcia, N. 298
Garfinkel, S. 313, 315
Garrett, N. 321
Gaskell, A. 325
Gebru, T. 163, 242, 302, 303,
    311, 312, 315, 321
Gelin, R. 295
Gelles, D. 285, 293
Gerling, K. 324, 325
Geurts, L. 325
Ghallab, M. 281
Ghosh, I. 320
Giodano, A. J. 319
Giuliani, M. 286
Glanz, J. 285, 293
Goethe, J. W. von 118
Goldstein, D. F. 324
Gomez, P. 295
Gompels, L. 309
González, D. 312
Goodman, B. 303, 316
Gordon, L. A. 318
Gore, J. 282
Gorelick, M. 321
Gottlieb, U. 297
Grandio, J. 301
Grant, T. D. 289
Gray, T. 306
Green, S. E. 319
Gregorio, M. 296

Gregory, M. 285, 312
Gresham, J. S. 285, 293
Griffin, A. L. 297
Griffin, W. 254–5, 323
Grishko, A. 324
Groom, V. 105, 292
Grossi, D. R. 300
Gruen, D. 304
Guerrero, L. A. 296
Guldenmund, F. W. 285, 308
Gutenberg, J. 34
Gutiérrez, F. 307

Haavik, T. K. 308
Hadfield, G. 298, 301, 310,
    313, 323
Hadfield-Menell, D. 308
Hafer, C. C. 285, 308
Hagemann, L. 291
Haibe-Kains, B. 289
Hale, A. 308
Halevy, A. 235, 320
Hamilton, E. P. 303
Hancock, J. T. 297
Hancock, P. A. 113, 248, 284,
    293, 294, 322
Hansen, K. 187–8
Hanson, D. 119
Harambam, J. 283, 306
Harman, D. 241
Harman, M. 153, 301
Harper, F. M. 306
Harrell, D. F. 164, 303
Hauck, J. C. R. 312
Haughey, M. M. 320
Havens, J. C. 281
Hawley, J. K. 284, 294
He, C. 307
Head, A. 306
Heckman, R. 321
Heer, J. 58, 103, 286, 291
Hegde, N. 306
Heilweil, R. 299
Heller, K. 322, 323
Hendry, D. G. 290
Henson, J. 124
Herodotou, C. 319
Herschel, M. 302
Higgins, L. 319
Hill, R. A. 319
Hilligoss, H. 299, 313, 322
Hilsabeck, R. C. 324

Hind, M. 303, 304
Hinton, G. 40
Hipp, J. 306
Ho, D. E. 317
Hoey, J. 324
Hoffman, G. 120, 294
Hoffman, R. R. 49, 50,
    112–13, 248, 282, 284,
    292, 294, 304, 322
Hoffman, S. C. 303, 304
Hohman, F. 169, 306
Hollnagel, E. 286, 308
Holstein, K. 302
Hong, J. I. 296
Hong, S. 304
Hong, T. 302
Honig, S. 130, 296
Hopkins, A. 308
Hopper, G. 137
Horne, N. 296
Horvitz, E. 70, 287
Hosny, A. 289
Houde, S. 312
House, S. 303
How, T. V. 325
Hsu, F.-h. 88, 289
Hsu, S. 307
Htun, N. N. 307
Hu, X. 166, 172, 305
Hull, R. 305
Hullman, J. 304
Hume, D. 19
Humphrey, W. S. 312
Hung, L. 296
Hurley, P. M. 323
Hutchinson, B. 302, 311, 315

Irvine, J. 310
Ishiguro, H. 292
Iyer, R. K. 310

Jablanski, D. 318
Jacobs, D. W. 319
Jacobs, M. 301
Jacobs, S. 288, 309, 326
Jaquet-Droz, P. 117–18
Jin, H. S. 297
Jin, Y. 307
Jirotka, M. 148, 299
Jobs, S. 83, 278–9
Johnson, J. 324

Johnson, M. 49–50, 112–13, 284, 294
Johnson, R. F. 319
Jones, M. L. 294
Jordan, K. 291
Jordan, M. I. 51–2, 285
Juels, A. 310
Jung, E. H. 290
Jung, M. F. 120, 292, 295

Kahn, P. H. 292
Kalbarczyk, Z. 310
Kalluri, P. 299
Kamar, E. 299
Kamhoua, C. 301
Kaminskiy, M. P. 285
Kanda, T. 292
Kane, A. 314
Kane, S. K. 292
Kankanhalli, M. 304
Kanna, K. 303
Kant, I. 18
Karahalios, K. 176, 307
Karaman, S. 294
Kasparov, G. 88
Kaufman, S. B. 324
Kavi, K. M. 300
Kay, A. 39
Kaye, J. 290, 297
Kelvin, Lord 245
Kember, S. 292
Kennedy, R. 286
Khadpe, P. 297
Khan, N. 285, 308
Khanna, R. 310
Khodakarami, F. 289
Kim, B. 305, 306
King, G. 286
Kitroeff, N. 285, 293
Klein, G. 160, 180, 282, 292, 304, 308
Kline, J. 231
Knight, I. 297
Knoll, A. 286
Koch, J. 291
Koch, L. 295
Koenemann, J. 171, 306
Konstan, J. A. 286
Koopman, P. 314
Krakovna, V. 309
Krämer, N. C. 292
Kress, W. J. 319

Krishna, R. 297
Kristensson, P. O. 288, 309
Krivtsov, V. 285
Krueger, G. 298, 301, 310, 313, 323
Kulesza, T. 305
Kumar, B. 305
Kumar, N. 319
Kunkel, J. 283
Kuo, L. 295
Kuyda, E. 133
Kwait, K. 301

La Porte, T. R. 308
Laborie, P. 289
Lacerda, T. C. 285, 312
Lahmar, H. B. 302
Laine, M. 291
Lam, K. H. 310
Lambert, A. 296
Landon, P. 308
Landwehr, C. E. 200, 314
Lanier, J. 282
Lazar, A. 325
Lazar, J. 324
Lazer, D. 58, 286
Lee, K.-F. 316
Lee, N. T. 318
Lee, S. 307
Lee, S. A. 298
Lefrancq, A. 309
Legg, S. 309
Leike, J. 309
Lennon, M. 303
Lenz, C. 286
Leonardo da Vinci 17, 19, 39
Lerman, K. 302
Letham, B. 305
Leveson, N. 181, 286, 299, 308, 310
Levy, C. 324
Lewis, J. E. 303
Lewis, J. R. 323
Li, F.-F. 51, 285
Li, J. 306, 324
Liang, X. 301
Liang, Y. 298
Liao, Q. V. 304
Licklider, J. C. R. 100, 276, 290, 326
Lieb, L. M. 285, 308
Lieuwen, D. 305

Lim, B. Y. 304
Lin, H. 318
Lin, Z. 310
Lindauer, A. 324
Lins, S. 322
Lisak, B. 324
Little, J. J. 325
Liu, N. 166, 172, 305
Liu, Y. 153, 301
Llorens, A. 294
Lobosco, K. 289, 297
Locke, J. 19
Löffler, D. 295
Lopatovska, I. 297
López, G. 296
Lopez, I. C. 319
Lovelace, A. 7
Lucero, A. 291

Ma, H. 320
Ma, L. 153, 301
Macintyre, P. E. 287
Mackay, M. 323
Mackay, W. E. 291
Mackenzie, D. 283
Mackworth, A. 84, 93, 288, 289, 325
Madigan, D. 305
Maes, P. 101–2, 291, 326
Magazinius, A. 310
Maharaj, T. 298, 301, 310, 313
Mahmud, S. 324
Mai, T. 310
Makhortykh, M. 283, 306
Mané, D. 309
Manic, M. 301
Mann, J. 296
Marcus, G. 89, 94, 289, 290
Marino, D. L. 301
Mark, G. 306
Markoff, J. 69, 101, 287, 291
Marks, P. 303
Martic, M. 309
Martin, C. D. 286, 290
Martin, D. 99
Martinez, A. 297
Marvel, J. 302
Maslow, A. 262
Matthews, J. 313
Matthies, S. 295
Mayer, R. 276

McAllister, B. 294
McBride, N. 122, 295
McCaffery, F. 312
McCarthy, J. 89
McCormick, T. H. 305
McGregor, S. 187, 281, 311
McGrenere, J. 324
McLuhan, M. 275–6, 326
Mehrabi, N. 302
Mellegård, N. N. 310
Mello, M. M. 311
Messom, C. 312
Metz, C. 314
Meurer, J. 295
Michael, K. 294, 319
Milhailidis, A. 324, 326
Milios, E. E. 306
Millecamp, M. 307
Miller, A. E. 319
Miller, S. 304
Miller, T. 165, 304, 318
Miller, V. 318
Miller, W. C. 325
Mindell, D. 36, 283, 284, 293
Minghim, R. 306
Minsky, M. 89
Mishra, K. 296
Mitchell, M. 302, 311, 315
Mitresvski, A. 300
Mittelstadt, B. 299, 303, 304, 316
Mochizuki, T. 295
Modarres, M. 285
Mojsilovic, A. 305
Moldovan, D. 322, 323
Montessori, M. 278
Moon, Y. 292
Moore, T. 270
Moran, T. 324
Mordvintsev, A. 30–1, 283
Morgenstern, J. 302, 312
Morley, J. 316
Morris, M. R. 162, 302
Morse, S. 4
Morstatter, F. 302
Mortenson, W. B. 325
Mou, Y. 294
Mouloua, M. 284
Moultrie, J. 285, 312
Mueller, A. S. 287
Mueller, S. T. 304
Mullainathan, S. 302
Muller, M. 304

Müller, T. 286
Mumford, L. 97, 98, 108, 229, 290, 293
Munson, J. C. 300
Muralikumar, M. D. 320
Murphy, R. 50, 112, 136, 284
Murphy, R. R. 290, 298
Musikanski, L. 281

Nadella, S. 204, 314
Nagar, S. 303
Nagel, P. 300
Nagy, A. 299, 313, 322
Nass, C. 105, 119, 135, 292, 298
Natale, S. 99, 282, 290, 292, 297
Nathan, P. 301
Naveed, S. 306
Newell, A. 275, 276
Nicas, J. 285, 293
Nieto, M. 300
Nissenbaum, H. 161, 302
Njilla, L. 301
Noble, S. U. 303
Norman, K. 276
Norouzi, N. 296
Norvig, P. 14, 93, 282, 289
Nourashrafeddin, S. 306
Nugent, C. 324
Nunes, I. 196
Nushi, B. 287, 309

Obermeyer, Z. 302
Obstfeld, D. 309
O'Connell, F. 306
Olah, C. 309
Oliver, J. L. 319
Olivier, P. 324
Olsson, L. 310
Olteanu, A. 321
O'Neil, C. 14, 160, 290, 302
Oron-Gilad, T. 130, 296
Ortega, P. A. 309
Osborne, M. 283
Oulasvirta, A. 291
Ovide, S. 283
Ozertem, U. 320

Packer, R. 291
Page, L. 278
Pandey, A. K. 295
Pantel, P. 320
Parasuraman, R. 284
Park, H. 306
Parra, D. 307
Pasquale, F. 223, 281, 303, 313, 317
Pasteur, L. 239
Patel-Schneider, P. F. 305
Pauli, L. 294
Paulk, M. C. 312
Pearl, C. 132, 297
Pearl, J. 19, 282
Pedraza, J. L. 300
Penzias, A. 45
Pérez, A. 300
Perez, C. C. 302
Perrow, C. 179–80, 308
Perry, W. J. 14
Peters, D. 286
Petrie, H. 261, 324
Pettersson, O. 300
Piaget, J. 278
Pichai, S. 204–5, 314
Pielke Jr, R. 316
Piorkowski, D. 312
Pitt, M. 309
Plaisant, C. 288, 301, 306, 309, 326
Plöger, P. G. 300
Plutchik, R. 27, 27f
Polyzotis, N. 302
Poole, D. 84, 93, 288, 289
Powers, B. 302
Prassler, E. 300
Preece, J. 301, 309, 319
Prescott, T. J. 294, 295
Pringle, R. 294
Pritchard, G. 324
Putin, V. 234

Quesada, L. 296

Ragan, E. D. 302
Raines, K. 297
Raji, I. D. 311, 315
Rakova, B. 303
Ramakrishnan, V. 238
Raman, J. 310

Rathi, S. 305
Ray, M. 324
Raymond, E. 187
Reagan, I. J. 287
Reddy, S. 309
Rees, J. P. 319
Reeves, B. 292, 298
Reichardt, J. 30
Reif, E. 306
Reisman, D. 314
Resnick, P. 318
Reynolds, E. B. 36, 283
Richards, J. 312
Richardson, K. 295
Rickert, M. 286
Rickman, A. 307
Riedl, J. 286
Riedl, M. O. 304
Rink, K. 297
Robert, L. 292
Robert, L. P. 106, 292
Roberts, H. 316
Roberts, W. S. 301
Robillard, J. 294, 295, 324
Robinson, C. 306
Rocha, Á. 312
Rock, C. 297
Rodríguez, S. 300
Roesler, A. 285, 293
Roger, E. 319
Rogerie, J. 289
Rogers, W. A. 323
Rogers, Y. 301, 309
Rosenberg, F. 299, 305
Rosenfeld, A. 278
Rosness, R. 308
Rossi, F. 290
Rotenberg, M. 317, 318, 323
Roth, D. 303
Roth, E. M. 282
Roy, S. 302
Rubinovitz, J. B. 310
Ruckert, J. H. 292
Rudin, C. 166, 305
Rus, D. 101, 115, 294
Russell, C. 299, 303, 316
Russell, S. 14, 87–8, 93, 135, 282, 289, 298
Ryan, R. M. 286

Saeidi, M. 320
Sahuguet, A. 305

Saini, A. 296
Sáinz, A. O. 300
Saltz, J. 321
Salviano, C. F. 312
Sands, K. 311
Santoni de Sio, F. 282, 298
Sanyal, J. 302
Sarid, D. 31, 283
Saxena, N. 302
Scassellati, B. 292
Scheidegger, C. 303
Schiff, D. 281, 303
Schöbel, M. 300
Schraagen, J. M. 282
Schulaman, J. 309
Schultz, J. 314
Schwarting, W. 294
Schwenger, C. 283
Sciuto, A. 296
Sculley, D. 322, 323
Sebo, S. 292
Seddon, J. J. 300
Severson, R. L. 292
Shapiro, S. S. 313
Sharkey, C. M. 317
Sharp, H. 301, 309
Shaw, P. 289
Sheehan, B. 297
Shelley, M. 118
Shen, T. 294
Sheridan, T. B. 47–8, 49, 59, 114, 284, 294
Sherkat, E. 306
Shetty, S. 301
Shi, C. 294
Shibata, T. 123*f*
Shields, J. 284
Shneiderman, B. 282, 286, 288, 289, 290, 291, 293, 297, 298, 299, 301, 305, 306, 309, 313, 316, 317, 320, 326
Shortliffe, E. H. 305
Shrobe, H. 294
Shull, F. 312
Siau, K. 292
Siegel, G. 300
Simon, H. 89, 275
Singh, V. K. 320
Skirpan, M. 321
Smart, A. 311, 315
Smilkov, D. 306
Smith, B. C. 282, 290

Smith, E. M. 325
Smith, J. M. 313
Smith, P. 322
Smulowitz, P. B. 311
Soares, J. V. 319
Sokol, K. 193, 312
Sonagara, D. 320
Spiel, K. 325
Spinoza, B. 18
Spring, N. 306
Sprinkle, T. 297
Srikumar, M. 299, 313, 322
Starbird, K. 320
Steinhardt, J. 309
Stephens, P. A. 319
Stevens, T. 126*f*
Stewart, M. 271
Stokes, D. E. 239, 320
Stoll, B. 292
Stone, M. O. 285, 293
Strait, M. K. 298
Strauch, B. 285, 293
Stray, J. 177, 307
Stumpf, D. 305
Sukis, J. 290
Sundar, S. S. 290
Sunyaev, A. 322
Sutcliffe, K. M. 309
Sutherland, I. 278
Sylla, C. 286
Szafir, D. 64, 169, 287, 305, 306

Taddeo, M. 316
Taffin, N. 291
Tamboli, A. 309
Tao, C. 324
Taylor, A. 324
Terry, M. 306
Theodorou, A. 300, 304
Thiebes, S. 322
Thimbleby, H. 62–3, 286
Thoduka, S. 300
Thompson, H. J. 325
Tintarev, N. 307
Tittle, J. 285, 293
Toews, R. 291
Toffler, A. 35, 283
Topcu, U. 294
Tosh, D. 301
Traeger, M. L. 292
Tramèr, F. 310

Trump, D. 236–7
Tsai, J. Y. 290, 297
Tsaneva-Atansova, K. 309
Tukey, J. W. 19, 279, 326
Turing, A. M. 4, 87, 99, 288, 290

Ueda, K.-i. 231
Unbehaun, D. 295

Vaccaro, K. 307
Vallor, S. 259–60, 323, 324
Van den Hoven, J. 282, 298
Van Hoboken, J. 283, 306
Van Horn, G. 233
Van Wynsberghe, A. 323
Varadarajan, S. 305
Vargemidis, D. 325
Vasconcelos, J. 312
Vasserman, L. 302
Vaughan, J. W. 302, 312
Vayena, E. 322
Vecchione, B. 302, 312
Velazquez, M. 297
Veloso, M. 290
Venkatasubramian, S. 303
Verbert, K. 173–4, 307
Vermeulen, J. 304
Verplank, W. L. 47–8, 59, 284
Vespignani, A. 286
Vest, C. M. 14
Vilím, P. 289
Vines, J. 324
Viswanathan, P. 325
Vogeli, C. 302
Vold, V. 286
von der Pütten, A. 292
von Wangenheim, C. G. 285, 312
Voorhees, E. 241
Vorvoreanu, M. 287, 309
Vought, R. T. 220, 221, 307, 318
Vyas, A. 305

Wachter, S. 299, 303, 316
Waddell, T. F. 290
Wakunuma, K. 295

Wald, I. Y. 324
Waldron, L. 289
Waldrop, M. M. 89, 282, 289
Walker, D. 324
Wallach, H. 241, 243, 302, 312, 321
Wallsworth, C. 296
Wang, D. 304
Wang, F. 307
Wang, J. 298, 301, 310, 313, 323
Wang, Q. 287
Wang, R. 287, 306
Wang, R. H. 325
Wang, S. 287
Wang, V. 316
Wang, W. 292
Ward, P. 282
Watson, D. 122, 295
Watts, J. 4
Wears, R. L. 282
Weaver, P. 308
Weber, C. V. 312
Weber, M. 318
Weick, K. E. 309
Weisz, J. D. 304
Weizenbaum, J. 133, 277, 326
Welch, G. 296
Weld, D. S. 165, 170, 287, 304, 306, 309
Wenskovitch, J. 299, 306
Wessel, M. 297
West, D. M. 214, 316
Westbrook, A. 320
Weyrich, M. 301
Whang, S. E. 302
White, R. N. 311, 315
Whittaker, M. 314
Wickens, C. D. 284
Wickramasinghe, C. S. 301
Williams, H. 297
Wilson, H. J. 183, 309
Winfield, A. F. 148, 292, 299
Winograd, T. 277–8, 326
Wolcott, J. 308
Wong, E. 70, 288
Wong, W. K. 305
Wood, C. A. 320

Woods, D. D. 49–50, 112–13, 180, 284, 285, 286, 292, 293, 308
Woodward, A. C. 311
Wortham, R. H. 300
Wortman Vaughan, J. 302
Wright, O. and W. 4
Wright, P. 324
Wu, S. 302
Wulf, V. 295

Xie, B. 324
Xu, K. 294, 299, 306
Xu, S. 323
Xu, W. 298

Yampolskiy, R. V. 187, 311
Yan, D. 307
Yang, H. 306
Yang, Q. 304
Yao, Y. 300
Yeh, T. 321
You, S. 292
Young, A. N. 319
Yue, Y. 307

Zacarias, M. 292
Zaldivar, A. 302
Zamorano, J. 300
Zhang, J. M. 153, 157, 301
Zhang, Y. 304
Zhang, Z. 306
Zhou, M. X. 299, 306
Zhu, D. 307
Zhu, H. 306
Ziegler, J. 283, 306
Ziemke, T. 295
Zimmermann, T. 299
Zinkervich, M. 302
Zoucas, A. 312
Zuboff, S. 220, 318
Zuck, L. 294
Zuckerberg, M. 236
Zuckerman, O. 324

SUBJECT INDEX

Figures are indicated by an italic *f* following the page number.

AARON 30, 31
AARP 259
Accenture 199
accounting and auditing
    firms vi, 11, 55, 198–9,
    202
ACM 196, 211
    Computer-Human
        Interaction
        conference 240
    conference (2017) 279
    Intelligent User
        Interface 102
    Technology Policy
        Committee 203
ACM SIGGRAPH Lifetime
    Achievement Award 30
ACM Special Interest
    Group on Computer-
    Human Interaction
    (SIGCHI) 102, 278
    Lifetime Achievement
        Award 277
acoustic recognition 232
active appliances v, 10, 12,
    40, 78, 84, 90f, 91–2,
    117, 127–31, 137, 138
    user interface design 72,
    73f
active measures 234
advanced driver assistance
    systems (ADAS) 21
ageing in place 260–1
Ageless Innovation 124
Agile Alliance 155

agile models 154–6
agriculture 34–5
AI 100 Report 94
AI Magazine 99
AI Now Institute, New York
    University 208
AI Research Centre (AIRC),
    Japan 244
AI Social Contract Index 256
AI4ALL 208
AI4Good 7–8
AIBO dog robot 123, 124f
airbags 47, 60, 61f
Alan Turing Institute 165,
    216
Alexa 29, 96, 131, 132
algorithmic auditing 189
algorithmic bias 160–4
algorithmic hubris 58
algorithmic impact
    assessments 197
Algorithmic Justice
    League 163, 202, 208
Alibaba 213
All of Us 269
AlphaFold 2 237–8
AlphaGo program 4
alt-tags 96
Amazon 96, 130, 131, 132,
    136, 150, 168, 245
    labor issues 33–4
American National Standards
    Institute 190
Ananova 119
animal robots 122–7

animism 97
Anki 119–20
APGAR scale 250
Apple 96, 102, 131, 169, 199,
    220, 268, 278–9
    Human Interface Design
        Guidelines 76, 102, 135,
        183
    Knowledge Navigator
        video 119
Apple Watch 269
artificial intelligence (AI)
    belief in rationalism 18, 21
    belief that computers are
        in same category as
        people 25, 95
    cautionary voices 14–15
    enthusiasm for 14
    vs. intelligence aug-
        mentation (IA) 69,
        101
    shift to empiricism 19,
        22–3
    skepticism about HCAI 40
    and un/employment 33–7
    Artificial Intelligence (Russell
        and Norvig) 14
artificial intelligence (AI)
    algorithms 12, 98, 196,
        235
    detecting hate speech 236
    and elder care 260, 267
    and HCAI 3, 7, 15, 39, 43,
        69, 78, 85, 146, 150

artificial intelligence (AI)
 algorithms (*Continued*)
  intellectual property rights
   and patents 31
  in powered
   wheelchairs 265
  and predictability 168–9
  in recommender
   systems 103
  safety 182
  and SEEK 233
  and surveillance
   capitalism 220
  three properties of
   dangerous 161
  verification and
   validation 157
artificial intelligence (AI)
 research goals v, 10,
  84, 87–92, 137 *see also*
  innovation goal; science
  (emulation) goal
arXiv 242, 243
Asimo robot 119
assessment, trust-
 worthiness 154,
 245–57
Association for Advanc-
 ing Automation
 (AAA) 152, 190, 212
Association for the
 Advancement of
 Artificial Intelligence
 (AAAI) 196, 211–12,
 240
assured autonomy v, 10, 84,
 90*f*, 91, 111, 114, 137
astronauts 106
audit data analysis
 tools 152–3
audit trails (product logs) vi,
 10, 20, 22, 47, 53, 77, 96,
 114, 151–3, 218
auditing firms *see* accounting
 and auditing firms
auditory interfaces 71
Augmented Human
 Conference 102, 279
autism therapy 122
automatic doors 46–7
automation *see* computer
 autonomy/automation
autonomous design 20–1, 22

aviation 83–4, 188
 control centers 115
 incident and accident
  reporting 184
 interlocks 63
 security testing 159
 verification and validation
  testing 157
 see also Federal Aviation
  Administration (FAA);
  flight data recorders
Aviation Safety Agency,
 EU 219
Aviation Safety Reporting
 System 184

Baidu 213
banks and banking 36, 119,
 135
Berkman Klein Center
 report 147, 147*f*
bias testing 160–4
bicycle riding 60, 61*f*, 83
Bill and Melinda Gates
 Foundation 230
biodiversity loss 233
Bloomberg Terminals
 109–10, 110*f*
BOB 119
Boeing 737 MAX crashes 15,
 50, 58, 61–2, 112
book production 34
Boston Consulting
 Group 199
Boston Dynamics 120, 121*f*,
 125
bot farms 234, 236
Brookings Institution 207
bug reporting 186–7
Bugcrowd 186
Bugzilla 186
building codes 200
Bureau of Labor Statistics,
 US 37
business management
 strategies vi, 11, 53, 54,
 80, 141–2, 148, 148*f*,
 149, 150, 179–93, 223

Cambridge Analytica 235–6
Campaign Against Sex
 Robots 120

Canadian government 107,
 215
cancer diagnosis 169–70
Capability Maturity
 Model 54, 191–2, 191*f*
Captain Tom Foundation 270
carebots 260, 262–4
caregivers 259–60
Carnegie Mellon
 University 54,
 240, 275
cars and driving 63–5, 66*f*, 91
 automatic
  transmissions 115
 breath alcohol levels 47
 see also safety-first cars;
  self-driving cars
case-based testing 158
causality 19–20
Center for Advancing
 Research Impact in
 Society, US 215
Center for AI and Digital
 Policy *see* Dukakis
 Center for AI and
 Digital Policy
Centers for Disease Control
 and Prevention, US 260
chair design 68
Challenger Space Shuttle
 disaster 180
chatbots 133–4, 277
China 133, 213–14
 Next Generation Artificial
  Intelligence Plan 213
citizen science 230–4, 270
Clippy 119
Cloudflare 187
coaches 103
Code of Practice on
 Disinformation,
 EU 235
Coded Bias 163
cognitive computing 100
collaborative software 97
Committee of Sponsoring
 Organizations 199
computer art 30–1
computer autonomy/
 automation 45–7,
 111–13
 autonomy vs.
  automation 94–5

dangers of excessive 15, 50, 61–2, 62f, 63, 96, 112–13

deadly myths of 15, 49–50, 112–13

fair distribution of benefits 34, 36, 37

high automation/high human control v, 9, 43, 45, 56, 59–60, 60f, 61f, 62f, 66, 66f, 67f, 71, 74, 79, 84, 95–6, 109, 265–6, 265f

high automation/low human control 60, 61f, 62f, 66, 66f, 67f, 265, 265f

and inequality 34, 35

one-dimensional levels of levels of 47–50, 48t, 49t, 59, 59f

low automation/high human control 60–1, 61f, 62f, 66, 66f, 67f, 265, 265f

low automation/low human control 61, 61f, 62f, 66, 66f, 67f, 265, 265f

stages of 48

ubiquity 12

and un/employment 33–7

and worker protection 40

see also assured autonomy

computer-generated music 31

Computer Power and Human Reason (Weizenbaum) 277

Computer Professionals for Social Responsibility 277

computers
as "bicycles for our minds" 83

in different category from/same category as people 25–31, 39–40, 79–80, 94, 106–8, 276, 277

emotional reactions by 28

emulating humans 29, 39, 87–9, 93–5

as moral and ethical actors 95

unique features 79–80, 107–8, 110

see also intelligent agents; teammates

Computing Research Association workshop (2020) 114

Conference Board Consumer Confidence survey, US 252

conferences 240–2

consequential applications 58, 79, 85

audit trails 20, 22

bias testing 160–1

continuous monitoring 77

explainable user interfaces 164–5

government regulation 218

industry standards 190

lack of assessment and failures 254

safety-first 47, 113

understandability 156

constraint solving 268

constructed emotions 27–8

Consumers Report 55

continuous monitoring 197, 197f, 253

control centers v, 10, 15, 40, 64–5, 66–7, 68f, 84, 90f, 91, 111, 114–15, 137, 138

control panels 15, 56, 58, 77, 91, 101, 103, 114, 128, 146, 177

corporate capture 191, 203, 218

corporate social responsibility 149, 205

Cortana 96, 131

Coursera 97, 240

courses 239–40

COVID-19 crisis 121, 197, 217, 237, 262, 270

contact tracing 199

misinformation 234

and tele-conferencing 97, 280

tests 249

and unemployment 33

and working from home 98

Critical Assessment of Techniques for Protein Structure Prediction (CASP) 237–8

customer service chat-bots 133, 134, 136

Cybernetic Serendipity exhibit, London (1968) 30

cybersecurity
red teams 159–60

reporting systems 185–7

Da Vinci surgical robot 108, 109f

Data and Society 208

DataKind 7

datasheets for datasets 193

de-skilling 62, 80

Deep Blue 88

deep fakes 234

deep learning 3, 13, 146, 280
AlphaFold 2 237–8

failures in real world applications 89

and radiology 40

DeepDream 30–1

DeepMind 237

Deepwater Horizon oil spill 201

Defense Science Board, US 50, 111

Deloitte 199, 252–3

Delphi method 252

Department of Health and Human Services Agency for Healthcare Research and Quality, US 188–9

design
combined strategy 10, 48, 53, 85, 89, 90–1, 90f, 92, 103, 109, 112, 113, 115, 126, 136, 137–8

design (*Continued*)
  implications of rationalism
    and empiricism 20–3
  see also user interface
    design
design guidelines 69–71, 102,
  183
design metaphors v, 10, 11*f*,
  12, 83–5, 90–2, 90*f*,
  105–36, 137, 227
design thinking 9, 48–9, 68,
  78, 137, 146, 225
Designing the User Interface
  (Shneiderman) 70, 278
*Designing Voice User
  Interfaces* (Pearl) 132
differential testing 158
digital cameras 4, 9, 12, 18,
  73–4, 74*f*, 84, 103, 137–8
direct manipulation
  designs 22
direct manipulation user
  interfaces 278
disability
  accessibility
    guidelines 190
  people/users with disabil-
    ities 78, 96, 102, 132,
    162, 260–1, 266, 267,
    268
disaster relief 136
disease treatments 237–9
dishwashers in dinner
  tables 266–8, 267*f*
dissociation 97
dolphins 232
dopamine 262
Down Dog Yoga 268–9
drones 15, 107, 108
Dukakis Center for AI and
  Digital Policy 209, 224,
  256

e-commerce 12, 33–4, 115
eBird 231
echocardiograms 109
educational choices 172–3,
  173*f*
edX 97, 240
Eight Golden Rules 70–1,
  71*f*, 76, 78, 81

Electronic Privacy In-
  formation Center
  (EPIC) 207
elevators, user interface
  design 72–3
ELIZA chatbot 277
emergent bias 161
emotions 26–8, 26*f*, 27*f*
empathy 20, 260
Empirical Methods in Natural
  Language Processing
  conference 19, 242
empiricism 17, 18, 19, 39
  design implications 21–2,
    23
employment and
  unemployment 33–7
Encounters with HCI Pioneers
  (Shneiderman) 279
Engineering and Physical
  Sciences Research
  Council (EPSRC),
  UK 243
Enron 198, 253
entrepreneurship, older
  adults 271
environmental issues 8, 230,
  233–4
environmental reports 252
Ernst and Young 199, 252–3
ethics 80, 239
  bridging the gap to
    practice 145–50
  checklist for
    journals 242–3
  courses 239, 240
Etsy.com 271
Europe 149, 216
European Commission White
  Paper on AI 216
European Research Council
  (ERC) 243
European Union (EU) 214,
  216, 220
evaluation of troubling
  technologies 13–14
Ex Machina 100
exercise machines 129
exoskeletons 98
Expert Committee on
  Liability for New
  Technologies, EU 195
explainability 54

explainable AI (XAI) 14–15
explainable user
  interfaces 164–77
explanations, preventing the
  need for 167–8
Exploratory Data Analysis
  (Tukey) 279
exploratory user interfaces,
  prospective visual
  designs 168–77
extensive reporting of failures
  and mean misses 184–8

Facebook 98, 196, 220, 234,
  237, 244
  hate speech detection 236
  misinformation 235–6
Facebook News Feed 176,
  235
Facebook Oversight
  Board 190, 235
facial recognition technolo-
  gies 28, 149, 159, 220,
  242
  racial and gender
    bias 162–3, 202
Fair Credit Reporting Act
  (1970) 219
fairness 54, 223
  bias testing 160–4
Fairness, Accountability
  and Transparency in
  Machine Learning
  conference 161
Fall Joint Computer
  Conference (1968) 101
Federal Aviation Adminis-
  tration (FAA), US 115,
  219
  Hotline 184
  Safety Reporting
    System 23
Federal Communications
  Commission, US 197
Federal Reserve Board,
  US 197
Federal Trade Commission
  (FTC), US 219

feedback
    from computers 22, 71, 80,
        269
    from users 78, 166
financial flash crashes 15, 58,
    112
Fisca robot dog 125, 127*f*
Fitbit 269
Fiverr 260
flight data recorders
    (FDRs) vi, 10, 53, 77,
    151
Fluid Interfaces Lab 279
Food and Drug Administra-
    tion (FDA), US 123,
    197, 219
    Adverse Event Reporting
        System (AERS) 23,
        184–5, 185*f*, 186*f*
    Manufacturer and User Fa-
        cility Device Experience
        (MAUDE) 185
ForHumanity 208
Foundation for Responsible
    Robotics 208
Frankenstein (Shelley) 118
Future of Life Institute 209
Future Shock (Toffler) 35

Galaxy Zoo 231
Gather.town 98, 280
gender bias 162, 163, 202,
    242
General Data Protection and
    Regulation (GDPR),
    EU 14, 149, 165, 216,
    240
Generative Adversarial
    Networks (GANs) 30
GitHub 157, 186
Global Partnership on AI
    (GPAI) 217
global/local explanations 172
Google 163, 169, 186, 199,
    220, 243, 278
    countering commercial
        deceptions 236
    design guidelines 69, 183
    internal algorithmic au-
        diting framework 189,
        205

People and AI Research
    (PAIR) 100, 244
search system 74, 75*f*
seven objectives for
    artificial intelligent
    applications 204–5
Google Docs 97
Google Flu Trends 58, 254
Google Health 269
Google Home 96, 131, 132
Google Images 163, 164*f*
Google Maps 107
Google Model Cards 160,
    193, 248
Google Nest 71–2
    Learning Thermostat 128,
        128*f*
Google Play 102, 268
governance structures 10–11,
    11*f*, 12, 141–2, 148, 148*f*,
    151–225, 227
government regulation vi,
    11, 40, 53, 55, 80, 142,
    148–9, 148*f*, 150, 202,
    213–21, 223
Grand Challenges 230
Group of Twenty (G20) 216
Gulf Coast Claim Facility 201

HackerOne 186
hate speech 236–7
HCI International
    Conference 240
healthcare 214, 219
    algorithmic bias 162
    internal review
        boards 188–9
    older adults 262
    see also disease treatments;
        personal health records;
        vaccines
HealthKit 269
Her 100
HIBAR Research Alliance,
    US 215
hierarchy of human
    needs 262
High-Level Expert
    Group principles
    for trustworthy AI,
    Europe 216

high reliability
    organizations 180
hiring, safety-oriented 182–3
hiring committees 251
Honda 119
Honeywell thermostats 72*f*
hospitals 188–9
housing, older adults 262
human autonomy 53, 114,
    146
Human-centered AI (HCAI)
    aspirations, goals and
        human values 11, 11*f*
    attributes 55, 56*f*, 244, 245,
        246*t*, 248, 249, 251, 254
    belief in empiricism 23, 39
    belief that computers are in
        different category from
        people 25, 79–80
    dangers and threats 4, 8,
        11–12, 11*f*, 41, 145, 224,
        273, 280
    driving forward 229–44
    growing interest in 7–8,
        15, 51–2, 274
    high expectations 7–16
    principles 147–8, 147*f*
    process 9
    product 9
    skepticism about shift
        to 40–1
    stakeholders 11, 11*f*, 13,
        13*f*
    as synthesis 7, 39, 40, 43,
        85, 89, 146, 150, 223
    system complexity 146–7
    trustworthiness
        assessment 253–7
    trustworthiness assessment
        process 254, 255*t*
    trustworthiness
        scale 256–7, 256*t*
    what it is 3–41
Human-centered AI (HCAI)
    framework v, 9, 11*f*,
    12, 43, 45, 48–9, 52, 56,
    57–68, 60*f*, 61*f*, 62*f*, 66*f*,
    67*f*, 79–80, 83–4, 227,
    265, 265*f*
    skepticism about 80–1
Human-centered AI (HCAI)
    pattern language 76–8,
    77*t*, 81

human-centered
    approaches 275–80
Human + Machine
    (Daugherty and
    Wilson) 183
human–computer
    competition 94
human–computer interac-
    tion 52, 96, 102, 154,
    276, 278–9
Human–Computer
    Interaction Lab 278
human control
    and automation in
        one-dimensional
        models 48, 59, 59*f*
    dangers of excessive 62–3,
        62*f*, 96
    and design guidelines 76
    design quality, and use 51
    high human control/high
        automation v, 9, 43, 45,
        56, 59–60, 60*f*, 61*f*, 62*f*,
        66, 66*f*, 67*f*, 71, 74, 79,
        84, 95–6, 109, 265–6,
        265*f*
    high human control/low
        automation 60–1, 61*f*,
        62*f*, 66, 66*f*, 67*f*, 265,
        265*f*
    and human mistakes 51,
        80
    low human control/high
        automation 60, 61*f*, 62,
        62*f*, 66, 66*f*, 67*f*, 265,
        265*f*
    low human control/low
        automation 61, 61*f*, 62*f*,
        66, 66*f*, 67*f*, 265, 265*f*
    and reliability, safety and
        trustworthiness 46–7,
        55–6
    and stages of
        automation 48
    supertools 102–3
    see also control centers;
        control panels
human creativity 12, 25, 56,
    108–9
    support tools 30
human responsibility 57,
    106–7, 114, 122, 195–6,
    198

human-robot interaction
    (HRI) 105, 106, 120
human-to-human com-
    munication 29,
    77
human values v, 7, 11, 11*f*,
    39, 225, 273, 277, 280
human vigilance problem 62,
    80, 112
human well-being 9
humans
    amplification of abilities 4,
        9, 12–13, 15, 25–6, 30,
        39, 40–1, 78, 98, 108,
        145–6
    communication and
        connection 97–8, 280
    in different category
        from/same category
        as computers 25–31,
        39–40, 79–80, 94, 106–8,
        276, 277
Humans in the Group;
    Computers in the
    Loop 21, 22*f*, 77, 280
humans in the loop 91, 96,
    157
humility 20, 22, 47, 77, 247,
    273
Hyperties 278
Hyundai 120

IBM 88, 100, 102, 150, 155,
    244
    AI Explainability 360 166
    AI Guidelines 62
    Design for AI website 70,
        183
IBM FactSheets 193, 248
IBM Fairness 360 162
IBM Watson AI XPRIZE
    Foundation 7
image understanding
    research 96
iNaturalist 231, 233
incident reporting 23, 47, 78,
    184–8
    appliance robot
        failures 130
    databases 12, 153, 187
independent oversight vi, 11,
    14, 53, 55, 80, 98, 107,

142, 148, 148*f*, 149, 150,
    195–205, 223, 252–3
Indiana University 276
Indigenous people 163–4
industry standard practices,
    alignment with 190–3
Information Commissioner's
    Office, UK 165, 216
information retrieval
    research 241
information visualization 13,
    14–15, 76, 279–80
innovation (application)
    goal 10, 84, 89, 90, 90*f*,
    91, 92, 95–8, 100, 101,
    102, 112, 135–6, 137,
    138, 145
Instagram 234
Institute for Electrical and
    Electronics Engineers
    (IEEE) 196, 211
    Ethically Aligned
        Design 147, 147*f*, 161
    Ethics Certification Pro-
        gram for Autonomous
        and Intelligent
        Systems 203
    Global Initiative on
        Ethics of Intelligent
        Systems 211
    P7000 series of
        standards 190, 203
    P7010 standard 9
    P7001 standard 255
Institute for Ethical AI and
    Machine Learning,
    UK 192
insurance companies vi, 11,
    55, 199–201, 202
intelligence augmentation
    (IA) 69, 101
intelligent agents v, 10, 84,
    90, 90*f*, 99–102, 103, 137
intelligent tutoring
    systems 168
interdisciplinary teams 55
interlocks 51, 63, 66, 96, 115
internal review
    boards 188–90
International Atomic Energy
    Agency (IAEA),
    UN 217

International Joint
    Conference on AI
    (IJ-CAI) 240
International Standards
    Organization (ISO) 190
International Telecommuni-
    cations Union (ITU),
    UN 217, 223
Internet connectivity 187
inter-rater reliability 250
iRobot 129

Japan 121, 123
Jibo 119–20
John Hopkins Institute for
    Assured Autonomy 114
*Journal of Responsible
    Innovation* 242
journals 242–3
Joy for All dog robot 123–4,
    125f

Khan Academy 97
Kiva Robotics 33
knowledge-based expert
    systems 167–8
KPMG 199, 252–3
Kumospace 98, 280

laptop accessibility 102
law of autonomous robots 50,
    112
leadership commitment to
    safety 181–2
lethal autonomous weapons
    (LAWS) 20–1, 113, 217,
    224
life-critical appli-
    cations 58–9,
    79
    audit trails 20, 22
    data on unsuccess-
        ful/inadvertent
        deployment 47
    government
        regulation 218
    industry standards 190
    interlocks 63
    safety-first 113
    understandability 156
Likert-like scales 251
Loebner Prize 99

Luddite revolt 35
Lyft 260

Machine Intelligence
    Research Institute
    (MIRI) 212
machine learning 3, 13, 30,
    66, 72, 128, 152, 169, 183
    vs. causality 19–20
    data set documen-
        tation 157, 160,
        193
    differential testing 158
    explainability 166
    five problem types 153–4
    for integrity 235
    poor behaviour in
        real-world domains 254
    software engineering
        workflows 156, 156f
    three forms of 157
    training data bias
        testing 163
    underspecification 243
    verification and
        validation 157
    and wheelchair
        refinements 266
Machine Learning Maturity
    Model 192
Machines of Loving Grace
    (Markoff) 101
malicious actors 4, 8, 29,
    57–8, 78, 224, 235, 237
man-computer
    symbiosis 100
management strategies *see*
    business management
    strategies
*Manifesto for Agile Software
    Development* 155
Mars Rovers 15, 107, 108
massive online open courses
    (MOOCs) 97–8, 168
The Matrix 100
Mattell 133
Mayfield Robotics 119–20
MCI WorldCom 198
McKinsey and Co 199
Meals on Wheels 267
medical devices 62–3, 129,
    160, 219

medical reports 18
medication devices for older
    adults 264–5
mental health 133
Mercedes-Benz Active
    Parking Assist 64
metamorphic testing
    158–9
Microsoft 96, 102, 119,
    131, 150, 224,
    241, 244
    AI and Ethics in Engineer-
        ing Research (AETHER)
        Committee 190
    chatbots 133
    Datasheets for
        Datasets 160,
        193, 248
    *Guidelines for AI-Human
        Interaction* 70, 183
    nine-stage software engi-
        neering workflow 156,
        156f
    Office of Responsible
        AI 190, 244
    six principles for respon-
        sible use of advanced
        technologies 204
Microsoft Teams 97
military applications 21, 106
    see also drones; lethal
        autonomous weapons
        (LAWS)
MiRO-E dog robot 123
misinformation 234–7
MIT 115, 276
    Media Lab 119
    Sloan School of
        Management 239
    Work of the Future
        project 36
MITRE Corporation 160,
    185
    ATT&CK matrix 159
Montreal AI Ethics
    Institute 212
Montreal Declaration for Re-
    sponsible Development
    of AI (2017) 7
mortgage loan ex-
    planations 169,
    171f
MYCIN 167

NAO robot 121
NASA 15, 91, 108, 180, 231
National Academy of
    Engineering, US
    230
National Academy of
    Sciences panel
    (2006-2008) 13–14
National AI Research
    Institutes, US 215,
    243
National Algorithm Safety
    Board, US 218
National Highway Traffic
    Safety Administration,
    US 188
National Institute of Stan-
    dards and Technology
    (NIST), US 185, 219,
    241, 257
    conference, 1982 278
    Text Retrieval Conference
    (TREC) 158
National Natural Science
    Foundation of China
    243
National Safety Council,
    US 184
National Science Foundation
    (NSF), US 215, 243
National Security Com-
    mission on AI,
    US 157
    Final Report 219
National Transportation
    Safety Board (NTSB),
    US 63, 148, 184, 197,
    217–18, 251
National Vulnerabilities
    Database, US 185
natural language trans-
    lation 58, 75, 76f,
    96
natural language
    understanding 277
navigation systems 4, 9, 12,
    169, 170f
Neural Information Process-
    ing Systems Conference
    (NeurIPS) 240–1
neural network strategies 88
neuroscience 100
news recommenders 46, 171

Newsweek 100
non-governmental organiza-
    tions (NGOs) and civil
    society organizations vi,
    11, 55, 149, 201–2,
    207–8
normal accident
    theory 179–80
novels recommender 174–5,
    176f
nuclear non-proliferation
    reviews 254
Nuclear Non-proliferation
    Treaty (1970) 217

objective
    measurement 248–9
older adults
    caring for and learning
    from 244, 259–71
    diverse users 261
    needs 262, 263t
    and social robots 121,
    124–5, 136, 260, 261,
    262–4
    tasks 261, 263t
Open AI 212
Open Community for Ethics
    in Autonomous and
    Intelligent Systems
    (OCEANIS) 190
Organization for Economic
    Cooperation and
    Development (OECD)
    AI Policy Observatory
    212
    Better Life Index 174,
    175f
    Policy Observatory 224
    Principles for responsible
    stewardship of trust-
    worthy AI 216–17,
    256
organizational responsi-
    bility 114, 179–80,
    195
orthotics 98
Oxford University
    report on the future of
    employment (2013) 33
    Zooniverse 231
oxytocin 262

pacemakers 58–9, 60, 61f
pain-controlled analgesia
    (PCA) devices 65–7,
    67f, 68f
PARO therapeutic
    robot 122–3, 123f
Partnership on AI 153, 177,
    187, 212, 244
Pasteur's Quadrant
    (Stokes) 239
pasteurization 239
PatientsLikeMe 269
Patriot missile systems
    failures 15, 50, 112
People Magazine 279
Pepper robot 120–1
personal health
    records 269–70
photography 35–6
phrenology 28, 242
piano playing 60, 61f, 103
planning oversight 197, 197f,
    253
pneumonia detection 157
popular culture 100
positive train control
    systems 63
Postal Buddy 118–19
post-hoc explanations 166–7
predictability
    principle 168–9
preexisting bias 161
PricewaterhouseCoopers 199,
    252–3
privacy 13–14, 98, 119, 199,
    207, 214, 220
product logs see audit trails
professional organizations
    and research insti-
    tutes vi, 11, 55, 149,
    202–5, 211–12
Project Sidewalk 266
prosthetics 98
protein folding 237–8

quantified self 269

racial bias 162, 163, 164f,
    202, 224, 242
radiology 40
randomized clinical
    trials 238

rationalism 17–20, 39, 275
  design implications 20–1
Rebooting AI (Marcus and
  Davis) 94
recommender systems 45,
  46, 57–8, 79, 85, 270
  combined design 103
  exploratory user
    interfaces 169, 172–6
  government
    regulation 218
  matching older adults with
    service providers 260,
    267
red teams 159–60
Reddit 234
reliability 56f, 149
  and data collection on in-
    advertent/unsuccessful
    use 47
  high human control/high
    automation 59, 60f, 61f,
    62f, 66–7, 66f, 67f, 265f
  high reliability
    organizations 180
  and human control 46, 55
  inter-rater 250
  life-critical applications 96
  vs. safety 181
  and sensor accuracy and
    data fairness 61
reliable systems vi, 10–11,
  53–4, 80, 148, 148f, 150,
  151–77, 223
Replika chatbot 133, 134f
Research and Innovation
  Council, UK 114
research directions 229–39
research excellence
  framework (REF),
  UK 252
research funding 243–4
research groups 239
research partnerships 215
resilience engineering 180
retrospective analysis of
  disasters 197, 197f, 253
rewilding 233
robophobia 135
Robot & Frank 100
robot arm design 118
robotaxis 65

robotic process automation
  (RPA) 35
robots
  audit trails 152
  human-like 15, 87, 95,
    105–6, 108
  predictability 169
  as teammates 105–6, 107,
    108
  and un/employment 33–7
  see also animal robots; law
    of autonomous robots;
    social robots
The Robots Are Coming
  (Ford) 33
Roomba robotic vacuum
  cleaner 17–18, 129–30,
  130f, 131f
Rossum's Universal Robots
  (Capek) 118
Royal Society, UK 216
Russian intelligence
  services 234

safety 56f, 149
  consequential ap-
    plications 47,
    113
  and data collection on in-
    advertent/unsuccessful
    use 47
  and high human
    control/high automa-
    tion 59, 60f, 61f, 62f,
    66–7, 66f, 67f, 84, 265f
  and human control 46, 55
  life-critical
    applications 113
  vs. reliability 181
  and sensor accuracy and
    data fairness 61
safety culture vi, 10, 11, 53,
  54, 80, 141–2, 148, 148f,
  150, 179–93, 223
safety cultures
  approach 180–1
safety-first cars 21, 64–5, 115
Sarbanes-Oxley Act
  (2002) 198, 199
Science, The Endless Frontier
  (Bush) 215

science (emulation) goal 10,
  84, 89, 90, 90f, 91, 93–5,
  97, 99, 102, 136, 137,
  138, 145
scoring by
  components 249–51
scrum 154
search auto-completion 58,
  74, 75f
Securities and Exchange
  Commission (SEC),
  US 152, 198
Seek app 232–3, 232f
self-driving cars 21, 58–9,
  113, 159
  audit trails 152
  insurance 200–1
  six levels of autonomy 49,
    49t
  see also Tesla car crashes
Senior Olympics 270
Senior Planet website 271
sentiment analysis 28
September 11 Victim
  Compensation
  Fund 201
sex robots 120
SHRDLU robot 277
SIGCHI conference
  (2017) 279
Siri 29, 96, 131
smartphone applications 15,
  95, 267
social media 29, 115
  challenges 12, 29, 98, 221
  misinformation 234–7
social processes, assessment
  by 251–3
Social Robotics 119
social robots v, 10, 21, 28, 29,
  40, 84, 90f, 91, 95, 97,
  137, 138
  future of 134–6
  history of 117–22
  for older adults 121,
    124–5, 136, 260, 261,
    262–4
Society of Automotive
  Engineers, US 49
Softbank 120–1
Software Engineering
  Institute (SEI) 190

software engineering
practices vi, 10–11,
53–4, 80, 141, 148, 148f,
149, 150, 151–77, 186,
192, 223
software engineering
workflows 153–6
Software Psychology
(Shneiderman) 276,
277
Software Robotics 121
SONY 123
Sophia/ Little Sophia
robots 119
speech recognition
research 96
spellcheckers 58, 75, 75f
sports
for older adults 270
scoring systems 250
Spot dog robot 125–6, 127f
Spotify 173–4, 174f
Stanford University 105, 146,
167
AI-100 report 25
Institute for Human-
Centered Artificial
Intelligence 51, 239
Star Wars 100
State University of New York
(SUNY) 275
statistical methods 19–20
stock market
audit trails 152
flash crashes 15, 58, 112
Superintelligence
(Bostrom) 14
supertools v, 4, 9, 10, 12,
25–6, 78, 84, 90, 90f, 95,
101–3, 107, 137, 138
surgical robots 55, 97, 108,
109f
adverse event
reporting 185
surveillance, China 124
surveillance capitalism 12,
98, 220, 224
SWOT analysis 252

Talking Barbie 133
talking dolls 133
TaskRabbit 260

teammates v, 10, 105–8, 84,
90f, 91, 109, 110, 137
technical bias 161
Technics and Civilization
(Mumford) 97
tele-bot cars 64–5
tele-bots v, 10, 12, 40, 84, 90f,
91, 97, 108–9, 110, 136,
137, 138
tele-conferencing 97
Tencent 213
The Terminator 100
Tesla crashes 20, 112
NTSB report 63, 218
reports on deaths 187–8
text classification ap-
plications 166,
167f
Text REtrieval Conference
(TREC) 241
text user interfaces 133–4
thermostats 71–2, 72f
tight coupling 179
Time Magazine 100, 279
toilet flushing 46
Tombot dog robot 124–5,
126f
training, safety-oriented 183
transparency 223, 254–5, 256
Travelers Insurance 200
trust 54, 245
*Trust: The Social Virtues and
the Creation of Prosperity*
(Fukuyama) 54
trustworthiness 56f, 149
assessment 154, 245–57
and data collection on in-
advertent/unsuccessful
use 47
high human control/high
automation 59, 60f, 61f,
62f, 66–7, 66f, 67f, 265f
and human control 46, 55
measures 242
and sensor accuracy and
data fairness 61
seven principles 216
vs. trust 245
vs. trustedness 247
Trustworthiness Maturity
Models (TMMs) 192–3

trustworthy certification vi,
10, 11, 53, 80, 142, 148,
148f, 150, 195–205, 223
trustworthy systems 54–5
TurboTax 168
Turing Test 87, 99
Twitter 98, 234
Twitter Rules 236
2001: A Space Odyssey 100

Uber 260
underspecification 243
*Understanding Computers and
Cognition* (Winograd
and Flores) 277
Understanding Media
(McLuhan) 275–6
Underwriters Lab-
oratories 55,
207
United Kingdom (UK) 216,
220, 240, 252, 267
United Nations (UN) 217
AI for Good Global
Summit 8
Convention on Certain
Conventional Weapons,
Geneva 113
Declaration of Human
Rights 256
Sustainable Development
Goals (SDGs) 8–9, 8f,
81, 217, 224, 230, 273,
280
United States (US) 149, 201,
213, 231, 239–40
AI policy 214–15
Capitol
insurrection 236–7
government
regulation 217–21
United States (US) Access
Board 190
United States (US) Air
Force 107
United States (US)
Army After-Action
Reviews 187
University-Industry Demon-
stration Partnership,
US 215

University of California at Davis 250
University of Maryland 276
University of Michigan Consumer Sentiment Index 252
University of Toronto Centre for Ethics 239
usability questionnaires 251
user experience design 7, 9, 19, 39, 138, 146, 151, 154, 155, 227, 268
User Experience Professionals Association 102
user experience testing 146, 156, 159
user interface design 12, 29, 58, 91, 98, 276
  Eight Golden Rules 70–1, 71*t*, 76, 78, 81
  visual use interface examples 71–6
user interface help systems 168
user interfaces 56, 102, 103, 135, 146
  and privacy protection 220

see also direct manipulation user interfaces; explainable user interfaces; text user interfaces; visual user interfaces; voice use interfaces

vaccines 237–8
verification and validation testing 157–60
Vietnam War 275
visual user interfaces 13, 22, 166, 167*f*, 279–80
  design examples 71–6
  see also exploratory user interfaces
voice user interfaces 29, 131–3

Wall-E 100
waterfall model 154, 156
Waymo 65
Weapons of Math Destruction (O'Neil) 14, 160–1
Webex 97
WeChat 213

Weibo 98
whales 231, 232
wheelchairs 265–6, 265*f*
White House reports and memoranda 172, 214, 220–1
Wikipedia 28, 96, 233
wine scoring 249–50, 249*f*
Wine Spectator 249
Woebot 133
World Masters Games 270
World Usability Day 102
World Wide Web 4, 28, 41, 237, 275, 278
World Wide Web Consortium (W3C) 190

Xiaoice chatbot 133
Xinhua 119
XPRIZE Foundation 230

yoga instruction 268–9
YouTube Community Guidelines 236

zebras 231
Zoom 97, 98, 280